DEBRAHMANISING HISTORY

Debrahmanising History . . . can serve as a text for an alternative history of India – the first 'history from below' in recent times which subaltern theory suggests is needed but subaltern scholars never attempted themselves.

GAIL OMVEDT

. . . [A] coherent, well-argued work . . . passionately argues an oppositional point of view and is persuasive at the same time.

UMA CHAKRAVARTI

This book – expected and required to be translated into many Indian languages – can be of great help to the struggling people in the 'search of good ideas' for the reconstruction of a new society.

Mainstream

Unconventional work of this kind provides the much needed 'cutting edge' which leads to debates of a new kind that may give an entirely new twist to the direction of research.

Summerhill: IIAS Review

DEBRAHMANISING HISTORY
Dominance and Resistance in Indian Society

Extensively Revised Edition

BRAJ RANJAN MANI

MANOHAR
2024

First published 2005
Revised edition 2015
Reprinted 2022, 2023, 2024

© Braj Ranjan Mani 2005, 2015

All rights reserved. No part of this publication may be reproduced or transmitted, in any form or by any means, without prior permission of the author and the publisher.

ISBN 978-93-5098-110-8

Published by
Ajay Kumar Jain *for*
Manohar Publishers & Distributors
4753/23 Ansari Road, Daryaganj,
New Delhi 110 002

Typeset by
Ravi Shanker
Delhi 110 095

Printed at
Replika Press Pvt. Ltd.

Do not believe in anything (simply) because you have heard it.

Do not believe in traditions because they have been handed down for many generations.

Do not believe in anything because it is spoken and rumoured by many.

Do not believe in anything (simply) because it is found written in your religious books.

Do not believe in anything merely on the authority of your teachers and elders.

Do not believe in specious reasoning, or a bias to which you have become attached by habit.

Have deliberation and analyse, and when you find a proper reason for accepting something which is conducive to the good and benefit of one and all, accept it and live up to it.

GAUTAM BUDDHA
(Kalama Sutta in *Anguttara Nikaya*
Woodward and Hare 1932–6, vol. I: 188–93;
also see Holder 2006: 19–25)

Contents

Preface to the Second Edition   11

Preface to the First Edition   17

Introduction   19
    Concomitance of Dominance and Resistance—Symbiosis of Brahmanism, Caste and Communalism—Dalit-Bahujan Resistance—Foregrounding the Contest in History—Colonialism Within Colonialism—The Hindu and Nationalist Makeovers of Brahmanism—Gandhi–Nehru Upholding of the Oppressive Tradition—Freedom Struggles of Phule, Ambedkar and Periyar.

1. **Historical Roots of Brahmanic Dominance and Shramanic Resistance**   59
    Violence and Domination Underpin Vedic Ideology—Caste Indoctrination—Pseudo-Religion as Engine of Oppression—Caste, Karmayoga and Swadharma in the Gita—*Dandaniti* Central to Brahmanical Polity and State—Popular Resistance Debunks Elite Historiography—Shramanic Counter-Tradition of Egalitarianism—The Contested Past: Romance versus Reality.

2. **Buddhist India: Against Caste and Brahmanism**   98
    The Buddha's Synthesis of Mind and Matter—The Antithesis of Upanishadic Absolutism— Indictment of Caste—Paradigm of Human Liberation—Alternative Vision of Social and Political Institutions—Buddhist Ascendancy and India's Past Greatness—The Counter-Revolution and Brahmanical Revivalism—Forgeries to Recast Indian Culture in the Brahmanical Mould.

3. **Medieval Mukti Movements of the
   Subaltern Sant-Poets** 140
   Social Resistance in Religious Idiom—Kabir and
   Monotheistic Radicalism in the North —Siddha Rebellion
   in Tamil Nadu—Virashaiva Socialism in Karnataka—
   Varakari Struggle in Maharashtra—Social Dimension of
   Bhakti and the Brahmanic Backlash.

4. **Colonialism and the Birth of
   Vedic-Brahmanic Nationalism** 189
   Orientalism, Aryan Race Theory and Neo-Hinduism—Roy,
   Reforms, Renaissance: Facts Against Fiction—Dayananda's
   Aryan Race and Vedic Culture—The Modernisation of
   Brahmanical Tradition—Nationalist Vindication of Caste
   Ideology—Vivekananda's Polemics—The Facade of
   Cultural Nationalism.
   Appendix: *Parallel Fascist Thinking in East and West:
   Nietzsche, Nazism and the Hindu Nationalism*

5. **Phule's Struggle against Brahmanical Colonialism** 253
   Power and Oppression of the Time—Emergence of
   Anti-Caste Radicalism—Satyashodhak Samaj: Vision of a
   New Society—Rewriting of History and Mythology—
   Education as Emancipation and Empowerment—Against
   Patriarchy and Women's Subordination—Engagement with
   Agriculture, Peasantry and Labour—Critique of Nation and
   Nationalism.

6. **Guru, Iyothee, Periyar, Achhutanand:
   Different Strategies, One Goal** 291
   Dynamics and Dimension of Egalitarian
   Emergence—Narayana Guru and Kerala's Liberation
   Movement—Dravidian Upsurgence: Iyothee Thass
   and the Justice Party— Periyar and the Self-Respect
   Movement—The Battle in the North: Achhutanand and
   Mangoo Ram—Movements from Below Signal the End of
   Colonialism.

7. **Nationalist Power Politics, Excluded Masses,
   and the Gandhi–Ambedkar Debate** 337
   The Myth of the Mahatma—Ambedkar's Revolt—The

True Story of the Poona Pact—Anatomy of Gandhian Paternalism —Varna Swaraj and an Obscurantist Critique of Modernity—Tagore, Nehru, Roy, and Ambedkar on Gandhism—The Nation as Social Democracy— Radical Realism Amidst the Euphoria of Freedom: The Constitution and the Hindu Code Bill.

8. **Epilogue: Institutionalised Discrimination from the Past to the 'Democratic' Present**   397

Bibliography   407

Index   437

Preface to the Second Edition

This is not the place to rehearse or condense the arguments that will be elaborated in this volume, but a few clarifications about the need of doing—and now redoing—such a book may be in order.

It is no secret that there are intellectual weapons in the arsenal of the powerful—in theology, in philosophy, in social sciences. Their function is to conceal systemic violence or injustice in order to maintain the established power and cultural equilibrium. Even fair-minded intellectuals who come from the top of the social pyramid (in which the many are miserable at the bottom) take safety in academic subterfuge. A social psychology made worse by inherited traditions of classicism, cultural conservatism, and obfuscatory religiosity does not allow the pandits to see the obvious. For example, even a cursory familiarity with the ancient brahmanic texts leaves little doubt that the Itihasa-Purana and Dharmashastras were written by the enemies of dalit-bahujans who were stigmatised as shudras and atishudras. The shudra (the debased caste of servants) was so constructed by the historical power of brahmanism. But the scholars who spend a life-time in researching the past remain forever blind to this reality, and the historical truth of upper-caste violence, both social and ideological. Their scholarship somehow never comes to grasp the point that brahmanical forms of knowledge were critical in the establishment and maintenance of caste. The pattern does not change when we move forward to the history of modern India. A benign amnesia shrouds the conservative and anti-dalit-bahujan strands of Indian nationalism, which permits academic and popular projections of the essentially upper-caste leaders such as Gandhi, Nehru and Tilak-Savarkar as non-partisan leaders.

Nothing can be more hypocritical than the claims of academic neutrality and objectivity (with the tantalising premise of not 'stating' anything) that is often invoked by 'disinterested' social science. There is a writer behind every writing, and it matters from where one writes, to whom one writes, and with what objective and perspective. As I have argued elsewhere, being neutral in an unjust society is to actively support injustice. The 'neutral narratives', their plurality and intellectual splendour notwithstanding, provide the mental furniture, even the life-blood, of reproduction of caste–class inequalities (Mani 2014). In India, this problem is particularly pernicious due to the longstanding brahmanic control over knowledge, despite some challenging attempts from below in recent times. That the higher echelons of academia and knowledge-construction have been monopolised by vested interests is a fact—and this fact is the problem.

This applies to the whole intellectual grove that reproduces India's history and culture in the brahmanic mould in a variety of ways. It explains the absence of any fundamental questioning of traditional structures; normalisation of caste and brahmanism; the identification of the privileged-caste culture with Indian culture; institutionalised exaltation of the Mahatma and the Pandit; and new fabrications to legitimise the dominant ('Indian') ideology. If you are critical of caste and brahmanism, you are Euro-centric and guilty of denigration of the civilisational ethos of India. Any suggestion that caste and race, brahmanism and colonialism are beastly kith and kin is still heresy. Wonderful theories, rich with erudition and documentation—such as caste is a colonial construction: almost a fabrication of the Population Surveys and Census Reports (Inden 1990; Dirks 2002); communalism is an 'Orientalist term', produced as 'a form of colonialist knowledge' (Pandey 1990); secularism constitutes an 'alien cultural ideology', 'a gift of Christianity', and 'there are no fundamentalists or revivalists in traditional society' (Madan 1987: 748–9)—are being invented under the banner of postcoloniality of the 'indigenous' to 'justify and defend the innocence which confronted modern Western colonialism' (Nandy 1983). The 'innocence' here involves a complete elision of centuries of violence of caste, class, and patriarchy (as this book will show in detail). In other words, the colonial tragedy returning now as the postcolonial farce (to paraphrase Marx's famous phrase) allows the brahmanic elite to mystify the caste–class exploitation and masquerade as the oppressed rather than the oppressors.

One can well imagine how comforting such 'primal innocence' can be to the custodians of 'community' and 'culture' because colonial crimes pale in comparison with the crimes of caste and brahmanism which have victimised, stigmatised and inferiorised the dalit-bahujans (who constitute more than 80 per cent of Indian people) for almost three thousand years. In other words, a deeply devious, neo-brahmanic impression is being created (by the resource-rich academics, many of whom are, ironically, ensconced in the Euro-American universities) that all the problems of contemporary India emanated from the Western colonialism. As Aijaz Ahmad (1992: 196–7) articulates it, 'Colonialism is now held responsible not only for its own cruelties but, conveniently enough, for ours too.'

The influence which entrenched interests still exert over all channels of communication—from the elite academia to the mass media—ensures a perpetual ambience of brain-washing. The opinion business, the persuasion industry range from sophisticated academic treaties to the stereotyped crudities of the infotainment industry. Invented histories, myth-making, and armoury of stereotypes merge seamlessly to create convenient narratives and myths which masquerade as history of India.

If any historical discourse is badly in need of deconstruction, an unravelling of its social and ideological roots, it is the established history of caste and brahmanism. Its roots may be traced to entrenched interests who benefited most from the brahmanical social order, but the ideology they projected with cunning and persistence have taken in a surprisingly wide variety of people ranging from the very victims of the caste–class nexus to foreign academics who accept the views projected in brahmanic narratives, both ancient and modern, at their face value. The seduction and insidious nature of the brahmanic indoctrination is truly amazing. Swami Vivekananda, who, like many of his castemen, was humiliated for his 'shudra' identity (see Chapter 4), remained convinced—fanatically—about the superiority of the brahmanic religion and classical caste system. Arnold Toynbee, a British historian, who was certainly not an Orientalist propagandist like Max Müller, ignored cruel social structures and cultural reality, and put on record his sublime belief that Hinduism and the Hindu worldview 'is at once more natural, more human, and more scientific' than all other religions. One finds the same superlative statements from many famous and not-so-famous figures about the Vedic–brahmanic achievements of India surpassing the West in the fields of naturalism, humanism, and scientific rationalism.

As the myths about India penetrated beyond the borders of India in modern times, the idle and empty cant of brahmanism (that hides now behind the hydra-headed facade of Hinduism or Indian culture) persists in multifarious forms. The obscurantist notions about India—such as Hinduism is 5,000 years old; Vedanta contains the ultimate truth, and has the answer to the most complex challenges of humanity; Hindu culture is inherently tolerant and peaceful, it is more emotionally alert to fellow beings, and cares more for women and family; Hinduism alone is capable of producing an 'apostle of truth and non-violence' like Gandhi (see Attenborough's *Gandhi* and the usual hagiographical portrayals in the global Gandhi industry), and, is, thus, the culmination of the cultural evolution of mankind—are taken seriously not only by an army of illiterates but also the august gatherings of academics.

It seems there is an intrinsic connection between the political Hinduism (of the semi-literate, vulgar fanatics who demand that the past, present and future of India be constituted around a notion of Hinduness or Hindutva) and the brahmanic Hinduism of academic study that we find in the writings of highly learned scholars who are in command of the pure epistemology and classical Sanskrit tradition. Where there is any cognizance of caste, class and patriarchal oppressions, they are finely wrapped in explanations produced by masters in the art of explaining away. Even those who accept the injustices of caste and brahmanism in the past, hasten to add the pointlessness of raking them up, as if those things and their consequences have become history. There is little awareness about a more or less institutionalised arrangement of normalising, if not glorifying, the oppressive past from which the privileged continue to derive profit and pleasure.

The untold–suppressed story mothers the lies. That is why the stories of Ekalavya, Shambuka, and Sita should not be forgotten. (Symbolic characters like them are few in the epics, but there must have been millions in the real life. Above all, their descendants have barely risen above the struggle for survival and they constitute a significant part of India's billion-plus population.) That is why the distorted history should be countered wherever one encounters it. Above all, history and culture should be reconstructed by the dispossessed, with the clear understanding that 'the master's tools will not bring down the master's house'.

The child who reads in her history book of Dronacharya's brilliance as a teacher and Kautilya's wonderful statecraft should also be told that those men were crooks by any definition. The representation of Hindu dharma as a uniquely indigenous way of dispensing 'righteousness', 'justice' and 'equality of all' should not conceal the fact of its exclusionary norms of caste and patriarchy that glorified the suppression of dalit-bahujans and women. Hagiographical accounts of Gandhi's life should not omit his support for caste and brahmanism, and his charming suggestion that 'a shudra who serves the higher castes as a matter of religious duty and who will never own any property is worthy of the world's homage. . . . The gods will shower their choicest blessings on him' (Gandhi [1934] 1993: 220).

Our history, as we shall see on the following pages, is replete with spectacular frauds of 'the good and the great'. Perhaps it would do the resilient 'Indian psyche' no damage if the false gods are a little mocked, if the great foundation of lies and ignorance on which our civilisation rests is a little unsettled, if the glorification of Veda-Upanishad is at least a little counterbalanced by some knowledge of how brahmanism was constituted and institutionalised, and how there has been a long contestation against it from the days of the Buddha to the present. The dominant narrative of a spiritual culture, communicated for centuries through brahmanic discourse, has apparently succeeded in its effort to brush under the carpet the red tooth and claws of brahmanism. But hiding the hideousness of caste and brahmanism serves only the hideous purpose: the subject needs to be opened, debated and discussed. Not just because they are responsible for so many of continuing inequalities, divisions and brutalities, but mainly to inoculate, unite and emancipate the oppressed because that past is not yet past.

The reasons that impelled me to write *Debrahmanising History* have intensified, not lessened, since its first publication in 2005. This spurred me to revise and update the book. I have avoided the fashionable academic practice of stuffing the writing with obscure original sources and technicalities. I have not followed, deliberately, many academic conventions in order to be a little more purposeful and accessible. This extensively revised book also has an extended and up-to-date bibliography. I hope that the book, besides presenting an alternative history of India, will be of some help to the people who struggle and dream for an exploitation-free humanity.

BRAJ RANJAN MANI

Preface to the First Edition

The world over, the dominant classes have invoked harmony without snapping their ties with the oppressive structures of class, caste, and gender hierarchies. Hollow, hypocritical advocacy of justice and equality becomes necessary for the power elites, especially in the democratic times in which we live. Therefore, those who aspire to build a more humane, more inclusive society have perforce to take off the elitist mask of generosity and solidarity in the name of seamless cultural unity or nationalism. Such deconstruction for an egalitarian reconstruction runs the risk of gross misconception and distortion at the hands of entrenched interests. I would like to make it clear, therefore, that this work is not intended to target any particular caste or group but to present historical wrongs in a perspective that pitches for the greater good. Thomas Szasz (1974: 20) says, 'In the animal kingdom, the rule is, eat or be eaten; in the human kingdom, define or be defined', and I had no choice but to write this book.

This work reflects the creativity not of one author but of many engaged social scientists. My thanks go first to all the people whose perspectives—articulated here in indigenous terms—militate against the colonisation of minds and bodies. I am also grateful to friends who read parts of the manuscript and offered their suggestions. I owe a special debt to G. Aloysius. Also in the debt department are Gail Omvedt, Arun Kumar, Namrata, and Anil.

My thanks to Mr Ramesh Jain who went against the conventional academic wisdom and decided to publish the work.

No words can express my gratitude to my parents, brothers and sister. This work would not have happened without their love and support. I dedicate *Debrahmanising History* to my mother.

New Delhi   BRAJ RANJAN MANI
January 2005

Introduction

> The impulse to oppose cultural norms appears as inarticulate revolt, as social criticism, as vision, as ideology, as completed revolution; it may spring from logic, disillusionment, or the experience of oppression. In short, it is part of the continuing dialectic of history, as much our cultural heritage as what it opposes. What I mean, then, by 'counter-tradition' is not 'that which opposes tradition', but 'the tradition which opposes'.
>
> Louis Kamp, see Delany 1971: 4

Classes and masses, and their understanding of the world, do not exist in isolation but in conflict. This is not to deny the role of the powerful in the production of knowledge that affects the life of all, but to make clear the fact that contradictions are inherent—and pervasive—in an unequal society as its order and power relationships are manufactured by manipulation and coercion. The inherited status of high and low and arbitrary distribution of material and cultural resources remain unacceptable to the devalued and the deprived. The contradictions run deep, and they are not only economic but also intellectual and moral. Though they may not be always explicit, mutual suspicion and antipathy are endemic in a hierarchical society.

Concomitance of Dominance and Resistance

Social divides, however, cannot be fully grasped without grasping the 'hidden transcripts' of the powerless and powerful. The 'public' transcript—the standard narrative—is unlikely to reveal the depth and dimensions of conflict in history and culture. 'Unless one can penetrate the official transcript of both subordinates and elites, a reading of the social evidence will almost always represent a confirmation of the status quo in hegemonic terms' (Scott 1990: 90). The weak, however, have their weapons: as Scott (1985) shows, hegemonies are never legitimate within the horizons of their consciousness and thinking. The tactics of ordinary people, seen in their everyday transgressions of rules, are tantamount to a de facto and wholesale negation of the dominant discourse (ibid.).

Subordinate groups do not share the understanding of history and society doled out by elites, and have their own traditions and ideologies of resistance. Precisely for this reason, the master narrative conceals, distorts, or misrepresents the contest in culture and history. Elites validate the existing order by either concealing or normalising the existence of social cleavages. Class conflict is a concept that upsets them since they do not see themselves as part of the exploitative racket. Viewing the world from the top, elites construct and interpret events or evidence in ways that trivialise or ignore the resistance. When they recognise resistance, they do so reluctantly—even grudgingly—and only when it attacks the formal institutions of power. On the whole, they do not take notice of the protests erupting in everyday life without the fanfare of open defiance. Moreover, studies of acknowledged protests, of popular rebellions and uprisings, are distorted in several 'scholarly' ways, misrepresenting events as instances of token or misguided resistance (MacGuire and Paynter 1991: 10–13).

Concomitance of dominance and resistance is a phenomenon that prevails as much in social life as in the intellectual–cultural realm. Injustice—inherent in the structures of caste, class and patriarchy—destroys the possibility of cooperation and consensus in society. History is replete with instances that show that struggle against oppression is as old as oppression. Such conflicts lead to the emergence of at least two distinct worldviews. Following Marx, Bryan S. Turner (1983: 78) argues that 'each mode of production will give rise to at least two significantly separate ideologies corresponding to the class position of subordinate and superordinate classes.'

Dominant ideology unifies the elite groups and fragments the subordinated mass by subverting the counter-ideology that can enable the people to change their submission into a transforming force. The elite design is to obscure the whole situation of socio-economic and political domination that perpetuates ignorance, disunity and lethargy among the suppressed. The ruling ideas of society ensure that the people do not see through the dominant ideology and strategy, lest they unite and engage in a struggle for liberation (Freire [1970] 1996: 126–7).

Viewing history as a class struggle, Marx theorised dialectical materialism to grasp the formation of class society and its disastrous consequences. His was a revolutionary attempt to deconstruct the nexus between economics, politics, and ideology. He strove for a liberating understanding of how the dominant class in a society, in the conditions of 'open competition', is able to secure its dominance. He explains that the ideas of the ruling class are, in every epoch, the ruling ideas, and the reason for this is that the class which is the ruling material force in society is at the same time its ruling intellectual force (Marx [1845] 1970: 64). That is why Marx called dominant ideology a 'false consciousness' and unravelled its role of hiding the economic factor (the determinant factor) in legitimising class exploitation. Although the famous base–superstructure formulation subjects the realm of ideas and culture to the dominion of economics and social relations of production, the real thrust of Marxism is to highlight the dialectic of given structures and to transform human agencies, and visualise a revolutionary task of knowledge in the liberation of humanity. The task of philosophy, as Marx stated, is not merely to understand the world but also to change material conditions and reconstitute society so that the few are not able to exploit the many.

It is not often grasped that Marx sometimes overstressed the economic base as a reaction to the prevailing bourgeois ideology which tended to ignore it. Sadly, for many Marxists the base–superstructure model became a dogma which tended to obscure the cultural–religious sources of exploitation such as patriarchy, caste, and race. As early as the 1930s, Ambedkar, the anti-caste revolutionary, pointed out the 'illusion of communists' and refuted the notion of social, cultural, and religious factors as 'superstructural' features. Underpinning the nexus of caste, religion, and ideology with devastating brilliance, he turned the architectural metaphor upside down.

> Yet the base is not the building. On the basis of the economic relations a society builds its religious, social, and political institutions. This building has just as much truth (reality) as the base. If we want to change the base, then first the building that has been constructed on it has to be knocked down. In the same way, if we want to change the economic relations of society, then first the existing social institutions will have to be destroyed.
> (Ambedkar [1938], see Omvedt 1994: 228)

Power has at least three prominent facets—political, economic, and ideological. Whereas political power is the power of physical coercion and economic power is the power of rewards and deprivation, ideological power is the power of ideas, opinion, beliefs, culture, traditions, through which our mental consciousness is moulded. Picking threads from Marxism, some creative thinkers undertook a more critical study of the ideological dimension of power. Gramsci expounded a relatively autonomous role of ideology through what he termed the phenomenon of hegemony. Derived from the Greek *hegemon* (leader) and *hegemonicos* (capable of commanding), hegemony is domination by consent. It is the process whereby dominant class indoctrinates the masses and manufactures a consensus in civil society through largely peaceful means. The Gramscian concept articulates a mechanism of ideological dominance over the whole complex of societal relations in a given social formation. Elite-controlled agencies and apparatuses—religious institutions, political parties, academia, the media, art, and literature—sell the status quo by presenting it as natural and good for everyone (Gramsci [1971] 1996). Elite institutions, as Fanon (1963: 38) put it, generate 'expressions of respect for the established order [that] serve to create around the exploited person an atmosphere of submission and of inhibition which lightens the task of policing'. Ideological indoctrination not only produces docile subjects, it also helps the ruling elite to mask or mystify its repressive machinery—police, law courts, the military. In a famous essay Althusser (1971: 121–73) establishes that ideology is the fulcrum of the state mechanism through which the dominant class is able to reproduce its class domination. Moulded into subjects through ideological state apparatuses, succeeding generations continue to conform to the norms of the existing class relations.

However, the crux of the Marxist-Gramscian dialectic is that dominance or hegemony is not forever. This is because a class society—fundamentally divided along power and powerlessness—is riven with oppositions. Dominant culture and ideology always remain contentious. The ideas of the ruling class are never fully accepted; the human spirit is never crushed permanently, and its overt or covert assertion marks the rhythm of history. Injustices are continuously interrogated, dissented, and contested by the sufferers; thus keeping alive the cycle of *subordination-exploitation-protest-continuum* that carries the hope of a revolutionary turnaround.

Extending the Gramscian conception of ideology to the realm of culture, Stuart Hall (1996) resituates ideology in a strategic relation to culture. Hegemony for Gramsci is a 'process by which a historical bloc of social forces is constructed and the ascendancy of that bloc secured'. Taking this forward, Hall says it is in the field of culture that social action and intervention take place, and 'power relations ... both established and potentially unsettled'. Hall defines ideology as 'the *mental frameworks*—the languages, the concepts, categories, imagery of thought, and the systems of representation—which different classes or social groups in order to make sense of, define, figure out and render intelligible the way society works' (Hall 1996: 26). So, far from being an aspect of culture, ideology is a means through which culture is defined.

In this book, I will attempt to demonstrate that contest against caste and brahmanism arose simultaneously with their emergence, in both secular and religious realms, occupying and struggling over the same historical space and cultural terrain—a contest that never ceased, and continues still in multifarious ways. 'A bit of open-mindedness, normal intelligence and healthy scepticism', to borrow the famous words of Chomsky (1998), will make this abundantly clear. Contrary to the formulations of foreign and brahman academics such as Louis Dumont and M.N. Srinivas, brahmanism since its very inception has been an intensely contested ideology in India, and perhaps will remain so as long as it survives. This understanding is not based on some pure epistemology, but on *mental frameworks, hidden transcripts* (of the privileged and lowered castes), *practical reason,* and *lived experience* grounded in the perspective to grasp the past through the present and vice versa—the kind of eclectic and subversive 'methodology' that was ingeniously adopted by the dalit-bahujan stalwarts such as Phule, Ambedkar, and Periyar in their enquiries into Indian society and culture. As Ambedkar said, 'Religion, social status and property are all sources of power and authority.... One is predominant at one stage, the other is predominant at other stage' (*BAWS*, vol. 1: 45) It will be in order first, however, to grasp the ideology and institutionalisation of caste and brahmanism.

Symbiosis of Brahmanism, Caste and Communalism

Ideology as an instrument of domination, of ensuring that the common people think and behave as the scheming few want them to, finds its archetypical expression in brahmanism. Named after those at the top of caste hierarchy, brahmanism is the main agency of caste indoctrination. As this book will demonstrate, the brahman's *brahma-astra* (ultimate weapon) was *shastras* (canons) such as the Dharmashastras (law-scriptures). (It is striking that the words in Sanskrit for arms [*shastra*] and canons [*shastra*] have the same etymology.) The classical brahmanic ideal of knowledge is the sublimation of self for attaining the supreme self, but translated into the social context, it implies performing predetermined caste duties for attaining salvation from ignorance or illusion. 'There is sanction of the caste system in the [brahmanic] ideology of knowledge itself' (Acharya 1996: 105).

The classical and scriptural texts preserve the idea that varnas (literally 'colour, class', or social hierarchies) are real universals rooted in the original—Vedic—ontological make-up of humankind. Veda means 'knowledge' and the Vedic past, as a model of timeless truth and righteousness, is credited with epistemological power of all knowledge. It is notable that the Sanskrit word for education is *siksha* (literally 'practice'), the science which teaches phonetics and euphony, and the word for 'study' is *adhyan*, whose etymological meaning is to utter or to recite and hence to hear it also. According to Mimamsa interpretation, shruti (*heard* from guru) and smriti (*remembered*, or reproduced from memory) both refer to Veda. 'Smriti is so called because by means of it the dharma of the Veda is remembered.' Knowledge or shastra-production is viewed in the classical texts themselves as a process of 'remembering' ancient, pre-existing truth. The axiom on which this knowledge production rested was 'that the improvement of any given practice lies, not in the future and the discovery of what has never been known before, but in the past and the more complete recovery of what was known in full in the past' (Pollock 1985: 512).

The classical texts view themselves 'as either the end-point of a slow process of abridgement from earlier, more complete, and divinely inspired prototypes; or as exact reproductions of the divine prototypes obtained through uncontaminated, unexpurgated descent from the original, whether through faithful intermediaries or by sudden revelation' (Pollock 1985: 512). Thus, practice is authorised by a knowledge made authoritative by its antiquity, and this is done in a manner which reflects the relation between the eternal Veda, as a blueprint for creation, and the material world, as its manifestation (ibid.: 518).

To produce knowledge was to recapture the pristine knowledge of the past alongside its vision of social hierarchy as a natural phenomenon. Thus, the past was continuously invented and kept alive by the present. The practical function of this process was to establish a flexible source of intellectual authority for perpetuating hierarchical social structure and brahmanic hegemony over society. This way, far from being an agent of change, the knowledge-production was committed to buttress the status quo of the past. The brahmanic texts constantly refer to rules in still earlier texts and never problematise the relation between the norms of the past and actual contemporary practices. This way, everyday the brahman literati recreate the social world with its species of caste together with their inherent caste characteristics (Aktor 1999).

A clarification on the word 'caste', however, is in order before we resume the main discussion. The term 'caste' is not problematic (contrary to the purists' assertion) simply because it derives from the Portuguese *casta*—'race', 'descent'. In fact, it perfectly captures the connotations of the Indian terms for (what is commonly called now) caste—*varna* ('colour') and *jati* ('descent'). 'Caste attaches to the body, not to the soul', as it is the 'biological reproduction of the human species through procreation within endogamous caste groups which ensures the permanence of ascribed marks of caste purity or pollution' (Chatterjee 1989: 203). Yes, caste is not race and class; it is more vicious than them. Lay people understand it perfectly when they say, 'What comes by birth and can't be cast off by dying—that is caste.'

Put briefly, those who called themselves brahmans proposed that the hierarchy of caste must exist as the sole form of social organisation, or not exist at all. The hierarchy was brought into existence on the religious principle of purity and pollution, reflected in the graded hierarchy of caste ranks, the highest belonging always to the brahmans, who are the purest and in command of *dharma* (religion) and its rituals. 'The essence of caste ... requires that the labouring bodies of the impure castes be reproduced in order that they can be subordinated to the need to maintain the bodies of the pure castes in their state of purity. All the injunctions of dharma must work to this end' (Chatterjee 1989: 203).

Brahmans gave a sacred aura to this fraud. The dharma they envisioned was the cosmic order maintained by the correct performance of sacrifice, which in turn was dependent on maintaining the requisite social hierarchy. The brahman would not establish dharma (which implied righteousness as well as justice) unless he himself presided over it, unless dharma upheld caste hierarchy, unless righteousness was bound to the caste order and polity, unless justice was one with *dandaniti* (the rule of force) and *matsyanyaya* (the law of big fish swallowing small ones).

Thus, by integrating the caste doctrine into *dharma*, the brahmans overcame several kinds of resistance and gradually succeeded in universalising the caste system within the subcontinent. It is this fact that Dumont, despite all his bias for brahmanism, has clearly brought out. 'In the last analysis, the [caste-based] division of labour shows not a more or less gratuitous juxtaposition of religious and non-religious or "economic" tasks, but both the religious basis and the religious expression of interdependence. Better, it deduces interdependence from religion' (Dumont [1970] 1998: 108).

However, what Dumont does not comprehend is the reality that the concentration of purity and privilege at the top and humiliation and disabilities at the bottom—intrinsic to caste system—is not simply a system of interdependence, or a mere division of labour, but implies a structure of organised violence, which also makes clear the strong material basis of caste. The lowered castes laboured, developed and preserved their knowledge of food, plants, animals and domestic livestock, of weather, soil, of tools used in agriculture, and crafts such as tanning, weaving, carpentry, black smithy, gold smithy, etc. Yet these productive skills and knowledge were denigrated as inferior and polluting, as compared to ritual and intellectual activity. In other words, the brahmanic control and exercise of knowledge, both religious and secular, and the exclusion of the lowered castes from the domain of knowledge, as we would see later, played a crucial role in institutionalising the caste hierarchy. Vividly grasping caste from their lived experiences and social reality around them as well as the brahmanical canon, Phule (1873) and Ambedkar (1916; 1936) wrote on the symbiosis of religion, culture and caste (Chapters 5 and 7), and also underlined (unlike Dumont, Srinivas and other mystifying sociologists) the role of violence and coercion in the origin and the functioning of the caste system. The 'holistic' and 'Sanskritising' shams of Dumont and Srinivas (who practice academic *untouchability* by never engaging with Phule–Ambedkar's critique of caste) are more popular because they are convenient for the privileged castes as they obfuscate the exploitation implicit in the structure of caste besides erasing their own location within that structure.[1]

Brahmanism represents, above all, a cultural–religious construction of power. It stands for the aggregate of the sacerdotal literature, hierarchical social structure, and religio-political institutions that have kept the masses ignorant, servile and disunited. Traditionally, it has been propelled by the ruthless pursuit of self-aggrandisement based on caste, priest-craft and false philosophy—caste representing the scheme of domination, priest-craft the means of exploitation, and false philosophy a justification for both (Dharma Theertha [1941] 1992). The most remarkable thing about brahmanism (which is generally not taken note of) is that it has never stood for any consistent philosophy, doctrine or ethics, but has adjusted its ideas and strategies to changing situations for maintaining power. Historically, it used the ideology and structure of caste to dehumanise and divide the productive majority. Ambedkar, perhaps the greatest thinker on caste and its consequences, saw caste not as a class-like division of labour but a *division of labourers* in a system of graded inequality (*BAWS*, vol. 1: 47). Many castes among a single class (occupying a similar position within the division of labour) will fragment and divide that class. No wonder, Ambedkar saw brahmanism as 'a diabolical contrivance to suppress and enslave humanity' (ibid., vol. 7: 239).

The 'diabolical contrivance' involves the 'graded inequality' between and among hundreds of mutually antipathetic castes and sub-castes, which explains why the stranglehold of caste, despite resistance from the lowered castes, has survived till now. Graded hierarchy embodies a built-in mechanism to guarantee the perpetuation of the social system 'and prevents the rise of general discontent against inequity' (*BAWS*, vol. 7: 307; vol. 5: 102). Examining the different kinds of social inequalities in world history, Ambedkar points out the crucial difference between inequality (class) and graded inequality (caste), and contends that the latter is at least twice as dangerous as the former (*BAWS*, vol. 3: 320).

Summarising, the caste system is a form of social stratification in which castes are hierarchised, occupationally specialised and separated from each other (in matter of marriage, physical contact, food) by rules of purity and pollution. The birth-based segregation is reinforced by endogamy and strict control over women's sexuality. Caste is fundamentally different from class and other forms of stratification in the sense that while the latter is a system of production, caste is a system of both production and reproduction, as Uma Chakravarti demonstrates in an illuminating work:

The structure of marriage, sexuality, and reproduction is the fundamental basis of the caste system. It is also fundamental to the way inequality is sustained: the structure of marriage reproduces both caste and class inequality, and thus the entire production system through its tightly controlled system of reproduction. . . . Under brahmanical patriarchy women of the upper castes are regarded as gateways—literally points of entry into the caste system. Lower caste male whose sexuality is a threat to upper caste purity of blood has to be institutionally prevented from having sexual access to women of the higher castes, so such women have to be carefully guarded. (Chakravarti 2003: 27–35)

Malicious and misogynist statements such as *na stri swaatantryamarhati* (women should not be given freedom) and *striyo hi mool doshaanaam* (woman is the root cause of all evil) abound in the caste canon. Women are seen in Dharmashastras as inherently lascivious and requiring male control from the cradle to the grave (*Manusmriti* 5.147–9, 9. 2–3).[2]

There are frequent co-references to women and shudras in the brahmanical literature—both are life-long slaves from birth to death (R.S. Sharma 1983: 45–8). Manu and Yajnavalkya, the premier law-givers, hold that even when released from slavery they are not emancipated because slavery is inherent to them. As we shall see in Chapter 1, the anti-woman, anti-shudra epistemology is enshrined in the brahmanical sacred texts.

Merit was made an attribute not of individuals but of castes—being born a brahman was in itself a mark of greatness. Manu says, 'The name of a brahman should connote auspiciousness and happiness; of a kshatriya strength and protection; the name of a vaishya should connote wealth and prosperity; and the name of a shudra should breed disdain and servility' (*Manusmriti* 2: 31–2). Hierarchy of purity and power culminates in the brahman. 'When a brahman is born he springs to light above the world; he is the chief of all creatures, entitled by eminence of birth to the wealth of the world' (*Manusmriti* 1. 99–100). The brahman's anti-thesis is the shudra, the category under which come peasants, artisans and workers. The shudra is the most impure, born in sin. Caste-and-order, theorised and made sacred and sacrosanct as Varnashrama Dharma by its beneficiaries, is an institutional arrangement of social closure in which knowledge, wealth and dignity are denied to the 'impure' groups.

Thus the characteristic attribute of the caste system is not only 'hereditarily appointed work' but also 'unequally divided rights'

(Bougle [1908] 1991: 64). In Ambedkar's words, caste is a system of graded inequality in which castes are arranged according to 'an ascending scale of reverence and a descending scale of contempt' (*BAWS*, vol. 7: 26). Other upright sociologists perceive caste in the same vein: higher the caste, greater its status, power, privilege, affluence, and security; lower the caste, greater the degree of contempt, humiliation, deprivation, want, and anxiety (Berreman 1991: 84–92; Mencher 1991: 93–109). Caste, more than anything else, is an 'institutionalised inequality' that guarantees 'differential access to valued things in life'.

The shudra, 'born in sin' and 'the untruth itself', was degraded and saddled by several disabilities. 'The sight of mere possession of wealth by a shudra injures the brahman', says Manu, who also declares that an attempt made by shudra to acquire knowledge is a crime. If he listens to a recitation of the Vedas his ears are to be filled with molten lead; if he recites the sacred texts his tongue is to be torn out; and if he remembers them, his body is to be split. The brahman was divinely entitled to insult, beat, and enslave a shudra but let the latter murmur a protest and he would have a red hot iron thrust into his mouth. Hundreds of such violent utterances against shudras are scattered through the brahmanic texts, for example in Shankara's *Brahma Sutra*, in the *Gautamdharmasutra* (12: 4), and in the *Manusmriti* (8: 270). According to the law-givers, the killing of a shudra by a brahman was equivalent to the killing of a cat, frog, lizard, owl, or crow. Holy books like the *Bhagavad Gita* condemn shudras and women as *paapyoni* (born in sin). The *Gita* glorifies caste in the name of *karma* and killing in the name of *dharma* (see Chapter 1). After reading these texts, Ambedkar was compelled to write,

What goes by the name of Sacred Books contains fabrications which are political in their motive, partisan in their composition and fraudulent in their purpose.... They [who defend such writings] are more selfish than any other set of beings in the world, and are prostituting their intelligence to support the vested interests of their class. (*BAWS*, vol. 7: 14–15)

Historical evidence suggests that the pedigree of hate and discrimination in India (that manifest themselves in contemporary caste-or-religion-based exploitation and violence) goes back to a time when a class of people with claims of purity of blood attempted to accord divine sanction to the caste system and to the pre-eminent position of the brahmans therein. Simultaneously there were concerted efforts to demonise the shudras and those outside the pale of varna society, who either did not observe or refused to conform to the rules of caste. The word shudra is derived from *kshudra,* which literally means contemptible, without worth or value. But shudra, as a scholar of Dharmashastras makes clear, was also the code word for anyone, especially the Buddhists, Jains, and foreigners who would not accept the superiority of the brahman. The word identified the enemy and it encompassed a wide cross-section of society. 'The reason why foreign ruling classes, such as the Greeks, Shakas, Persians, and Chinese, have fallen to the level of Shudras ... is their lack of devotion to Brahmins' (Olivelle 2005: 39).

Another term coined to demonise the other was *mlechchha,* the 'dirty, unwashed other', which has a history going back to around 800 BCE and occurs originally in a Vedic text. One who did not know the sacred tongue, did not accept the Vedas, or did not acknowledge brahman supremacy, was mlechchha. 'Viewing an antagonistic group as dirty, and thus subhuman, whereas one's own cleanliness is not only humanely civilised but next to godliness, is commonplace in ethnic conflict' (Kakar and Kakar 2007: 32). Contrary to the brahmanic claim that the term mlechchha was essentially one of contempt for the invading, barbarous foreigners, especially Muslims, it was used originally and frequently by the privileged castes to refer to shudras and ati-shudras, considered the enemy. According to Romila Thapar, demonisation/*rakshasisation* of the enemy—irrespective of who the enemy was—has been a constant factor with reference to many pre-Islamic enemies and going back to earlier time.

Sayana's commentary of the fourteenth century AD refers to the dasas of the Rigveda as rakshasas and asuras. Inscriptions of this period freely use the terms rakshasas and Ravana for enemies who are Hindu. In later centuries, the reference to some Muslims as mlechchhas was an extension of the term to include them among the many others who were denied varna status. This usage is more common in sources which come from the upper castes, such as Sanskrit texts and inscriptions, and was more easily used for the lower castes who were, even without being Muslim, marginalised, moved to the fringes of society and treated with contempt. (Thapar 1999b: 17–18)

Thus the construct of a benevolent Indic religion centred around 'Hinduism' alongside the normalisation of caste is, contrary to popular perception, a supremacist fabrication that obscures or erases India's heterogeneity, contradictions, and the contested past. Above all, the construction of an all-encompassing and five-millennia-old Hinduism hides the fraud and violence of brahmanism. The supposed cultural unity of Hinduism—and the bid to make it synonymous with Indianness and cultural nationalism—is in fact an elitist ploy to conceal the divisiveness of brahmanism by normalising caste and its consequences along with the hidden agenda of keeping the oppressed majority ignorant, fragmented, and demoralised. Brahmanic Hinduism has a history of targeting other religions—Buddhism, Islam, Christianity, Sikhism—but its worst offensive has always been reserved for its own supposed co-religionists, the oppressed majority consisting of erstwhile shudra-atishudra and adivasi (tribal) communities. As the suppressed castes sought shelter in other religions, those religions and the converted people incurred the wrath of the caste elites. Organised violence against the perceived enemies—as reflected in the 1990s slogan of *Aaj Kasaai, kal Issaai* (First kill Muslims, then Christians)—becomes necessary for the brahmanic forces because the consolidation of Hindus cannot be forged unless there is a bloody conflict based on religious affiliations (see the Appendix to Chapter 4).

One of the brahmanical means of political control is through the use of force in the name of religion—*dharmadanda*—to offset the festering and unresolved question of caste, especially when the suppressed castes strive to escape the prison-house of brahmanism. In this sense, what is called the Hindu backlash (against the 'alien' religions of Islam and Christianity) is actually a brahmanic backlash against the dalit-bahujan democratic clamour for change. The violent 'Hindu' opposition to dalit-bahujan struggles for justice—along with trivialisation/marginalisation of their freedom fighters such as

Phule, Ambedkar and Periyar—calls the bluff of 'Hindu majoritarianism'. The upper-caste minority, no more than 15 per cent of the Hindu population, hides behind the politics of Hinduism, using it as a powerful political tool to deflect the immense inequality and resultant mass frustration, anger, and violence within the 'Hindu' fold by employing a section of dalit-bahujans as the foot-soldiers against Christians, Muslims, and other 'aliens'. The design is to drive a wedge between each of the 'minorities' (who together constitute a majority)—dalits, adivasis, OBCs, Christians, Muslims, Sikhs, etc.—and pit them one by one (as per the exigencies of realpolitic) against the imaginary majority, thus keeping them divided, ghettoised and demoralised.

Dalit-Bahujan Resistance

While the oppression of 'others' in the name of religion or nationality is not confined to India, no other society can match the record of brahmanic bigotry against its supposed co-religionists, bigotry maintained for centuries and buttressed by every cultural resource and social sanction. No religion other than Hinduism discriminates against the majority of its own co-religionists on scriptural authority. The infringement of human rights and dignity of common people on religious grounds is unique to Hinduism. In a stinging assessment of Hinduism, born out of lived experience, a dalit-bahujan thinker writes:

[T]his religion, from its very inception, has a fascist nature, which can be experienced and understood only by the dalit-bahujans, not by brahmans who regard the manipulation and exploitation as systemic and not as part of their own individual consciousness. But the reality is that every 'upper' caste person takes part in that exploitation and manipulation and contributes towards the creation and perpetuation of such cultures in the Indian context. (Ilaiah 1996: 72)

Caste elites vehemently contest such claims and instead credit their Hinduism for creating a uniquely plural and peaceful culture in India. But some of them, in moments of rare candour, concede that 'Hinduism . . . constructed a deep, enduring and disfiguring ideological edifice of inequality. This framework, with its fusion of coercive, ideological, economic and religious power, pitilessly condemned large masses to the most insidious forms of subordination mankind has known' (Mehta 2012). The title of the essay, 'Breaking the Silence: Why We [the elite] Don't Talk About Inequality', from which these words are excerpted is revealing. Apparently, vested interests do not allow the elite to talk honestly about massive inequality in India. It is astonishing that brahmanism does not figure in 'serious' debates on inequality, caste, Hinduism, and communalism.

As an exploitative ideology and practice, brahmanism has been kept hidden in modern India under a cleverly designed 'cultural' or 'national' discourse which obfuscates (in a variety of ways) the historical reality of caste and its consequences. Mere economism—reflected in the history-as-study-of-succession-of-advancing-modes-of-production approach—does not help much to grasp the hydra-headed brahmanism. As in the past, so in the present, it works at several levels in a multiplicity of forms—all of which empower the brahman and allied castes, and disempower the rest, engendering massive inequalities, human rights abuse, gender discrimination, mass illiteracy, etc.

Not surprisingly, brahmanism and its consequences have divided Indians into two broad categories—those who support it, and those who oppose. This divide has a long history, the roots of which can be traced in the existence of an ancient dual tradition. The history of India can be seen a story of struggle for hegemony between the brahmanic and anti-brahmanic traditions. Discarding the long-held myth that passes as Indian history even in the works of most credible of Indian and Western scholars, an incisive new book, drawing on archaeological and brahmanic sources themselves, sees

> India as the only civilisation of the ancient world that generated two opposing models of social and economic relations that coexisted for a long time in conflict, whatever the attempts to reduce or mask the incompatibilities. Far from being a history with a low level of conflict, it was highly confrontational. (Verardi 2011: 11)

The brahmanic canon is crammed with stringent injunctions and punishment to make the people fall in the caste system. Caste elites destroyed the records of their opponents, especially of the shramans, Lokayatikas and Buddhists (Chapter 2), but the anti-caste views and attitudes are still discernible in the tradition of Buddhism and in various heterodoxies, in the strands of regional cultures, and in the surviving Pali and Prakrit literature. The views expressed in these sources are sharply critical of brahmanic religion and culture. Opposition to caste and brahmanism is also apparent from the fact that

When the Sanskrit literature, whether the Dharmashastras, the epics, or any other, refers to varna and caste, the attempt is not to realistically *describe* the society but to *prescribe* for it. The references represent projections; the brahmanic texts are an attempt to delineate an ideal model and impose it on the society. They are a manifesto for a particular form of social inequality. (Omvedt 2003: 133)

Contending with the conventional—falsified—history of caste, Omvedt comes to the conclusion that the 'real history of caste in India is still to be written!' (ibid.: 134).

These are the views of a sociologist who is sympathetic to the struggle of the caste-oppressed. The dalit-bahujans, who have suffered humiliation and exclusion due to their caste, know the history of caste from their lived experience. Breaking the imposed 'culture of silence', they have started telling their stories in their own words. Their narratives refute their conventional representation in history and culture. The dalit-bahujan ideology—inspired by Phule, Ambedkar and Periyar, heroes of the social justice movement in modern India—rejects the brahmanic version of caste and culture (Rodrigues 2008).

In his groundbreaking *Gulamgiri* (Slavery), Phule showed that brahmanism enslaved the people in caste system through a deceptive web of socio-religious ideology. The main purpose of 'fabricating these [temporal and spiritual] falsehoods was to dupe the minds of the ignorant and to rivet firmly on them the chains of perpetual bondage and slavery which their selfishness and cunning had forged' (Phule [1873] 2002: 30). Following Phule, Iyothee Thass, Periyar, Ambedkar, and other dalit-bahujan leaders (Chapters 5–7) brought out the vicious role of brahmanic ideology and religion in the design of dominance.

Now, the dalit-bahujan intellectuals acutely feel the need for the deconstruction and construction of history. Ilaiah, following Phule, Ambedkar, and Periyar, suggests that all that has been written by brahmanical thinkers 'must be re-examined thoroughly' for the simple reason that they cannot be at once judge and party to the lawsuit. Conflating the Hindu with the brahmanic, he argues:

[T]he life-world of the Dalit-bahujans of India has hardly anything in common with the socio-cultural and political environment of Hindu-Brahmanism. The Dalit-bahujans live together with the Hindus in the civil society of Indian villages and urban centres, but the two cultural worlds are not merely different, they are opposed to each other. Hindu thinking is set against the interests of Dalit-bahujan castes; Hindu mythology is built by destroying the Dalit-bahujan cultural ethos. Dalit-bahujan castes were never allowed to develop into modernity and equality. The violent, hegemonic, brahmanical culture sought to destroy Dalit-bahujan productive structures, culture, economy and its positive political institutions. Everything was attacked and undermined. This process continues in post-Independence India. (Ilaiah 1996: 114)

Indeed, the brave new India retains the exclusivist structure of the past. The basic substance of the past is sustained, even when the environment appears to be changing dramatically.

Belief in the inherent inferiority of an hereditary population has dangerous economic and psychological advantages for all individuals in the dominant society: a vast pool of cheap, legitimately degraded labour; limits on competition for the goods and positions that shape modern prestige and power—land, white-collar professions, political leadership; limits on competition for scarce loans to marginal farmers and scarce jobs for industrial labour; an automatic boost to the self-esteem of all in the dominant society. (B. Joshi 1986: 6)

The same or similar understanding is shared by most dalit-bahujans, but the grand narrative of India, a common knowledge of which is taken for granted, does not reflect this. Led astray by brahmanic information and formulations, scholars, Indian as well as Western, with an exception here or there, interpret India in ways that either ignore or trivialise the dalit-bahujan perspective. The studies of subalternised castes or communities, their understanding of history and caste, and their aspirations and struggles have been misinterpreted in several 'scholarly' ways. Mainstream sociological study of India has been so brahmanised that it has made even the 'upper'-caste Marxist scholars blind to caste under the class-alone-matters dogmatism. It is astonishing that caste has been a non-factor in the Left's doctrinaire politics in India. Brahmanism, in other words, has rendered even some of the most radical ideologies redundant.

Foregrounding the Contest in History

The history of India may be described as a story of the struggle for supremacy between the traditions of shraman (Pali: samana), the ascetic truth-seekers with their origin in the Indus civilisation, and the brahman who came from within or without the subcontinent and strove to establish their religio-cultural dominance. After their arrival in the subcontinent around *c.* 1,400 BCE, the Aryans came into conflict with the indigenous communities and their cultural leaders, the shramans. The Aryans fought many battles with the local people, pejoratively called Dasas and Dasyus of which we get graphic descriptions in the Vedic corpus. The shraman-brahman contest stretched over centuries, but finally the brahmans—with their divisive caste principle and politics—were able to rope in many local kings and chieftains (as kshatriyas) and with their help established their dominance.

After remaining dormant in the wake of Vedic-Aryan onslaught, the shramans came to the fore around the sixth century BCE. We find a significant number of fiercely independent shramans by the time the brahmans were discarding the old Vedic moorings and accepting the new metaphysical speculations recorded in the Upanishads. Many religio-philosophical questions—such as the uncertainty and fragility of human existence, and the meaning or purpose of life—that the shramans sought to answer were not very different from those raised and speculated in the Upanishads, but one vital and enduring issue divided them sharply, giving birth to a perpetual mutual hostility. The shraman believed in universal egalitarian ethics which radically 'differed from the tendency to segment religious practice by caste which was characteristic of brahmanism' (Thapar 2001: 58).

It was from this intellectually fecund community that Buddhism and Jainism arose, and posed the most powerful challenge to the authority and normative prescriptions of brahmans. The shraman-brahman antagonism was so acute that Patanjali, the second century BCE grammarian, likened it to the hostility between the mongoose and the snake (Chapter 1). The Buddhist and Jain texts, the inscriptions of Ashoka, the description of Megasthenes and the account of the Chinese pilgrim Hsuan Tsang, covering a period of a thousand years, all refer to shramans and brahmans as two main religious categories. In the eleventh century too Alberuni noticed 'this indigenous view of the dichotomous religions of India' (Thapar 2001).

For several reasons, Buddhism emerged as the mainstay of shramanic tradition. Referred to as Samana Gotama in the Pali canon, the Buddha objected to brahmans' self-glorification, belittling of others, and lack of concern and compassion for the toiling people whom they degraded as the base born and despicable. He opposed the brahmans 'not because he wished to win a philosophical point but because he saw their claims to exclusivity and supreme authority as pernicious to people's well-being' (Hamilton 2001: 55). He also rejected the brahmans' reliance on tradition and inherited words of wisdom, advocating instead to accepting or rejecting an idea or proposition in the light of rationality and one's own experiences.

The Buddha was also a pioneering political thinker. Envisioning the connection between public works, economic welfare and moral elevation, his theory of state—represented in the idea of the Great Elect (*Mahasammatta*)—went beyond the concepts of divinity of kingship and the authoritarian monarchical state conceived by brahman ideologues such as Manu and Kautilya. The early republican states and political systems influenced Buddhism, which in its turn reinforced the republican spirit, vividly visible in the democratic order within its assemblies and institutions (Chapter 2).

Above all, the Buddhist view that *karma-kanda* (rituals) was useless posed a threat to its champions who were trying to build their cultural supremacy. The threat to the *karma-kanda* was seen as a threat to the Veda, and threat to the Veda was perceived as a threat to the supremacy of the brahman. The threatened brahman came forward with a range of arguments to defend his hierarchical worldview. In this running battle with the contesting ideologies, the brahman erected defences first to reinforce the social hierarchy—evidence of this attempt at caste reinforcement can be seen in Dharmasutras and Dharmashastras, enjoining each member of society to strictly adhere to his/her caste and gender duties—and then to justify and preserve the metaphysical fundamentals of Vedic worldview by developing the six specialisms of Vedic knowledge, known as Vedanga (Hamilton 2001).

At a different level, this worldview was also carried in the Upanishadic metaphysics which tried to discover the same eternal reality behind all the 'illusion' of changing phenomena of the world. The quest of the absolute led to the concept of an eternal soul and its Almighty Creator. Upanishadic absolutism can be, and has been, used to defend caste hierarchy as divinely designed because nothing happens in the world without the Almighty's concord. Thus, the leitmotif and common strands woven intricately to the brahmanic knowledge-system were, above all, the defence of social hierarchy.

The brahmanic belief that the Buddha was 'born, grew up, and died a Hindu' (Radhakrishnan [1956] 1997: IX) is ridiculous, if not mischievous. The Buddha rejected the Vedic-brahmanism, and his views against caste and pretensions of the brahman are scattered through the Pali canon (Rhys Davids [1899; 1910; 1921] 2000a and 2000b; Chakravarti 1996). His dialectics, atheism, and denial of soul remain a permanent antithesis of the Upanishadic absolutism, as we will see in Chapter 2. His teachings differed radically not only from the teachings of brahmanism, but also from the later absolutist forms of Buddhism (Kalupahana 1976: 9).

Though Buddhism remained a major religion of India for close to a millennium, it was eventually overcome by the hostile and violent politics of brahmanism (Omvedt 2003; Verardi 2011). The Buddhist–brahmanic conflict, the transformation of the Buddhist heritage, and the disappearance of Buddhism as a living faith from India during the early medieval centuries were 'largely responsible for the growth of misconceptions about ancient Indian civilisation and also for the propagation of the brahmanical standpoint during medieval through modern times' (Joshi [1969] 2007: 3). The period following the rise of aggressive brahmanism witnessed wholesale fraud, forgery and fabrication to recast the whole Indian culture in the brahmanic mould (Chapter 2).

Buddhism was destroyed, but it continued to have a subterranean existence in a new garb. Some of its inclusive features were carried alive in later centuries by a range of socio-religious campaigns like that of the Natha-Siddhas and the medieval Mukti (liberation) movements of the sant-poets, as well as anti-ascriptive movements such as Sikhism and Sufism. These challenged, sometimes openly and sometimes less openly, the politics and culture of caste.

In the dominant historiography, there is a deliberate cover-up of the anti-caste thrust of medieval socio-religious movements, which were a spectacular site of creativity and resistance from below. While their contemporary adversaries saw the shudras' *bhakti* (devotion) not only as an aspiration to religious autonomy but also socially subversive and a threat to brahmanism, the modern elitist researches highlight their religious fervour, projecting them as mystical or spiritual entities. But (as their surviving verses attest) they repudiated the superiority of the brahman, and also rejected ritualism, temples and monasteries of the organised religion. Their radical monotheism envisioned a god who resided within their own beings in the form of individual and social conscience. Their god stirred up rebellion against injustice in the hearts of the devotees. In other words, in spite of the religious idiom, the cut and thrust of the debate they generated was social and political. This forced the brahmanic champions such as Tulsidas to infiltrate the movement in order to sabotage it from within, while the more reactionary elements tried to crush it with the feudal-kingly support (Chapter 3).

Colonialism Within Colonialism

Despite resistance, brahmanism retained its ideological–cultural hold, and its prescriptions went on to become cultural common sense. By allowing all regimes to pass over its head, it ensured its spectacular survival. Brahmanic social order continued in the middle ages under the absolutism of Muslim rulers who found the caste system useful for mass subjugation. Later, during colonialism, the British rulers carried caste and brahmanism on their back for the same reasons (Chapter 4). To both overseas and Indian ruling classes, a neat division of society between the rulers and the ruled was the natural order; both were bonded by the 'sacredness' of categories like caste, class, race, and patriarchy. Thus brahmanism got a new lease of life during colonialism, first by colluding with the colonial powers (which allowed it to rejuvenate and refurbish its old cultural resources), and then by emerging as the politico-ideological engine of nationalism and capturing power after Independence.

History books hide the enduring nexus that existed between the colonial power and the Indian elite. The dominant trajectory of colonialism constructs two civilisational absolutes of India and the West which subsume the voices of the marginalised in both societies as well as the reality of collusion between the British and Indian elites on which colonialism was founded. To speak of colonialism in India as if the British controlled everything that happened during the colonial rule is really a myth. Even at the height of British power at the beginning of the twentieth century there were hardly more than 1300 British civil servants in the whole of subcontinent. Below them they had a vast army of Indian subordinates, most of them from brahmanic backgrounds. The Army, too, was predominantly Indian. In other words, the Indian elites who colluded with colonialism were in the privileged position of being able to accommodate and manipulate the language of colonial power.

The echo of colonialist narratives and policies is nowhere more evident than in the writings of those who either took it upon themselves or were pushed into that role by the colonial authorities to represent Hindu and Muslim communities. This tradition begins in the nineteenth century, and continues in one form or the other in contemporary India, although it has been adapted and transformed, depending on specific contextual factors. (Baber 2006: 53)

Recently, some Euro-American scholars, suffering from the guilt induced by the postcolonial works of Indian intellectuals, have written sympathetic tomes to establish that caste and other contraditions in Indian society were more or less invented during the colonial period (Inden 1990; Dirks 2002). Their researches assume one way or the other that colonialism affected all Indians—privileged as well as downtrodden—in a similar manner. The problem with such researchers is the same as that of the Orientalists they deride: their interlocutors, informers, and Indian friends consist only of the caste elites. They forget that all of colonial caste–tribe volumes, gazetteers and censuses relied heavily on the work of privileged-caste assistants. The process of redefining, updating, and reinforcing caste during colonialism was not simply a Western project. Caste elites, the main beneficiaries of these measures, were complicit in the colonial construction of caste. The criminal complicity of colonialism in strengthening brahmanism and vice versa is a sordid story which remains largely unknown (Chapter 4).

The Aryan race theory (which gained currency during colonial rule) had resulted in the stereotypes of arrival of Aryans in India, the composition of the Vedas, and the subjugation of the indigenous dasa-shudras, first through necessary violence and then through the seductive instrument of caste, etc. According to this theory, the higher one's caste, the more Aryan (i.e. of 'European' descent) one was. The race and Indo-European language theory fired the imagination of many Europeans who saw themselves as distant cousins of the upper-caste Indians. Max Müller, who brought out the first printed edition of *Rigveda* and popularised the word *arya* [Aryan], fancied that the same blood ran in the veins of English soldiers as in the veins of the dark Bengalis. It was this feeling of kinship which inspired the European romantics to take upon themselves the task of recovering the 'lost glory' of India with the help of Sanskrit pandits. They would derive immense pleasure in 'discovering' the spiritual–intellectual achievements of their Indian ancestors. In spite of some critical writings of the Utilitarians and Evangelists, who had been to India and had seen the reality for themselves, the spiritual myth about India, thanks to those racist romantics, survived in Europe. The myth was built into the concept of the mysterious, spiritual East as drastically different from the rationalistic, materialist West.

In a variety of ways, the Aryan theory and East–West dichotomy were useful for the elites of both societies. To the colonialist, they provided legitimacy to colonial rule (spirituality-intoxicated Indians were not supposed to take care of the material side of life). To the caste elites, the notion of their racial superiority—certified by the 'European authorities'—legitimised them as 'natural leaders' of Indian society. Both swore by the caste system which had allegedly created a harmonious society where everyone was given a job based on his natural tendencies and aptitudes! The degeneration, and here, too, there was broad agreement, began with the dilution of caste and establishment of Muslim rule. With so much crucial consensus, colonial historiography had to be twisted only a little—to ward off colonial arrogance—and it was ready to be employed in the service of brahmanic nationalist reconstruction.

The Hindu and Nationalist Makeovers of Brahmanism

A 'Hindu' was born when the Muslim entered the Indian scene; and with the rise of British colonialism (and Indological scholarship in which the Indian pandits contributed their mite) was born a movement from the 'Hindu' to 'Hinduism'. It is significant that Rammohun Roy used the term 'Hinduism' for the first time in 1816–17 for a faith that was earlier called, as Roy himself said, Varnashrama Dharma, Sanatana Dharma, or simply Brahmanism (see Killingley 1993: 62–3). Though the word Hindu (emanating from the river Sindhu) had been in use in the pre-modern India, more as a cultural and geographical marker than as a religious category, Hinduism, as we know it today, is a modern construction of the upper-caste literati, aided and abetted by the colonial rule and Oriental scholarship. Romila Thapar terms this phenomenon 'syndicated Hinduism', a construct which was more political than religious. This Hinduism seeks to encapsulate all the indigenous religious sects, denominations, and practices into one entity in a hegemonic manner. Drawing largely on brahmanism in thought, scriptures, and rituals, it identifies the essential beliefs, ritual, and practices of a Hindu, thereby aiming at uniformity, centralisation, and monotheism of the Semitic religions. It attempts to firmly take all the lowered castes and tribes within this standard Hinduism, and encourages proselytisation through reconverting Muslims and Christians. It supports the inequality of brahmanic social order, and advocates Hindu nationalism—Hindus being the majority must rule the country, and must lord over the minorities, that is, adherents of other religions. Syndicated Hinduism is thus a hegemonic attempt to reinterpret and remake Hinduism to gain a hold over the masses (Thapar 2001).

In other words, brahmanism got a new makeover during colonial rule, and in due course went on to nationalise itself into octopus-like Hinduism. Simultaneously, the brahmanic forces developed the idea of cultural nationalism and turned it into a political–cultural campaign that justified caste in the name of patriotism, making brahmanism synonymous with Hinduism and Hinduism with Indianness. It was this betrayal of the wider nation, the marginalised majority, by the wily caste elites that was challenged by the dalit-bahujan stalwarts such as Phule, Periyar, and Ambedkar (Chapters 5, 6 and 7).

The basic orientation of upper-caste-centric reform movements that Rammohun Roy pioneered was such that it became inseparable from brahmanic revivalism. Later, combining piecemeal reformism with revivalism, charismatic leaders such as Dayananda and Vivekananda attacked, periodically and in patches, some odious aspects of 'degraded' caste culture but at the same time vigorously defended the classical caste system and brahmanism under the fig-leaf of 'glorious Indian tradition' (Chapter 4).

Gandhi–Nehru Upholding of the Oppressive Tradition

Since its foundation in 1885, the Indian National Congress, the umbrella organisation of nationalist politics, remained in the grip of brahmanical vested interests. Political socialisation—through which civil values, symbols and cognitions are learned and internalised, through which operative social norms regarding politics are implanted, and political consensus created—that took place in India under Congress' overarching leadership, was grounded in the politics of deception and double-speak (Chapter 7). From the very beginning, elite reformism and nationalism had the potential of being co-opted into visceral communal politics and that is exactly what happened. It is notable that K.B. Hedgewar, the founder of militant Hindu organisation Rashtriya Swayamsevak Sangh (RSS), was a prominent Congress leader. Many top Congress leaders such as B.G. Tilak, M.M. Malaviya, P.D. Tandon had always flirted with the RSS-type Hindu chauvinism, antagonising the dalit-bahujan leaders, and alienating the Muslim leadership which soon built its own Islamist politics and separatist agenda. The partition of India was, thus, inscribed in the brahmanic DNA of the national movement. In this sense, the 1947 vivisection of India and the truncated freedom that came with it was not an individual failure of this leader or that, it was the failure of the brahmanic nationalism of which Gandhi and Nehru were an integral part.

Gandhi and Nehru have been deified—mythified—as the founding fathers of a uniquely inclusive nationalism, secularism, and democracy. Before one accepts this textbook glorification, one must read their own writing and give due attention to the existence of the Phules, Periyars and Ambedkars, from the other spectrum of society. While Gandhi used vague religious idioms and Nehru resorted to socialist–secular rhetoric, both of them, contrary to the popular myth, romanticised caste and brahmanism which were to them the life-blood of Indian culture, the fulcrum of the wonderful unity in diversity, the very basis of Indian nationalism.

It is indeed amazing how dexterously Gandhi and Nehru swept away the 'red tooth and claw' of the brahmanic social order which perpetrated the most barbaric practices against the lowered castes. They used an anti-colonial ideology to put on a great nationalist show, full of democratic sound and fury, while actually promoting the brahmanical perspective of Indian culture. Except their emphasis on the Hindu–Muslim amity, which too was envisaged on the notion of unity of elites from the two communities, their socio-cultural construction of the past and the nationalism animated by that bore a startling similarity to the 'Hindu nationalism' envisioned by the caste chauvinists of the earlier and contemporary times. Communal fanatics have derived much comfort from the Hindu revivalisms, 'but considerable sections of what we call our secular nationalism have never been quite free of that kind of rhetoric, so much so that [Gandhi's] *Hind Swaraj* is of course a major document of that fantasy of the past but even Nehru's *Discovery of India* tends sometimes to rehearse precisely those themes' (A. Ahmad 2002: 87).

Gandhi was a faith-intoxicated man, a self-declared 'Sanatani Hindu'. His winning formula of defending, and then glorifying, caste-bound Hinduism, was simple: he never spoke of Hinduism as it was but what it might be. Anyone who loves Hinduism, has, necessarily, to justify caste since caste is central to Hinduism—there can be no Hindu without a caste. No one knew this better than the 'Sanatani Hindu' who throughout his life defended caste and brahmanism by resorting to devious logic, tortuous explanations, and select examples to prove that varna and caste have nothing to do with each other—and this was, and is, the main reason for his popularity among the dominant castes. Offering within the Sanatana Dharma a language for change and redress, Gandhi had the staggering ability to emotionalise and obfuscate all issues. He expeditiously shifted—without changing—his definitions of caste, freedom, and nationalism, all of which were embedded in his trademark obscurantism. Always speaking from the high moral ground in the name of the poor and invoking truth and non-violence, he never lost his zeal to perform miracles—in the manner of a Mahatma—liberating the oppressed with the consent of the oppressor and raising the poor with the wealth of the rich. He invested his self-righteousness with a revolutionary fervour and assumed that the virtues of the powerful would compensate for the latter's structural complicities in oppression. This is enough for his hagiographers to project him as a redeemer of the poor and an enemy of the establishment. It is never unravelled how, through his constant evocation of Varnashrama, Ram-rajya and Trusteeship, Gandhi supported the hierarchical order and the whole matrix of socio-economic injustice associated with it (Chapter 7).

Gandhi pioneered a brahmanic–bourgeois politics that ignored the structural and intellectual roots of caste–class oppression. He mistook the order imposed by hegemony (which ensures the absence of war) for peace, ignoring that authentic peace is not possible without justice and genuine concord. Refusing to see any discrimination, let alone violence, in caste hierarchy, he consistently declined, despite being reminded by social radicals like Ambedkar and Periyar, to apply the same ethical principles against the internal injustice that he so effectively employed against colonialism. Instead, Gandhi declared his determination to defend the princes and landlords by all means should ever any attempt be made to confiscate their property (Chapter 7).

The elite intellectuals conceal the reality of Gandhi's brahmanic bias and conservative orientation of his politics, and glean from him some uniquely Eastern ideas of redeeming holiness. The obfuscatory wordsmithery of the likes of Bipan Chandra (1989), Ashis Nandy (1980; 1983), Bikhu Parekh (1989) and Richard Attenborough's cinematic biography are classic examples of Gandhi's mythification. His devotees recount his historic role in mobilising the masses, without recognising that his politics was oriented against the very masses whom he used as his foot-soldiers. He never approved of the autonomous activity of the oppressed masses. They had to be always guided by the privileged-caste notables. In their turn, the caste elites projected Gandhi within the framework of brahmanic faith, tradition, and mythology as an *avatar* whose *darshan* was an ennobling end in itself.

To behold the Mahatma in person and become his devotees were the only roles assigned to the *sadharan janta* or ordinary people, while it was for the urban intelligentsia and full-time party activists to convert this groundswell of popular feeling into an organised movement. Even in the relationship between peasant devotees and their Mahatma there was room for political mediation by the economically better off and socially more powerful followers. (Amin 1996: 4)

In the *avatar* of half-saint and half-politician, Gandhi allowed himself to be manipulated by his 'trustees', the caste elites. No wonder, Ambedkar and Periyar saw Gandhi as an orthodox moralist whose pacifism actually enhanced his authoritarianism, and whose renunciations rid none of his desire to control and coerce the traditionally subjugated. Gandhi's defence of caste and brahmanism under the cover of spiritual–cultural nationalism was the secret of his popularity among the elite intelligentsia. The grateful pandits have created a fabulous industry around his mass of platitudes emerging from a conception of morality based upon a dogmatic faith. Hagiographic accounts of the 'saintly-godly' Gandhi and his 'ism'—with his own tacit consent and complicity—have been cunningly used by the exploiting classes as an apparel to cover their hideous nakedness. With the government's propaganda machine at its command since Independence, the neo-brahmanic forces have succeeded in spreading an apostolic image of Gandhi in all corners in the world. Billions of rupees—all public money—have been squandered on creating and disseminating the image of Gandhi as 'father of the nation' and the 'Christ of the East'.[3]

In contrast to Gandhi, Nehru was a self-conscious intellectual, a secularist and a propagator of scientific temper. A student of 'scientific' history, he wrote *The Discovery of India* in the dying days of the British rule, to present a systematic nationalist history. The recurrent themes of Nehru's discovery—the assertion of a national unity from very ancient time; India's genius for seeking a synthesis in apparent contradictions; and, the amazing staying power of the Indian civilisation—are envisaged in the brahmanic myth of the golden past. In fact, Nehru attributes, directly or indirectly, the national synthesis to brahmanism and caste system throughout his narrative.

Stuffed with acknowledged as well as free borrowings from 'European authorities' and local luminaries like Radhakrishnan, Nehru's imagined India rests on the same thesis of earlier Hindu nationalists from Dayananda and Vivekananda to Tilak and Savarkar that the nation and nationalism in 'Bharatvarsha' is ancient. Its genesis he traces, like his predecessors, in the remote past when the Sanskrit-speaking Aryans came into India from the north-west, conquered (without an invasion?) the natives—the Dravidians to whom they considered themselves 'vastly superior' and the 'backward aboriginal tribes, nomads or forest-dwellers' and constructed a social synthesis through the varna/caste ideology, thus laying the foundation of the civilising current of Indian history ([1946] 1996: 84). The indigenous backward people were included 'at the bottom of the social scale' as shudras in Aryan society, that is, the 'nation', according to their natural disposition and inclination (p. 85). Despite occasional protestations (caste 'brought about degradation in its train afterwards', p. 84) and claims to the contrary (caste as 'a device to keep the Aryan conquerors apart from and above the conquered peoples', p. 246), he celebrates the 'cohesiveness and stability of the social organisation' (p. 247).

The institution of caste, Nehru argues, evolved as an answer to the 'national' challenge of organising the co-existence of different races. It proved to be a unique and lasting solution to conflict between various groups. It has stood through the ages, and its power and cohesiveness, he stresses, derives from its functions. Brahmans, he holds, were 'honoured and respected by all' because of their high intelligence which they used to 'determine values and the preservation of ethical standards' and 'their record of public service and personal sacrifice for the public good' (pp. 86–7). The brahmans were the brain behind the *dharma*—'a conception of obligations, of the discharge of one's duties to oneself and to others', which 'stands out in marked contrast, with the modern assertion of rights, rights of individuals, of groups, of nations' (p. 87). Attempting to prove that this brahmanic dharma went on to become the national religion and culture, Nehru cites the Vedas from which

> flow out the rivers of Indian thought and philosophy, of Indian life and culture and literature, ever widening and increasing in volume, and sometimes flooding the land with their rich deposits. During this enormous span of years they changed their courses sometimes, and even appeared to shrivel up, yet they preserved their essential identity. (Ibid.: 80–1)

The Vedic ideals of the Indo-Aryan race became enshrined, Nehru asserts, in all aspects of national life, religious and social, despite the 'successive waves of invasion and conquest by Persians, Greeks, Scythians, Mohammedans, and remained practically unchecked and unmodified from without down to the era of British occupation'. Thus the continuity 'between the most modern and the most ancient phases of Hindu thought' (p. 88).

Interestingly, the exalted theories of India's genius to 'create unity out of diversity' (Joad), 'the wonderful assimilative power of Hinduism' (Vincent Smith) and the unparalleled intellectual glories of the Vedic-brahmanic tradition (Max Müller) which keep Nehru enthralled through his narrative, were all discovered for him and other brahmanic ideologues by European scholars. No wonder the basic formulations of the nationalist historiography bear an uncanny resemblance to the colonial imagination of the Indian past. Nehru's myth-history, too, was erected on the architecture of European scholarship and Orientalism, which championed the Aryan theory, the associated linguistic symbiosis between Sanskrit and European languages and the spiritual myth about India. In some basic ways these formulations served the vested interests of both British and Indian ruling classes, as we saw earlier.

Over a period of time, such brahmanic outlook was fine-tuned in the nationalist idiom by Rammohun Roy, Dayananda Saraswati, K.C. Sen, Bankimchandra Chatterjee, R.C. Dutta, B.G. Tilak, Vivekananda, M.G. Ranade, Lajpat Rai, B.C. Pal, Aurobindo, M.K. Gandhi, V.D. Savarkar and S.P. Mookerjee. Nehru took the brahmanic myth-history forward in a sophisticated way and in elegant prose. Paraphrasing many Western authors (pp. 73–107),[4] he argues that brahmanism lies at the core of Indian genius for seeking and shaping unity-in-diversity, and has saved the nation throughout its long and turbulent history:

Other foreign elements came and were absorbed. They made little difference. . . . [after periodic invasion] The reaction was essentially a nationalist one. . . . That mixture of religion and philosophy, history and tradition, custom and social structure, which in its wide fold included almost every aspect of the life of India, and which might be called brahmanism or (to use a later word) Hinduism, became the symbol of nationalism. It was indeed a national religion, with its appeal to all those deep instincts, racial and cultural, which form the basis everywhere of nationalism today. (Ibid.: 138)

Nehru adds here that Buddhism, though native to India, became a world religion, and as it developed and spread it became irrelevant in the national arena. 'Thus it was natural for the old brahmanic faith to become the symbol again and again of nationalist revivals' (p. 138).

Thus, the Nehruvian discourse of secular nationalism, too, is replete with those claims of cultural particularity which trace themselves back to the Aryan-brahmanic glories of the past. To build the brahmanic monolith of Indian culture, the caste elites ignored the more inclusive traditions represented by Buddhism and other heterodoxies and the contribution of Islam, Sikhism and other faiths, thus undermining the real plurality of India. For purposes of rhetoric though, for the nationalists like Nehru, the legacies of Buddha, Ashoka, Kabir and Nanak could safely be assimilated to a loudly proclaimed eclecticism by juggling around with the laws of logic.

The slogan of nationalism enabled the dominant castes, strategically placed with different levers of power in their hands, to project their selfish interests as national interests. The intellectual elite coopted other exploiting sections, and together they came forward to speak in the name of the nation as its sole representative. This gave them a handle to crush dissent from below as 'anti-national' with accusations of lack of faith in the 'nation' itself. Thus, the old brahmanic religion was effectively supplanted by the new nationalist politics of hegemony. As the ancient faith was sacred and supreme, so became the new religion of nationalism. Despite a variety of formulations of the past, the common denominator and trajectory in all of them was clear and sharp: a preference for the Aryan races, their ideologies of hierarchy, 'their constant historical role in developing the identity of the nation', and the necessity hence of 'shaping the nationalist future by salvaging as much of these ideals as possible from multifarious modern attacks' (Aloysius 1997: 162). The result was,

[T]he sheer persistence of Brahminical revivalisms at the very heart of what were expected to be structures of our modernity and which never did give us any kind of modernity, precisely because of the extensive compromises they made with colonial representations of Indian history and because of their interest in representing their caste cultures as our 'national culture'. (A. Ahmad 2002: 87)

Freedom Struggles of Phule, Ambedkar and Periyar

It is precisely this neo-brahmanism in the name of nationalism that was challenged and exposed by the dalit-bahujan leaders who saw themselves as heirs to the other tradition, the tradition of resistance to caste and brahmanism. They argued that the brahmanic socio-religious system was a form of colonialism and, therefore, its annihilation must constitute an integral part of nation-building. Phule, the first person to articulate this view, declared war on the internal colonialism and its ideological matrix, arguing that smashing its intellectual defences was essential even before targeting its material basis of exploitation (Chapter 5). Later, Periyar (Chapter 6) and Ambedkar (Chapter 7) took this struggle forward in their distinctive ways, seeking freedom from not merely colonial rule, but also from humiliation and exploitation of the brahmanic social order.

The agenda of the dalit-bahujans, like that of the counter-traditions to which they attached themselves, was to demolish social disabilities and barriers, to restore dignity among the caste-oppressed and to establish a new order based on inclusive values. In a significant shift from the elitist approach, they tried to understand the past by the present as their understanding of history and culture was animated by objective reality and their own experiences. While fighting for their citizenship rights—the right to enter public and religious places; access to educational centres; the right to wear shoes and carry umbrellas; the right of their women (in the south) to cover their breasts; the right to give up agricultural bondage and the freedom to choose an occupation—the dalit-bahujan leaders approached history in search of the roots of contemporary reality and discovered India in a way that tore apart the basic formulations of elite ideology. Ilaiah makes a pertinent point in this regard by stressing that personal experience brings out reality in a striking way.

Instead of depending on Western methods, Phule, Ambedkar and Periyar spoke and wrote on the day-to-day experiences of the dalit-bahujan castes. I would argue that this is the only possible and indeed the most authentic way in which the deconstruction and construction of history can take place. (Ilaiah 1996: XII)

On the nation issue, Phule, Ambedkar and Periyar hammered home the point that the nation is nothing if it is not the people. Unravelling the caste–class structure of society, they argued that a society divided by discrimination could not constitute a genuine nation. The caste elites claiming to represent the nation were actually its destroyers, since they not only rationalised or masked the glaring inequalities of the past and present, but actually sought to maintain them as their power base. Exposing the conflicts and crimes of history, the dalit-bahujan leaders held brahmanism responsible for enslaving the minds of toiling people through a fake religion and a false philosophy. They attacked brahmanism for creating caste ideology to exploit the productive majority. They rejected Hinduism itself by arguing that it was symbiotically bonded with brahmanical tyranny, superstition, and irrationality. They felt that the new India required an egalitarian and rational religion that could not be provided by reconstructed Hinduism.

The search for an alternate religion as an ethical foundation of an alternate culture was a common concern of the dalit-bahujan radicals (Omvedt 1994). Phule formulated the *sarvajanik satyadharma* (the universal religion of truth); Iyothee Thass and Ambedkar returned to 'their old dhamma' Buddhism and fashioned a new Buddhism out of it; many in the south found solace in a radicalised version of Shaivism; Narayana Guru formulated 'one religion, one caste, one god' while his more radical follower Ayyappan, in the manner of the atheist Periyar, proclaimed 'no religion, no caste, no god for mankind'. Some preferred to convert to Christianity and Islam while subalterns in the north sought to create independent religions out of the teachings of their cultural icons such as Kabir and Ravidas.

Recognising the power of culture in the politics of transformation, Phule, Iyothee Thass, Periyar, Acchutanand, and above all, Ambedkar spent a significant part of their intellectual energies on the task of developing the counter-tradition, and strove to link it to their struggles for a casteless and democratic society. These tireless documenters of atrocities against the lowered castes and women used this knowledge to expose the hollowness of the elitist version of history, culture, and nationalism. They asked the nationalists to change their brahmanic mindset before claiming to represent the nation. Challenging the patriotic pretensions of those who were presenting the oppressive past as the site of national glory, Phule wrote as early as 1873: 'If the ancestors of these progressive and liberal men had really understood the meaning of patriotism, they would not have written essays in their books in which their own countrymen, the shudras, were regarded as lower than animals.' Ambedkar and Periyar asked the same question in different ways: Was it patriotic to suppress one's own countrymen, the toiling majority, while one might be eloquent in contesting colonial rule? Could Hinduism's vicious, vindictive, violent content vanish merely by labelling it 'cultural nationalism'?

In a famous essay 'The Politics of Recognition', Charles Taylor has argued that 'contemptible images' of a cultural community, consistently projected by a dominant group and refusal of equal recognition can actually distort and oppress that community. What can be more dehumanising than being labeled 'shudra', 'untouchable' and 'low caste'? The greatest of privileged-caste nationalists (such as Gandhi and Nehru) refused even to recognise this, let alone forging a social unity for cultural reconstruction, forcing the dalit-bahujan leaders to wage their autonomous struggles for freedom. Since Phule, Ambedkar, and Periyar represented the suppressed majority, there was greater democratic depth, intellectual reasoning, and empirical thoroughness in their dalit–bahujan ideology than in the brahmanic nationalism of Tilak, Gandhi and Nehru.

Hegel once said that only the slave can understand the whole of society because he must understand himself as well as the conditions of his exploitation, and hence his master; whereas the master can rest his laurels on understanding merely himself and the terms on which he can exploit his slave. It is in this specific sense that the consciousness of the subjugated is always superior to the consciousness of the rulers. ... [I]n the multiplicity of our reform movements, it was only the reform movements of the oppressed castes, and the efforts of some valiant women, that were substantially free of those kinds of revivalisms and had some fundamental understanding of the social whole, and therefore of the 'nation' conceived as 'the people', because the overwhelming majority of 'the people' were neither upper class nor upper caste. (Ahmad 2002: 85)

This cognition can help us grasp the significance of Phule envisioning a new Satyadharma, Periyar standing out as an avowed atheist, and Ambedkar ultimately undertaking a formal religious conversion 'not as merely a personal act, living his conversion not as a personal salvation, but as militant repudiation of caste society and as an invitation to mass repudiation of the same' (Ahmad: ibid.).

However, the cultural revolution that the dalit-bahujan leaders initiated, remained not only incomplete but also ignored in mainstream historiography. Those who could have been India's liberators were marginalised as leaders of 'lower castes' and 'untouchables'. The modernity, nation state and democracy that came to India (on the back of selective Westernisation and neo-brahmanism) failed to break the spell of caste and brahmanism.

The brahmanical grip on Indian society was established through suppression of mass education. *Na shudray mati dadyat* (do not give education to the ordinary people) was a common refrain in the Dharmashastras. The custodians of society devised a multi-pronged system of domination and sought to stifle all expression and creativity from below. Those who tried to overcome the system were suppressed. Ekalavya lost his thumb and Shambuka his life for breaches of caste rules. Dronacharya tricked the tribal boy to cut off his own thumb so that Arjuna, the Pandav prince, could become the best archer. Dronacharya is revered in the 'great tradition' as the exemplar of a teacher—a national award for sports coaches has been instituted in the name of this perfidious teacher. The Prince of Ayodhya, who beheaded the meditating Shambuka because he was striving for spiritual excellence in violation of his *shudrahood*, has become the greatest cultural icon of the Hindu nationalists. In their narrative, Rama the Shambuka-slayer, who also exiled his wife Sita on suspicion of infidelity, is presented as the protector of the weak and the undefended.

History and culture have been fictionalised to show that the lowered castes were the willing collaborators in the making of caste culture. The coopting or coercing the powerless into accepting the oppressive culture, and thus become a participator in their own oppression, have been done both politically and ideologically. Caste elites writing on India, despite a lot of internal differences or debates among them, have conditioned the minds of people, both scholars and commoners, to think about India in a brahmanical way. Experts on the epics and scriptures have built a brahmanic cultural stranglehold on the people's psyche. Their fabrications overwhelm the entire ideological spectrum of the upper-caste intelligentsia. All the stereotypes in which they encapsulate India are designed to preserve vested interests and structures of power, as this book will show.

When the powerful can no longer withhold education from the powerless, they see to it that the education imparted to the people does not encourage critical thinking. They ensure that people at large remain in the dark about larger social and cultural reality. It is extremely difficult even for the educated people with minds of their own not to succumb to the constant repetition of cultural constructs and images that reinforce the dominant ideology. Visionary leaders that they were, Phule, Ambedkar and Periyar had keenly felt the need to democratise education and culture. What they meant by education was not just the competence to read and write but the power to see through hegemonic ideology, which Phule termed *tritiya ratna* (the third eye) in his eponymous 1855 play.

Summarising, egalitarianism is neither alien to India nor the gift of the West. Common people everywhere have a tradition of aspiring to build an egalitarian world. In India, this tradition is to be found in the heterodoxies of diverse inclinations, particularly in the inclusive strands of shramanism, Buddhism, the movements of subaltern sant-poets, Sufism, and Sikhism. This creative and anti-hierarchical legacy was carried forward in modern India by, more than anyone else, Jotiba Phule, Iyothee Thass, Narayana Guru, Ambedkar, and Periyar.

In some micro studies, the emanciaptory orientation of this tradition is recognised, but it is seldom integrated with macro-level theoretical studies on Indian culture and society. This book is an attempt in that direction. The effort is to debrahmanise India's social history by revisiting some of the major episodes of people's resistance and creativity. This book is meant for all those who are—or want to be—part of the ongoing struggle for human liberation.

Notes

1. M.N. Srinivas, considered a disinterested authority on caste, is known for his characterisation of social change in India under the rubric of Sanskritisation (which has become part of the academic folklore and cited often as a theory of caste not driven by ideology). This thesis of Sanskritisation and Westernisation claims that the lower castes Sanskritise—imitate and adopt upper-caste, especially brahmanic, practices so as to move up in the caste hierarchy—and the upper castes modernise and westernise. Thus, Srinivas normalises, even glorifies, caste and brahmanism, locating caste in the past with the implicit optimism that whatever remains of it is on its way out—upper castes have shown the way; the lower castes will follow suit. Implicit in his theory and his overall scholarship is the idea that caste is amazingly fluid and fair; caste is not the problem; in fact, it never was (caste had more or less been a fair division of labour based on function and merit); the only problem which produces all problems in modern India is the politicisation of caste, especially the caste-based policy of affirmative action. Srinivas earned his livelihood by theorising and talking about caste but never revealed his own brahman identity, except in a rare burst of honesty (in response to a provocative query by social anthropologist E.R. Leach) that his Sanskritisation was indeed inspired by his being a brahman. In a review of Srinivas' *Caste in Modern India*, Leach found the Sanskritisation theory representing 'Brahminocentric' viewpoint, and asked 'If Professor Srinivas had been of Shudra origin would this have coloured his interpretation'. Srinivas (who never engaged with Phule, Ambedkar, and Periyar's critiques of caste and never entertained any question from dalit-bahujan critics) responded to the British anthropologist, admitting his brahman positionality and the fact that his views on the effects of reservations could not but be related to his sensitivity as a south Indian brahman and his affinity with his brahman 'friends and relatives' and 'their distress' (Srinivas [1966] 1972: 148–52). After admitting this, Srinivas again rides the high horse of academic neutrality and objectivity, speaking a language of common good in terms of efficiency and development as his logic for opposition to reservation (ibid.: 153), forgetting that measures like reservation actually fit his Sanskritisation theory like a glove. Nothing can be more corrupt than opposition to reservation for encouraging casteism by scholars like Srinivas, to use Sumit Sarkar's words (1996: 292), 'who spent a life-time writing in fairly sympathetic terms about Sanskritisation: surely the kind of caste movement that is the most casteist, in the sense of encouraging narrow sectional loyalties through the quest for mere positional mobility on behalf of a caste group, while maintaining and even strengthening the basic hierarchical order.'

2. 'Even in their own homes, a female—whether she is a child, a young woman, or an old lady—should never carry out any task independently. As a child, she must remain under her father's control; as a young woman, under her husband's; and when her husband is dead, under her sons. She must never seek to live independently.... Day and night men should keep their women from acting independently; for, attached as they are to sensual pleasures, men should keep them under their control.... A woman is not qualified to act independently.' (*Manusmriti* 5.147–9, 9. 2–3, tr. Olivelle 2005: 146, 190).

3. Academia in India and Euro-America, has been, with some exceptions, an integral part of this Gandhi industry. No one has bothered to investigate the fact that a significant part of Gandhi's writings, especially his translated writings (now available in the 100 volumes of *Collected Works*), have been massively edited, reworked and redacted—to hide or obscure his original crude support of caste, conservatism, and vested interests.

4. The following roster of European statements faithfully quoted by Nehru in his *Discovery* within a space of a few pages may give us an idea of how closely his construction of history was embedded in the Western reading of the Indian past: 'India ... infinitely absorbent like the ocean' (Dodwell, p. 73); '... the wonderful assimilative power of Hinduism ' (Vincent Smith, p. 74); '... Vedic literature goes back to 2000 BC or even 2500 BC ...' (Winternitz, pp. 76–7); '... India here [in the Vedic verses] set out on a quest which she has never ceased to follow' (Macnicol, p. 79); '... the country most richly endowed with all the wealth, power and beauty .... I must point to India' (Max Müller, p. 88); '... Where all the dreams of living men have found a home from the earliest days ... it is India' (Romain Rolland, p. 89); '... no important form of Hindu thought, heterodox Buddhism included, which is not rooted in Upanishads' (Bloomsfield, p. 92); '...The Mahabharata ... the idea of a single centralised India' (Margaret Noble, p. 107).

CHAPTER I

Historical Roots of Brahmanic Dominance and Shramanic Resistance

> Dominant human groups have long defined themselves as superior by distinguishing themselves from groups they are subordinating. Thus whites define blacks in part by differing melanin content of the skin; men are distinguished from women by primary and secondary sex characteristics. These empirical distinctions are then used to make it appear that it is the distinction themselves, not their social consequences, that are responsible for the social dominance of one group over the other.
>
> JEFFREY MASSON AND SUSAN MCCARTHY 1996: 40–1

We cannot comprehend the myths of caste and brahmanism unless we clear the cobwebs of fiction and fantasy that have been woven around the Veda and Vedic culture. The Veda (from the root *vid*, 'know') is the primary canon of the Aryan-brahmans, venerated as *apaurusheya* (not of human origin), eternal, and infallible. Supposedly revealed to certain inspired *rishis* (sages)—hence called *shruti* (heard, implying revelation)—it is claimed that the Vedas existed in divine form from the beginning of time. They comprise four collections (*samhitas*)—*Rig*, *Sama*, *Yajur*, and *Atharva*—of hymns, sacrificial formulas and detached verses, of which the *Rigveda* is the oldest and most sacred. Its nucleus is believed to be the parts known as the *Mantras* and *Brahmanas*. The appendages to the *Brahmanas* are known as *Aranyakas* (forest books), and the concluding portions of the *Aranyakas* are called the *Upanishads*. The Aranyakas, connected with mysticism and symbolism, form a transition to the philosophical texts of Upanishads. The four Vedas and the Brahmanas together are known as *shruti*, while the Aranyakas and the Upanishads are called *Vedanta* (the last portion of the Vedas).

Actually, the Vedas are the creation of several generations of those Indo-Europeans who came into India from Central Asia in several waves beginning about 1400 BCE. According to a credible work remarkable for synthesising data from a variety of sources—archaeology, linguistics and literature, the history of technology, geomorphology, and astronomy—the original Rigvedic hymns were composed in *c.* 1700 BCE in Afghanistan before the Rigvedic Aryans arrived in the Ganga-Yamuna doab. '. . . The composition of the *Rigveda* was taken up in south Afghanistan a few centuries after the demise of the mature Harappan phase. The later parts of the *Rigveda* as well as the later Vedic texts were however composed in India.' Under the circumstances, some correspondence between the Vedic texts and the later Harappan cultural phases is to be expected, but there is no evidence to show that Mehrgarh, or the early or mature Harappan cultures had any cultural trait in common with the Rigvedic and Avestan people (Kochhar 2000: 225). Instead studies have shown the remarkable ties of language, culture, mythology and rituals between Rigvedic and Avestan Aryans. Both formed part of one group—the Indo-Iranians—of Indo-Europeans (who got divided into the European and the Indo-Iranian), moving around the second millennium BCE from their original home in the steppes north of the Black and Caspian Seas, southwards into the territories now called Europe and Central Asia respectively.

Parts of the Vedas composed in India reveal that the Vedic Aryans fought many battles with the indigenous inhabitants whom they called *dasa* and *dasyu,* and succeeded in subjugating them due to their use of horses and possibly better weapons. Gradually, the invaders settled down amongst the native people, but antagonism persisted, a fact amply attested by several verses in the *Rigveda*. Either during this tumultuous transition, or, more likely in subsequent centuries, the Aryans devised the system of caste—primarily to retain their racial purity and impose their authority over the 'low-born' aborigines. Even if caste, or something approximating it, existed before the Aryan arrival in the subcontinent, as some historians claim (for obvious reasons), the graded hierarchy of caste was the creation of the Aryan-brahmans. In the later Vedic period (i.e. after 900 BCE), their descendants attributed the genesis of caste to divine will to give it a religious halo. Most historians are categorical that the *Purusha-sukta* in the tenth book of the *Rigveda,* which gives a religio-mythical explanation for the origin of caste, is a later interpolation.[1]

Originally, the Vedas consisted only of a few hundred verses but increasingly the samhitas were inflated by additions and interpolations, into a massive hotchpotch of history, legends, religious beliefs and ceremonies of the early Aryans. This because the verses were handed down the priestly tradition by word of mouth for centuries before they were finally written down.

Amidst the bewildering maze of rituals, sacrifices, nature-worship, and stray depictions of contemporary material life, it is difficult to decipher the exact Vedic worldview—'hidden as it is behind the thorny wall of an ancient and cryptic language'. In many places, as a translator points out, 'a difficult idea is couched in a simple language; in others, a simple idea is obscured by difficult language' (O'Flaherty 2000: 14). There is no uniformity in the quality and subject matter of the hymns. 'To take an extreme example, there are a few late passages in the *Rigveda* which nineteenth-century British prudery would print only in Latin translation' (Kochhar 2000: 19). (Many of those sexually explicit passages are now available in O'Flaherty's translation.)

The task of interpretation is made difficult by the interested pandits who tend to make the Vedas more and more esoteric in order to present them as the ultimate holy book. Marx once sarcastically remarked that the brahmans preserved the holiness of the Vedas by reserving for themselves the right to read these. Besides large-scale revisions and redactions, the language, much older than Sanskrit, is ambiguous, and open to contradictory interpretations. The verses are so full of allusions and passing references for which no contexts are available, that a determined Sanskritist can read anything into them.

A perceptive study by Kumkum Roy (1996) suggests that Vedic cosmogony was never far from an attempt to control the social and the political. Though the concept of the cosmic sacrifice—*yajna*—encouraged an understanding of cosmogonic activities, the exercise of such privilege was open only to priestly experts and, to some extent, the *yajamana*, the male sacrificer or patron of the sacrifice. Given the wide range of sacrifices, a participatory role was perhaps available to patriarchs of the first three varnas. And, of course, it was eminently accessible to, and frequently exercised by, ambitious or victorious men such as *rajas* who would perform the *rajasuya* or *ashvamedha* to show off their exalted status.

Yet, there were many who were excluded from an independent role in the sacrifice. These included shudras, junior members of the households of men belonging to the first three varnas, and women.... Thus access to or lack of access to the sacrifice as a cosmic act could have been one (but by no means the only) means of enforcing social stratification—between priests and non-priestly categories, between sacrificers and others, and between men and women. (K. Roy 1996: 17–18)

Despite multiplicity or fluidity of Vedic cosmogonies, and the possibility of some tension or contestation over them, the socio-ritual differentiation had taken roots. Although Roy concludes that 'the attempt to reduce cosmogonic speculation into an ideology of dominance was probably only partially successful' (ibid.: 19), the picture she paints gives a hint of how the cultural foundation of caste culture was laid by the priest, prince, and patriarch.

In brief, the basis of brahman supremacy over all others was established through control over the all-important ritual sacrifice. The brahman contended that it was from a cosmic and primordial sacrifice that the universe was created, and it was because of the repeated sacrifices that the universe continued. The intent behind the logic is clear: by presiding over the sacrifice the brahman plays the role of mediator between the divinities above and humans below, and, thus keeps the world going. So anyone from the upper varnas who is desirous of well-being must turn to the brahman who will offer sacrifices on his behalf.

Violence and Domination Underpin Vedic Ideology

There are very few dispassionate studies which have tried to grapple with the Vedic conundrum. The pandits, both Indian and Euro-American, continue to perpetuate the myth that the Vedic corpus comprise sublime and humane values within the cultural context of a complex cosmology. More objective studies, however, point to the fact that ethics have little place in the system of Vedic sacrifice. Hidden in the mystery of nature, sacrifice is a mechanical act that is brought out by the magic art of the priest, who performs it for a fee. Some scholars contend that self-aggrandisement and violence stand out as dominant Vedic themes in both religious sphere of ritual as well as in the material life. Sylvain Levi says, 'It is difficult to imagine anything more brutal and more material than the theology of the Brahmanas. Notions which usage afterwards gradually refined, and clothed with a garb of morality, take us aback by their savage realism' (cited in Rhys Davids [1902] 1981: 240).

Hiṁsa ('the desire to inflict injury'), or violence, is indeed the Vedic leitmotif. Violence and power exercised over others were not only glorified on their own terms, but represented as an 'integral part' of the natural order of things. They are manifest in the recurrent metaphor of 'food' and 'eaters'. As the *Shatapatha Brahmana* puts it, 'The eater of food and food indeed are everything here.' This was not merely a culinary metaphor, but was meant as a depiction of the natural and social world organised into a hierarchically ordered food chain. In fact, the nutritional chain exactly described the order of the species, as Doniger and Smith (1991) point out. At the top of Vedic 'natural' order were the heavenly deities feeding on sacrificial oblations that were clearly represented as a substitute for the human sacrifices, next in the line on the menu. Then, humans consume animals, the next life-form; animals eat plants, who, in turn, consume 'rain' or 'the waters' from which all food is generated.

Eating and killing were regarded as two sides of the same coin. But eating was also frankly envisioned as the perpetual re-enactment of the defeat and subjugation of one's rival.... Eating was the triumphant overcoming of the natural and social enemy, of those one hates and is hated by.... Consumption was, in sum, the ultimate victory of the consumer over the consumed, of the victor over the vanquished, and of the self over the rival. (Doniger and Smith 1991: XXV–VI)

The Vedic order is defined and guided by the principle by which the strong consumes the weak. Like nature, society too is neatly divided into classes of eater and eaten—the lower orders are nothing but food and fodder for the higher orders. The supposedly 'immutable', 'natural' and 'eternal' hierarchical distinctions between the higher and the lower orders, which provide the basis of caste ideology, are drawn on this Vedic principle. It is for this logic that Prajapati, the Lord of All Creatures, is portrayed in a brahmanic text as manifest on earth in the form of a series of mouths: 'The priest is one of your mouths. With that mouth you eat rulers.... The king is one of your mouths. With that mouth you eat the commoners' (ibid.: XXVI). In this hierarchical division, the brahman or priest eats the next most important being, the kshatriya or warrior/ruler, who in his turn eats vaishyas and shudras. Thus the higher orders live, feed, and thrive on the lower.

The Veda depicts a life where I gain only at your loss, my prosperity entails your ruin, my continued existence depends on your death, my eating requires that you become food. It is an order of things seemingly most advantageous to the one with the greatest physical strength and military might—the biggest fish, the top dog. The rank order of eaters and food in the natural world is straightforward: the physically more powerful eat the physically less powerful. And the principle supposedly holds when it comes to the social world. (Ibid.: XXVII)

The Vedic celebration of power and violence is retained in the later-day brahmanism. This is manifest in the famous metaphor of the *matsyanyaya,* 'the law of the fishes', whereby the bigger fish (the strong) devour the small (the weak), and the obsessive and constant glorification of *danda,* the force of punishment, as the king's main instrument of rule over the masses, in the *Mahabharata*, the Dharmashastras and Kautilya's *Arthashastra*. The brahmans, however, were in a minority, and knew that they could not physically subjugate the multitude. Therefore, they devised the hegemonic caste ideology and strove to institutionalise it, socially and religiously, to establish their supremacy. If they could not conquer the 'others' physically, they could enslave them mentally and psychologically, by breaking their confidence in themselves by constantly underlining their worthlessness and base birth under the cloak of religion.

Caste Indoctrination

This the brahman supremacists achieved through developing the crude Vedic cosmology of nature and society into a complex and obscurantist Upanishadic metaphysics which came to be known as Vedanta. As Meera Nanda (2002) has explained, the non-dualistic ontology of Vedanta (hence also known as Advaita, 'non-duality') does not separate matter or physical nature from the spirit or moral realm. It discounts any separation between the subject—mind or consciousness—and the object—nature or the physical world. Its holism introduces a supernatural element by insisting that nature and culture are mere reflections (or illusions, as the leading exponents of Advaita such as Shankara would say) of the supreme spirit, Brahma. In their view, human culture is modelled on the order of nature. And the order, whether natural or social, is eternal, sacred, inviolable. The Vedantic philosophy holds that the order of caste and patriarchy mirrors the order of nature. Thus, the much-celebrated holism in brahmanic metaphysics lies at the very heart of caste and gender hierarchy in India.

This imposes the claims of the natural and the sacred order on human subjectivity, ethics and morality: transgressions against the social codes simultaneously become transgressions against the natural and sacred order. Nowhere is the naturalisation (and sacralisation) of social order more evident than in the institution of caste. The caste hierarchies . . . are supposed to mirror the order of nature. Whether one is born a female or a male, a dalit or a brahman, is not an accident at all, but the working out of the natural laws of karma and rebirth that regulate the embodiment of Spirit. Castes, genders, animals, plants and inanimate objects are simply different forms of the same spirit, arranged in a chain of being, depending upon their karma or moral deeds. In this non-dualistic, inter-connected world, objects of nature take on moral significance (e.g. diseases are goddesses, animals and plants are auspicious for human life and purposes) while human morals have consequences for the natural order (e.g. women's sins can bring about death of her husband). (Nanda 2002: 55)

Beginning with the Upanishadic time, *atma* and *brahma*, *karma* and *dharma*, *varna* and *jati*, *punarjanma* (rebirth) and *moksha* (salvation) became links in a chain and the entire chain became an unbreakable whole. Not for nothing have the champions of Vedanta supported caste, and the champions of caste have valorised Vedanta (Sardesai 1994: 209).

But how was the idea of human hierarchy, or social inequality of caste, established at the popular level? To institutionalise the idea of hierarchy and inject it into the life-blood of culture and people's psyche (at conscious, subconscious, and unconscious levels), a varna-based religion—Varnashrama Dharma—was founded; new rituals and sacrifices were invented; mantras, *dakshinas* (gifts) and *prayashchita* (penances) were multiplied; fictions of caste-loving gods were created and passed off as history; and, above all, mass ignorance was consciously encouraged and consolidated. Brahmanas were piled upon Brahmanas, Upanishads upon Upanishads, Aranyakas over Aranyakas, Smritis over Smritis, and then endless interpretations and commentaries upon them—commentaries and chopping inconvenient facts and adding new verses or passages dictated by the exigencies of time. In short, false knowledge and a pseudo-religion were promoted in place of real knowledge and humanist thinking. The caste order was given cosmic and spiritual sanctity—mere mortals could not challenge it.

The *Purusha-sukta* (the creation hymn) in the *Rigveda* (10.90) gave a supernatural origin of caste: the brahmans came from the mouth of the Divine Man; the kshatriyas (warriors) from his arms; the vaishyas (commoners) from his thighs; and the shudra (servants) from his feet. This mythical theory was made the basis of the fourfold division of society, known as the *chaturvarnya*. Etymologically, the word 'varna' means colour, and initially, to a large extent, caste had the implications of colour of the skin. The association of the four colours white, red, yellow, and black respectively with the four varnas shows this and the social hierarchy implicit in this *rangbhed* (R.S. Sharma [1958] 1990a: 282). Supposedly, the first two varnas or castes, the descendants of Aryans, were fairer than the non-Aryans and Dravidians, the dark-skinned original inhabitants, who were branded and stigmatised as shudras. This is why the top two varnas are known as *savarna* (literally, with colour) and the last two are despised as *avarna* (without colour). Varna order meant a graded inequality in which brahmans were the controllers of society and custodians of culture, religious rites and intellectual pursuits in general; kshatriyas were warriors and rulers; vaishyas were the producers of wealth as cattle-rearers, agriculturists, and later, as traders; and, shudras (some of them were later relegated as ati-shudra and branded as 'untouchables') were the servants of all the three higher classes, especially of the brahmans and kshatriyas.

The system was sustained by brahmanic mind and kshatriya brawn, a permanently organised force. Canon, enforced consent, and coercion gave caste ideology 'an interiorised force', making it an 'external law taken into the psyche', so that culture became nature and the individual learnt to affirm and reproduce the caste principle from within himself through his instinct. Each person was born into a caste and was thereby either superior or inferior to someone else. The brahman was by birth endowed with all the great qualities, but the shudra was by birth unfit to come to the level of humanity. While a brahman may fall from his superhuman status, the shudra was innately subhuman (Haq 1997: 17). The shudra cannot become human—in fact, he does not want to become human as he has killed the human in his self. He has the mind but he does not think; he has a will to act but he chooses not to act. The shudra is passivity personified: he does not act but is acted upon. This is so because, as Manu says, 'slavery is inborn in the shudra'. He has to submit to the brahmans and gods who will oppress him and bring to him all the miseries of the world.

The shudra was given the name *padaja* (born from the feet) implying thereby that God created the shudra to be the eternal slave. Initially, the lot of the vaishyas, the producing class, was slightly better than the shudras, though later these two were often clubbed together as *paap-yoni* (born in sin). The vaishyas were seen, like the shudras, as servants of the brahmans and kshatriyas. The later Vedic period, during which various Arayankas and Brahmanas were composed, witnessed the systematic segregation of all productive communities—peasants, artisans and labourers—as shudras, who were *krishnayonih* (black people), *tvacham krishname* (black skinned), and *dasyun vishah* (descendants of dasyus). Shudras were to be supported, to be fed, to be clothed with the remnants and castaways of food and clothes of the higher orders. They were not to hear the

Vedas or wear the sacred thread. They were to be kept out of all *yajnas* and *anusthanas* (religious ceremonies).

We can assume that superior in number and physical strength than the higher orders, the shudras resented their humiliation and subordination. They could have attempted to join hands with the *Vratyas* and other non-Aryans to destroy the brahmanical order. But the sources of the ancient period do not reveal this. All we know is, the shudras failed to subdue their opponents. Most probably their subjugation was ensured by the divide-and-rule mechanism of caste. The brahmanical order, both at material and ideological levels, gradually consolidated its position, and eventually emerged triumphant after a prolonged process of conflict, hierarchisation and exploitation.

In retrospect, it appears that, besides other factors, the shudras had to pay a heavy price for their inability to develop an alternative knowledge-system and a language like Sanskrit which the brahmans used with deadly effect to demean, divide, and destroy the shudras. The brahmans invented thousands of words to proclaim their supremacy and glorify themselves: *brahmajnani, vedagya, acharya, upadhyaya, devavani, shastragya, pandit, manushyadeva, bhudeva,* etc. Simultaneously, they coined scores of pejoratives—*danav, daitya, rakshasa, pishacha, chandala, mlechchha, kshudra, nikrishta, dwijadasa*—for the shudras. The *Manusmriti* (2.31) instructs the shudras to adopt names which should breed disgust, repulsion, and hatred. The Dharmashastras prescribe the respectful vocative terms which the shudras must use to address brahmans; and in reverse, they also mention the derogatory terms with which the brahmans were to address the shudras. *Manusmriti* (9.33) says, 'Speech is the weapon of the brahman, and with it he can slay his enemies.'

The writers of the Smritis or Dharmashastras envisioned their religion in terms of strict adherence to endogamy, hereditary occupation, and the rules of purity-pollution. The shudras were supposed to be treated, on religious ground, as two-footed beasts and bonded labourers. Entitled only to work and produce, they were debarred from acquiring education, collecting wealth, and carrying weapons. Echoing the Dharamshastras, the *Shanti Parvan* in the *Mahabharata* stipulates that the shudra can have no property; his wealth, if 'illegally' amassed, can be appropriated by his master at will.

Despised as ritually impure, a section of shudras, known variously as ati-shudras or *antyaja* or *panchama* came to be regarded as a source of pollution, which gave birth to the practice of untouchability. Not only goldsmiths, blacksmiths, washermen, carpenters, physicians, but also singers, dancers and actors were considered untouchables (*Manusmriti*: 4.210–15). In course of time, the difference between the labouring class (shudra) and the agricultural class (vaishya) got blurred because of the brahmanical contempt for physical work of any kind. Thus was the caste system organised in favour of the two upper varnas who lived off the labour and fruits of the two productive varnas.

Pseudo-Religion as Engine of Oppression

In the Sanskritic lore, the word *brahma(n)* denotes the sacred—in the form of hymn, prayer, formulation of truth—and the title brahman is accorded to everyone born in a particular caste believed to possess the qualities suggested by the word. Says the *Shatapatha Brahmana*, 'Verily there are two kinds of gods: the gods themselves who are absolutely gods, and the brahmans who have studied Vedic lore' (see Walker 1983a: 167). It is significant that the pre-eminent god of the post-Vedic period was named Brahma, and the brahmans were regarded as his sons, and, therefore, described as brahmans. It simply meant according *brahma* power to the brahmans. In texts such as the Brahmanas there was a tendency to identify the brahman caste as symbolising the Brahma power (Varma 1974: 60). All this was a ploy to make the Brahma and the brahman one and the same. Expressions such as *Brahma-hatya* (killing of the Brahma) and *Brahma-bhoj* (feast in honour of the Brahma) were commonly understood only as murder of a brahman and community meal for brahmans (Dhani 1984: 152). Another such word, which came later, is *Brahmadeya*, widely used for land grant to a brahman. Considered the embodiment of Brahma, a brahman's body and property was made inviolable in the Dharmashastras (see *Manusmriti:* 11.72–82).

To top it all, a metaphysical connotation was developed around the word 'Brahmana'. Brahmana was the name given to the 'Supreme Spirit', which subsumed all beings and all deities, the individual soul as well as the divine. The Upanishads taught that the man who knows the Brahma(na) becomes the Brahma and has complete sway over what he desires (Varma 1974: 62). The intention was to present the brahmans as both gods and humans endowed with exceptional abilities. This becomes apparent from epithets like *Bhudevata* (the lord of the earth) and *Jagatguru* (the master of the universe) which they coined to glorify themselves (Dhani 1984: 152–4; Walker 1983a: 172–3). Such self-glorification was inspired by the desire to dominate the 'others'. To this end, they devised the caste system as the key instrument to institutionalise their domination, and accordingly they developed a religion as a cloak to legitimise their supremacy.

The caste ideology was founded on the twin doctrines of *karma* and *dharma*. The doctrine of karma expounded that one's caste was the consequence of deeds done in past existences; birth in a 'high-caste' was a reward, and birth in a 'low-caste' a punishment. A person born in a 'high-caste' was intrinsically superior in intellect, ability, and morality to a 'low-caste' person. The karma theory thus justified the 'lowly-born' to his degraded condition. The related concept of dharma was to reinforce one's caste-duty. Dharma is generally understood as the religion of the highest moral order; it is often used as a suffix after the word 'Hindu' to show the humane, compassionate face of Hinduism. But it was not used in the same sense by the brahmanic literati who coined it. Etymologically and originally, the word dharma means that which holds or sustains (society). What is to be held and sustained? The answer: the socio-religious structure centred around caste. The Dharmashastras graphically describe the duties of the four classes, and prescribe unswerving adherence to one's caste-duty in all circumstances; any action contrary to one's prescribed caste-duty is declared *adharma* (prohibited action).[2]

Historical Roots of Brahmanic Dominance

To institutionalise caste and the concepts of karma, dharma, and *punarjanma*, the brahman literati authored a large number of Smritis or Dharmashastras in the post-Upanishadic times, roughly from 300 BCE to 600 CE. The Dharmashastras were claimed to be based on the Vedas, implying thereby that they too, like the Vedas, are sacred and inviolable. The *Manusmriti* is the best-known of all such Dharmashastras, the law-codes presented as religious injunctions and integral to the brahmanical canon, as the very word denotes.

Although Manu wrote the *Manusmriti* many centuries after the last Veda was composed, a famous, and apparently interjected, Vedic verse declares, 'All that Manu said is medicine, curer of all diseases.' The interpolation shows the brahmanical eagerness to push back the date of its compilation to give it the aura of the 'Vedic sacredness'. It was claimed that everything prescribed in the *Manusmriti* was in perfect congruence with the divine knowledge. It was to illuminate the entire dharma, the nature of good and bad karma as also the unalterable duties of all the four varnas (*Manusmriti*: 1.107).

Caste, according to Dharmashastras, is the creation of gods, and the brahmans embody the gods on earth—*bhudeva*. 'A brahman is a great god whether he is learned or imbecile . . . He should be respected in every way, even if he indulges in a crime' (*Manusmriti* 9.317–19). Manu instructs peasants, workers, even kings to religiously serve the brahmans. He stresses that the greatest virtue for shudras and women, who are born in sin, is to play the role of willing slaves, ever ready to be exploited without a murmur of protest, so that in the next life they may get a lift up the caste ladder. Shudras are not entitled to education, to amass wealth, or to bear arms. A brahman can take away any possession from a shudra, since nothing at all can belong to him as his own (8. 417). Women, similarly, are debarred from property and other rights. Manu places all women, irrespective of caste, in the category of the shudra and expects them to surrender their body and soul to men. The supreme duty of the king is to enforce this varna-dharma under the guidance of brahmans. No matter how mighty a king be, he is inferior to even a brahman child. 'A ten-year-old brahman and a hundred-year-old ruler should be regarded as father and son, and of the two of them the brahman child is the father' (2.135).

The *Manusmriti* is crammed with all kinds of abuse and injunctions against shudras and women.³ Aimed at establishing a brahmanical social order, it carries forward the caste spirit of the earlier works such as the *Gautama Dharmasutra* and *Apastambh Dharmasutra*. It is a representative work as its social philosophy is followed by other influential law-books such as the *Yajnavalkya Smriti*.

Written by various authors at different times, according to the exigencies of different circumstances, there are obvious external differences in the sacerdotal texts but in their core and essence all these works converge to uphold the brahmanical self-interest. If we read these texts in their contexts, the exquisite *shlokas, suktis,* and *subhasitaanis* are alluring only for the chosen few. In the brahmanical canon, ethics is selective, not universal.

The brahmans knew, as we shall see shortly, that there were other social principles and paradigms in existence, championed by their critics and challengers. Which is why they kept parroting that there was no greater sin than to question the authority of the Vedas. Proclaiming that 'one who speaks ill of the Vedas is an atheist' *(nastiko vedanindakah)*, they claimed that other philosophical and religious thoughts—devoid of any intrinsic merit—invariably lead to disastrous consequences. The message was loud and clear that anyone following a different path other than Vedic-brahmanism would come to grief (*Manusmriti*: 12.95; *Bhagavad Gita*: 3.35).

All evidence suggests that the brahmanical texts we have cited were produced by those who were wary of the multitude and rival socio-religious groups. Contending with intellectual challenge from critics, they couched their social views in vague religious terms so that it was difficult, if not impossible, to expose their ethical and intellectual vacuity. They kept their metaphysics sufficiently open and opaque to multiple interpretations by referring to contradictory sources and authorities, one after the other. And they composed their tracts in Sanskrit, the so-called *devabhasa* (the language of the gods), a language that was understood only by the gods above and themselves. The 'others'—commoners, shudras, and women—were debarred from learning it.

Yet the brahmanical leadership had to compromise on many issues with the people. They had to, for instance, adopt only black-skinned deities as their greatest gods. It is significant that all the three popular gods—Shiva, Rama, and Krishna—are black-skinned. And Shiva, as is well-known, has two consorts: the first one being Kali (of black colour), the brahmans had to procure him a second one, Gauri (of white skin). In other words, in the later period, especially during the Gupta rule, the wily brahmans appropriated several uniquely indigenous beliefs, superstitions, deities, and sacred places, and mischievously oriented them to buttress the brahmanical culture. This, in brief, is the background to the Puranic religion.

Caste, Karmayoga, and Swadharma in the *Gita*

The *Bhagavad Gita* is the finest philosophical treatise of brahmanic Hinduism and its most popular and oft-quoted scripture. Like the Veda-Purana, the *Gita,* too, is 'honoured oftener than read, and understood far less than it is recited' (Kosambi [1965] 1992: 209). A far cry from the claims that it is the greatest moral code for the guidance of humanity, a dispassionate study shows it is not gospel. This is not however to deny that this metaphysical interlude in the *Mahabharata* by some unknown hand does hold lofty prescriptions for excellence in mental discipline. But its precepts are dazzling only in their splendid isolation, for, if one delves beneath its surface, the *Gita*, like other brahmanic works, abides by the same caste mantra for salvation. Its much-glorified concepts of *swadharma* (one's own duty) and *nishkama karma* (dispassionate activity) are embedded in the idea of unwavering performance of duty of the caste to which one is born.

The karmayoga as espoused in the *Gita* is the principle of faithful and joyous performance of caste duty. Its anonymous authors keep drumming the message that nothing is nobler than observance of one's caste duties, and nothing more heinous than the breach (*Bhagavad Gita* 3.35; 18.45; 18.47). The duty of the brahman is to attain religious and intellectual perfection (18.42); the kshatriya is obliged to rule the masses (18.43); and, tending to cattle, agriculture, and trade are duties of the vaishya (18.44). However, it is on the 'natural' slavery of the shudra that the *Gita*, like the Dharmashastras, lays the maximum emphasis: 'Service is the natural duty of the shudra' (18.44). Its famous doctrine of *nishkama-karma* expressed in the dictum *karmany eva'dhikaraste ma phaleshu kadachan* (2.47)—'your business is only with the work, not the fruit'—is loaded with the implication of shudras' subservience.

The *Gita* stresses that *swadharma*—one's duty (i.e., the duty of one's caste)—even performed imperfectly, is better than *paradharma*, another's duty or the duty appropriate to another caste, even if well performed. Another's duty brings disasters, one's own brings salvation (3.35). There is no crime bigger than abdicating one's hereditary occupation and marrying outside one's caste because 'mixture of castes leads to nothing but hell' (1.42) and 'destroys all family and caste values' (1.43).

This collection of 700-odd verses, presented in the form of a dialogue between Krishna and Arjuna, was in all probability written in response to the growing defiance of caste rules by the lowered castes and women, which is termed in the Puranic literature as the *Kaliyuga,* a decadent era marked by indiscriminate mingling among castes in marriage and occupation. In the very beginning of the dialogue (1.41), Arjuna says, *strishu dushtashu jaayate varnasamkara*, 'women's wickedness is responsible for intermixture of castes'.

An interpolation in the epic, the *Gita* dates to around the fourth century CE. It draws heavily on the earlier Yoga and Vedanta philosophies as well as the Buddhist teachings. Some of its finest teachings—such as 'remain steadfast even in trying circumstances as a lamp in a windless place'—have the indelible imprint of Buddha's teaching of careful cultivation of the mind. Similarly, its famous injunction of conquering desire, man's deadliest foe, is quintessentially Buddhist. No wonder Kosambi says the *Gita* summarises a great deal of Buddhism quite efficiently in the mouth of Krishna ([1965] 1992: 208). However, while the Buddha's stress on surrendering one's desire is linked to universal compassion, Krishna is not bothered by such ethical concerns since this world, as he keeps repeating, is an illusion created by 'Him'. 'Neither yoga, nor knowledge, nor kindness, nor austerity, nor renunciation captivates Me so much as devotion to Me', he insists. There is no place for love and ethics in his universe. It is this point that Albert Schweitzer (1936:193) makes effectively:

> Hinduism in the Bhagavad Gita does not yet take the actual step of demanding ethical deeds. Love to God is for it an end in itself. Hinduism does not make love to God find expression in love to mankind. Because it fails to reach the idea of active love, the ethic of the Bhagavad Gita is like a smoky fire from which no flames flare upward. One must ever bear in mind, that in the Bhagavad Gita there is no question of love.

As we saw, the *Gita*'s overriding concern, like other brahmanic texts, is to extol the varna ideology, though here it is couched in delicate equivocation and splendid Sanskrit. Here, the divine singer of the song is prepared to grant salvation to even those 'born from the very womb of sin: women, vaishyas and shudras', provided they repose their faith in his divinity. In the words of Kosambi,

> That the song divine is sung for the upper classes by the brahmins, and only through them for others, is clear. We hear from the mouth of Krishna himself (9.32): 'For those who take refuge in Me, be they even of the sinful breeds such as women, vaishyas and shudras. . . .' That is, all women and all men of the working and producing classes are defiled by their very birth, though they may in after-life be freed by their faith in the god who degrades them so casually in this one. Not only that, the god himself had created such differences (4.13): 'The four-caste (-class) division has been created by Me'; this is proclaimed in the list of great achievements. ([1962] 2000: 15)

The *Gita*'s teaching is essentially the teaching of caste-feudalism camouflaged as devotional spirituality. It extols the virtues of sticking to one's birth-based duty in the name of spirituality. Krishna does not invoke justice for the sake of which wars are generally justified. Instead, he prepares the reluctant Arjuna for war by appealing to his caste duty and to the fear of loss of social face. It is the holy duty of Arjuna, born into a kshatriya caste, to battle without being troubled about the consequences. Krishna exhorts Arjuna to find and kill his enemies without scruples since creatures are destined to perish. Krishna the Lord has himself already slain them all, and Arjuna will be only the apparent cause of their death.

The *Gita* attempts to transform the discredited idea of ritual sacrifice into one of self-sacrifice, the dedication of all one's acts to God as a form of penance. It induces one to obey the dictates of God reposed in his priestly-feudal agents on earth. Its stress on action without expectations of any change is hardly an encouragement for work. Undermining any need for social action, Krishna propounds the doctrine of *avatara*—the idea that gods are born in many forms many times—to reassure the devotee. 'For whenever dharma, or morality, declines and wrong increases, then I create myself. I am born again and again to protect virtue and to destroy evil' (4.7).

The *Gita*'s theory of karma, dharma, and avatara teaches social conservatism in the name of the religious self-surrender. Its notions of good and evil, morality and immorality are embedded in the brahmanical ascription. Its overall social philosophy is ranged against the producing and labouring classes. Its elitist glorification is chiefly due to this and the feudal doctrine of bhakti that extols loyalty to the ruler and acquiescence in the established order.

It is not fortuitous that the composition of *Gita* and the emergence of Indian feudalism in the Gupta took place almost simultaneously. Also, the appearance of the *Gita* coincided with the resurgence of brahmanism and a decline and eclipse of Buddhism. While the pre-*Gita* period, with a strong Buddhist presence in the land, was marked by a vibrant cultural and economic life, the post-*Gita* period is marked by the rise of feudalism characterised by a closed economy, excessive caste conservatism, and the growing tentacles of insularity.

The devotee-commentators of the *Gita*—right from Shankara, Ramanuja, Gyaneshwar, Madhav, Vallabh and Nimbaraka to Tilak, Aurobindo, Gandhi, Rajagopalachari and Radhakrishnan—have read the epic poem out of context to project their own notions and concepts into its verses. Taking advantage of the contradictions and verbal jugglery that pervade the text, they have made the *Gita* highly mystifying. In fact, to interpret and reinterpret, unravel and illuminate the supposed layers and layers of *rahasya,* supposedly hidden in the *Gita* verses, has for centuries been a favourite pastime of the brahmanic literati. Shankara wrote the *Brahma Sutra* in the ninth century and Gyaneshwar his *Gyaneshwari* in the thirteenth to illumine its esoteric meanings. Many lesser luminaries followed suit, delved into the *Gita* and discovered their own pearls of wisdom from its depths.

Tilak, however, was not satisfied with the commentaries of his illustrious predecessors, and tried to dispel the confusion by authoring the *Gita-Rahasya*. For him, the *Gita* mirrored karma-yoga, ceaseless action without desire for results. He stressed that the holy text also taught *shatham prati shaathyam* (paying the villain in his own coin). In a speech in 1897, Tilak claimed, as part of his anti-British rhetoric, that the *Gita* sanctioned the killing of enemies for 'unselfish' and 'benevolent' reasons. (Later, Nathuram Godse, a Tilak acolyte, who knew the entire *Gita* by heart, also gave a similar interpretation of the 'sacred text' to justify his assassination of Gandhi.)

Close on Tilak's heels, Gandhi claimed to penetrate the heart of the matter through his own treatise on the *Gita*, which supposedly anchored his principles of truth and non-violence. The Gandhian Vinoba Bhave, in thrall to the 'celestial treasure-house of timeless wisdom', recorded his own *Gita-Pravachan,* while C. Rajagopalachari, another Gandhian, paid homage through his book *Bhagavad Gita*. Aurobindo Ghosh even left the national movement to delve into the elusive truth in the mystical verses. In his *Essays on the Gita,* Aurobindo fancies that its influence is not merely philosophical or academic but immediate and living—its ideas are actually at work as a powerful shaping factor in the revival and renewal of the Indian nation and culture. (Having pontificated so, he retired to Pondicherry to concentrate on his spiritual quest, cutting himself completely off from the national life.) Radhakrishnan, who saw nothing but spiritual splendour in the brahmanic wonder that was India, followed suit and came up with his own impassioned *Gita*-glorification in his trademark hagiographical style.

All these devotional works in the name of commentaries—from Shankara's to Radhakrishnan's—reveal little more than their brahmanical biases. The modern interpreters discovered a 'dynamic doctrine for action' in the *Gita*, and claimed that it was of eternal value for India. After pronouncing that the *Gita* was the holiest scripture for 'the Hindu people', they went on to extend the claim to include the entire nation. One scholar wrote, 'The *Gita* has thus become the scripture of the new age. The main foundation on which its social doctrines, and even its political action depends.... No one can understand the developments which are taking place in India who has no appreciation of this fundamental fact' (K.M. Panikkar 1961).

Contrary to these lofty claims, the *Gita* has strengthened orthodoxy and the fiction of 'sacred' antiquity. It has aided reactionary obscurantism.

The *Gita* has been repeatedly invoked to fight the forces of revolution. If Shankaracharya sought its assistance in the ninth century AD to deal a death-blow to declining Buddhism, Mahatma Gandhi utilised its teachings to annihilate the rising tide of secular democracy. This is true even though Shankara was dubbed as a crypto-Buddhist and Gandhi acclaimed as the champion of democratic freedom. (Bazaz 2002)

It is claimed that the *Gita* is the life-blood of Indian civilisation, and that every Indian believes in its ennobling message of selfless service. The *Gita*-lovers do not tell the world why Indians lagged behind socially and civilisationally, deteriorated intellectually and morally, lost freedom and suffered so much and for so long after they had decided to abide by its principles. The argument that the Indians accepted the *Gita* as their scripture but failed to live up to its ideals is vacuous. When one argues that its teachings are etched in the heart and mind of every Indian, it is absurd to contend that the sufferings of the people have not been caused by the acceptance of such scriptures (Bazaz 2002).

The truth is, the *Gita* sees worldly life as 'transient and joyless' (9.33). This is not surprising since brahmanic cosmogony is basically insipid. According to its mythology, creation began with *Satyayuga,* a golden age, when everything was perfect, men attained excellence in all respects and dharma existed as a four-footed able creature. Then degeneration set in: the next *yuga,* the *Treta,* was not so glorious as it had only three feet to support it. In the third *yuga,* the *Dwapar*, there was further decline as dharma was reduced to subsist only on two feet. Dharma was almost destroyed and crippled in *Kaliyuga*, the present era, as it is left with only one foot to hop about in this dark age, the period of crisis, chaos, and catastrophe.

The secret of the mesmerising appeal of *Gita* for the caste elites is its unique ambiguity. Riddled with contradictions, tautology and rhetoric, it slides into vague philosophical concepts. Ambivalence and prevarication are its hallmark. Vedic polytheism is accepted in some places, in other places ridiculed and rejected. The idea of monotheism is affirmed categorically (4.6) only to be rubbished in the next verse by the idea of avatar in a human body (4.7). Similarly, Krishna at one place disapproves the path of renunciation, while at another place recommends it as a way to realise the Brahmana, and at third place he advocates *bhakti-marg* (path of devotion) as the best path. Kosambi demystifies the *Gita* mystique thus:

> Practically anything can be read into the Gita by a determined person, without denying the validity of a class [caste] system. The Gita furnished the one scriptural source which could be used without violence to accepted brahmin methodology, to draw inspiration and justification for social actions in some way disagreeable to a branch of the ruling class upon whose mercy the brahmins depended at the moment. ([1962] 2000: 15)

The utility of the *Gita* to the caste elite derives from its fundamental defect, its dexterity in seeming to reconcile the irreconcilable. Krishna praises the virtue of non-violence, yet his entire argument is an incentive to war. It is not possible to kill or be killed, the god tells Arjuna and then opens his 'innumerable voracious mouths' that have swallowed up all the warriors of both sides; Arjuna's killing of his kin is thus a mere formality as the demoniac god himself had already killed all of them (Kosambi, ibid.: 17).

Above all, Krishna himself as depicted in the *Mahabharata* is unfit to teach morality. During the war he comes across as a ruthless politician revelling in the violation of the prevailing codes of fair play. He resorts to the dirty tricks at every critical turn of the war. The killing of Bhishma and Dronacharya, Karna and Duryodhana—which had a crucial bearing on the outcome of the war—were ensured through unethical means. Bhishma was disarmed by the duplicity of placing Shikhandi (a eunuch) before him. Yudhishthira the Dharmaraj deceives Drona without batting an eyelid, saying Ashwathama, the latter's son, has died, muttering *sotto voce* that it was actually an elephant. Near the end of the war, at Krishna's instance, Duryodhana was literally hit below the belt by Bhima. Karna, the greatest warrior on the Kaurava side who had the potential to defeat Arjuna and the Pandavas, was killed in a blatant violation of the war rules when he was unarmed and engaged in pulling the wheels of his chariot out of the mud. Earlier, Krishna's use of a crucial nugget of information about Karna's personal life (that he was the first born of Kunti) to wean him away from the Kauravas traumatised Karna enough to force him to promise Kunti he would spare all the Pandavas (Yudhishthira, Bhima, Nakula, and Sahadeva) except Arjuna. Jayadratha, the killer of Abhimanyu, was ensnared by the 'divine' illusion of sunset—assured that the sun had set, Jayadratha came out of hiding and was killed by Arjuna, who had promised to kill him before the sun set for the day.

All this was done with Krishna's approval. He explained them away with the argument that had he not resorted to such tactics, the victory would never have been won. Elsewhere too, the *Mahabharata* is replete with the evil committed by its heroes. Drona asking for Ekalavya's thumb as his *guru-dakshina* is an example of how outstanding talent in the subaltern strata was crushed by brahman gurus. It is perhaps in the same ruthless spirit that a devotee of the *Gita* and Gandhian non-violence, C. Rajagopalachari, extolled the virtues of non-violence as a method to gain and retain power but 'when in the driver's seat, one must use the whip' (Kosambi [1962] 2000: 19).

With its deceiving equivocation, the *Gita* remains a perennial source of inspirational quotations to justify almost any action while shrugging off the consequences. 'This slippery opportunism characterises the whole book. Naturally, it is not surprising to find so many *Gita* lovers imbued therewith. Once it is admitted that material reality is gross illusion, the rest follows quite simply; the world of "doublethink" is the only one that matters' (Kosambi, ibid. 17).

Dandaniti Central to Brahmanical Polity and State

Dharma expounded in the brahmanical literature, as we saw, was centred on caste, and following this dharma meant fulfilling one's ascriptive social responsibility along with a trivialised individual morality. Facts and fiction, legends and myths, fables and fantasies, stories and superstitions, were rendered in a way to create and perpetuate caste culture and mindset. The brahmanic precepts—upholding varna-dharma, patriarchal family values, and rights of private property for the first two varnas—were to be made effective by the political elite led by a kshatriya king. For maintaining varna-dharma and containing social conflict, the brahmans propagated the divinity of kingship alongside a caste-feudal ideology (R.S. Sharma 1983: 68ff).

Thus, brahmans and kshatriyas came together to form the ruling alliance. Both lived off tax, tribute and labour supplied by the productive lowered castes. There were occasional fights between them for power and privilege, but the conflicts were made up in the face of any opposition from below. The need for brahman-kshatriya bond is repeatedly stressed in the brahmanical texts. The *Shanti Parvan* in the *Mahabharata* and the *Manusmriti* (9.322) make clear, 'the brahmans cannot prosper without the support of the kshatriyas and the kshatriyas cannot prosper without the support of the brahmans'. But there was no doubt who was in the driver's seat: the brahman elite controlled the kings and feudal lords. The king was duty-bound, on religious ground, to bow to brahmans and act according to their instruction. In the *Mahabharata*, Bhishma preaches:

> The highest duty of a crowned king is to worship brahmans; they should be protected ... respected, bowed to and revered as if they were one's parents. If brahmans are contented, the whole country prospers; if they are discontented and angry, everything goes to destruction. They can make a god not-a-god, and not-god, a god. One whom they praise, prospers; and one whom they reproach becomes miserable. (See Dharma Theertha [1941] 1992: 90–1)

The 'Hindu polity' was founded on the religio-political bedrock of brahmanism. The divine origins of kingly power and social order made any rational and humanist political thought impossible. The princes found in caste and priestcraft an effective system to keep people submissive and divided. Caste as an institution and ideology had been fervently patronised by ruling groups down the ages. As Dharma Theertha observes:

> The scheme of castes and priest-craft was wide enough to afford scope for numerous exploiting groups, so that despotic monarchs, adventurous kings wishing to become emperors, usurpers to thrones desirous of priestly support, new invaders such as the Scythians, the Chinese, the Turks, the Greeks, the Rajputs, the Muhammadans and the modern Europeans, and Indian princes aspiring to Kshatriyahood and relying on Brahman help, all have patronised it in turns when it served them in their conquest or exploitation. ([1941] 1992: 7)

The brahmans made inherited or acquired kshatriyahood mandatory for according legitimacy on kings and aspiring rulers. In fact, kshatriyahood was put on sale: anyone (including those from the lowered castes or casteless tribals or foreign groups) could buy it—and they did—from the brahmans for a price and promise to rule according to the varna-dharma. Kosambi has demystified the *hiranya garbha* (golden womb), the ceremony for symbolic rebirth into caste society, by which tribal chiefs and aspiring rulers acquired kshatriya status, agreed to maintain the caste order, and converted the rest of the tribe into a subject peasantry:

> A large vessel of gold was prepared into which the chieftain would be inserted doubled up, like the foetus in a womb. The brahmin ritual for pregnancy and childbirth was then chanted by the hired priests. The man emerged from the 'womb of gold' as if reborn, having also acquired a new caste, or even a caste for the first time; this was not the caste of the rest of the tribe when they were absorbed into society, but one of the classical four castes, usually kshatriya, with the gotra of the brahmin priest. . . . The brahmin priests received the golden vessel as part of their fee, which made everyone happy. . . . All this amounted to keeping down a newly created set of vaishyas and shudras by brahmin precept and kshatriya arms. (Kosambi [1965] 1992: 171)

To keep the masses down, kings were given power and divinity, making the *danda* (coercion) central to the state. In the brahmanical polity, *dandaniti,* rule by force, was the chief principle of state management. The Dharmashastras proclaim that the whole world is governed by the *danda*—Agni burns through fire, Surya sends forth his beams through fear, through fear Vayu blows. According to the *Manusmriti*, the *danda* is the king and the man, he is the inflicter and he is chastiser. The *danda* alone chastises all subjects. Justice is the *danda* (7.17–18).

Other brahmanical authorities vie with Manu to eulogise the role of *danda*. Among the precepts of the *Mahabharata* there is one which states, 'Right leans on might (*danda*) as a creeper on a tree. As smoke follows the wind, so might follows might' (see Walker 1983a: 267). The drone of *danda*-devotees goes on and on: *Danda* moves the universe, piercing, cutting, wounding, maiming, afflicting, causing panic in the hearts of all; it is *danda* and *danda* alone, irresistible and terror-striking, that makes the earth prosper, that brings about morality and makes virtue possible (ibid.). The following paean to the *danda* in the *Mahabharata*, addressed to the king, celebrates what is now known as Social Darwinism:

All the limits established in the world, O King, are marked by danda. . . . No man will sacrifice if he is not afraid, nor will he give gifts or hold to his promise. . . . I see no being which lives in the world without violence. Creatures exist at one another's expense; the stronger consume the weaker. The mongoose eats mice, just as the cat eats the mongoose; the dog devours the cat, O King, and wild beasts eat the dog. Man eats them all—see dharma for what it is! Everything that moves and is still is food for life. (See Doniger and Smith 1991: XXXI)

The *Mahabharata* exalts the *Dandaniti* so much that it interchangeably uses it with *Rajadharma*, the policy of the state:

When Dandaniti becomes lifeless, the triple Veda sinks, all the Dharmas howsoever developed, completely perish. When traditional Rajadharma is departed from, all the bases of the divisions of the Ashramas are shattered. In Rajadharma are realised all the forms of renunciation, in Rajadharma is revealed all knowledge. In Rajadharma are centred all the worlds. (Cited in Varma 1974: 102)

In the *Arthashastra*, the much-acclaimed treatise on statecraft, Kautilya is concerned with the preservation of varna-dharma through *danda* in the same way. '*Danda* and *danda* alone protects this world and the next' (*Arthashastra* 3.1). His *danda* is employed to uphold the 'brahmanical social organisation which rests for its validity on the Vedas'. Kautilya, the alleged 'architect of Hindu secular statecraft', requires every varna to perform its functions, and declares that the person who observes his duty attains heaven and infinite bliss. The world can be destroyed, he warns, by a violation of caste duty. He instructs the king that he should never allow the people to deviate from their caste duty (R.S. Sharma [1958] 1991a: 253 ff). He accords—and justifies—three important privileges to the brahmans: exemption from physical torture and capital punishment for any crime; protection and special treatment from the state; and, the right to demand honour and gifts from everyone. The *Arthashastra* says that brahmans are *bhudeva,* deities on the earth: *ye deva devalokesu cha brahmanaha,* 'brahmans occupy the same position among human beings as gods occupy in heaven' (ibid.: 255).

In contrast to the favours granted to the brahmans, Kautilya imposes restrictions on non-brahmanic faiths and sects. There are several instances in the *Arthashastra* which show his intolerance towards Vrishals, Pashandas, Sakyas, Ajivikas, the lower orders, and other groups opposed to the brahmanical system of life. Vrishals, Pashandas, and Buddhists were particularly marked out by him for harassment and discriminatory treatment (Sharma [1958] 1991a: 261). Kautilya also recommends separate living quarters for supporters of heretical sects and those who followed 'unclean' occupations. The Pashandas and Chandalas were required to live near cremation ground of a town or village.

Like other brahmanic works, *Arthashastra* never urges the king to provide support to the poor; all that matters is the protection of brahmans and varna-dharma. It is concerned with the strategies of winning war but hardly ever with social welfare; it is interested in taxing irrigation without bothering to build dams. To admire the *Arthashastra* as representing the fine flower of Indian political thought is either rank ignorance or brahmanic mischief.

Popular Resistance Debunks Elite Historiography

Caste and brahmanism did not go unchallenged. The political economy and social order structured in favour of the higher varnas were not endorsed by the victims. The lowered castes, in fact, strove to throw off the yoke of oppressive order. Which is why the brahmanical texts, especially the Dharmashastras, are full of exhortations to maintain the varna-dharma, repeating ad nauseum that the vaishyas and shudras should never be allowed to deviate from the functions allotted to them, otherwise chaos—terrible and unmanageable—would descend on the world. *Sama* (manipulation), *dama* (coercion), *danda* (punishment), *bheda* (discrimination), *niti* (morality), *aniti* (immorality)—everything was legitimised in the naked quest of power and invoked to be employed to keep the lowered classes in order and discipline. The intellectual and political elite adopted the strongest measures to quell eruptions of rebellion from below.

No matter how savagely the ruling classes dealt with the people's protests, social crises kept erupting at intervals. One major crisis occurred during the third century CE described in the Puranas as *Kaliyuga* (the age of anarchy) characterised by large-scale *varna-samkara* (literally, intermingling of blood between castes). R.S. Sharma (1983; [1958] 1990a) has argued that *varna-samkara* did not merely mean the intermixture of blood between four varnas; it also meant the lower orders refusing to carry out their caste duties.

Emphasis on the importance of coercive mechanism (danda) in the Shanti Parva and the description of anarchy (arajaka) in the epics possibly belong to the same age and point to the same crisis. The Kali age is characterised by varna-samkara, i.e. intermixture of varnas or social orders, which implies that vaishyas and shudras, i.e. peasants, artisans and labourers, either refused to stick to the producing functions assigned to them or else the vaishya peasants declined to pay taxes and the shudras refused to make their labour available. (Sharma 1983: 31)

Since the shudras and ati-shudras never fully reconciled to the brahmanical social order, they kept registering their protests in one form or another. Not for nothing they are referred to in the brahmanical literature as hostile, violent, boastful, short-tempered, greedy, ungrateful, undependable and unfit for any responsible work. Sharma says that there are at least nine verses in the *Mahabharata*'s *Shanti Parvan* stressing the necessity of joint action by brahmans and kshatriyas to offset the challenge. He cites one revealing passage, in which it is bitterly complained that at one stage shudras and vaishyas, acting most wilfully, began to unite with the wives of brahmans (Sharma [1958] 1990a: 280). This is a striking instance of vengeance of the victims—shudras, vaishyas, and women—against their oppressors.

Like the *Manusmriti*, the *Shanti Parvan* defines a *vrishala* (i.e. a shudra) as one who defies *dharma* (Sharma [1958] 1990a: 281). The *Anushasan Parvan* portrays the shudras as 'destroyers of the king' (ibid.). Shudra rebellion can also be inferred from a passage of the *Narada Smriti* which declares that, if a king does not exercise coercive force, all castes will abandon their obligations, the shudras surpassing all the rest. Yajnavalkya repeats the provision of Kautilya that the shudra who 'pierces' the eyes of others, pretends to be a brahman, and acts against the king must be heavily fined. A passage from a manuscript of the *Shanti Parvan* ordains that dasas and mlechchhas must be dealt with by the state agencies, and that force must be used against them (ibid.).

All these provide clear suggestions of caste war in ancient India. This explains why the king is repeatedly enjoined in the brahmanical texts to uphold the caste system, and keep the vaishyas and shudras in their place by forcing them to fulfil their obligations. As Sharma shows, terms such as *Kaliyuga, varna-samkara* and *arajaka* (anarchy) are described in the brahmanical literature as conditions in which what collapses is the caste order when the authority of the first two varnas is eroded and caste rules are flouted on a massive scale.

Instances of social conflict cited above are culled from the brahmanical literature. When one takes into account other sources, especially the Jain and Buddhist Pali texts, one comes across the deep antagonism between brahmans and non-brahmans. The former, despite their claims to be worthy of worship by the latter, had not attracted much love. A popular ancient saying, still current all over India, is 'if you meet a snake and a brahman, first kill the brahman'. Another ancient saying, still popular in northern India, mocks the superiority claimed by the priestly class: *anna manna swaha, panditji bauraha* (chanting mantras is useless and the pandits who do that have gone raving mad). Villagers in the north use a genial though highly sarcastic word *Babaji* to address the brahman.

Its subtle connotation is one who is fatuous or empty-headed. A more explicit term to mock the 'foolish priest' is *ponga pandit*. These are just a few examples: a great deal of shudra-subaltern subversive expressions lie undiscovered in the maze of folk and oral traditions. Hardly any of them have been recorded in writing, in Sanskrit or the other standard languages.

To rewrite a credible history of ancient India demands an honest and imaginative use of existing material from folk culture and unorthodox sources. R.S. Sharma, after examining early Indian social history, suggests that 'on the whole the social structure from the sixth century BC to the fifth century AD in mid India may be called vaishya-shudra based society in the sense that vaishyas were peasants and shudras were artisans, slaves and hired labourers' (2001: 17). Later, the difference between vaishyas and shudras was blurred and both worked mainly as cultivators. Shudras, however, have invariably been portrayed as serving the three higher classes in the dominant historiography. Hsuan Tsang, the Chinese pilgrim who visited India during 629–45 CE when Harsha was the most important ruler of the north India, has categorically contradicted this stereotype. In his vivid account of the time, he calls the shudras agriculturists.

Similarly, brahmanic historians deny the fact that Buddhism was conquered through a violent process (see Chapter 2). The Buddhists were targeted by the resurgent brahmanical forces in post-Mauryan India. In fact, Buddhism and brahmanism had been locked in a combat for many centuries before the former was finally driven out from the land of its birth, as a recent study has convincingly shown (Verardi 2011). One telling incident is narrated by Hsuan Tsang: he narrowly survived an assassination bid on his life. The brahmans wanted to kill the Chinese pilgrim because he was able to convert the Shaivaite Harshavardhan to Buddhism. Harsha became a patron of Buddhism and convened a grand Buddhist conference at Kannauj, his capital, which was attended by the kings of twenty countries, including the Kamrupa ruler Bhaskarvarman. Hsuan Tsang, who initiated the discussion, eloquently spoke of the virtues of Buddhism and challenged his audience to refute his arguments. 'But none came forward for five days and then his theological rivals conspired to take the pilgrim's life. On this Harsha threatened to behead anybody causing the least hurt to Hsuan Tsang. Suddenly the great tower caught fire and there was an attempt to assassinate Harsha. Harsha then arrested 500 brahmanas and banished them and some of them were also executed' (Sharma 1990b: 173).

That the Buddhist-brahmanic conflict stretched over centuries is corroborated by historical evidence. One such case involves the Shaivite king Shashank of Gauda, a contemporary of Harsha. Shashank cut down the Bodhi tree at Bodh Gaya where the Buddha attained his enlightenment. He removed the Buddha image from the shrine near the tree and replaced it with a *Shiva-linga*. For their part the Pala rulers of Bengal, staunch supporters of Vajrayana, a contemporary form of Buddhism, declared war on brahmanism. The Palas and Vajrayanis declared that what was righteous to the followers of the shruti-smriti would be unrighteous and irrelevant to them and what was unrighteous to the smriti-worshippers would be righteous to them. It was a sequel to this mutual hostility that gave birth to social rebels like the Kapalikas and Aughars who led a life which was utterly disrespectful of the caste codes. 'The leaders of this great movement of the underdog were the famous Siddhas who were either low-caste thinkers or broken brahmans. All restraints were defied, all bonds with the codes snapped and men revelled in cultivating the forbidden' (Upadhyaya 1989: 89). Throwing all social and sexual prohibitions to the wind, they led an unrestrained life, believing that the best way to conquer temptation was to yield to it. Their movement represented an extreme rejection of the ascriptive brahmanism. Their subversive thoughts helped prepare the ground for the egalitarian Bhakti and Sufi movements which engulfed India in the succeeding centuries (Chapter 3).

Shramanic Counter-Tradition of Egalitarianism

One can discern in the course of Indian history a 'dialectical interweaving' of two types of ideological attitudes—shramanic and brahmanic—which are apparently contradictory (Pande 1978). The former (under which rubric come Buddhism and Jainism) is not a reformist or heterodox school within the Vedic tradition, but precedes and contradicts the latter. India's 'great ascetic movements' belonged to 'an ancient tradition independent of the Vedic Aryan tradition' (Pande 1978: 5; L.M. Joshi [1969] 2007). India has in fact a deeply dual tradition, represented by struggle for supremacy between the traditions of the indigenous shramans[4] (Prakrit: samana), the ascetic truth-seekers generally associated with the pre-Aryan Indus Valley civilisation (manifest in archaeological evidence like the Indus seal that depicts a meditating ascetic) and the Aryan brahmans who appeared on the scene later and strove to establish their cultural dominance. The Aryan-brahmans were not at ease with the 'strange' religious practices of the shramans. In the *Keshi-sukta* of the *Rigveda* (10.136), a Vedic poet expresses awe at the sight of the long-haired ascetics. Though relegated to the background by the more mundane Vedic-brahmanic culture, the shramans never accepted the religious power and social hierarchy of brahman priests. The ascetic tradition of the non-Aryans could not be completely wiped out. 'After remaining dormant for a while, it seems to have reemerged with fresh vigour and vitality. The history of Indian philosophy may be described as the story of the struggle for supremacy between these two traditions' (Kalupahana 1976: 3-4).

The shramans had a variety of philosophical positions, but they held in common a non-hierarchical position, arguing that all people were subject to the same social and spiritual laws. On this common matrix, they admitted anyone interested in spiritual accomplishment, irrespective of their social location, in their ranks. Just because they mocked the brahman's pretensions of pre-eminence does not mean they were only reacting against the latter's supremacist politics. As carriers of an autonomous tradition, inherited from a non-Vedic, non-Aryan past, they were one of the principal builders of the Indian cultural tradition. In this sense, the tendency to term them as 'heterodoxies'—as has been the trend in the dominant historiography—is preposterous, to say the least.

In an illuminating monograph on shramanism, G.C. Pande has delineated its moral and social outlook, establishing that it constitutes a system of universal, rational and ethical system which is remarkably open-ended and 'as relevant today as it was 2500 years ago'. Critiquing shramanic criticism of casteism, Vedism, and idea of God, he concludes,

> Shramanic atheism is not a variety of irreligion but of religion. It faces the evil and suffering of life squarely and attributes it to human failings rather than to the mysterious design of an unknown being. It stresses the inexorableness of the moral law. No prayers and worship are of any avail against the force of karman. It emphasises self-reliance in the quest for salvation. Man needs to improve himself by a patient training of the will and the purification of feelings. Such purification leads to an inward illumination of which the power is innate in the soul or the mind. This is quite different from the Vedic view where illumination comes from outside, either from an externally revealed word or from the grace of God. Shramaism represents a sterner variety of religion where the consolation of a personal God is replaced by the guidance of a spiritual teacher which must be practiced by the individual himself on the basis of his own resources. (Pande 1978: 73)

This fair assessment dispels many confusions, among them the smug notion that shramanic religions like Buddhism *also believed* in *karma* without realising that Buddhist concept of karma was fundamentally different. By presenting a powerful critique of the Vedic *karmakanda* and Varnashrama Dharma, the shramans in fact forced the Vedic cosmogony to evolve into a better-formulated metaphysics in the Upanishads. This analysis also helps us better grasp why the historical roots of the anti-caste movement can be traced to the shramanic tradition (Chakravarti 1996; Thapar 2001).

There were other challengers to the Vedic school. Even before the emergence of the most renowned shraman teachers, the Buddha and Mahavir, in the sixth century BCE, materialists such as Kautsa and Brihaspati contested the claims to supernatural power of the Vedic hymns. They challenged the brahmans to produce their Brahma in flesh and blood. They were perhaps the earliest proponents of the materialist school of Lokayata. Lokayatikas, also known as Charvakas, dubbed the Vedic rituals and ceremonies as outright frauds (Chattopadhyaya 1992, 2001; Sardesai 1994). They declared that the mantra-chanting priests were rogues out to cheat and fleece the common people. Productive occupations of peasants and artisans, they stressed, were dignified, whereas those who smeared their bodies with ashes and chanted the Vedic mantra were good-for-nothing idiots.

Etymologically, Lokayata means prevalent in the world. The name suggests that its ideas were fairly well-known to the people. Sadly, there is little information about this school. In his pioneering work on the subject, D.P. Chattopadhyaya contends that Lokayatikas were pro-people, proto-materialist and sharply critical of the brahmanical way of life. He has cited several Lokayata verses and aphorisms culled from the writings of brahmanical idealists themselves. Even in rough translation, Lokayatika's biting satire and contempt for the brahmanical order are unmistakable:

Heaven and liberation are empty talk. There is no soul that is imagined to go to the other world. The actions prescribed for the caste-society (varnashrama) do not really yield their alleged results.

If (as claimed by the priests) the animal killed in the Jyotistoma sacrifice attains heaven straightway, why does not the sacrificer kill his own father (and thus ensure heaven for him)?

The authors of the three Vedas are just cheats and cunning thieves. All the learned formulas—the meaningless spells jarvari-turvari—like the wife taking the horse's phallus (i.e. a part of the Ashvamedha sacrifice), are nothing but the inventions of cheats for the purpose of obtaining their sacrificial fees. (Chattopadhyaya 2001: 214–15)

Sardesai (1994) has rightly argued that the driving principle of the Lokayata was more social than philosophical. Its views were strongly directed against caste order and brahman domination. Sardesai cites many Lokayata aphorisms from a Marathi work by Sadashiv Athavle:

The body, the face and all limbs (of all people) being similar, how can there be any distinctions of varna and caste? Such distinctions are unscientific and cannot be defended.

Agriculture, cattle-breeding, trade, state service, etc. are occupations of the wise. They should be followed. But those who smear their bodies with ashes and perform Agnihotra and other religious rites are devoid of intelligence and manhood. Hence, men should pursue sciences and arts which are of practical utility and based on practical knowledge.

Real bondage lies in servitude. Real moksha lies in freedom.

There is no such thing as moksha. Death is the end of life.
There is no rebirth. There is no other-world.
Dharma is the conspiracy of the crafty. Fools fall victim to it.
Those who composed the three Vedas were hypocrites, crafty people and devils. (Sardesai 1994: 219–20)

Traditionally, Indian philosophers are broadly classified under two heads, namely, *astika* and *nastika*, theists and atheists. In the cultural context, however, the words carry respectively the connotations of the conformists and non-conformists. Conforming meant accepting the scriptural authority of Vedas. An astika accepted the Vedic authority; a nastika controverted the Veda. Atheism of the shraman sects negated the Vedic idea of personal creator of the world, not the idea of a benevolent spirituality. Buddhism and Jainism, both nastika in the Vedic sense, developed their own religiosity. Thus, the ideologies of ancient India were not neatly divided between idealistic and materialistic systems, as argued by some Marxist scholars, but between the anti-Vedic and Vedic. The term *nastikata* (atheism) was used to denote opposition to the polytheistic superstitions and caste ideology that was the essence of the Vedic-brahmanism. Nastikata (in opposition to astikata) meant not simply atheism but 'denying the authority of the Vedas'. The casteist basis of the Vedic-Aryan philosophy and its supporters' preoccupation with their self-interest suggests that an astika (one who abides by the Vedas) had also to be one who believed in his own self-interest, served best through his caste interest. The caste interest could be served best by the secret knowledge embodied in scripture in the custody of the brahmans or those who 'knew'. On the other hand, anyone who questioned the authority of caste and *karmakanda* (rituals) was a nastika, a non-conformist, an outcaste. The phrase coined for this was *nastiko veda-nindakah*.

Seen from this perspective, the philosophies of *Lokayata*, Buddhism, and Jainism belong to the nastika or shramanic stream; and Vedanta, Nyaya and Vaisheshika schools of philosophy are astika or brahmanic. All shramanic systems, though differentially articulated, had their monastic order called *gana* (tribe) or *sangha* (organisation) which were casteless. Advocates of the shramanic worldview such as Buddhists, Jains, and Ajivikas explored areas of belief and practice different from the Vedas and Dharmashastras; they were opposed to caste and *karmakanda*.

In the Introduction, we saw the glimpses of shraman–brahman antagonism. In his *Mahabhashya*, Patanjali uses the example of shraman-brahman to illustrate an antagonistic compound—*samahaar dvanda*—and remarks that the opposition of the two was eternal—*yesham cha virodhah shashvatikah* (see Chakravarti 1996: 41). The two contending systems were so important before and during the Buddha's time that the period as a whole has been characterised by B.M. Barua ([1921] 1970), in his *Pre-Buddhist Indian Philosophy*, as the 'Age of the Shramanas and the Brahmanas'. In the succeeding centuries, the opposition between the brahmans and shramans (the latter typified by the Buddhist and Jain monks) is a constant feature of the literature of the two systems. The brahmanical literature has several instances of derogatory statements about the Buddhists and Jains as worthless heretics. On the other hand, the Buddhist and Jain texts, especially the Buddhist Pali texts, refer to brahmans as liars and exploiters whose vices include pride, deceit, greed, gluttony, and even crimes such as matricide and patricide. Denying any privileged position to the priestly class and rejecting the notion of any ascriptive qualifications for salvation, the shramanic ethic was egalitarian and universalist, though its lay followers, duped by the incessant brahmanical propaganda, later fell victim to the caste system.

The Contested Past: Romance *Versus* Reality

Besides the Shramanic–Lokayata rejection of the Vedic-brahmanic authority, there was resentment against the latter among non-Aryans, Asuras and Dasas. Examples are scattered in the Upanishads and the epics of defiant characters who opposed Vedic ritualism and beliefs. The *Chandogya Upanishad* speaks maliciously of the *Asura*-views against the brahmanical worldview. In Valmiki's *Ramayana*, there is a reference to Jabali who denounces the rituals and condemns the cult of sacrifice as an invention of interested, sinister, and fraudulent individuals. Later in the ninth century, Shankara mentions the anti-Vedic Kavsheya in his commentary on the *Brahma Sutra*. Such critics of the Vedic religion must have had popular support or else they would have been eliminated by their opponents who preached that *Vaidiki himsa himsa na bhavati*, 'the Vedic violence is no violence'. Not for nothing the Aranyakas, Brahmanas, Smritis are crammed with stringent injunctions against the challengers of Vedic religion. The threat from the people who were not willing to fall in the brahmanical line must have been serious.

In other words, the enslavement of the bulk of productive people into lowered castes and the latter's struggle to liberate themselves are the social context of India's troubled history. What was a dream project for the brahmans was a nightmare for the lowered castes. One's glory was another's ignominy. Almost all religious and secular literature in Sanskrit, one of the chief sources of the Indian past, are little more than the brahmanical propaganda which tells only one side of the story. There is no valid reason not to believe that the brahmanical sources do not give us the actual facts of life; they give and were meant to give what the brahmans thought the facts to be. Brahman records, to take an example, completely ignore the Mauryan king Ashoka except for referring to him in some texts as a despised Buddhist and a shudra. Besides maintaining a conspiracy of silence against the opponents, several evidences suggest that the Sanskrit texts were frequently subjected to interpolations, tendentious redactions, and plain fabrication.

There is hardly any Sanskrit composition which has not been tampered with, altered or added to by them. There is no famous rishi or teacher in whose name they have not concocted scriptures. There is no sacred book into which fiction and legend and imaginary history have not been interpolated....Veracity as to facts was never a feature of brahman authors, so much so that historical unreliability has become a universal literary characteristic of the Sanskrit language. The best critic would be unable to separate ... where facts end and fiction begins. This is even more the case in regard to the so-called sacred literature. (Dharma Theertha ([1941] 1992: 115–16)

Forgeries in Sanskrit texts remained undetected before the modern age because only brahmans could read and interpret them for others. The Sanskrit texts were held to be too sacred to be put to human reasoning. It is only in modern times that some scholars with an expert knowledge of the subject, have been able to unearth the forgeries committed by the brahman scribes, commentators, and thinkers. For example, pointing out the interpolation of the *Purusha-sukta* in the *Rigveda,* Max Müller has also shown that the brahmans 'mangled, mistranslated and misapplied' the original word *agre* to read *agneh* in order to provide Rigvedic support for the burning of widows. K.M. Panikkar (1938) has referred to the fabrication of a Shankara text by the brahmans of Malabar to sanction the custom of unapproachability. R.S. Sharma ([1958] 1991a) has pointed out rampant distortions in the epics to suit the brahmanical viewpoint. Didactic digressions on the superiority of the brahman in the *Shanti Parvan* in the *Mahabharata* are too obvious. While spurious records and fictitious dynastic pedigrees for brahmanised rulers abound in the sacerdotal texts, especially the Puranas, 'the Mauryas are described in these texts as *sudra-prayastv-adharmikah,* 'mainly shudras and unrighteous' (Thapar 1999: 12). Citing many examples of brahmanic forgeries (some of which we shall see in the next chapter), a scholar concludes that 'the full story of forged texts in Hinduism has yet to be written' (Walker 1983a: 364).

To sum up, a credible history of ancient India cannot be reconstructed without the context of social stratification, political economy, and cultural establishment. The brahmanical and non-brahmanical intellectual articulation cannot be grasped without context. The social and religious ideas generated by the elite were symbiotically related to its self-interest. Similarly, the thinking and ideology of the lower orders were crucially linked to their survival: this prompted them to reject, sometimes totally and at other partially, the norms and ideals of the brahmanic culture.

Notes

1. The *Purusha-sukta* in the *Rigveda* ([1981] 2000: 31) provides a supernatural origin of the varnas:
   When they divided the Man, into how many parts did they apportion him? What do they call his mouth, his two arms and thighs and feet?
   His mouth became the Brahmin, his arms were made into the Warrior, his thighs the People, and from his feet the Servants were born.

2. The very word dharma, however, could very well be of Buddhist origin, appropriated by brahmanism through a subtle slippage of meaning. The Sanskrit 'dharma', in all likelihood, was a later transcription of the Pali dhamma, used by the Buddha for a universal ethics, as we will see in Chapter 2.
3. To keep erring or defiant shudras in their place, Manu has prescribed exemplary punishment. Here are some instances. 'If a shudra hurls cruel words at a brahman, his tongue should be cut out, for he was born from the rear-end. If he mentions their name or caste maliciously, a red-hot iron nail ten-fingers long should be thrust into his mouth. If he is so proud as to instruct brahmans about their duty, the king should have hot oil poured into his mouth and ears' (8.270–2). '. . . If a shudra injures a man of the higher castes with some particular part of his body, that very part of his body should be cut off. If he raises his hand or a stick, he should have his hand cut off; if in anger he strikes with his foot, he should have his foot cut off. If a man of inferior caste tries to sit down on the same seat as a man of superior caste, he should be branded on the hip and banished, or have his buttocks cut off. If in his pride he spits on him, the king should have his two lips cut off; if he urinates on him, the penis; if he farts at him, the anus' (8.279–82). The list of such instructions—shared by other leading law-givers as well—runs long.

Like shudras, women, too, are at the receiving end of the most vicious attacks from the brahmanical authorities. Manu condemns all women to eternal surveillance by their male relatives because they suffer, he says, from uncontrollable lust and malicious nature. 'Good looks do not matter to them, nor do they care about youth; "A man!" they say, and enjoy sex with him, whether he is good-looking or ugly. By running after men like whores, by their fickle minds, and by their natural lack of affection these women are unfaithful to their husbands even when they are jealously guarded. Knowing that their very own nature is like this, . . . a man should make the utmost effort, to guard them' (*Manusmriti* 9.14–18).
4. Shraman (*Saman* in Pali) is derived from the root *shram,* 'to exert'. Shraman was a practitioner of spiritual exertions. A striver, literally. Of the two earliest references to the word *shraman* in the Vedic corpus, one is in the *Brihdaranyaka Upanishad* where it is used to denote a class of mendicants opposed to brahmans and brahmanism. While shraman in Sanskrit means one who exerts himself and performs austerities, Buddhist commentaries associate the word saman with 'quieting' (*samita*) of evil (*papa*). *Dhammapada* (verse 265) says, 'Someone who has pacified evil is called saman.' In the Pali Buddhist scriptures, we see the compound word saman-brahman, the former denoting the Jains, the Buddhists and the Ajivikas, and the latter

the upholders of the Vedic tradition. The Buddha is called a great saman, addressed often as 'Saman Gotam' (Shraman Gautam in Sanskrit), and members of his order referred to as the samans or shramans. In the Jain texts, Mahavir, too, is called a shraman, a term by which the followers of Buddhism and Jainism as well as all those opposed to the Vedic religion came to be identified.

CHAPTER 2

Buddhist India
Against Caste and Brahmanism

> When the whole country was basking in the sunshine of great ideals of brotherhood, when the king [such as Ashoka] and the commoner were co-operating . . . [and] producing glorious blossoms in the fields of science, literature, arts and architecture, when the people of India liberated from their bondage were carrying the joyful tidings of emancipation into distant lands and filling the world with the fragrance of the Buddha's teachings, alas! in the land of that Buddha, the brahman priests were studiously engaged in polishing the chains of imperialism and replenishing the armoury of aggression and exploitation with Manu Sastras, Sukra Nitis, Puranas, idolatrous temples, Kali worship and other literature and institutions of wily priestcraft.
>
> DHARMA THEERTHA [1941] 1992: 96

It was the intensity and multiplicity of resistance from below that facilitated whatever social mobility could exist in ancient (and for that matter in modern) India, not the in-built dynamism in the caste system as fondly held by the caste apologists. As we saw in the preceding chapter, proponents of inclusive ideologies, especially the shramanic leaders, came up with ideas that bypassed the brahmanic gods and beliefs. Some of them raised the banner of *chattaro vanna samasama honti* (all the four castes are equal). But the caste enthusiasts kept alive, in theory as well as practice, injunctions such as *shudram tu karyeta dasyam* (shudras would have to do slavery) and *na shudray mati dadyat* (shudras should not be given any knowledge).

The sixth century BCE was a period of momentous change in the Gangetic valley, not only in the material life—in the wake of the

Iron Age and what has been termed the 'second urban revolution' when the egalitarian tribal institutions were struggling to survive against the emergent monarchical states—but in the realm of ideas and culture as well. On the one hand, the brahmans were trying to establish their supremacy by floating fanciful socio-religious doctrines, and on the other, a range of non-conformists were coming up with ideologies—almost materialist or at least much less speculative—challenging brahmanic claims to higher knowledge and superior status. This surcharged milieu threw up a personality whose teaching—Buddhism—posed the most serious threat to brahmanism.

This period witnessed the emergence of a host of remarkable thinkers and strivers. Famous among them were six independent teachers—Ajit Keshkambal, Prakuddha Katyayana, Puran Kassapa, Sanjay Belathaputta, Niggantha Natputta, and Makkali Gosala. Popularly recognised as *saman* (*shraman*) or *paribbajaka* (Sanskrit, *parivrajaka*), these 'strivers' and 'mendicants' (which the two terms mean respectively) gave voice to a range of contesting opinions that reveal how contentious and cacophonous the society actually was.

The Buddha, Mahavir, and the above-mentioned thinkers had different philosophical visions but none of them believed in caste and brahmanism. They admitted whoever wanted to, irrespective of caste, to their ranks. In this and similar anti-ascriptive attitude, they carried forward the legacy of the earlier shramans and free thinkers who had rejected the exclusivist Vedic-brahmanism. As Pande (1978), Joshi ([1969] 2007), Carrithers (1992), and many others have pointed out, it was from this intellectually fecund community that Buddhism and Jainism arose.

There was also a vibrant school of anti-Vedic sceptics and materialists (Chattopadhyaya 1959). The Lokayata philosophy propagating thoroughgoing materialism was popular, as its very name suggests. The *Brihasapatisutra,* also known as *Lokayatasutra,* which expounded the classic matter-over-mind materialist thinking, existed in some form till the second century BCE as can be judged from Patanjali's references. Later, the Lokayata materialism became synonymous with Charavaka, who was supposedly a disciple of Brihasapati. Anti-brahmanic ideas were also present in Virochana's philosophy as mentioned in the *Chandogya Upanishad* and revealingly labelled there as *Asuropanishad*.

However, it was Jainism and Buddhism that represented the most powerful challenge to the Vedic-brahmanism. The Jain ideas were formulated by Parshva in the eighth century BCE, stressing non-violence, non-possession, and adherence to truthfulness. Vardhamana Mahavir, the celebrated contemporary of Buddha, added, among other things, self-mortification and absolute sexual abstinence to the list of Jain tenets. Atheistic in orientation, Jainism emphasised that self-purification could be achieved through asceticism, non-violence, truthfulness, and celibacy. The excessive stress on non-violence and self-discipline, however, proved a dampener and could not win a mass following for this religion.

Above all, Jainism failed to present a viable socio-religious alternative to brahmanism. Its emphasis on individual salvation through extreme austerities was unable to enthuse the common people. To counter the Vedic religion, Upanishadic metaphysics and the brahmanical social order, a balanced and effective philosophy was needed—a philosophy which grasped the people's consciousness, could appeal to the average human mind, and also give an impetus to social development. Buddhism was a product of these challenging conditions (Ilaiah 2000).

The Buddha's Synthesis of Mind and Matter

The outstanding figure that emerged from an array of shramanic truth-seekers was none other than Gautam Siddhartha (563–483 BCE). His leaving home in the bloom of youth with the resolve that 'I would enter a blazing fire, but I would not enter my home with my goal unattained' (as Ashvaghosha put it in his *Buddhacarita* [*c*. 100 CE]), and living up to this vow are the stuff legends are made of. His life story is fairly well-known. Born at Lumbini, Kapilvastu, situated in the foothills of the Himalayas, in the territory of the Sakya republic headed by his father, he took leave of his family at the age of twenty-nine, attained 'Enlightenment' at Bodh Gaya at the age of thirty-five, and died in Kusinara at the age of eighty. For forty-five years he traversed the kingdoms of Magadha and Kosala (corresponding to south Bihar and eastern Uttar Pradesh of today), as well as the adjoining republics and principalities, conversing, teaching, and converting people. Generating consciousness about compassion and holistic thinking for *bahujan hitaya, bahujan sukhaya* (the good and happiness of the many), he raised and trained a dedicated band of monk-brothers and sisters (bhikkhus and bhikkhunis). In a sharp break from brahmanic exclusivism, the Enlightened One (Buddha) recruited disciples from all castes and classes, both men and women. The Buddha's life, his thinking and his activities are recounted in detail in the historical records and Pali canon.[1]

The Buddha was unique in achieving an equilibrium between external activity and inner evolution by stressing both an acceptance of life and a detachment from it. He produced a synthesis by combining strands of shramanic thinking with the social challenge of the time. He rejected both the obsessive asceticism (by asserting that complete self-mastery is not an end in itself but a means to higher individual and social goals) and the absolutist Vedic-Upanishadic theology along with its essentialisation of caste by declaring that there is a better way and a better *dhamma* (by which he meant a universal 'standard' or 'norm' which is good for all humanity). He repudiated both the anarchic, excessive individualism of the ascetics and the Vedic-brahmanic regimentation of people in different caste groups. Charting a new course, he founded a dhamma and built a Sangh (organisation), which could only be entered on abandoning caste, and which offered conducive conditions for both individual and social development.

The pandits who confine religion to a belief in God, ritualism, and a set of dogmas have branded early Buddhism as an ethical system rather than a religion. But religion is essentially about our understanding of what life is about, and at its best represents an inspired search for higher truths and higher values to illumine our lives. In this sense, Buddhism, from the very beginning, was a religion. No doubt it was utterly unorthodox, and represented an 'antinomial system' against Vedic-brahmanism (Verardi 2011). Apart from its empirical and anti-metaphysical orientation, Buddhism embodied a universal morality by which it urged people to live. The Buddha rejected absolutist speculations, the fiction of caste, the theories of heaven and hell, and the metaphysics of *Atman-Brahmana*. For him, belief in heaven and hell was nothing but pleasurable and painful feelings one experiences in this life. Similarly, he regarded the belief in an immortal soul pernicious because 'it was a theory harmful to the religious life in that it tends to generate selfishness and egoism' (Kalupahana 1976: 41).

The Buddha was different from the know-all prophets and messengers of God. He admitted that he did not have answers to all questions. He objected to the charismatic cult being built around him by some of his followers. Not the one to give false hope, he advised his disciples to be their own path-finders: 'I never undertake to secure salvation for anybody under any circumstances; understand the dhamma and you will cross the ocean.' His immortal words, *atta dipo bhava attasaran*—'be a lamp unto yourself, be a refuge of yourself' (the *Mahaparinibbana Sutta*)—leaves little doubt that he did not want anyone to take his teachings on trust, but rather to test them in the light of personal experience and rational thinking.

The Buddha did not want his followers to stop thinking, as does Krishna in the *Gita*, claiming that every truth of any worth has already been revealed by him and the only need was to follow them faithfully. The Buddha's temper is different from the intellectual arrogance of the teacher-sages of the Vedic-Upanishadic tradition. In a well-known debate between Yajnavalkya and Gargi, recorded in the *Brihadaranyaka Upanishad,* the latter asks many searching questions, which enrage the sage who threatens Gargi with dire consequences: 'Shut up woman, or your head will break into pieces'.

The Buddha was humbler because he was not a prisoner of received wisdom, or inherited dogma. Logical and lucid, he was a rational thinker who discounted all metaphysical propositions as 'meaningless strings of words, sentences which conform to the rules of grammar but are lacking in meaning, even though they are capable of arousing strong emotional responses in the people'. Kalupahana's acclaimed study of Buddhist philosophy (1976) brings out the empiricist attitude of early Buddhism which rejects everything that cannot be experienced through the senses or sensory perception. Nowhere is this more clearly stated than in the *Sabba Sutta* of the *Samyutta Nikaya* where the Buddha says:

...What, monks, is 'everything'? Eye and material form, ear and sound, nose and odour, tongue and taste, body and tangible objects, mind and mental objects. They are called 'everything'. Monks, he who would say: 'I will reject this everything and proclaim another everything', he may certainly have a theory. But when questioned, he would not be able to answer and would, moreover, be subject to vexation. Why? Because it would not be within the range of experience. (Kalupahana 1976: 158)

The Buddha did not give any formulation; he gave an open-ended methodology to think rationally as well as compassionately. Talking to the people of the Kalama clan, he said:

Do not believe in anything (simply) because you have heard it. Do not believe in traditions because they have been handed down for many generations. Do not believe in anything because it is spoken and rumoured by many. Do not believe in anything (simply) because it is found written in your religious books. Do not believe in anything merely on the authority of your teachers and elders. Do not believe in specious reasoning, or a bias to which you have become attached by habit. Have deliberation and analyse, and when you find a proper reason for accepting something which is conducive to the good and benefit of one and all, accept it and live up to it. (The Kalama Sutta in *Anguttara Nikaya*, see Woodward and Hare 1932–6, vol. I: 188–93)

The Buddha takes an objective yet a deeply sympathetic view of life. His first discourse begins from the truth about suffering. His worldview evolves from this basic truth. The experience of suffering is so universal and pervasive that it forms the connecting link between all sentient beings—humans, animals, birds—who otherwise have little in common. The idea of suffering is conceived as an empirical reality, and becomes the basis of a world-embracing and life-affirming philosophy, because there does not exist any other experience that is as pervasive and universal. It provides the foundation of a human bond, visualised in the principle of universal love and friendship, *metta* (Sanskrit, *maitri*). In a moving and majestic exhortation (the *Metta Sutta* of *Sutta Nipata*), the Buddha defines *metta* as such:

Mata yatha niyam puttam ayausa ekaputtamanurakhe
Evam pi sabbabhutesu manasam bhavayet aprinamam.

(As a mother, even at the risk of her own life, loves and protects her child, so let a man cultivate love without measure towards all living beings.)

Similar passages abound in the Buddhist Pali literature, stressing that one should recognise oneself in the pain of others. The opening verse of the 10th Chapter of the *Dhammapada* says: 'All beings are afraid of pain, all beings are afraid of death. Recognising oneself in others, one should neither kill nor cause to kill.'

Based on values such as *ahimsa* (non-violence), *prajna* (humane application of knowledge), *karuna* (compassion), and *samata* (equality), the Buddhist quest of individual accomplishment is not divorced from social responsibility. In Buddha's discourses, as much emphasis is given to community awakening as to the awakening of the individual. He suggests that unless one comes out of one's selfish, egoistic self, one has very little chance of attaining peace and equanimity. The *Dhammapada* says: 'The cause of all disturbance is lack of compassion. It corrupts the body, speech and mind; it harms the family no less than strangers. If those who strive for virtue will only remember compassion, only good can result.' Unconditional love for all beings is the Buddhist way to heal worldly wounds. Such a love becomes the basis of compassion. By becoming compassionate, one can become a healing force in this world of misery. The Buddha lived up to this ideal—his life was an embodiment of universal *metta*. He inspired others to lead such a life. It was under such Buddhist influence that Ashoka set up hospitals for not only fellow humans but also animals and birds.

The Anti-Thesis of Upanishadic Absolutism

Independent of Vedic sacrificial culture and Upanishadic metaphysics, the Buddha enunciated Four Noble Truths. The first truth is there is sorrow and suffering (*dukkha*) in life. The second, dukkha is caused by an unbalanced life and endless desire—*trishna*. (Later in his life he took into account oppressive social conditions as well for human misery, see the *Digha Nikaya* 3.58 ff. and Kosambi [1965] 1992: 113.) The third, there is liberation—*nibbana* ('nirvana' in Sanskrit). The fourth points to the way to liberation, which he visualised in the *Atthangika Magga* or Eightfold Path. Centred around *majjhima patipada* (the middle path), the *Atthangika Magga* consists of Right View, Right Thought, Right Speech, Right Action, Right Living, Right Endeavour, Right Mindfulness, and Right Concentration, which leads to knowledge, to calmness, to awakening.

The Buddha explained the beauty of the middle path through the metaphor of the *sarangi*. If the strings of the musical instrument are too loose or too tight, will there be mellifluous melody? In Buddhism, awareness and compassion are the means, and wholesome, healthy transformation—individual as well as social—is the end. Individual happiness cannot be achieved in isolation and extremity. Individual and society are interdependent, and to be happy, one must create happiness around oneself. In this way, the 'middle path' is imbued with radical potential. The transformation it would usher in shall be peaceful, wholesome, avoiding the extremes of mindless materialism and obsessive spirituality. The Buddha insisted on avoiding extremes and treading cautiously in the middle, which would bring balance, symmetry, and beauty in life.

Since an unexamined life is not worth living, the Buddha lays stress on bringing awareness to life. He says that like kaleidoscopic images in a dream, a person is delusioned by fleeting emotions of all kinds. So long as the dream lasts, the images appear to be real, but on awakening they disappear. Awakening requires reflection and action to transform oneself at the very core, so that one is no longer blinded by delusive images or false beliefs. For this the Buddha himself does *vipassana* (literally 'to look within'), a simple and effective meditation, and recommends the same to others. *Vipassana*—aimed at stilling the mind and bringing insight—is his gift to humanity. Anyone who does *vipassana,* looks within and without, strives for one's own and others' welfare, aspires to be like the Buddha, is a Boddhisattva. The term Boddhisattva was perhaps originally used in this sense, though later its connotation got mired in superstitious belief in Buddha's incarnations.

The Buddha was an early, if not the first, proponent of dialectics, the art of investigating the truth of opinions. His dialectics led him to enunciate the law of causality and change that forms the core of Buddhist philosophy. In his first discourse at Sarnath, famous in history as the *Dhamma-Chakka-Pavattana*, or Setting in Motion the Wheel of the Law, he said:

> Let us put aside such unprofitable and unsolvable questions (*avayaktani*) as the questions of beginning and end. I will teach you dhamma. That being thus this comes to be. From the coming to be of that, this arises. That being absent, this does not happen. From the cessation of that this ceases. This is the dhamma. Whoever accepts dhamma, accepts the law of paticca samuppada (dependent origination). (See Rhys Davids [1910] 2000b: 45)

The Buddha says, *paticca samuppada* ('*pratitya* samutpada' in Sanskrit), the law of causation or dependent origination, is the truth about the world. All natural and social phenomena are to be understood in the light of this theory, not in terms of a Creator or transcendental reality. He also stresses that the world is not only a set of objects found in space and time, related or unrelated, but includes our feelings and dispositions, likes and dislikes. The world consists not only of mountains and rivers, trees and stones, but also of humans and animals with their behavioural patterns. A man's dispositions, likes and dislikes, influence his judgement about good and bad, truth and falsehood, which are relative rather than absolute (Kalupahana 1976: 63–4). Causality explains the pattern according to which all these things happen.

Paticca samuppada is the cornerstone of the Buddhist dialectic. Everything is relative, constantly changing, mutating, evolving, decaying, and disintegrating. This implies *anicca* ('anitya' in Sanskrit), the idea of impermanence, and that nothing exists by itself. Everything is the effect of some cause; cause and effect are interrelated. Buddhism, thus, explains the processes of bondage and freedom, unhappiness and happiness, both at the individual and social levels.

The Buddha developed the idea of *anicca* along with *anattavada* ('anatmavada' in Sanskrit), the theory of no-soul. He explains that what is called the soul is in reality a physical and mental aggregate of five *anicca khanda* ('impermanent conditions'): (a) *rupa* or form (the physical body), (b) *vedana* or feelings, (c) *sanna* (sangya in Sanskrit) or understanding, (d) *sankhara* (sanskara) or will, and (e) *vinnana* (Sanskrit vigyana) or pure consciousness. All these elements go into the making of human personality or what is called the soul. The

Buddha insisted that the soul was only a name for the constituent elements of experience and was the result produced by a simultaneous manifestation of these elements.

Some pandits refuse to grant Buddhism its philosophical distinctiveness. Radhakrishnan says, 'It was Buddha's mission to accept the ideology of the Upanishads at its best and make it available for the daily needs of mankind. Historical Buddhism means the spread of the Upanishad doctrine among the people.... Such democratic upheavals are common features of Hindu society.' He then contradicts his statement, '... the religion of Buddha is an aristocratic one. It is full of subtleties that only the learned could understand, and Buddha had always in view the Shramanas and the Brahmanas' (Radhakrishnan [1923] 1962). In this stereotype, Buddhism is foreshadowed by the Vedic-brahmanic worldview, especially Upanishadic ideology. Radhakrishnan asserts: 'Early Buddhism is not an absolutely original doctrine. It is no freak in the evolution of Indian thought' ([1923] 1962: 360). Elsewhere he declares, the Buddha was 'born, grew up, and died a Hindu' (Radhakrishnan [1956] 1997: IX). Jocobi, Oldenberg, and Rhys Davids hold similar views, attributing the Buddhist philosophy to a reformist school within the larger Vedic-Upanishadic tradition.

The underlying assumptions behind such misleading assessments, besides gross ignorance about the pre-Vedic shramanic tradition to which Buddhism owed its origin, are three—(a) the Buddha accepted the traditional Hindu doctrines of transcendental reality, karma and rebirth (b) he set out to 'reform' brahmanic Hinduism, and (c) all Upanishads are pre-Buddha. All are baseless. First, the Buddha did not accept anything without personal verification. There is no evidence to show that he accepted the theory of transcendental reality expressed in the Upanishadic *Atman-Brahmana*. Second, there is absolutely nothing in his life to indicate that his aim was to salvage an ailing brahmanism. The main thrust of his thinking and struggle stood in sharp opposition to brahmanic theology. His disregard for the Vedic sacrifice, Upanishadic speculation and the idea of caste left no doubt that his priority lay well beyond the Vedic-brahmanism.

Moreover, the Upanishadic philosophy was not yet crystallised as most Upanishads, contrary to the popular myth, were composed after the Buddha's time. Dharmanand Kosambi, a major scholar of Pali and Sanskrit, contends that not only all Upanishads but a major portion of the Aranyakas and Brahmanas too were composed after the Buddha's time. He cites the lineages given in the *Shatapatha Brahmana* and the *Brihadaranyaka Upanishad* which mention 35 generations of the post-Buddha writers who continued compiling these works. Historian H.C. Raychaudhury calculates 30 years for each generation but Kosambi brings it down to 25 years to be more realistic. This shows that these writings extended up to 875 (35 x 25) years after Buddha's death in 483 BCE. In other words, the last Upanishads were composed as late as the Gupta period, i.e. the fourth and fifth centuries CE. Shankara's famous commentaries on Upanishads were written in the ninth century. Even an *Allopanishad* was concocted by the opportunistic Sanskritists during Akbar's regime (see Kosambi's *Bhagwan Buddha: Jeevan aur Darshan*, pp. 25–6; for more detailed discussion of the subject, see his *Hindi Sanskriti Aani Ahinsa* in Marathi).

Even assuming that Buddha was familiar with the Upanishadic metaphysics, his thinking was its anti-thesis. Through a maze of theological, theosophical, and metaphysical conceptions, the Upanishads tried to discover some unchanging, eternal reality behind the changing and temporary phenomena of the world. The quest for the Absolute led Upanishadic thinkers to the concept of an eternal soul and its eternal Creator. Buddhist philosophy, characterised by the *paticca samuppada*, *anatta*, and *anicca*, remains, contrary to the fond beliefs of pandits like Radhakrishnan, the permanent antithesis of Upanishadic teaching. That is why Buddhism was called *anatmavada* as against the Upanishadic *atmavada*.

In his masterpiece *Pramanavarttika*, Dharmakirti, the seventh-century logician, has given a devastating expression to the Buddhist opposition to the brahmanic teachings:

Vedapramanyam kasyachit kartivadah
snane dharmechha jativadavalepah,
Santaparambhah papahanaya cheti
dhvastaprajnanam panchalingani jadye.

The unquestioned authority of the Vedas;
the belief in a world-creator;
the quest for purification through ritual bathing;
the arrogant division into castes;
the practice of mortification to atone for sin;
—these five are the marks of the crass stupidity of witless men. (See Jaini 2001: 47)

The Vedic-Upanishadic fixation on *Atman-Brahmana* and human life as a plaything of the Brahma make any human initiative or investigation utterly futile. The Buddha changed all that by bringing social, psychological and scientific factors into the human world. *Paticca samuppada* propounds the dialectics of change that characterise the world. Buddhism stresses that changeability is one of the basic principles of life. It underlines a process which is capable of bringing out new ideas to meet new challenges. The social message emanating from this is not hard to find.

The Buddha's prime purpose was to heal the festering wounds of humanity. His mission was to build a well-off society where new forms of creativity and compassion could blossom. The Buddha wanted his disciples to think creatively and contribute to the development of a compassionate dhamma. He wanted them to develop the *bodhi hradaya,* the awakened heart, the compassionate heart. The awakened individuals, he believed, would awaken and emancipate the enslaved. Buddhism believes in the power of social action.

The impression that Buddhism is a pessimistic religion is wrong. In Buddhism, the truth of suffering is only half the truth as it also propounds that there is a way out. The Buddha takes up human suffering only as the starting point of his thinking, after that he proceeds to its anti-thesis—the truth of the cessation of suffering. He urges people to avoid that which produces suffering and to do that which produces happiness.

In determining whether an action, physical or mental, is good or bad, the Buddhist criterion is whether or not that action leads to happy or healthy consequences, both individual and social. The Buddha's classic definition of good and bad is to be found in the *Ambalatthika–Rahulovada Sutta* of *Majjhima-Nikaya*:

Whatever action, bodily, verbal, or mental, leads to suffering for oneself, for others or for both, that action is bad (*a-kusalam*). Whatever action, bodily, verbal or mental, does not lead to suffering for oneself, for others or for both, that action is good (*kusalam*). (Kalupahana 1976: 62)

The Buddha stresses on acquiring mastery over the self by which one can get rid of selfishness, lust, possessive attachments and the resultant suffering and sorrow. It is not an invocation to the extinction of individuality: it is a plea to obliterate the untrammelled ego. It is a plea to give up not all activity but activity of the wrong type. Man has to remake himself, has to evolve into a transformed individual, a compassionate individual. This was the morality that the Buddha interchangeably used for dhamma. He coined the word 'dhamma' for a religion of morality. Later, it was appropriated by brahmanism as 'dharma' but to mean a religion which was founded on certain (sacrificial) rites and (caste) rules.[2] Contrarily, the core of the Buddha's dhamma is a universal morality; all else is subservient to morality. Here, one is required to reject everything, including the scriptures whose injunctions clash with the requirements of morality. On the other hand, in the case of brahmanism, the Vedas are *apaurusheya*—not of human origin—and hence infallible and inviolate. The Buddha had to reject the Vedas because they glorified violent and immoral 'gods' (who tortured and killed their enemies) and enjoined the performance of rituals involving animal—and in some cases even human—sacrifice.

The Buddha stood by reason, but insisted that only that reason is valid which is tested on the anvil of practice—reason divorced from practice degenerates into abstract absurdities. While the Upanishadic metaphysics strove to prove that the core of man is the *Atman* or *Brahmana* and the supreme aim of man is to discover it and merge his unreal individual self with the real cosmic self, the Buddha changed the logic by asserting that a heightened consciousness or personal perfection can be attained by doing good to people in distress. He warned his followers against getting trapped in abstruse hair-splitting discussions, and instead set out to discover the cause and cure of suffering.

Indictment of Caste

As manifest in his emphasis on *pragya, karuna* and *samata*, the Buddha wanted to evolve a new human character for *bahujan hitaya, bahujan sukhaya*. The term *bahujan* (the multitude) was his coinage for the commonality who despite their service to society were kept deprived and marginalised. The eloquent phrase 'bahujan hitaya' leaves little doubt that Buddha's ambition was to reconstruct the world where the few are not more precious than the many. Opposing the brahmanic idea that the common people have to be kept down for the benefit of the 'chosen few', he insisted that individual flourishing could be best ensured through social flourishing. He warned, 'Don't try to build your happiness on the unhappiness of others. You will be enmeshed in a net of hatred' (*Dhammapada* XXI: 2; tr. Easwaran 1986).

Based on such inclusive thinking, Buddha's opposition to the discriminatory ideology of caste and brahmanism was absolute. While brahmanism was constructing a cultural structure to support *brahman hitaya, brahman sukhaya,* Buddha came up with the proposition of *bahujan hitaya, bahujan sukhaya*. Shifting the paradigm from hierarchy to equality, he used strong words to describe those who threaten the people's welfare: *mogham sa ratthapindam bhunjati*, 'useless consumers of society's wealth' (see Sankrityayan 1990: 1).

The Buddha attacked in his discourses the fundamentals of caste and brahmanical theology. His opposition to injustice of caste and barrenness of rituals had been the main factors in his appeal to the common people (Chattopadhyaya 1992: 466–7). Buddhism became a rallying point for the lowered castes, the outcast, the women. From its inception, for multiple reasons, Buddhism was uniquely placed to become 'the biggest socio-religious movement in Indian history' (ibid.).

The Buddha was the first in history to visualise humankind as one biological entity. In the *Vasettha Sutta* of *Sutta Nipata*, in his answer to the question as to what makes a man a brahman, he reminds his questioner that whereas in the case of plants, animals, fish and birds, there are many species that can be distinguished, in the case of human beings there are no such species, no distinguishing marks. He brings home the point that caste distinctions made between individuals are arbitrary, a matter of sheer prejudice and custom. He stresses that it is wisdom and goodness that make the only real distinction; and it is only the ignorant who maintains that it is birth that makes a man superior or inferior.

The Buddha also points out that social divisions based on occupation developed at a certain stage in social evolution, but basically there were two interchangeable categories of people—masters and servants. A rich person could buy the services of the poor and the latter had to serve the former in lieu of wages. Discarding the notions of *jativada* (casteism) and *gottavada* (clanism) as superfluous divisions that hindered social and spiritual progress, he asserts *chattaro vanna samasama honti*, 'all the four varnas are equal' (the *Assalayana Sutta* of *Majjhima Nikaya*).

On tour in villages and cities, the Buddha had to face the brahmans' resentment for professing this view, and stressing that everyone, irrespective of caste or clan, has the potential to become virtuous. On several occasions, he and his followers had to face abuse and harassment on this count.[3] The *Digha Nikaya* mentions the story of Lohitya, a brahman of Salvatika village, who argued with the Buddha that an enlightened person like him should not share his knowledge with the commoners as it would confuse the simple folk faithfully following the traditional ways. The Buddha countered by suggesting that if a wise person had a flawless idea which could do good to humanity, he owed it to society to teach it to all, even if it went against the grain of established beliefs.

The Buddha's rejection of caste and brahmanism is eloquently expressed in the *Vasala Sutta* of the *Sutta Nipata* where he says that no one is lowly because of birth in a particular caste. It is one's deeds that decide if one is lowly or not. 'Not by birth does one become an outcaste, not by birth one becomes a brahman, by deeds one becomes an outcaste, by deeds one becomes a brahman.' The Buddhist Pali used the word 'brahman' as denoting acquired excellence, not a birth-based caste status. Uma Chakravarti's study of the early Buddhism makes this clear:

The Buddhists, as is usual with them, use the vocabulary of the brahmanas which they infuse with their own meaning. Chandala is used by the Buddhists to express a moral value and not to indicate low birth. In a hard-hitting attack on the brahmanas Buddha turns the table on them. He applies the term brahmana chandala for a brahmana who leads an immoral and depraved existence but claims at the same time that he can remain undefiled and pure, like the fire which burns unclean things but remains pure in spite of it. ([1987] 1996: 107)

During Buddha's time the brahmanical social order was in the formative phase and not yet fully crystallised. While the brahmans were asserting identity of individuals and professional groups based an ascribed caste status, the society at large had not yet accepted birth-based status groups. Chakravarti's study of the period establishes that the brahmanical varna stratification was more a theoretical concept than a social reality. In contrast to the brahmanical texts, the term varna (Pali *vanna*) appears in the Buddhist texts only in the abstract—here no one is ever described as belonging to any particular varna by birth. Chakravarti verifies that only two social groups, the khattiyas (kshatriyas) and brahmans of the brahmanical scheme, are verifiable as existing categories in the Buddhist texts. The categories *vessa* (vaishya) and *sudda* (shudra), occur seldom and only in passages where there is a theoretical discussion about caste.

In the brahmanical texts the vessa is associated with agriculture, cattle-keeping and trade, and the sudda with service. But nowhere in the Buddhist texts are people or groups occupied with agriculture, cattle-keeping or trade, referred to as vessas, or those associated with service referred to as suddas. Instead the Buddhist texts associated agriculture with the gahapati, the cattle keeper is described as a gopaka, and the term vanijja is used for the trader.... Similarly while there are no suddas there are innumerable references to dasas and kammakaras who are associated not with service of the higher vannas but with providing labour for their masters who are almost invariably gahapatis.... The significant factor in Buddhist society for purposes of identification, particularly for the service groups, were the occupational divisions among people. The function actually performed by a person provided the basic identity of individuals. (Chakravarti [1987] 1996: 106–7)

Though the society of Buddha's time was not yet a rigid caste society, the Buddha made it clear that a category like caste had no place in his organisation:

> As the great streams, O disciples, however many they be, the Ganga, Yamuna, Aciravati, Sarabhu, Mahi, when they reach the great ocean, lose their old name and their old descent, and bear the only name, 'the great ocean', so also my disciples (of all castes and social categories) when they, in accordance with the law and doctrine which the order has preached, forsake their home and go into homelessness, lose their own name and their old paternity, and bear only one designation, shramans. (*Udana* V. 5; *Vinaya Pitaka* II. 9; see Oldenberg [1882] 1927: 152)

It was its anti-caste character and its identification with the lowered castes that earned Buddhism brahmanical antipathy. Nowhere was this more candidly expressed than in the Buddha's dialogue with Vasettha, his brahman disciple, in the *Agganna Sutta* of the *Digha Nikaya*. Vasettha reveals that exceptional brahmans like him who embrace Buddhism are held in contempt by their relatives. The Buddha asks him to explain in 'what terms the brahmans blame and revile you'. Vasettha:

> Sir, the brahmans say this: 'The brahman is the highest caste, the others are low; only the brahmans are fair-complexioned and well-born, the non-brahmans are dark and low-born. Brahmans are own sons of Brahma, born of his mouth, offspring of Brahma, created by Brahma, heirs of Brahma. But you have forsaken the best social rank, and have gone over to the low-born . . . the shaven beggars, the menials, those black-skinned and footborn Buddhists, the offscouring of your kinsman's heels.' (See Rhys Davids [1921] 2000b: 78)

The Buddha laughs this off, and makes a sharp retort: 'Surely, Vasettha, the brahmans . . . forget their own heritage? For the women of the brahman are seen to have periods, to be pregnant, to give birth and to suckle babies, and yet those very brahmans born out of vaginas, say that they are born out of the mouth of Brahma.' Resorting to this rather combative style, very untypical of Buddha, he asserts that no one is inferior or superior by birth; there are good people and bad people in all ranks—'khattiya, brahman, vessa, sudda.'. . . 'Now seeing, Vasettha, that both bad and good qualities, blamed and praised respectively by the wise, are distributed among each of the four classes, the wise do not admit those claims which the brahmans put forward' (ibid.: 78–9).

The Buddha's arguments that followed thereafter in the *Aggañña Sutta* need some elaboration. There is more here than meets the eye. The Buddha was also known as Sakyamuni (the sage of the Sakyas) and his followers were often described as Sakyaputras (the sons of the Sakyas). The Sakyas, a distinct ethnic group, living in the outskirts of the Vedic civilisation regarded themselves as khattiya, but not in the brahmanical sense. It is notable that khattiya is derived from the word *khet* or *kshetra,* which means a field or land; in this sense, all those who lived or worked on their land were khattiyas. However, as Vasettha's description brings out, the brahmans would dismiss Buddha, his people and his followers as being in effect despised shudras, the lowest rank of menials. As Carrithers (1992: 128) points out, the brahmanic contempt of Buddha and his people smacks of what we would call racial prejudice. The brahmans saw the world as neatly divided into different races: a brahman is not just a priest by vocation, but inherently endowed with purity of birth, physical beauty, personal purity, virtue and wisdom. Likewise, calling someone a shudra not only brings out the image of a manual worker but someone condemned to misery and slavery. It is a worldview which has the vicious divisiveness of apartheid, where there are no individuals, only the whites (brahmans) and the blacks (shudras).

It was this mentality that Buddha opposed. Viewing the dialogue with Vasettha in perspective, his reply, containing some basic knowledge of biology against the brahman's theological knowledge (where he is born of Brahma's mouth) is, as Carrither says, not only 'extraordinarily apt' but also 'effective'. Stung by the brahmanical insult, the Buddha gives a befitting reply.

There are critics who argue that Buddha did not oppose caste; he merely tried to replace the superiority of the brahmans by the khattiyas, since he himself was a khattiya. They miss the point: what the Buddha seems to suggest is that the khattiyas are the best but only for those who believe in lineage; this is not *his* criterion of judging any individual or group. This is a ploy he employs at times to put the arrogant brahman in his place. At one level, in a rhetorical flourish, he is suggesting that even on the basis of birth you (the brahman) are not the best. He makes it clear by adding that the best individuals are those, irrespective of their lineage, who radiate wisdom and compassion. The Buddha tells Vasettha that he and others like him who have left their past identities of family, caste, and clan can say they are 'strivers [after truth], sons of the Sakyas'. The followers of Buddha can say with pride: 'We are true sons of Buddha, born of his mouth, born of the truth, made by the truth, heirs of the truth.' Buddha, as is well known, gathered followers from all castes and called them sons of the Sakyas, making no distinction between them on the basis of birth.

Devastating remarks against the pretensions of brahmans are scattered through the Pali canon. The early Buddhist texts refer to disputations of Buddha with Ambattha and other brahmans on the caste question. Buddha argues that an individual's assessment should take into account only his character traits, not his birth or lineage.

In the supreme perfection in wisdom and righteousness, Ambattha, there is no reference to the question either of birth, or of lineage or of the pride which says: 'You are held as worthy as I', or 'You are not held as worthy as I'. . . . For whosoever, Ambattha, are in bondage to the notions of birth or of lineage, or to the pride of social position, or of connection by marriage, they are far from the best wisdom and righteousness. It is only by having got rid of all such bondage that one can realise for himself that supreme perfection in wisdom and in conduct. (Rhys Davids [1899] 2000a: 123)

The Buddha remained firm in his commitment to the welfare of all, without the distinction of caste and later even gender. He supported the lowered and the despised in two ways—first, by taking an ideological position against caste; and second, at the practical level, by admitting persons of lowly origins, the 'untouchables' and women in his Sangha. *Theragatha* and *Therigatha*, the Pali texts which form part of *Khuddaka Nikaya*, mention many persons of the 'lowest' castes (including a scavenger) occupying key positions in the Buddhist order. Upali, accepted as the chief authority after the Buddha himself, was formerly a barber. There was a separate order of sisters, with their own organisation. Punna and Punnika were earlier slave girls, while Sunita was a Pukkusa, one of the 'low' tribes. Nanda was formerly a cowherd and Dhania a potter. The two Panthakas were outcastes as they were born of the union of a slave with a woman of 'high' caste. Sati, Kapa, Sumangala, and Subha were all born of parents belonging to 'low' castes.

Also received in the order were women like Ambapali, the royal courtesan of Vaishali, Buddha's foster-mother Mahaprajapati Gautami, as well as the 'low' caste girl Prakriti, vagabonds like the unnamed man of Rajgriha, and robbers like Angulimala.

On the basis of such evidence, Rhys Davids concludes that as regards his own order, over which alone he had an effective control, he ignores completely all advantages or disabilities arising from birth, occupation and social status, and dismantles all barriers and disabilities arising from the arbitrary rules of caste and status. Had the Buddha's views won the day, the evolution of social grades and distinctions would have gone differently and the caste system would never have been built up in India ([1899] 2000a: 102–7).

Paradigm of Human Liberation

The social dimension of early Buddhism that emerges from the historical records was remarkably progressive for that era. As Buddhism saw the world as a perpetual process of change, it focused on understanding this process, adopting a rational and open-ended attitude. The Buddha's last words to his disciples were: *vayadhamma sankhara, appamadena vattetha*, 'worldly objects are transitory; be on your guard' (*Mahaparinibbana Sutta*). It was a call for eternal vigilance and willingness to undergo desirable transformation. Without this, individual and social progress was not possible.

With mindfulness and diligence an individual could lead a good life and secure his salvation. Unlike brahmanism, the Buddha had a rational concept of *kamma* (*karma* in Sanskrit) which did not take into account divine intervention. In his view one cannot escape the consequences of one's actions by indulging in superfluous rites and performance. What one needs for liberation are self-awareness, self-discipline, and ceaseless efforts. The Buddha had to go through hell to attain enlightenment. The Buddhahood was his attainment after waging an epic struggle to get rid of worldly delusions and personal weaknesses. But there is no formula, no single illuminated path that can guarantee everyone's freedom. Which is why Buddha wanted everyone to be a light unto themselves—*atta dipo bhava*.

Speaking in people's language, using simple words to convey his ideas, the Buddha declared all rituals irrelevant and unnecessary for the good life. He attacked superstition and obscurantism wherever he found them. His discourses often took the form of questioning and parables in which he spurned metaphysical mysticism and abstract speculation. Aware of the mischief of brahmanic intellectualism, and of the immense pretensions of the clever, he warned his listeners that meaning was important, not the word—*arthah pratisaranama na vyanjanam*. His liberating ideas were addressed to the whole of society, especially to the weaker sections, who were more susceptible to the devious teaching of intellectual elite.

However, conditioned by the patriarchal spirit of the time, Buddha's views on women were far from enlightened. He saw them as weak and inferior. Ananda, his favourite disciple, who was more sympathetic to women, had to persuade him to allow women to join the Sangh. Though belatedly, Buddha accepted the woman's right to knowledge and liberation. His surrender to the women's demand to be admitted to the Sangh was commendable, and in keeping with the progressive and more inclusive culture than brahmanism that Buddhism was trying to create. Though women were not accorded equality with men within the Sangh, their arrival on the hitherto prohibited area was a welcome step.

As Mrs. Rhys Davids (1909) has underlined, it is difficult to imagine today the emancipative experience many women felt after joining the Sangh. The bereaved mother and childless widow found solace there; the wife of rich man left behind the emptiness of an idle life of luxury, the poor man's wife from the oppressive poverty; the young girl from the humiliation of being handed over to the highest bidder; the thoughtful woman from the ban imposed on her intellectual life by convention and tradition. Escape, deliverance, freedom from suffering—mental, moral, domestic, social—from situations that became intolerable, are poignantly expressed in many songs of the *Therigatha* (C.A.F. Rhys Davids [1909] 1980). It is remarkable that the percentages of bhikkhunis' hymns in which the goal achieved is envisaged as emancipation, is higher than the corresponding proportion in the hymns by the bhikkhus (ibid.). We see in the songs their celebration of the newly found freedom. Sumangalamata joyously exclaims:

O Woman well set free! How free I am,
How wonderfully free from kitchen drudgery,
Free from the harsh grip of hunger,
And from empty cooking pots,
Free too of that unscrupulous man,
The weaver of sunshades.
Calm now and serene I am,
All lust and hatred purged.
To the shades of the spreading trees I go
And contemplate my happiness. (See Tharu and Lalita 1991: 69)

Kisagotami portrays the Buddha as a kind and noble friend (*kalyan-mitta*), and some women intimately relate to their mentor and claim spiritual fatherhood in him. Uttama exults:

Buddha's daughter I,
Born of his mouth, his blessed word, I stand!
(C.A.F. Rhys Davids [1909] 1980: 37)

And so does Sundari:

Thou art Buddha! thou art Master! and thine,
Thy daughter am I, issue of thy mouth. (Ibid.: 141)

Considering women's subjugation of that era, the Buddha's sympathy gave the unhappy, harassed women a new hope. With the change came the energy and confidence to lead a new and promising life. Vasitthi's verse expresses this:

Now all my sorrows are hewn down, cast out,
Uprooted, brought to utter end,
In that I now can grasp and understand
The base on which my miseries were built. (Ibid.: 80)

The Buddhist recognition of human dignity and equality won the hearts of generations of people, especially from the subordinated communities. Symbolising an egalitarian alternative to the discriminatory brahmanism, Buddhism has an enduring appeal to the outcaste and the devalued. It was able to fire the imagination of Ambedkar in the twentieth century, inspiring him to author his classic *The Buddha and His Dhamma* and embracing it with millions of fellow dalits. Even before Ambedkar, many subaltern leaders had recognised in Buddhism an antithesis to caste and Brahmanism (Mani 2007). One such leader was Iyothee Thass (1845–1914) of Tamil Nadu (see Chapter 6). It was Thass who, by founding the South Indian Buddhist Association with several branches both within and outside India as early as 1910, had pioneered the movement of Buddhist regeneration in India (Aloysius 1998).

The engaged Buddhism of the dalit-subalterns does not see Buddha as a beatific mystic meditating under a banyan tree, but as a compassionate hero intensely engaged with the sufferings of the marginalised. See Daya Pawar's *Buddha*:

I never see you in
Jeta's garden
sitting with eyes closed
in meditation, in the lotus position,
or
in the caves of Ajanta and Ellora
with stone lips sewn shut
sleeping the last sleep of your life.
I see you
walking, talking,
breathing softly, healingly,
on the sorrow of the poor, the weak,
going from hut to hut
in the life-destroying darkness,
torch in hand,
giving the sorrow
that drains the blood
like a contagious disease
a new meaning. (Tr. Zelliot and Karve, see Joshi 1986: 159)

A similar sentiment is expressed in Bhagwan Sawai's poem *Tathagata*, where Buddha is artistically resurrected as a friend and redeemer of the oppressed:

Tathagata
I've come to you
my sorrows interred in my bones
bringing my darkness within the radius of your light
Take me within your fold, away from this darkness
Out there, I've worn myself out, slogging in their carnival
losing my self-identity.

Tathagata
Ask no questions, questions are alien to me,
I do not know myself
Out there, there was nothing but darkness and rocky muteness
So transmigrate into me from that picture
in flesh and blood, into my effusive being.
. . .

Tathagata
I do not want you in your yogic postures as in the pictures
before whom I could place my offerings of flowers and prayers
Pardon the slaves of fetishism
Who created idols in your name and festivals.

(Tr. Radha Iyer, see Dangle 1992: 29–30)

These poems show that the Ambedkar-led Buddhist movement strove to provide a cultural alternative to the dalits. For all its faults, religion remains a major source of power and culture as well as value system. Despite the modernist prophets of doom, religion has neither vanished nor lost its importance in social life. Ambedkar's decision to embrace Buddhism was animated by this reality. Like Durkheim (1912), Ambedkar argued that as religion embodies 'sacred morality' it serves the function of social integration. In rejecting Hinduism for its fundamental corruption, he did not abandon religion. He opted for Buddhism because he saw the necessity of a just religion, especially for people-in-distress to fight the terrible odds of life. That Ambedkar was not wrong in his hope is borne out by this eye-witness account of the Buddhist conversion that he led in 1956 at Nagpur:

All of them, even the poorest, came clad in the spotless white shirts and saris that had been prescribed for the occasion by their beloved leader. Some families had had to sell trinkets in order to buy their new clothes and meet the expenses of the journey, but they had made the sacrifice gladly, and set out for Nagpur with songs on their lips and the hope of a new life in their hearts.... By the end of the week 400,000 men, women, and children had poured into Nagpur, with the result that the population had nearly doubled and the white-clad Untouchables had virtually taken over the city. The Caste Hindus, who were accustomed to think of the Untouchables as dirty and undisciplined, gazed with astonishment at the spectacle of tens upon tens of thousands of clean, decently dressed, well behaved and well organised people in whom they had difficulty in recognising their former slaves and serfs. (Sangharakshita 1986: 129–30)

The liberating, exhilarating experience the dalits felt after embracing Buddhism is corroborated by many of them. The writer-critic Shankarrao Kharat gives one such description:

I have accepted the Buddhist Dhamma. I am a Buddhist now. I am not a Mahar nor an untouchable nor even a Hindu. I have become a human being.... I am not low born or inferior.... With the acceptance of Buddhism my untouchability has been erased. The chains of untouchability which shackled my feet have now been shattered. Now I am a human being like all other... I am now free. (See Shah 2001: 205)

Alternative Vision of Social and Political Institutions

The Buddha was not just a spiritual truth-seeker but also a pioneering political philosopher. Like his social thinking, his ideas of the state and kingship, too, were morally inspired. His ideal society had no place for inequality or poverty: it was the duty of those wielding power to ensure justice and a means of subsistence to everyone. His views on this, culled from the *Samyutta Nikaya,* are forthright: 'It is possible really to rule as a king in righteousness, without killing or causing to be killed, without practising oppression or permitting oppression to be practised, without suffering pain or inflicting it on another.'

The Buddha came from the Sakya clan which had a republican polity. His father was at one time the elected head or one of the heads of the state. Born and brought up in such a milieu, it was not unusual for him to become a champion of republicanism. Some scholars have demonstrated that the Buddha consciously modelled the Sangh's constitution and organisation on the democratic pattern of tribal republics of north India, and these principles were seen as a model for government for society in general (Ling 1981: 144–52; Ilaiah 2000).

The Sangh was founded on the principle which entitled all members to freely express their views. In his study of Buddha as a political philosopher, Ilaiah has shown that he had created the Sangh system as an institutional alternative to the brahmanical social order and authoritarian monarchical state. While for the brahman law-makers adherence to (discriminatory) caste rules was the cornerstone of justice, admission to the Buddhist Sangh was based on the sole criterion of character. Likewise, the maintenance of discipline and harmony within the Sangh was anchored in equalitarian values— one person one vote, and one vote one value. Every issue within the Sangh was decided either by consensus or majority opinion. The administration of monasteries—management, maintenance, recording of important items, accounting of money and grain collected as alms, and commodities produced collectively—bore a democratic functioning. Property was owned collectively. The Buddha had no quarrel with the division of labour as production needed expertise in each field, but he was opposed to the breaking up of society into immobile social groups, just as he was against the degrading of productive labour (Ilaiah 2000: 218–20).

It is notable that kings are held in contempt in the early Buddhist literature. The power-obsessed kings invoke the image of cruelty and stupidity, and they are put into a list of disasters—floods, fire, famine, etc.—to be avoided at all cost. This is understandable, both in historical circumstances of the time when monarchies were swallowing up the republics, and in the general trend of how kings exercised brute power. Early Buddhism, therefore, envisioned a state in which the ruler was chosen by people and worked at their behest. As the *Agganna Sutta* of the *Digha Nikaya* attests, Buddhism advocated the theory of *Mahasammat*, the Great Agreed On or the Great Elect. This was a polity based on agreement between the people and the person whom they elected as king (Rhys Davids [1921] 2000b: 77–94).

It was the people who fixed for the king a portion of their produce in lieu of his services. Elected to serve the state, the king was supposed to remain in office as long as he satisfied people's needs; and, in return he was entitled to collect taxes. The king's power was in direct proportion to his social responsibility. There was even a provision to dislodge the king who did not deliver the goods. There was a theory that tells how disaster strikes a kingdom in which the ruler fails to provide succour to the poor. Such a king was not allowed to be in office. One Aryadeva, a Buddhist ideologue, eloquently expresses this: 'What superciliousness is thine, (O King!) thou who are a (mere) servant of the multitude and who receivest the sixth part (of the produce) as thine wages' (see Varma 1974: 195).

The Buddha was unique in grasping the connection between economic justice and social harmony. In his view, anti-social activities could not be curbed merely through force and punishment, since poverty was a major cause of immorality and crime in society. Charity or donations to criminal elements in order to lure them away from crime would only exacerbate evil action. His recommendation, therefore, was to improve economic condition of people by providing seed and water to agriculturists and money-on-loan to traders. He also suggested that state servants should be paid adequately to stop corruption. He thought that only a holistic, integrated approach would generate a conducive atmosphere for development of the state and its citizens. His advice that the surplus accumulated should be spent in public welfare such as digging wells, water ponds, and planting groves along the trade routes is a remarkably modern view of political economy.

The Buddha was also the first major proponent of peaceful coexistence among states. He prevented a war between the Sakyas and Kolias, and tried, though unsuccessfully, to stop the fight between the king of Kosala and the Sakyas. Later, King Ashoka adopted this principle of peace. Under the Buddhist influence, the mightiest monarch of his time underwent a process of transformation, turned his back on violence, and strove for humane and efficient governance. To use his own idiom, he opted for *dhammaghosha* (affirmation of righteousness) and rejected *bherighosha* (proclamation of war).

Buddhist Ascendancy and India's Past Greatness

By striking a balance between the pursuit of personal excellence and the wider objective of liberating humanity from suffering, it was the Buddha and Buddhism that made India a great cultural force in the ancient world. India's remarkable achievements in republican statecraft, in the arts and literature, and in cultural contacts with the world could be traced to the movement started by Buddha. Giving respect to all life and the importance of *ahimsa* (non-injury) to others, it was the Buddhists who built the earliest hospitals for humans as well as animals.

In the middle of the third century BCE, Ashoka embraced Buddhism and sent missionaries far and wide to spread dhamma. His son Mahendra and daughter Sanghamitra went to Sri Lanka. In subsequent centuries, the Buddhists travelled to Greece in the west, to Tibet in the north, and to China and Japan in the east. Buddhism spread around the world on the strength of its universal message, without ever using force or coercion. Over the centuries it took the shape of a global movement. (The accompanying chronological table explains this.)

THE SPREAD OF BUDDHISM

c. 563–483 BCE	Life of the Buddha.
c. 370	The Vaishali Council registers divisions following rival interpretations of Buddhism.
c. 255	King Ashoka converts to Buddhism.
c. 240	Sri Lanka embraces Buddhism.
c. 150	Menander, the Greek king, promotes Buddhism in north-west India and Afghanistan.
c. CE 65	Buddhist missionaries arrive—and get a toehold—in China.

c. 120	Buddhist Council in Kashmir standardises major texts of the Mahayana school.
c. 120–62	Kanishka, the Kushana king, patronises Buddhism in Gandhara, Punjab and Sindh.
c. 200	Buddhism enters Indonesia.
c. 400	Buddhism arrives in Korea.
c. 400–10	Fa Hsien visits India at the behest of the Chinese emperor, to collect authentic Buddhist texts.
c. 400–500	Buddhism reaches Burma.
c. 540	Buddhism arrives in Japan.
c. 640–5	Hsuan Tsang in India; King Harshavardhan accepts Buddhism.
c. 850	Buddhism penetrates China.
c. 1300	Buddhism adopted in Thailand.
c. 1890s	Faint beginnings of Buddhist revival in India with establishment of the Mahabodhi Society and South Indian Buddhist Association.
c. 1900	Buddhism reaches America and Europe.
1956	The Ambedkar-led mass conversion in India.

Buddhism developed a system of logical inquiry and injected a rational outlook in Indian intellectual life. The brahmanic ideologues borrowed many strands from Buddhism, used them to strengthen their own defences, disclaimed indebtedness, and instead tried to write off Buddhism as a mere offshoot of the Vedic-Upanishadic tradition. Buddhist ethical verses in Pali were rendered into Sanskrit and interpolated in the Vedic-Upanishadic tradition to show a humane face. Such borrowed and isolated words are often recited by modern votaries of brahmanism to take on their critics. One famous example they never fail to cite is 'May all beings be well and happy ...'

Sarve bhavantu sukhinah, / sarve santu niramaya
sarve bhadrani pashyantu, / ma kashchid dukh bhag bhavet.

As Angar Ee (1994: 53) claims, the above lines in Sanskrit were taken verbatim from the original Buddhist verse in Pali:

Sabbe satta sukhi hontu, / sabbe hontucha khemino,
sabbe bhadrani passantu, / ma kanchi dukha magama.

Whatever reforms took place within the orthodox circles of brahmanic Hinduism, which played a crucial role in ensuring its survival, was largely a result of the intellectual and moral stimulus provided by Buddhism. 'The so-called high Hindu ethics and personal morality is very largely a Buddhist achievement; a lasting reform and refinement inherited by later forms of brahmanism' (S.C. Sarkar 1928). Blunt through it may seem to suggest, it was Buddhism that taught basic lessons in humanity to the brahmanic supremacists.

From the fourth century BCE to the sixth century CE (when India was at its creative best), the subcontinent was not 'Hindu India' but 'Buddhist India'. During the millennium Buddhism remained the major determinant of Indian civilisation, though in conflict throughout with brahmanism which it opposed (Omvedt 2003). The early republican states and many political and administrative systems are traceable to the Buddhist influence. Many outstanding kings—Ashoka, Kanishka, and Harshavardhan—were Buddhists. The first systematic historical records in India were kept by Buddhists. The universities at Taxila, Nalanda and Vikramashila were Buddhist institutions. In the realm of letters, practically every Indian language begins with Buddhist works (Walker 1983a: 186). The Brahmi script which Ashoka used in his inscriptions and from which the Devanagari of Sanskrit derives; the emergence of Prakrit as a vehicle of regional cultures; and the impressive communication system across the subcontinent, all owe their indebtedness to the Buddhist movement.

Even the first known poetry in classical Sanskrit was written by a Buddhist, Ashvaghosha, who also authored the first Sanskrit play. The fable (in the *Jataka* stories) is Buddhist in origin. Likewise, Buddhist architecture flourished centuries before the earliest-known brahmanical temples, and many features from the Buddhist models were incorporated into Hindu temples. The earliest sculpture at Bharhut, Sanchi, Bodh Gaya, Amaravati, etc., is Buddhist. The first paintings in the history of Indian art are the Buddhist frescoes at Ajanta.

Ashoka (269–232 BCE) was a product of the Buddhist ideology. Beginning as an emperor of conventional ruthlessness, he underwent a change of heart after his blood-soaked victory in the Kalinga war. His transformation is most visible in is his policy of dhamma which held together a vast and heterogeneous empire. His dhamma was aimed at building up an attitude of mind in which social responsibility and personal behaviour were of key importance; it was a plea for the recognition of human dignity and for a humanistic spirit in the activities of society (Thapar [1966] 1984: 85).

Ashoka was a dhamma-enthusiast, but he was not concerned with making Buddhism the state religion. He adopted a policy of impartiality to all communities and religious sects. He asked the people to respect both shramans and brahmans. His quest for a just order made him set aside discriminatory ritualism and brahmanical privilege, but he never attacked brahmans and their freedom to teach. All these lead Romila Thapar to wrongly conclude in an influential work ([1961] 1999a) that Ashoka's dhamma was not Buddhism. In her eagerness to show Ashoka in the modern secular light, Thapar misses the crucial point that Buddhism, unlike brahmanism, was a non-casteist and non-sectarian religion; in fact, Ashoka was able to rise above the narrowness of caste and creed precisely because of his personal faith in Buddhism. His broad-minded outlook and ability to grasp the requirements of ruling diverse groups of people made him an exemplar of what the Buddha called *chakkavatti dhammiko dhammaraja*, 'the righteous ruler'.

Proclaiming that *savve munisse praja mama* (all the people are my children), Ashoka stressed on kind consideration towards slaves, servants, aged people, and even animals. He made officials act with forbearance. The people cooperated. Rock Edict 5 reports that people were abstaining from the sacrificial slaughter of living creatures, and behaving properly with their relatives and elders. The Ashokan inscriptions mostly consisted of reports on the results achieved. Even allowing for official exaggeration, the achievements were impressive. The king and the commoner were cooperating for public order and civil decency. An inscription claims, 'Now by reason of the practice of piety by his Majesty the King, the reverberation of the war-drums have become the reverberation of dhamma.'

By pursuing a policy of peace and development-oriented

pragmatism, Ashoka succeeded in knitting together most of the subcontinent, a tremendous feat by any standards, especially in that period. His reign witnessed remarkable progress in economic and commercial activities, as well as cultural and artistic efflorescence.

Indian art and architecture, not the least valuable part of Indian culture, may be said to begin from Asoka in spite of Indus Valley construction. The ruins of the Asokan palace at Patna were still impressive to Chinese pilgrims in AD 400, seemingly the work of genii and supernatural agencies. Asoka spent a great deal on much more important public works that would give no profit to the state. Hospitals were founded all over the empire for men and beasts, with free medical attendance at state expense. Shady groves, wells with steps leading down to the water, fruit orchards and resting-places were systematically laid out on all major trade routes. ... These new constructions, which must have been an absolute godsend for the traders, especially because of the doctors and veterinaries available at many of the stations, were located not only in Asoka's domains but also beyond his frontiers. This agrees precisely with the duties of the benevolent chakravartin emperor which are mentioned in the Buddhist discourse. (Kosambi [1965] 1992: 160–1)

Kosambi underlines that such public welfare is not visualised in Kautilya's *Arthashastra,* the founding text of brahmanical statecraft. In fact, the Ashokan administration in the use of uniformity of civil and criminal laws along with the renouncement of violence and war was a repudiation of imperialist policies advocated by Kautilya who considered upholding of caste order and conquest of neighbouring territories as the duty of a king. Kautilya was interested in maximising taxes and winning wars, but not in social welfare. Sadly, it is the Kautilyan vision of state characterised by coercion and deception that has caught the imagination of elite historians and 'nationalists' who do not consider the polity of Buddha and Ashoka Indian enough to be admired and emulated.

The Counter-Revolution and Brahmanical Revivalism

The Mauryans were not interested in giving brahmans preferential treatment and certain immunities that they demanded as their birth-right. Ashoka introduced the policy of equality in civil law (*vyavahara-samata*) and criminal law (*danda-samata*) for everyone. The officials were instructed to implement this policy (4th Pillar Edict). In another edict, Ashoka exposed the Bhudevas (gods on earth) as the false gods. He appointed *Dhamma-mahamartya* (the superintendent of morals) which was a blow to the special rights and privileges so long enjoyed by the brahmans (Dutta [1944] 1983: 164). He also prohibited the killing of animals and birds and discouraged superfluous rituals performed by women (Inscription no. 6). This was the result of the Buddhist aversion to sacrifice that Ashoka had adopted. Also, there was indifference to Sanskrit, the language of brahmanic priestcraft. Such a policy hit the interests of the brahmans who depended on donations and gifts given to them in various rites and sacrifices. In other words, the superiority of brahmans and the credibility of their sacerdotal literature were under threat. Moreover, the royal genealogy and ancestry were not of any concern to the Mauryas, nor did they bother to claim a kshatriya status or even to belonging to a family of high status— a necessary brahmanic requirement for the kingly position. No wonder the brahmanic texts describe the Mauryas as the *shudra-prayastv-adharmikah,* 'mainly shudras and unrighteous' (Thapar [1961] 1999a: 12).

The brahmans retaliated. Led by Pushyamitra Shunga, the commander of the last Mauryan king Brihadratha, they hatched a conspiracy. Pushyamitra gave his daughter in marriage to the king, got the coveted post and cold-bloodedly beheaded his master during a military parade in 185 BCE. That the regicide was the brahmanical backlash is borne out by the fact that soon after his accession, Pushyamitra, who was a disciple of the grammarian Patanjali, revived Vedic sacrifice and performed the Rajasuya Yajna. Persecution of Buddhists and vandalisation of their monasteries became his top priority. After burning monasteries in and around Pataliputra he went up to Sakala (Sialkot in West Punjab) and offered a reward of 100 *dinars* or gold pieces for the head of every Buddhist monk (Burnouf, *l'Introduction a l'Historie on Buddhisme Indien*, see Ambedkar, *BAWS*, vol. 3: 269; also Sastri and Srinivasachari 1980: 139). That he unleashed a reign of terror against the Buddhists is corroborated by several sources including the Tibetan and Chinese records. According to the *Divyavadana,* and the account of the Tibetan historian Taranath, he destroyed and burnt monastries from Pataliputra to Sakala. Historian H.P. Shastri says, 'The condition of the Buddhists under the imperial sway of the Sungas, orthodox and bigoted, can be more easily imagined than described. From Chinese authorities it is known that many Buddhists still do not pronounce the name of Pushyamitra without a curse' (cited in Amdedkar, ibid.).

Rejecting the established trajectory of Indian history, Ambedkar in his incomplete work *The Revolution and Counter-Revolution in Ancient India* has made the conflict between Buddhism and Brahmanism the corner-stone of restructuring the past. He sees the 185 BCE regicide a turning point, heralding a brahmanic counter-revolution marked by virulent orthodoxy. (K.P. Jayaswal, too, in his *Manu and Yajnavalkya* [1930: 40–1], has termed the brahmanical reaction the 'orthodox counter-revolution'.) The objective was to destroy Buddhism, which was still powerful and popular and to replace it with brahmanism and its hierarchical principles of social and political organisation. Ambedkar's contention that the process of the decline of Buddhism in India was a violent one (not a process of gradual adjustment and absorption into Hinduism as is routinely portrayed by the elite historians) has been corroborated by ample archaeological and textual evidences in Verardi's brilliant work (2011).

Ambedkar links the brahmanical backlash with the beginning of Smriti literature, which was to provide the framework of the varna-jati system; the laws relating to *anuloma* (husband's caste higher than wife's) and *pratiloma* (wife's caste higher than husband's) marriages; and above all, the systematic subjugation of vaishyas, shudras, and women. He cites various sources to prove that ascribing the *Manusmriti,* the most important law-book, to the legendary name of Manu was an 'utter fraud':

> The author of Naradasmriti writing in about the 4th century AD knew the name of the author of Manusmriti and gives out the secret. Manu is the assumed name of Sumati Bhargava who is the real author of Manusmriti. ... According to scholars whose authority cannot be questioned Sumati Bhargava must have composed the Code which he deliberately called Manusmriti between 170 BC and 150 BC. Now if one bears in mind the fact that the Brahmanic Revolution by Pushyamitra took place in 185 BC there

remains no doubt that the code known as Manusmriti was promulgated by Pushyamitra as embodying the principles of Brahmanic Revolution against the Buddhist state of the Mauryas. (*BAWS*, vol. 3: 270–1)

Ambedkar cites some verses from the *Manusmriti* to show the author's antipathy to Buddhism. This was fully supported by the regime of Pushyamitra. He argues that the brahmans exploited their monopoly over religious literature to reassert their domination and crush Buddhism. Other brahman kings followed Pushyamitra's lead by persecuting Buddhists and destroying their monasteries and educational institutions. Ambedkar sees a parallel between the Muslim invasions of 'Hindu India' and the brahmanic invasions of 'Buddhist India'. Muslim invaders of various stock—Arabs, Turks, Mongols, and Afghans—fought for supremacy among themselves but were united in destroying idolatry. Likewise, the brahmanic invaders of Buddhist India, the Shungas, the Kanvas, and the Andhras, fought among themselves for supremacy but had one common goal to destroy Buddhism. The Muslim invaders, he argues, destroyed only the outward symbols of Hinduism—temples and *maths,* and did not cause any subversion of the principles which governed the spiritual life of the people. The effect of the brahmanic invasions, however, was to thoroughly destroy the Buddhist principles that had been accepted and followed by the masses as the way of life (ibid.: 273–4).

In his analysis of the destruction of Buddhism, Ambedkar also mentions a 'subversion' theory. He did not substantiate it as he could not complete the book but the tone and tenor of his argument suggests that subversion involved the insidious role of brahman-Buddhists. This can be better appreciated in the light of what a mainstream historian says: 'From the very beginning the Order contained brahmins who might have [outwardly] renounced caste but retained their intellectual traditions. The current brahmin ideology (not ritual or cults) was often taken for granted, just as the brahmins had given up beef-eating and accepted non-killing (*ahimsa*) as their main ideal. The higher philosophies of both Buddhist and brahmin began to converge in essence. Neither admitted the material world as real' (Kosambi [1965] 1992: 179). In other words, they continued to be brahmans despite accepting Buddhism and probably observed their caste exclusivism as well. They produced doctrines akin to the metaphysics of brahmanism which culminated in the Mahayana school, and they very nearly succeeded in smothering the basic epistemology and spirit of early Buddhism. The Buddha had not said that material things did not exist or wordly things did not matter. His theory of impermanence stated that things were constantly coming into being and going out of existence. The Mahayanists interpreted this to mean that since everything is momentary, nothing exists. This led to the exposition of *shoonyavad,* which said that the world was a void. Out of this void emerged all kinds of superstitions and obscurantist ideas which gradually elbowed out rationality and the materialist outlook of early Buddhism. Even Pandit Nehru seems to affirm this:

> Probably it was due to the Brahmins, who later joined it, that it developed more along ... metaphysical lines.... It may have been due also chiefly to the Brahmin Buddhists that the Mahayana form developed.... Mahayana doctrine spread rapidly but it lost in quality and distinctiveness what it gained in extent. The monasteries became rich, centres of vested interests, and their discipline became lax. ([1946] 1996: 175–9)

The Mahayanists transformed Buddha into a god, introduced his several incarnations, and brought deities and even hobgoblins into Buddhism which provided scope for ritualism and priestcraft. Speculation regarding the nature of the Bodhisattva (the Buddha after death), a question which Buddha himself had considered metaphysical and left unanswered, became the dominant theme of Mahayana. Buddha's original concepts of *kamma* and *nibbana* too were substantially distorted. To top it all, in a move of far-reaching consequences, the brahman-Buddhists also gave up the people's language Pali and adopted Sanskrit.

The magical, transcendental assertions of the Mahayana form of Buddhism was a travesty of the profound humanism and social radicalism of the early Buddhism. The brahmanical opponents found it convenient to quote contradictory strands from various forms of deformed Buddhism—such as the deification of Buddha and the Tantrism of the later periods—to prove that (between brahmanism and Buddhism) there was no fundamental difference. Some adventurous brahmans, in their eagerness to eliminate Buddhism, even tried to co-opt Buddha in the brahmanical mould by depicting him as the ninth avatar of Vishnu, even though they did not set up his statues in their temples nor construct any viharas or stupas.

In sum, various unsavoury developments in the later Buddhism gave the brahmanical elements a handle to use against the former. Later, ideologues like Shankara found the distorted doctrines of Buddhism attractive enough to appropriate and promote brahmanism. They established their *mayavada* (the theory of illusion) on the bedrock of *shoonyavada*. It is in this sense that the Vedantic Shankara, with his theorisation of *brahma satyam jagat mitthya* (this world is illusion; the Brahma, or the world beyond, is the only reality), is known as a crypto-Buddhist. This 'crypto-Buddhist' whose real ambition was to establish brahmanic supremacy described Buddhism as *sarva-vainashika,* the destroyer of all, and declared that the Buddha was an 'enemy of people'. A sworn campaigner against Buddhism, Shankara is said to have founded his Sringeri-math on the site of a Buddhist monastery.

Forgeries to Recast Indian Culture in the Brahmanical Mould

Post-Mauryan brahmanical literature and other sources bear out the revival of militant brahmanism. This had three elements—hostility to all languages not Sanskrit; an intolerance towards religions other than Vedic-brahmanism; and, a prejudice against all castes not brahman (Walker 1983a: 172). 'To the revival is due the sanskritisation of Indian thought and the brahmanisation of Indian social codes by the scribes' (ibid.: 363). The hallmark of the revival, and its only raison d'être, was the glorification, even the deification, of the brahman caste. The manifesto of the counter-movement was the *Manusmriti*.

With the rise of aggressive brahmanism, political and administrative developments after the Mauryan period tended to feudalise the state apparatus. The most striking development, R.S. Sharma shows in his study of Indian feudalism, was the practice of land grants to brahmans (*brahmadeya*) which was sanctified by the Dharmashastras, Puranas, and the epics. The *Mahabharata* devotes an entire section to praising such gifts of land (Sharma 1980: 1–2). The practice became quite frequent and subsequently, especially from the Gupta period, the grantees were given administrative rights as well. 'Thus the widespread practice of making land grants . . . paved the way for the rise of brahmana feudatories, who performed administrative functions not under the authority of the royal officers but almost independently' (ibid.: 4).

It was in this period of triumphant brahmanism that the Vedas, smritis, epics and other religio-secular works were thoroughly revaluated and tampered with. It was a time for the wholesale re-casting of Indian life and culture into the brahmanical mould. To this period belong the Sanskritisation of the *Mahabharata*, *Ramayana*, and other bodies of literature (Walker 1983a: 362–5). To buttress the brahmanical edifice, brahman authors suppressed facts, changed names, and confused places and periods. This period witnessed wholesale counterfeiting of the Vedas and other scriptures, the accumulation of false data, and the creation of fictitious dynastic pedigrees. So inextricably is fact interwoven with fancy in Indian 'historical' annals, that the shramanic traditions, especially Buddhism, were either suppressed, or at the best, grossly misrepresented in some fleeting references. King Ashoka is depicted and ignored as a hated Buddhist and a despised shudra. 'The brahman records completely ignore him until the time when, ten or twelve centuries afterwards, all danger from his influence had passed away.' Ashoka, whose name seems to have been expunged from Indian history, had to be discovered by James Prinsep in the nineteenth century on the basis of his rock edicts and other Indian and foreign records, especially the Ceylon chronicles.

The basis for a common law on the principles of equality was destroyed by the brahmanical laws which were never recorded or made public. Justice and jurisprudence were reduced to a farce. Kosambi says, 'Crime and sin stand hopelessly confused, while juristic principles are drowned in an amazing mass of religious fable which offers ridiculous justification for any stupid observance.' The use of Sanskrit as the language of the rituals, and royal genealogies concocted for the ruling chiefs and aspiring kings for a price (including the promise to defend the caste order) helped create a pan-India brahman elite. These pandits, however, never showed any interest in the study of the guilds and city records that existed through the ages, nor did they bother to develop social morality.

Indian culture lost the contributions that these numerous groups (tribal, clan, jati, guild, and perhaps civic) could have made. The civilising and socialising work of the Buddha and of Asoka was never continued. The tightening of caste bonds and of caste exclusiveness threw away the possibility of finding some common denominator of justice and equity for all men regardless of class, profession, caste, and creed. As a concomitant, almost all Indian history is also obliterated. (Kosambi [1965] 1992: 173)

The genesis of Sanskrit literature is traceable to the period of brahmanical revival. Up to then, there had been no literary work in Sanskrit. Sanskrit was revered as the sacred language of gods in which there was no place for 'profane' worldly literature. It was a contrived, inflexible and incommunicable language, jealously guarded by the brahmans who used it as a vehicle of sacerdotal gobbledygook. Pali and Prakrit, with their many regional varieties, were the spoken and written languages in the north, while Dravidian languages were the means of communication in the south of the Vindhyas.

The *Mahabharata* and the *Ramayana* were long current in the Prakrits before they were rendered in Sanskrit. According to Keith, they were re-written in Sanskrit, involving translations and elaborations of Prakrit originals, in the early years before and after the beginning of the common era. Tinkering with the earlier texts of the *Mahabharata* is evident from critical scrutiny. The conversion of the original heroic adventures into a sort of brahmanical bible was not always cleverly done, for in the Sanskrit redactions the priestly interest overshadows the heroic, and the legends related are often distorted to suit the brahmanical viewpoint. Sidhanta has written in *The Heroic Age of India* that everything is viewed from the angle of the priest, and instead of a straightforward narrative, there are many didactic digressions on the sanctity of the brahmans. Pargiter (1922: 60) is equally categorical: 'The brahmanical versions are a farrago of absurdities and impossibilities, utterly distorting all the incidents'.

It is not surprising that 'the whole of the Sanskrit literature has no historical works' (ibid.: 2).

The Sanskritised *Ramayana*, too, carries the indelible imprint of major editing. It is generally agreed that the 'pronounced brahmanical tone did not characterise the original work, but was given to it at the time of the revival, when much additional material was also introduced'. In the reworked text, to cite one example, Rama castigates Buddha as a 'thief', and warns people against accepting the thief's teachings (see Varma 1974: 297). The reference to Buddha clearly indicates that the *Ramayana* was recast in the post-Buddha period and represents the reassertion of resurgent brahmanism against Buddha's anti-Vedic teachings.

Like the epics, a great deal of secular literature in Sanskrit—the poetry, the fable, the fairy tale—are translations and elaborations from Prakrit originals. The *Katha-sarita-sagar*, the best-known Sanskrit collection of stories, is said to have been based on an earlier work composed in Prakrit (Walker 1983a: 364; Kosambi [1965] 1992: 203–4).

Benjamin Walker points out that the period of the brahmanical revival was the age that fixed the criterion for every subsequent interpretation of Hindu life and culture. It was at this time that the ancient Indian traditions as they existed in the regional languages were taken over, adapted to the brahmanic bias, and hammered into the new mould of Sanskrit. The earlier works were rendered into Sanskrit for the deification of brahmans and the damnation of all others, especially shudras and ati-shudras. The indigenous writings were first sanskritised and then the whole of Sanskrit literature was brahmanised. Local and original names were altered to fit the Sanskrit alphabet; native sentiments were put through the mill of Sanskrit syntax, and a great deal of indigenous material irretrievably lost. This wholesale change and substitution, Walker says, was nothing short of calamity:

Interpretations of pre-Sanskrit and what might be called 'un-Sanskrit' life were further distorted by wilful tendentiousness that shaped into orthodox from the mythology, history and even the geography of ancient India. Its corruptions crept into the regional languages by its insistence on its own sanctity and stilted rules. And in most instances it debased what it influenced. The noble early poetry of Tamil, characterised by simplicity and realism, never recovered its freshness after contact with Sanskrit, and Tamil literature was thereafter subjected to the artificialities of the northern tongue. Practically every vernacular literature has suffered in like manner as long as it lay under the shadow of Sanskrit influence. (Walker 1983a: 364).

That Sanskrit monopolised the intellectual and cultural space after this period is attested by an analysis of inscriptions. The brahmanical revival climaxed during the Gupta period (i.e., fourth to sixth centuries CE), after which Sanskrit symbolising the brahmanical hegemony gradually elbowed out Prakrit. Prior to the Gupta age, more than 95 per cent of inscriptions were written in Prakrit and concerned non-brahmanical shramanic sects, mainly Buddhist and Jain, and only five per cent in Sanskrit concerned brahmanism. 'The position is almost entirely reversed in favour of Sanskrit and brahmanism in the post-Gupta period. The power of the priesthood must have been tremendous, almost tyrannical, to have achieved the phenomenal reversal. The number and nature of spurious inscriptions after the seventh century confirm the continuance of this tendency' (ibid.).

Notes

1. The Buddha's speeches, conversations and discourses were compiled just after his death. Preserved in Pali, Buddhist hybrid Sanskrit and later classical Sanskrit, the literature of Buddhism (despite the fact that a significant portion of it is lost, or wilfully destroyed by opponents like Pushyamitra Shunga) is enormous, with various Buddhist schools such as Theravada and Mahayana having their own versions of the scriptures. Some ancient works survive only in Chinese or Tibetan translations. However, the earliest and authoritative canon of undivided and early Buddhism—the Pali *Tipitaka*—has been preserved in Sri Lanka. According to some scholars, Pali was either Magadhi Prakrit or an amalgam of various Prakrit dialects of the region corresponding to the modern south Bihar and eastern Uttar Pradesh. The Buddha spent most of his time in this region, and delivered his speeches in Pali which, in all likelihood, he fashioned by mixing various dialects of the region he visited in order to be communicable to a wider audience. It is natural that the early Buddhist literature was composed in the language

which the master himself spoke. The Pali canon, known as the *Tipitaka* (the Three Baskets) comprises *Vinaya, Sutta,* and *Abhidhamma Pitakas*. The *Vinaya Pitaka* contains the rules of conduct of the Buddhist order of monks and nuns. The *Sutta Pitaka* is the most important; it contains doctrinal expositions, discourses, and conversations attributed to the Buddha, divided into five sections, namely the *Digha Nikaya* (the Long Collection containing long discourses); the *Majjhima Nikaya* (the Medium Collection with shorter discourses); the *Samyutta Nikaya* (the Connected Collection, containing brief pronouncements on related topics); the *Anguttara Nikaya* (the Progressive Collection, short passages arranged in eleven sections); and the *Khuddaka Nikaya* (the Minor Collection, containing various works of varying type, including the exquisitely poetic *Dhammapada*, the 'Way to Righteousness', and *Udana*. The third basket, the *Abhidhamma Pitaka* (the Supplementary Doctrines), is a collection of work on Buddhist psychology and metaphysics.

2. There is no mention of the word *dharma* in the Vedic literature; its use in Sanskrit literature became popular only after Buddha's time. In the Vedic verses, another word is used to express 'cosmic law'—*ṛta*. It could be surmised that the brahman priests and grammarians stopped using *ṛta*. in order to adopt dharma to mean the same thing, because it needed to upstage Buddhist dhamma. The symbol of Buddha setting in motion the wheel of the universal dhamma, while pronouncing his first sermon in the deer park in Banaras, was to be overtaken by the dharma of four varnas. The Sanskrit word dharma would then be nothing other than the Pali word *dhamma* (see Deleury 2005: 95; and Angar Ee 1994).

3. There is an instance in the *Digha Nikaya* as well as *Khuddaka Nikaya* in which brahmans are reported to have attempted to harass Buddha and his companions by throwing garbage in a well.

CHAPTER 3

Medieval Mukti Movements of the Subaltern Sant-Poets

We'll set fire to divisions of caste,
We'll debate philosophical questions in the market place,
We'll have dealings with despised households,
We'll go around in different paths.

Pambatti Sittar, see Kailasapathy 1987: 391

Simmering tension between the liberal-humanist shramanism and the conservative-exclusivist brahmanism has been the defining feature of India's social history, manifested in many obvious and subtle ways. A classic site of this longstanding tussle is the Bhakti movement under which rubric comes a radical stream of socio-religious activities. It peaked in the fifteenth and sixteenth centuries in the north with the emergence of a remarkable line of subaltern sant-poets—Kabir, Ravidas, Dadu, and Nanak, among others. Starting in the south in the later half of the first millennium, gradually spreading northward through Karnataka and Maharashtra, and engulfing north India and Bengal from the fifteenth century onward, these movements from below represent a cultural revolt and scintillating examples of ordinary people's extraordinary creativity. Though the brahmans occasionally climbed aboard the Bhakti bandwagon, the radicalism of the movement was shaped and spearheaded by artisans, cultivators, and labourers who composed poems of exquisite beauty in people's languages. Their verses and activities represent 'a whole climate of opinion' that challenged the tenets of caste-feudalism in a caste-feudal age. If the Bhakti movement was a *jan-andolan*, a people's movement (Dwivedi [1959] 1997) and a protest movement (Ranade [1900] 1961), it was due to the challenging egalitarian proposition of its anti-caste proponents. Their lowly social origin and their transgressive and often iconoclastic attitude are a striking feature of the movement which was also animated by the presence of many lively women.

Though these movements stretched unevenly over centuries and differed widely on account of regional variations and individual sensibilities, opposition to caste, cultural insularity, and religious bigotry was a common thread that they shared. This egalitarian syncretism encompassed several strands of multi-cultural diversity of India, including liberal elements of what is called folk Hinduism and Islamic egalitarian thinking, especially of the Sufi variety. The striking point is, the God of people's sant-poets was not the transcendental brahmanic God; their God had an existence within their selves in the form of individual and social conscience. *Look within to realise God and decide what is right and wrong for you and others* was their common refrain. Envisioned in the mould of desirable transformation, both individual and social, this God was revered not for maintaining the hierarchical order but to change it all by gracing everyone who leads a virtuous life, irrespective of caste and status. So much so that when the God did not live up to these expectations, the sant-poets were not afraid to even question him! Thus their proposition of accessibility of God and mukti (liberation) to anyone and everyone passes through a social and secular process and involves subversive egalitarianism. When everybody is somebody, then nobody is low-caste or untouchable. It was precisely this secular aspect that made the Bhakti movement a social movement. And in this sense the Bhakti movement was a Mukti movement, as the following pages would make clear.

Seen from this perspective, these movements represented a resurrection of the earlier shramanic-Buddhist resistance to brahmanism. Of late, the dalit-subaltern radicals and those engaged in the work of rediscovery of the Indian past are increasingly stressing a close affinity between Buddhism and the radical streams of Bhakti. The movement of sant-poets, they argue, was influenced by the egalitarian ethos of Buddhism, and the difference between the two was more in appearance than in reality. They categorise both as movements against caste and brahmanism.

The sant-poets who shared a striking similarity on this count included outcaste brahman Basava, the leather-worker Haralayya, the proto-feminist Akka Mahadevi (Karnataka); the tailor Namdev, the village servant Chokhamela, the grocer Tukaram, the vegetable-grower Savata Mali, the potter Gora (Maharashtra); the weaver Kabir, the cobbler Ravidas, the barber Sena (Uttar Pradesh), the cotton comber Dadu Dayal, the rebellious princess Mira (Rajasthan), the khatri Nanak (Punjab). The Tamil Sittars or Siddhas such as Sivavakkiyar and Pambatti Sittar who sang subversive songs are not known to belong to the Bhakti movement, but they shared their cultural radicalism with Kabir, Ravidas, and Tuka, and as such must be seen as an integral part of this movement.

The general backdrop of the movement was the chaos in the wake of the defeat of Buddhism, Muslim invasions, bad economic conditions and mass poverty made worse by the brahmanic-feudal tightening of socio-religious restrictions. There was a multiplication of gods and goddesses; an unprecedented proliferation of castes by an unending process of permutation and combination involving all kinds of commensal and connubial prohibitions; a growing insistence on purity-pollution rules; and, an increasing feudalisation of land and land-relations.

Such explosive situation provoked protest and a revaluation of prevalent values. The ferment thus generated, especially among the downtrodden, threw up many cultural heroes, popularly recognised as sant-poets, whose belief in one-God-and-one-humanity inspired them to fight against injustices of caste, brahmanism, and feudal order. Their emphasis on spiritual equality was emblematic of their vision of social justice and identification with the suffering humanity. Though they used religious idioms, they shaped the terms of the debate in a secular context. Though religious in style, the cut and thrust of their discourse was political. Not for nothing most of them took recourse to free thinking and rationalism embellished with an exquisite humane touch, instead of pedantic parroting, to drive home their point.

Without much ado, the movement relegated the brahmanical deities, rites and rituals to the background, replacing them with a *nirguna, nirakara* (formless) God as the ultimate symbol of universal compassion and justice. This God stood on the side of the oppressed and the defenceless. In fact, the sant-poets laid greater emphasis on the devotee than on the deity. Ultimately, God, or religion for that matter, they argued, was for the devotee. Kabir and Tuka, two charismatic poets, would say that there was no duality between God and his glorifier because by entering into a holy alliance, they had become one.

Social Resistance in Religious Idiom

The sant-poets, who came from the downtrodden class, clothed their rebellion in obedience to God. Kabir would say, whoever uses force commits a crime (*Kabira jor kia so juluma hai*) and God will punish him severely. Their love and loyalty was to a God who stirred up rebellion in the hearts of devotees. This God begged his people to free him from the idolatrous—and ignominious—fetters of a pseudo-religion founded and jealously guarded by the pandits and maulvis. In their concord, the deity and the devotee were determined to rescue society from the clutches of corrupt elements. Striving for true religiosity was thus not an end in itself but a means to bolster inclusive values and a just society. This becomes clear from the way the sant-poets brought into play the monotheistic radicalism to engineer a revolution.

The sant-poets did not advocate detachment from worldly life as a prerequisite for salvation. They set examples by leading normal, productive and balanced lives. Most of them were married, and worked for a living—Kabir did weaving and Ravidas worked with leather. Unlike the brahmans, they accorded dignity to labour, and invested it with social service and spiritual value. Guru Nanak, for example, exhorted the religiously-inclined to seek God 'in the fields, in the weaver's shop, and in the happy home' instead of the temple and the mosque. They rejected renunciation, asceticism, and celibacy as the means of enlightenment. Kabir poked fun at the yogi who in his quest of heaven tonsures his head, takes a vow of celibacy, and shuns worldly life.

Moreover, the sant-poets grasped the need to democratise language and culture. In the north, they produced poetry of great beauty and excellence in a composite colloquial language, which came to be known as *Saddhukari*. If Sanskrit is *devabhasha* (the language of gods), they asked, is the *janbhasha* (the people's language) the language of thieves? Kabir mocked the 'sacred' language, saying, 'Sanskrit is like *koop-jal* (well-water), a stagnant pool of water, and *bhasha*, or the people's language, like *bahata nir* (water of the brook)'. This was, by and large, the stand taken by the sant-poets in different parts of the country. The result was, Sanskrit lost its dominance. Top brahman authors such as Gyaneshwar and Tulsi were forced to write in local languages. This led to a remarkable efflorescence of thought and imagination in regional languages that were fresh, authentic, and imbued with people's sentiments.

Caste was the main target of the sant-poets. It was to them what the Church, the symbol of corrupt Christianity, was to the eighteenth-century French philosopher Voltaire. Those who attacked caste as fundamentally wrong and inhuman announced their arrival on the scene. In a dramatic development, the cultural leadership shifted from the pandits well-versed in *karmakanda* and Sanskrit scripture to those who composed verses in vernaculars and debated socio-spiritual issues with the people. Energised by fresh leadership and new ideas, Bhakti unleashed new creativities, and became a campaign for socio-cultural change. Writing in 1900 (even though from a brahmanic perspective), M.G. Ranade saw the Bhakti upsurge as a rebellion against brahmanic dominance, and compared it (in significance) with Europe's Protestant movement against papism.

[L]ike the Protestant Reformation in Europe in the sixteenth century, there was a Religious, Social and Literary Revival and Reformation in India. This . . . was not Brahmanical in its orthodoxy, it was heterodox in its spirit of protest against forms and ceremonies and class distinctions based on birth, and ethical in its preference of a pure heart, and of the law of love, to all other acquired merits and good works. This was the work of the people, of the masses, and not of the classes. At its head were Saints and Prophets, Poets and Philosophers, who sprang chiefly from the lower orders of society—tailors, carpenters, potters, gardeners, shop-keepers, barbers, and even mahars. (Ranade [1900] 1961: 5)

The exceptional brahmans who joined the movement—a Ramananda here, a Gyaneshwar there—had been influenced by the humane religiosity of the subaltern sant-poets and not the other way round as is made out in the dominant historiography. A case in point is Ramananda, who is credited to have brought the Bhakti to the people of all castes in the north. Ramananda was supposedly the guru of all the sant-poets of the north including Ravidas (the cobbler), Sadhana (the butcher), Dhana (the Jat), Sena (the barber), Pipa (the Rajput) and also Kabir (the weaver). It was this outstanding line of sant-poets which spearheaded the Bhakti radicalism in the north, and, thus, Ramananda—by virtue of being their mentor—is accorded the status of the father-figure of the movement in the region. This myth was fabricated to showcase the brahmanical broadmindedness which actually amounted to draining those sant-poets of any radical fervour and, then, presenting them, with a little bit of doctoring their texts, either as self-contradictory mystics or conventional followers of the Veda-Purana.

The Ramananda story is untenable on chronological grounds. Those sant-poets appeared in different times and it was not possible for him to have had all the disciples attributed to him. Second, there is no mention of Ramananda in the available utterances of his so-called 'disciples'. Third, and most important, the affinity or similarity between the radical poets and the sanatani pandit Ramananda is next to nothing. After all, why would a champion dissenter like Kabir, who had nothing but contempt for the brahmanical culture and religion, 'trick' a shastric brahman, as the legend goes, into accepting him as a disciple?[1] It is not hard to see that the brahmanical mind concocted Kabir's obeisance to Ramananda in order to blunt his attack on brahmanism. The fabrication was an instrument of containment, mythologising Kabir in a brahmanic way to wipe out his anti-caste radicalism. This is a classic case of forgery, and an instance of co-option of intellectual opponents, not a benign example of reconciliation and community formation, as the brahmanic scholars and their foreign imitators facetiously argue (Dwivedi [1941] 1999; Chaturvedi 1950, 1954; Lorenzen 2006). The hidden brahmanic contempt for Kabir, however, sometimes spills over and can be seen in the abusive comment of a renowned nineteenth-century 'reformer':

> Kabir went to a Pundit to learn Sanskrit with him, but he insulted him by saying that he would not teach a weaver. In like manner, he went to several other Pundits but no one would teach him. Thereupon, he began to compose hymns in incorrect and unidiomatic language and sing them to weavers and other low-class people to the accompaniment of a tambura. He especially spoke ill of the Vedas, the Shastras and the Pundits. Some ignorant persons were ensnared into his net. After his death, his followers made a great saint of him. His disciples kept on reading whatever he had composed in his lifetime. (Dayananda Saraswati [1875] 2002: 442)

A well-researched Marathi book *Sahitya Setu* by the linguist-scholar Shridhar Kulkarni has convincingly proved that it was not Ramananda but the Maharashtrian sant-poet Namdev (c. 1270–1350) who played the role of 'bridge-builder' between the north and the south. Namdev, in his later years, had become itinerant but finally settled in Punjab, composing his poems and spreading the radical devotionalism among the locals. As many as 61 of Namdev's 300 odds poems have found a niche in the *Guru Granth Sahib*, and all major sant-poets from the north including Kabir, Nanak, Ravidas, and Dadu Dayal speak highly of Namdev. Kulkarni's book also shows that it was the Maharashtrian poets, particularly Namdev, who first realised the potential of Hindi as a possible common language of the country.

In the north, the movement consisted of several streams and regional variations, all close in spirit to the shramanic offshoots such as Sahajyani Buddhism, the Tantrik and the Nathpanthi. The nonconformist Siddhas (who were drawn mainly from the lower orders of society) expounded the Sahajyani, Tantrik, and Nathpanthi ideas. The Bhakti leaders' attack on Sanskritic tradition and scriptural authority was rooted in this shramanic tradition represented by the Sahajiya Buddhists and Nath-Yogis who were popular in Bihar and eastern India. From the eighth or ninth century, the Siddhas and Yogis had been communicating their ideas in the *bhasha* that had developed from a form of western Apabhransha or old Bengali. Despite ambiguities about many things about them, there is little doubt about their iconoclastic radicalism. Anyone, irrespective of caste, creed, or sex, could be initiated into the Tantrik and Nath-panthi orders. There are instances of women from the category of 'untouchables' being accepted as gurus. The Tantrik indulgence in forbidden food, drink, and free sex as a means to attain higher awareness could be interpreted as a revolt against the repression of patriarchal and puritanical culture.

Although the Nath-Siddhas enjoyed popularity among the masses, they had to bear the brunt of priestly-feudal wrath due to their heretical beliefs and practices. The esoteric nature of their faith and the secretive manner in which they transmitted their ideas and conducted their activities could be a device to escape political persecution. Faced with increasing hostility, the Nathpanthis, under Gorakhnath's charismatic leadership, organised themselves in a well-knit community. They were able to set up their centres not only in different parts of the northern and western India but also in the deep south, glimpses of which we will see later.

It was these or similar forces which provided favourable atmosphere for the movement to take root in many parts of the country. On a broader historical canvas, the movement may be interpreted as a spontaneous, unstructured opposition to the ascendancy of the priestly-feudal alliance in the wake of liquidation of Buddhism. The spectre of Vedic-brahmanic supremacy, kept in check for a millennium by Buddhism, had come to haunt the caste-oppressed. Bhakti was perhaps the subliminal attempt of the suppressed castes to offset the danger of a belligerent brahmanism (reflected in the writings and activities of Kumaril Bhatta and Adi Shankara who pulled out all stops to revive the Vedic-brahmanism). As Satish Chandra says, reactionary revivalism was manifested most clearly in the persecution of Buddhists and Jains, with almost all Buddhist shrines being forcefully converted into Hindu temples. By all indications, this revivalism was carried out in an organised manner by the priestly-feudal leadership.

It was also reflected in the Hinduisation of many tribes and the consequent growth of many new jatis or sub-castes, which had to be fitted into the existing structure by putting forward the theory of varnasankar, i.e. the growth of mixed castes. The rise of image worship, often accompanied by gross superstitions, and the elaboration of a religion of work (karma) were other features of the religious ideas of the period. This socio-religious order was supported and buttressed by the Rajput-Brahman alliance. Thus, any effort to disturb the established social order ... would not only have to face the opposition and hostility of the entrenched brahman class, but also invited repression at the hands of political authority. (S. Chandra 2001: 118)

This may explain why, despite its early stirrings, the radical bhakti in the north could not broaden its base or become a movement in the initial stage. The movement emerged in the south where the brahmans were in lesser number and alliance between them and the feudal forces was still being forged. As the kshatriya caste hardly existed in the south, it was easier for the shudras to take on the brahmans. But in the north the movement did not take root until the arrival of Islam which somewhat slackened the grip of the brahman-kshatriya combine over the masses.

Kabir and Monotheistic Radicalism in the North

As in the south and Deccan, in the north too, the movement transcended its religious confines and established itself as a platform for socio-cultural changes. Many factors were responsible for this development. First, the prestige and power of the brahmans was on the wane following the defeat of their feudal patrons and the establishment of the Delhi Sultanate. Second, at about the same time, the movements of the Nathpanthis and Siddhas were openly challenging caste and supremacy of the brahmans. The third factor was the coalescence of the Bhakti thought with Sufi philosophy. Sufi ideas, rooted in the Islamic concepts of equality and brotherhood, echoed and invigorated the social vision of the movement. It is notable, however, that the Bhakti leaders did not encourage the mysticism of the Sufis.

Kabir, the first major sant-poet to emerge in the northern India after two centuries of Hindu-Muslim interaction, is the greatest figure of the movement. In his poetry the movement achieves its creative apogee. He is also the most controversial. In absence of authentic documentation, his life, his activities, and his philosophy have been *free-for-all* since his death, made worse by the dominant scholarship which tends to domesticate him in the brahmanic mould. Attempts and anxiety to prove that Kabir was actually a brahman by birth, or at least was initiated into legitimate spiritual life by a brahman guru, and that his teachings were nothing but a mystical or rustic version of the Veda-Purana still persist, but now there is a consensus among serious Kabir-scholars about his non-brahman origin and the strongly anti-brahmanic orientation of his thinking (Vaudeville 1993; Hess and Singh 1986; Dharwadker 2003). This is also the view of the earliest portrayal of Kabir by Nabhadas, alone among the early orthodox commentators who did not attempt to brahmanise Kabir. This is what Nabhadas writes in his *Bhaktamal* composed around 1600:

Kabir didn't honour the world's conventions, such as caste, the four stages of life, the six philosophical systems [of brahmanism]. . . . He showed that yoga, ritual sacrifice, fasting and charity were trivial and base without the practice of devotional worship. His ramainis, shabdas, and sakhis are the truth about Hindus and Muslims. His words didn't belong to a faction: what he said was good for everybody. The world's disposition is inflexible: he didn't say things to please someone. Kabir didn't honour the world's conventions. (Tr. Dharwadker 2003: 23; also see Vaudville 1993: 43)

It was his outright rejection of caste and brahmanism which prompted the pandits to mythologise, mystify and appropriate Kabir. As part of the design to misrepresent and coopt Kabir came the hagiographical works of Anantdas who composed *Kabir Parachai* (*c.*1625) and Priyadas who composed *Bhaktirasbodhini* (*c.*1712). Both the fabricators belonged to the Ramananda community, and they tried their best to make Kabir a *Ramanandi* and thus absorb him into the conservative Vaishanav devotion. As we saw, neither Kabir nor any other radical poet was a disciple of any brahman guru. According to Vaudville, one of the most credible scholars on the Bhakti movement, 'Kabir was never a Ramanandi' and 'the fact remains that he never named a human guru'. None of the other sants did either as their concept of Satguru was not in the human form.

Kabir and the other Sants undoubtedly inherited from Nathism their claim to divine spiritual awareness not from a particular guru, but from direct experience, an experience which Kabir calls *paracha* (Sanskrit parichaya). *Paracha* is conceived as the hearing of a mysterious Word or Sound (*shabda*) spoken in the depth of the soul by the *Satguru*. The silence Kabir and the other Sant poets maintained about their human gurus was certainly for them not only a matter of tradition but also of conviction. Yet, it was not understood by later Vaishnav writers, who interpreted their silence as some accident due to forgetfulness. By the time of Nabhaji [*c.*1600], the older Sants' narrow connection with the Yogic tradition was somewhat obliterated, so that a number of apparently guru-less saints, beginning with Kabir, had to be fitted with a suitable guru, in the person of Ramananda, a high-caste, very respectable and dignified saint. (Vaudeville 1993: 92)

Though confusions about Kabir's life and poetry still persist, now there is unanimity about at least the dates of his birth and death (1398–1448) and the fact that he was born and brought up in a family of weavers in the Banaras-Magahar region of Uttar Pradesh. His family, identified as julaha (weaver), had converted to Islam a generation or two earlier from the lowered-caste kori (weaver) community. In earlier times, the weavers, the creators of the fabled Indian textiles, were organised into guilds and enjoyed social respect. Evidences suggest that the weavers and other artisan castes were followers of Buddhism in the north-eastern India (Vaudeville 1993: 71). After the decline of Buddhism, they were absorbed in the orthodox caste system, and their systematic degradation as a 'low caste' began. The weavers, however, never reconciled to their humiliation, and when the opportunity came, they revolted; they embraced Islam in the age of the Delhi Sultanate. The change of religion, however, did not change their social status. Snubbed by the Muslim ruling class, their aspiration to social equality remained unfulfilled. In Kabir's time, the people treated his caste contemptuously, which he underlined in a famous couplet:

Everybody, O Kabir, reduces my caste to a laughing stock:
But it devotes itself to the Creator, and I martyr myself to its cause.

(Tr. Dharwadker 2003: 8)

Born and brought up in such a milieu, it was not unusual for Kabir to rebel against caste and brahmanism. Vaudeville (1993: 73) contends that it is difficult to say whether the julahas of the area (from where Kabir came) were 'converted to Islam from Hinduism or from Buddhism, since at that time and at that social level, both religions were amalgamated'. Later forms of Buddhism, as we saw earlier, had survived from the earlier medieval India in the movements of Sahajiya Siddhas and Nath Yogis. The Gorakhnathi Yogis were referred to simply as Jogis—also known by respectful titles like Avadhut, Gosai, Sadh, even Faqir and Pir. All Jogis were not ascetics, and in Bengal, the Jogis constituted a caste of weavers. Based on the researches of K.M. Sen and H.P. Dwivedi, Vaudeville (ibid.: 76) suggests that 'Nathism itself, as a kind of anti-brahmanical, half-Buddhistic creed, was already widespread among weavers and some other artisan castes at the time of the Muslim conquest.' According to K.M. Sen, the Jugis (or Jogis) of Bengal were already outside the pale of Hinduism before most of them became Muslims—as was the case with julahas. Similarly, Dwivedi (1941) considers that the Nath-Yogis were nearer to Islam than to Hinduism in their religious outlook. Kabir came from such a background, and though he did not confine himself to Nathpathi tradition, he was deeply familiar with the ideology and vocabulary of this essentially Buddhist, anti-brahmanic tradition, which he made use of brilliantly in his social and philosophical critique.

Kabir had no formal education, but even a cursory glance at his poetry reveals that he was superbly educated in the university of life through what he called *sahaj sadhana* (accessible meditation which requires no mediation of priests and texts of the organised religions) and *parakh pad*, which means testing empirical knowledge acquired through experience by intellect and rational thinking. It was his empirical knowledge and rational thinking that led him to *anabhai sancha* (fearless truth) which enabled him to reject with supreme confidence the solutions offered by the elites and their canons. His dismissal of all received education made eminent sense in a social context where education was a caste privilege, where the lowered castes were denied access to the Veda-Purana. Obviously, the contents of such canons were bound to be caste-oriented, and nothing could be more corrupt than such theology and epistemology. Kabir rejected the entire brahmanic literature on this basis. He would call his knowledge *suchchham veda* (critical knowledge), which was in contention against *sthool veda* (the vulgar knowledge of the brahmanic canons).

Kabir, thus, transgressed the conventional *mantra*, *tantra* and *yantra*. A challenging philosopher of life, he was a merciless critic of received ideas, and gifted with a rare ability to articulate his complex ideas in a simple and striking way. In an age dominated by orthodoxies of all kinds, he put to use his experience, observation, and intellect to critique the system. In a magnificent poem, addressed to his brahmanic adversaries, he proclaims that his criteria for assessing reality is *aakhin ki dekhi* (one's own observation) while the shifty-eyed pandit takes recourse to *kaagad ki lekhi* (fabricated knowledge) to pull wool over people's eyes.

How can ours, yours and mine, mind meet!
I say what I have seen.
You say what you have read.
I want to disentangle the complexity of truth.
And you keep it under wraps to
Further complicate the matter!

(For the Hindi original, see Dwivedi [1941] 1999: 247)

Kabir, thus, comes across as a rationalist par excellence, not a mystic (as alleged by many critics). With *parakh pad* and *anabhai sancha*, the sant-poets like him were in search of an alternative knowledge which was emancipatory for both the self and society. Kabir gives voice to this great ambition in his sakhi *fahama aage, fahama paachhe*:

Knowledge ahead, knowledge behind,
knowledge to the left and right.
The knowledge that knows what knowledge is:
that's the knowledge that's mine.

(Tr. Dharwadker 2003: 183)

Such quest of knowledge demanded removal of all falsehoods and fabrications, whether social or religious. And this is what Kabir did adroitly in his life and letters. He ridiculed caste and brahmanism, and mocked the pretensions of Muslim clerics. He questioned the beliefs and ritualism of established religions with a brilliance unprecedented in history. Kabir's

> constant effort was to strip away disguises, force confrontation, expose lies, promote honesty at every level. His socio-satirical poems, his psychological probes . . . his crazy and paradoxical and mystical poems, do not inhabit separate categories. They are unified by a principle of radical honesty that sweeps through marketplace, temple, body and mind, that will no more allow you to delude yourself than to cheat others. (Hess 1986: 21)

In a fragmented and insular society steeped in caste and religious bigotry, Kabir's advocacy of human unity and equality was nothing less than revolutionary. He tried to demolish all barriers that separated human from human. He either dismissed the Hindu and Muslim ideas of religion or else equated them, saying that Rama and Allah were identical. Kabir's God is 'neither in the temple nor in the mosque'; he is *ghat-ghat mein,* 'in every heart'. For him, God is not an object, nor the sort of reality that one can speak of and conceptualise, certainly not the sort one can see and worship. He found sacrifice to the gods hideous, and he thought it was utter nonsense to picture God in a succession of animal and human incarnations 'whose form could then be worshipped and adored and whose stories could spawn an industry of religious texts, complete with their brahman interpreters' (Hawley and Juergensmeyer 1988: 43).

Kabir's spirituality did not require religious institutions and priesthood. 'The religion he knows, if religion it is, is of a totally different order from the admonitions and assurances that put bread and butter on the tables of qazis and pandits.' He says that religious rituals and textual authority are created by the wily elite to fool and rule the masses:

Veda and Koran are traps laid
for poor souls to tumble in. (Tr. Hess and Singh 1986: 52)

Emphasis on religious externals perpetuates animosity among adherents of different religions. From this viewpoint, institutionalised Islam is not very different from Hinduism, despite its advocacy of a different theology. Hence, Kabir pours scorn over both the mullas and the brahmans. In poem after poem he makes a mockery of their injunctions, admonitions, and pious assurances to the people. This he does, apparently, to liberate the people from the priestly-feudal thrall.

For Kabir, the brahman was 'the craftiest, the most unkind, the most status-conscious and vanity-ridden man on earth'. Even his bhakti was a pretence, since that bhakti had no compassion for the other creations of God. In Kabir's eyes, it was the brahman, more than anyone else, who was in need of basic education in humanity and kindness. One major agenda of his life, therefore, was to make the brahman aware of his ignorance, his dishonesty, and his callousness towards fellow humans, especially the 'untouchables'. He did this using that most potent weapon he was so marvellous at wielding—ridicule.

Tearing into the claims of the birth-based superiority, he asks: *'Re baman tu bamani jaya, aan baant se kahi na aaya'*.[2] Elsewhere he asks: 'Do you have milk in your veins while we have blood? If not how are you a brahman and we shudras?' He sees refractions of the divine in all humans, and has nothing but contempt for those who don't see this essential unity of humanity:

It's a heavy confusion.
Veda, Koran, holiness, hell, woman, man,
a clay pot shot with air and sperm...
When the pot falls apart, what do you call it?
Numbskull! You've missed the point.
It's all one skin and bone, one piss and shit,
one blood, one meat.
From one drop, a universe
Who's Brahman? Who's Shudra? (Tr. Hess and Singh 1986: 67)

Kabir shows up the pandit who projects himself as the repository of all knowledge, as 'a rank ignoramus, a pompous fool lacking insight into reality'. He scorns the brahman's babble and compares his holy books to 'a cell made of paper' in which to imprison fools. The pandits were to him 'lovers of lust and delusion' who had the temerity to 'laugh at the (real) lovers of God'. In his poem *Pandit Baad Badante Jhhutha* (The Pandits' Pedantries are Lies), he sarcastically asks: 'Read, read, pandit, make yourself clever/ Does that bring freedom?' The *Kaliyuga* was to him 'the age of phoney brahmans', and Veda and Puranas 'a blindman's mirrors'. The pandit, he says, is a 'buffoon' who searches the sky but can't find out how to quell his pride. The pandit's meaningless rituals and prayers, ignorance and pride have made him a laughing stock; no one could be lower than such a creature.

The pandit got lost/ in Vedic details
but missed the mystery/ of his own self.
Worship, prayers,/ six sacred activities,
four ages teaching Gayatri,
I ask you: who's got liberty?
You splash yourself/ if you touch somebody,
but tell me who/ could be lower than you.
Proud of your quality, / great with authority,
such pride never brought anyone good.... (Ibid.: 85)

Some people erroneously see Kabir as an eclectic reformer of Hinduism and Islam. Some have even tried to portray him in the brahmanical mould. Attempts have been made to create an image of Kabir that complies with the Vedic-Puranic tradition. He has also been branded as an 'individualistic' and a 'mystic' and denied recognition even as a social critic. Kabir's poetry, however, brings out his radical credentials. He attacks the dogmas and cruelties of the dominant culture. He ignites a similar subversiveness in his follow-travellers. In a well-known couplet he announces:

I've burned my own house down,
the torch is in my hand.
Now I'll burn down the house of anyone
who wants to follow me. (Ibid.: 5)

Kabir trod an untrodden path, singing *Apanee raah tu chale Kabira*—'Go your own way, Kabir'. His way—made luminous by his experience, observance, and reflection—was not hamstrung by the rules of established religion, custom, or caste. His hunger for truth, regardless of the cost, often brought him in confrontation with the people in power and the custodians of Hinduism and Islam. Despite threat to his life, he never desisted from telling what he saw around him. What he saw around him—people killing souls and worshipping rocks, or worse, the sectarian zealots killing each other in the name of religion—deeply troubled him; he could not reconcile himself to this 'mad' world:

Saints, I see the world is mad.
If I tell the truth they rush to beat me,
If I lie they trust me.
I've seen the pious Hindus, rule-followers,
early morning bath-takers –
killing souls, they worship rocks.
They know nothing.
I've seen plenty of Muslim teachers, holy men
reading their holy books
and teaching their pupils techniques.
They know just as much.
The Hindu says Ram is the Beloved,
the Turk says Rahim.
Then they kill each other
They buzz their mantras from house to house
puffed with pride. (Ibid.: 42)

Pioneer of a new culture, Kabir's stress was on an enlightened remaking of society. He fought against caste and religious bigotry wherever he encountered them. And so did his followers in many regions of the north India. Joining a non-caste group was one of the ways to escape the caste boundary, as many sects and organisations had done in the past. Kabir's followers, too, founded an independent religious community, the Kabir-panth, which received enthusiastic response from the artisans and cultivators. His ardent followers, millions in number, are still scattered all over the north India, especially in the states of Uttar Pradesh, Bihar, Madhya Pradesh, Rajasthan, and Punjab.

Since compromise or half-way solutions were not his way, and his fight against the forces of oppression relentless, Kabir has an enduring appeal as a symbol of anti-establishment. It is notable that Kabir was a hero to two of modern India's greatest revolutionaries—Phule and Ambedkar.[3] The colourful stories of Tagore and Gandhi's great admiration for Kabir are also well known, though their brahmanic understanding of Kabir was very different from the Kabir that we have seen here. Kabir is also acknowledged as the father of Hindi literature, and he is perhaps the most quoted and most sung poet ever of India. His popularity remains undiminished: the very name Kabir radiates images of a colourful revolutionary, a people's poet, and a cultural hero who lives forever.

Ravidas or Raidas (fl. 1450) was another Bhakti stalwart in the north. Born into a community of leather-workers, he indicates his wider family to which he belonged by mentioning some of his illustrious predecessors. The names he gives are that of Namdev, Trilochan, and Kabir (Hawley and Juergensmeyer 1988: 12). While the first two hailed from western India, Kabir lived in Banaras, Ravidas's home turf. 'In mentioning these three as recipients of divine grace along with himself, Ravidas underscored his sense of solidarity with a tradition of bhakti that flowed with particular animation in the lower ranks of society' (ibid.). Like his kindred souls, Ravidas' spirituality is tinged with an egalitarian ethos. In his moving and mellifluous words, *Tohi mohi, mohi tohi antar kaisa* (Between you and me, me and you/ How can there be a difference?). He visualises God as 'deliverer of the poor', 'uplifter of the lowly', and 'purifier of the defiled'. He raises crucial questions about the social hierarchy and speaks of an ideal society 'where none are third or second—all are one'. He dreams of an earthly paradise in his poem 'Begumpura', the City without Sorrow:

The regal realm with the sorrowless name:
they call it Begumpura, a place with no pain,
No taxes or cares, nor own property there,
no wrongdoing, worry, terror or torture.
... where none are third or second—all are one;
... They do this or that, they walk where they wish,
they stroll through fabled palaces unchallenged.
Oh, says Ravidas, a tanner now set free,
those who walk beside me are my friends.

(Tr. Hawley and Juergensmeyer 1988: 32)

His disdain for those who proudly uphold the shastras and discriminatory socio-religious order often comes to the fore. He chastises them for denigrating people belonging to castes and communities other than their own. He argues that even the lowest can rise to great heights by acquiring noble qualities—he considers such a self-realised person superior than the priests, heroes and kings:

A family that has a true follower of the Lord
Is neither high caste nor low caste, lordly or poor.
The world will know it by its fragrance.
Priests or merchants, labourers or warriors,
halfbreeds, outcastes, and those who tend cremation fires—
their hearts are all the same.
He who becomes pure through love of the Lord
exalts himself and his family as well.
Thanks be to his village, thanks to his home,
thanks to that pure family, each and every one,
For he's drunk with the essence of the liquid of life
and he pours away all the poisons.
No one equals someone so pure and devoted—
not priests, not heroes, not parasolled kings.
As the lotus leaf floats above the water, Ravidas says,
so he flowers above the world of his birth.

(Tr. Hawley and Juergensmeyer 1988: 25)

It was Ravidas who gave the call of *Jaat-paat poochhe nahi koi, hari ka bhaje so hari ka hoi* (Don't ask about caste, whoever is a devotee of God belongs to Him). He often refers to his humble birth and leather-work, stressing the dignity of an occupation and caste that had come to be regarded as disgraceful. He defies the conventional wisdom by arguing that despite his allegedly 'low' occupation he too is as important as the 'well-born', many of whom come to him to pay their homage:

Oh well-born of Benaras, I too am born well known:
my labour is with leather. But my heart can boast the Lord. ...
I, born among those who carry carrion
in daily rounds around Benaras, am now
the lowly one to whom the mighty Brahmans come
And lowly bow. ... (Ibid.)

In a poem *With What Can I Worship?*, Ravidas mocks the ideas of purity and pollution. He pictures an innocent and bright young girl asking questions about the offerings to be made to the deity.

Mother, she asks, with what can I worship?
All the pure is impure. Can I offer milk?
The calf has dirtied it in sucking its mother's teat.
Water, the fish have muddied; flowers, the bees—
No other flowers could be offered than these.
The sandalwood tree, where the snake has coiled, is spoiled.
The same act formed both nectar and poison.
Everything's tainted—candles, incense, rice—
But still I can worship with my body and my mind
and I have the guru's grace to find the formless Lord.
Rituals and offerings—I can't do any of these.
What, says Ravidas, will you do with me? (Ibid. : 26)

Another remarkable sant-poet was Kabir's Rajasthani follower, Dadu Dayal (d. 1603). It is significant that Dadu calls his path *nipakh* or non-sectarian. This was a bid to rise above the disputations of religious communities and establish harmony among the masses. Calling himself 'neither a Hindu nor a Muslim', he dismisses all revealed scriptures, valuing only personal devotion to God and to humankind. In many of his poems which possess great beauty and force, Dadu asserts that all humans have the same essence, and that differences based on colour, caste, or race are superfluous. It pains him that the world is divided among antagonistic sects and castes as few dare to defy the sectarian traditions.

Writing towards the end of the seventeenth century, Dharmadas, Darya Saheb and Yari Saheb of Bihar also underlined the same sentiments. Dharmadas stresses the fundamental unity of humanity and irrationality of the birth-based caste. Darya Saheb says, 'All humans suffer from hunger or thirst, or feel pain or pleasure in the same way'. Different rituals and beliefs, he says, cannot make a difference to the status of humans. Similarly, Yari Saheb insists that 'Gold is the same everywhere whether it is in melted form or an ornament. Who can say which is higher and which is lower?' (Savitri Chandra 1978: 141).

Towering above his contemporaries is the charismatic personality of Guru Nanak (1469–1546), the founder of Sikhism. He rejected caste Hinduism and preached an egalitarian monotheistic faith, shorn of idolatory and based on the equality of all men and women. In a lucid and interactive language Nanak drew the people's attention to the true relationship between humanity and divinity and and human and human. Brahmanism looked down upon the Punjab as a fallen land—out of bounds for the Varnashrama Dharma. The region indeed saw the admixture of many ethnic identities and cultures. Nanak's arrival on the scene further invigorated the assimilative trend and gave a fillip to the cultural blending. The movement he led unleashed the forces that brought about a major change in the religious, social, and political outlook of the Punjabi people.

Guru Nanak campaigned for a universal religion, and attacked divisive caste rites and rituals. He laid stress on the importance of true knowledge manifested in compassion for fellow humans as a necessary means of spiritual awakening. Religion, for him, consists not in a string of words but in high thinking and noble behaviour. Only those who look on all humans as equal—and treat them humanely—are truly religious.

He shows no appreciation for the ruling classes, whether Hindu or Muslim. He displays no sympathy for the religious elite. He identifies himself with the ruled, the common people. What moves him deeply is their misery, ignorance and helplessness.... That they should not be denied the means of liberation was, for Guru Nanak, the supreme purpose of human life. His message, therefore, was meant for all. The universality of his message is the obverse of his idea of equality. (Grewal 1999: 19–20).

Guru Nanak's was a vision which clashed with all ascriptive and sectarian ideology. He rejected the brahmanic scriptures, incarnations, and idolatry, and rebuked the priests who sold superstition and false hope to the gullible masses. His path was based on humanitarian concern, in which the theological was not divorced from the sociological. In his eyes, truth was not only an abstract notion of the Supreme Reality but also a practical principle of social conduct. Guru Nanak—and the Gurus who succeeded him—stressed that we can't shirk our family and social responsibility by branding the world as illusion. We are responsible for our life and endowed with the ability to remake ourselves through reflection, action and ethical discipline. Nanak laid stress on virtuous living: 'Truth is higher, but higher still is truthful living.' The steps he prescribes to his followers to achieve self-actualisation are simple: participation in productive activities and proper human conduct. 'Those alone know the right path who earn their bread by the sweat of their brow and share it with others.' The personality so developed, he said, must wage a ceaseless struggle, not only with one's selfish ego, but also in the realm of social relations.

The *Adi Granth*, which contains the teachings of Nanak and constitutes the core of Sikh theology, incorporates several poems of the subaltern sants. The social philosophy of Nanak bears a striking similarity to that of Kabir and Ravidas, whom he held in great esteem. He challenged caste distinctions by precept and example. A case in point is a well-known incident that has become a part of the folk memory. At Sayyidpur he stayed and dined with Lalo, a carpenter, and declined the feast of Malik Bhago, a 'high-caste' landlord, on the ground that the latter had accumulated his wealth by exploiting the poor while the former earned his bread by hard work. He also established a radical practice: he made his followers eat in a common kitchen—*langar*. In a rare frisson of empathy for those held in contempt for their 'lowly birth', he says that his followers of humble origin 'may wear shoes made from my skin'.

The rise of Sikh community as a hardworking and prosperous people in a country teeming with the poor is largely the result of egalitarianism and dignity of labour enshrined in the ideology of Nanak and his successors. At the instance of the last Guru, Gobind Singh, every male Sikh bears—and shares—the surname Singh, as does every female the surname Kaur. The objective behind this was to make the traditional caste identities unimportant. In this and other respects the Sikh Gurus were harbingers of ideas which have contributed in making Indian culture more humane and democratic.

The Bhakti leaders transcended sectarian boundaries and incorporated bright elements of all faiths in their teachings. They protested against the low position given to women, and encouraged them to participate in social activities. When the followers of Kabir, Ravidas, and Nanak gathered together, women were included in the gathering.

Mirabai (1498-1565), the Rajasthani Rajput princess, the author of some of the finest hymns in Hindi, broke out of her gilded prison to become a disciple of Ravidas. A 'high-caste' princess taking a guru from the class of 'untouchables' is an act of rebellion in itself. According to a remarkable research (Parita Mukta 1997), Mira after leaving her princely home found a new community among the marginalised of Rajasthan and adjacent regions. She forged a bond with the despised and toiling people. In her new life, companionship made up for material deprivation. Mira made a radical reversal in which manual labour, even the skinning of animals and dyeing of skin, became noble and dignified. All this is exquisitely expressed in her own words:

Mira found a guru in Rohidas.
She bowed at his feet, and asked his blessings.
    Refrain: Mira's Mohan, come to the Mertni's desh.
I have nothing to do with caste or other divisions.
Let the world do what it will,
I offer you my body, mind and soul.
    Mira's Mohan, come to the Mertni's desh.
I skin animals and dye the skins.
My work is to dye.
This dyeing is dear to me, this dyeing is dear to me,
Dye my soul in it. (See Mukta 1997: 112)

Mira's abandonment of her feudal husband, her acceptance of the 'untouchable' Ravidas as her guru, her audacity in joining the company of saints, her love affair with the despised communities, all paint the picture of a sublimely rebellious character. There are stories about her insulted husband, the Rana, how he tried everything he could to 'reform' his wayward wife, to bring her back. When he failed to win her over, he sent her poison. Mira disappears, or dies, under uncertain circumstances. Many contend, and so does Parita Mukta, that Mira, in all likelihood, was eliminated in revenge on the orders of her outraged husband.

Siddha Rebellion in Tamil Nadu

The poetry of the sixth century Tamil sage Tirumular who sang 'Caste is one and God is one' and equated Love with God—instead of defining God as Love—marked the beginning of a distinct socio-spiritual movement in the south. This movement reached its high-water mark between the fourteenth and eighteenth centuries in which the Siddhas played a leading role. The Siddhas or Sittars, who hailed from subaltern groups and sang subversive songs, mocked the rites and rituals and extolled love and compassion. In this sense, they carried forward the legacy of Tirumular as well as two other native icons Thiruvalluvar (*c.* CE 300–400), the 'low- caste' author of poetical classic *Kural*, and Nandnar, the ninth-century 'untouchable' who dared to enter the sacred realm of religion.

Combining spiritual excellence with social regeneration, the Siddhas scaled the caste-class barriers and championed the radical inclusiveness of their predecessors, one of whom sang 'every village is the village of my birth and all are my kith and kin'. With a blending of wisdom and compassion, remarkably similar to the Buddhist ethos and akin to the Siddha ideal in the north, they sought yogic–spiritual experience for a blissful consciousness. The Tamil Siddhas' resemblance to the Nathpanthi movement is unmistakable, although there is no authentic study yet on this subject. It is surprising—and revealing—that the various streams of Tamil Siddhas count Gorakhnath as one of their illustrious elders (Kailasapathy 1987: 387).

As believers in the unity of humanity, the Siddhas were 'implacable opponents of the caste system and the gradations of orthodoxy and respectability that it gave rise to'. Considered dangerous for their non-conformist views and lifestyle, they were persecuted by the powerful. The anti-establishment thrust of their poetry is so similar to the verses of northern radicals like Kabir that they appear to be carbon copies of each other. Regarded as heretical like Kabir, the Siddhas too were hated and hounded by reactionary forces, who stigmatised them as religious *panchamas*, or outcastes as they 'challenged the very foundations of medieval Hinduism: the authority of the shastras, the validity of rituals and the basis of the caste system' (Kailasapathy 1987: 389).

It was the Siddhas, not the fabled Shaivaite Nayanars and Vaishnavaite Alvars, who carried the torch of radical humanism in the south. The Alvars and Nayanars confined themselves to religious-theological concerns within the precincts of Vedic-brahmanism. Traversing the Dravidian land with scriptures in Sanskrit, they built the brahmanical temple cult with the associated settlements and tenants, and, thus, played the role of catalysts in the processes of Aryanisation/Sanskritisation of the Dravidian culture. They were also instrumental in driving out Buddhism and Jainism which had had a significant presence in the region for centuries. Contrary to the elitist propaganda, the Alvars and Nayanars galvanised the brahmanic-feudal combine for the cultural subjugation of the Tamil people, a process which was quite violent.

Tamil literature makes it painfully clear that the foundations of the medieval synthesis were soaked in blood from battles that established the temple-centred, devotional Brahmanical religious ceremonial practice at the centre of the agrarian order.... The Sanskritic and temple-centred character of Tamil verse during medieval times distinguishes it sharply from earlier epochs and nourishes a popular belief in Tamil Nadu today that medieval South India succumbed to an invasion of Brahmans from the north. (David Ludden, see Omvedt 1994: 41–2)

Historians relate the origin of caste, slavery, and the segregation of people as untouchables to the process of Aryanisation of south India which reached its peak during the period of imperial Cholas. The Chola regime brought about basic changes in land relations. Large sections of original inhabitants like Paraiyars and Pallars were unsettled from their land due to large-scale land grants to brahmans (known as the *brahmadeya* and *agrahara*) by the kings during the seventh to eleventh centuries. The institution of caste system and slavery in the south is related to this process. As S. Manickam (1993) observes,

It is difficult to say when the institution of slavery originated in the south. Perhaps the conquest of southern India by the Aryans and the consequent fusion between them and the inhabitants of the land could have been the possible cause of the birth of caste system and the institution of slavery which is closely allied with the former.

Oppression of those pushed down to the bottom of social hierarchy grew in intensity in pace with the Aryanisation process. And with it grew a tradition of protest against the oppressive system.

The Siddhas were in the forefront of a cultural fight-back from below. Critical research on the Siddhas is hampered by lack of reliable editions of Siddha literature, and this is not fortuitous. The powerful tried their best to distort and destroy the Siddhas' works. The brahmanical Shaivism excluded the Siddha views from its vast canonical corpus. As a scholar points out, their poems have been left to the common man to preserve as best as he can. Whatever little material we have suggests Siddhas' detachment from the brahmanical way of life. Their verses manifest a protest against the forced formalities of life and religion. Antithetic attitude to the beliefs and practices of the ruling class is a major strand of their poetry.

Their social location and diverse backgrounds played a role in shaping the Siddha radicalism. Most of them came from families of shepherds, temple-drummers, potters, fishermen, hunters, etc. There are also stories that some of them came from other cultural traditions, Chinese or Arabic. The stories are based on the evidences of connection with those cultures in the fields of medicine, alchemy and astronomy (Kailasapathy 1987: 406). There is also the belief that the first major Tamil Siddha, Tirumular, came from Kashmir. These stories are apocryphal, but they point to the inter-mingling of Siddhas with some Muslim saints. It is significant that two Sufis—Pir Muhammed and Mastan Sahib—are included in the list of Siddhas. All this must have widened their cultural horizons and contributed to their inclusive philosophy. Irrespective of whether their egalitarianism was ideology-driven or not, they were strongly opposed to the caste distinctions practised by the higher castes—brahmans, vellalas (affluent peasants) and vanigas (merchants).

The most powerful voice in the community of Siddhas is that of Sivavakkiyar. Believed to have lived in the ninth century, he was capable of writing a couplet like 'Shall the stone be God? What shall I do but laugh?' (Meenakshi 1996: 111). Like Kabir, he is merciless in mocking priestly pretensions. His poems bring out the strong anti-brahmanical sentiments, which are so characteristic of the Siddhas.

The chanting of the four Vedas
The meticulous study of the sacred scripts,
The smearing of the holy ashes,
And the muttering of prayers,
Will not lead you to the Lord!
Let your heart melt within you.
And if you can be true to yourself
Then you will join the limitless light
And lead an endless life.
You dumb fools performing the rituals
With care and in leisureliness.
Do gods ever become stone?
What can I do but laugh?
Of what use are temples,
And of what use are sacred tanks?
Slavishly you gather to worship
In temples and tanks! (Tr. Kailasapathy 1987: 390)

Sivavakkiyar employs simple similes to convey his ideas. He cites quotidian domestic instances to drive home his point. This is what he does in the following verse while trashing the theory of eternal soul and transmigration:

Milk does not return to the udder,
Likewise butter can never become butter-milk;
The sound of the conch does not exist once it is broken;
The blown flower, the fallen fruit do not go back to the tree;
The dead are never born again, never! (Ibid.: 401)

Like the Bhakti stalwarts in other regions, celebration of monotheism and condemnation of idolatry were emblematic of the Tamil Siddhas:

When once I knew the Lord,
What were to me the host
of pagan deities,
Some fixed in temple shrines,

Or carried in the crowd;
Some made of unbaked clay,
And some burnt hard with fire?
With all the lying tales
That fill the sacred books,
They've vanished from my mind.
But yet I have a shrine—
The mind within my breast.
An image too is there—
The soul that came from God.
I offer ash and flowers—
The praises of my heart;
And all the God-made world
Is frankincense and myrrh
And thus where'er I go
I ever worship God. (Jordens 1985: 278–9)

The poems of Pambatti Sittar are modelled on the songs of snake-charmers. With wit and verve, he attacks the brahmanical ideology:

The four Vedas, six kinds of Shastras,
The many Tantras and Puranas,
The Agamas which speak of the arts,
And various kinds of other books
Are of no use; just in vain.
So dance snake, dance!
In a statue of stone whanged with a chisel
D'ya think there's understanding?
D'ya think the idiots of the world
Have any understanding?
Will a flaw in a pan go away
If you rub it with tamarind?
Ignorance won't go away from the idiots
So dance snake, dance! (Kailasapathy 1987: 390–1)

Such poems—popular in Tamil Nadu to this day—are testimony to the fact that egalitarian culture was deeply cherished. Pambatti's verse, cited above, ends on a note where he talks of 'setting fire to divisions of caste' and 'taking philosophical questions to the market place'. This leaves no doubt about the real intention of the Siddhas.

The Siddhas' songs radiated an attitude that was empathetic and life-affirming. The Siddhas played their part as singers, magicians, healers, physicians—all rolled into one—and tried to mitigate people's miseries, keeping alive the tradition of the great shramans who gave out their all for the welfare of the multitude. Their love of humanity can be summed up in their elder Tirumular's celebrated words—'May the world be as happy as I am'.

The language of the Siddhas is said to be rough, rugged, and paradoxical. Interestingly, it bears a resemblance to Kabir's *saddhukari* (mixed language), rough rhetoric and *ulat baansian* (upside down language). This can be interpreted thus. First, as outcastes and wandering recluses rebelling against all forms of establishment including the literary, which was particularly oppressive in Tamil, the Siddhas had a strong preference for the people's diction, the colloquial. Secondly, because of their multiple yearnings including a passion for spiritual accomplishments (that had to be attempted at individual basis) and their desire for social awakening and transformation (that demanded popular participation), they had to invent a language that could best be appreciated in its milieu. Divorced from the context, their idiom and diction become esoteric and contradictory, which give their cultural adversaries an excuse to label them (like Kabir again!) as mystics. But the Siddhas were not interested in nurturing mysticism. Their objective was to bring about a revolution in personal and social affairs. If we read them closely, their seemingly difficult language becomes luminous. The Siddhas abhorred Sanskritised Tamil and their poems brimming with popular epigrams, witticisms, earthy adages, and wisecracks carry the colloquial expression of the common people. Their vocabulary does not accept a distinction between the sacred and the profane, the refined and the coarse. Interestingly, like Rabindranath Tagore who was profoundly influenced by Kabir, Subramania Bharathi (1882–1921), the brahman Tamil poet, was in thrall to Siddha poetry. He frequently employed Siddha folk metres and colloquialism in his poetry and went on to declare in his autobiography, 'There were many Siddhas before me, I too am one in their line.'

Virashaiva Socialism in Karnataka

A remarkable episode in medieval history is the rise of Virashaiva movement in Karnataka. 'Heroic followers of Shiva', or Lingayatas, arose in the twelfth and thirteenth centuries under the leadership of Basava. A brahman by birth, Basava had refused to undergo the *upanayan* (sacred thread) ceremony that entitles high-caste male to become *dvija,* the twice-born. Having thus *decaste* himself, he gained the people's confidence, and spearheaded a campaign against brahmanism that sanctified inequalities and exploitation. Adopting a multi-pronged strategy aimed at a cultural transformation, Basava, who later rose to become the prime minister of the Kalachuri king of Kalyan, gave the movement a radical orientation.

The movement strove, through competition and confrontation, to change established social relationships. It was a quest for equal access to political and economic resources, and, thus, for limiting the arbitrary powers of the brahmans (Bali 1978: 67–100). It evolved as a mass movement as men and women cutting across castes joined the experimental community. They created their sacred literature *vachanas*, lyrical poems and devotional hymns. Over two hundred writers who composed vachanas used the colloquial idiom of Kannada, and advocated ideas extraordinarily progressive for the time. They lambasted caste, and laid stress on spiritual and social value of every kind of labour.

The Virashaivas engendered a new morality that accepted converts from the lower strata as equals. The leadership encouraged commensality and connubium within the community. One such incident, a sparkling cameo in India's social history, involves the violation of that most 'sacred' law laid down by the Dharmashastras—a marriage of a brahman woman with an 'untouchable' man. Madhuvayya (or Madhuvaras), a patrician brahman who (like Basava) was a minister in the court of King Bijjala at Kalyan, gave his daughter in marriage to the son of Haralayya, who did leatherwork to earn his living. The marriage represented the worst form of *pratiloma*, the most maligned connection of a brahman female and a shudra male. An *anuloma* relation involving a higher-caste man and a lower-caste woman was somewhat forgivable, but a *pratiloma* marriage was the stuff of utter opprobrium in the brahmanic eyes.

Outraged by the marriage, the reactionaries, led by King Bijjala, launched a witch-hunt against the Virashaivas. Both fathers together with the bridegroom were arrested, blinded, chained to the leg of an elephant, and then dragged to death along the streets of the town. Large-scale persecution followed, forcing the Virashaivas to flee the town and take shelter in safer places (Schouten 1995: 48–50). Many contemporary and later works in Kannada celebrate the martyrdom of Haralayya and Madhuvayya. Haralayya went on to become an iconic figure in the history of the Virashaivas. Many regard him as the forerunner of the dalit fight for emancipation.

Faced with terrible odds, Basava showed exemplary leadership and kept the movement alive. Renouncing his office, he declared himself the relative of the subaltern devotees in the community. He described his new family ties in a number of fascinating vachanas. One such is testimony to his unique radicalism.

The boy of the servant in Cannayya's house
and the girl of the maid in Kakkayya's house—
they both went to the field to gather dung
and then they made love.
A child was born to them—that was me.
So say the Lord of the Meeting Rivers be my witness! (Schouten 1995: 51)

Basava thus discards his background, his family, his caste, and hopes to be admitted to the new circle of people who share the same spiritual and social values. He sketches a family portrait which includes only devotees from the most humble origins. He uses his 'low' status as a plea to compel God to show mercy.

Our Cannayya, the untouchable, is my father,
and our Kakkayya, the tanner, is my uncle;
See, Cikkayya is our grandfather,
and our Bommayya, the lute-player, is my elder brother.
So why do you not know me,
O Lord of the Meeting Rivers? (Ibid.: 52)

The 'untouchable' Madar Cannayya, idolised by Basava in the above vachana as his father, was a major Virashaiva sant-poet. He castigates caste in one of his vachanas by presenting an impressive array of cultural heroes from the despised castes:

Sankhya was a sweeper;/Agastya, a huntsman;
Durvasa, a cobbler;/Dadhichi, a locksmith;
Kasyapa, a blacksmith;/Romaja, a coppersmith;
Kaundilya, a barber;
So, why should you then,
In ignorance of this,
Insist on caste? (Ray et al. 2000: 480–1)

The Virashaiva leaders entreat people to give up their caste identity and loyalty. In a poem, Allama pinpoints the 'six errors' one must overcome in order to become a good Virashaiva. The first, he says, is *jati* that hinders people from realising their true worth. The second fallacy is the Varnashrama Dharma that gives sanctity to caste divisions. The other errors are pride in one's own family (*kula*), lineage, name and native land (Schouten 1995: 54–5). In other words, one simply cannot become a Virashaiva without forsaking one's caste and other narrow identities. Siddharama articulates this thus:

What does it mean to belong to the system of the four castes?
Look, he is a Virashaiva who transcends the four castes. (Schouten 1995: 54)

Comparing vachanas like the ones cited above with some Buddhist texts, Schouten points out that Basava seemed to be familiar with—and fascinated by—the Buddha's egalitarian teachings. This, he says, was not surprising since Buddhism had a powerful presence in Basava's native region.

In 1095, only about ten years before Basava's birth, a large Buddhist monastery was founded in Dambal (in the present Dharwar district). Dambal later became one of the most important religious centres of Virashaivism.... The strong resistance against the caste system, as it occurred in the Buddhist tradition, was still preserved in the last strongholds of Buddhism in northern Karnataka when Basava tried to find an alternative for the strict Brahmana values of his family. It is an obvious suggestion that he also acquainted himself with the Buddhist tradition. In that tradition, he would certainly have been fascinated by the egalitarian philosophy that rejected discrimination on the basis of caste. (Schouten 1995: 61)

A sparkling feature of Virashaivism is the strong presence of women. There are instances of female ascetics as well as women who joined their husbands in the community on an equal footing. The movement rejected female subordination and strove to build a new man–woman relationship. It was characteristic of Virashaivism that there was a place in it for the most unconventional of women such as Akka Mahadevi and Muktayakka. A leading composer of vachanas, Mahadevi was fiercely independent and her quest for personal emancipation had subversive social implications. This poem of hers is an exquisite and typical example:

Those who have become equal by love,
Should they heed background or pretensions?
Those who have gone mad,
do they know shame or restraint?
Those who are loved by the Lovely Lord of the Jasmines,
Could they have loyalty to the world? (Schouten 1995: 30)

Akka says that those besotted with divine love are insane people who do not care for the established rules and traditional distinctions, for which she uses the word *kula* which includes all factors which are determined by birth, such as family, gender, and caste.

The Lingayatas came up with alternative rituals, ceremonies, taboos: they constructed new religio-cultural symbols. Rejecting the core values and social institutions associated with the brahmans, the movement tried to develop an egalitarian institutional framework:

In its desire for 'human relationships', it felt it was necessary to break down interpersonal barriers and conventional norms that prevented interpersonal contact on issues like interdining and intercaste marriage, i.e. it discarded the notions of purity and pollution between brahmans and non-brahmans. It revealed the realities hidden by rituals, practices, conventions of brahmans, in order to be liberated from the oppression of brahman domination. (Bali 1978: 69)

The movement laid special emphasis on the dignity of labour and connected it with social progress and spiritual uplift. Social mobilisation was taken up vigorously, and people were recruited to the community through the institution of *math*. In sum, the movement was a 'social upheaval by and for the poor, the low-caste and the outcaste against the rich and the privileged ...' (Ramanujan, cited in Bali, ibid.).

The aims and achievements of the Virashaiva movement were ahead of other such movements. And despite its later decline and disintegration as the movement fell victim to rigidity and hierarchy in its own ranks against which they once fought so heroically, the Lingayatas today form the single largest ethnic group in Karnataka. For all its faults and limitations, it was this community that provided the core structure for the backward classes movement in the Madras Presidency in the twentieth century.

Varakari Struggle in Maharashtra

From the thirteenth to seventeenth century in Maharashtra flourished an essentially subaltern upsurge, known as the Varakari movement. Here too, the sant-poets from the lower spectrum of society struggled for religious uprightness and social justice. Though they resorted to religious symbols and activities and did not mount a direct attack on the powerful, their identification with the oppressed signalled a strong disapproval of the vested interests of the power groups (Sardar 1978: 102). Since socio-economic control was then exerted through the control of religion and culture, the Varakaris' emphasis on spiritual equality implied an attempt at opening the gates of knowledge and power for the hitherto excluded castes, and thus pushing for social change that such opportunities entailed. Since they wanted to make knowledge, even the most sacred one, available to everyone in people's own language—a hallmark of the Bhakti movement everywhere—they also made a historic contribution in the growth of Marathi language and literature.

The religious upheaval in Maharashtra had strong social undercurrents which carried the seeds of the anti-caste campaigns that submerged the region in the nineteenth and twentieth centuries. Ranade was forthright in calling the Bhakti 'unbrahmanical' and 'heterodox' protest movement 'of the masses, and not of the classes' ([1900] 1961: 5). The 'occasional brahmans' like Gyaneshwar and Ekanath who joined the movement were shunned by their caste members. For instance, when Gyaneshwar, his brother and sister (the children of a brahman ascetic) returned to the mainstream, they were boycotted by the community. Earlier, their parents, who had scandalised the fellow brahmans by returning to lead a normal family life, had to expiate their 'sins' by giving up their lives—they were forced to drown themselves in a river. Similarly, Ekanath, who dared to feed the 'untouchables' at a community dinner, had to undergo a purificatory rite.

Even a conservative brahman sociologist like Ghurye concurs with the view that the brahman sants 'cannot be regarded as being wholly in a direct line of this movement. They still laid much emphasis on the philosophical aspect of religion' ([1932] 2000: 103). Their continued attachment to the varna-jati tradition, which Ghurye euphemistically calls 'philosophical aspect of religion', was due to their inability to come out of their caste cocoons. Ghurye, however, is candid in admitting that, 'Almost everywhere the Brahmans figured as opponents of the new movements which appeared to them to upset the good old Brahmanic way of salvation through proper rites and ceremonies and to undermine the system of caste' (ibid.: 104).

The task of cultural and social transformation in Maharashtra, as elsewhere, was left to the shudra sant-teachers who invented a new religio-political language to challenge the caste-based power structure. Religion at that time was shamelessly used by the caste elite to extract material benefits and free services. Like their counterparts in other regions, the prime target of the Varakaris was this pseudo-religion and its dogmas that had become a tool of the exploitative system.

The movement in Maharashtra produced three outstanding figures: Namdev, a *shimpi* or tailor by profession, who flourished in the first half of the fourteenth century; his contemporary Chokhamela who hailed from the 'untouchable' Mahar caste; and perhaps the greatest of them all, Tukaram (1608–50), who came from a kunbi caste. All three belonged to the Varakari school with its main deity Vitthal at Pandharpur. In the orthodox version, the cult of Vitthal as a young cowherd merges imperceptibly into the cult of brahmanised Krishna. Elite chroniclers conveniently seek its roots in orthodox Vaishnavism and portray the Varakari luminaries within the Vedic-brahmanic tradition. Underlining such brahmanic distortion, an important research points out:

> In modern times, a renewed enthusiasm of the literate, and especially of the Brahman elite, for the Varakari poet-saints, has accentuated the tendency to view the medieval literary tradition of Maharashtra as essentially orthodox and Vaishnava. Furthermore, books were written from this point of view in both Marathi and Hindi, comparing the sants of Maharashtra with their counterparts in northern India and Karnataka. This has led to considerable confusion and to erroneous interpretations, particularly concerning the northern sants, who cannot be said to fit into an orthodox Vaishnava pattern at all. (Vaudeville 1996: 246)

Vaudeville views the Maharashtrian bhakti centring around the Vitthal cult as 'nominal' Vaishnavism, and delineates its roots in Tantric form of Shaivinism inherited from the Nathpanthi tradition. In fact, the very icon of Vitthal was originally a Kannada deity, revered by the Lingayatas and Nathpanthis, with a close resemblance to the Shiva character which is suggested by the *Shiv-linga* as its headgear:

> The mysterious apparition of Vitthala on the bank of the Bhima river at Pandharpur did not, however, result in the immediate conversion of the population to Vaishnavism. Shiva remained the supreme deity—as attested to by the most ancient temple in Pandharpur, the Pundalik temple, now half submerged in the river bed. To this day, it remains a Shiva temple, in the hands of low-caste Koli fishermen. (Ibid.: 251)

The earliest texts written in Marathi, the *Vivekadarpana* and the *Gorakha-Gita*, belong to the Nath tradition which traces Gorakhanath's spiritual heritage to Adinath or Shiva. There is evidence, Vaudeville says, suggesting the strong presence of Nathpanthis in the region. While the pandits never mixed with the 'low' caste people, the Nathpanthis freely fraternised with them.

Contrary to the brahmanical myth, the founder of the Varakari lineage was Namdev, not Gyaneshwar. In one tradition Namdev is said to be the disciple of one Nagratha—a name that clearly suggests a connection with the Nathpanthi lineage. Others link Namdev with Visoba Khechara, whom the former is believed to have accepted as his guru. The name Khechara—literally 'one moving in the air'—too refers to a Siddha, an accomplished master endowed with supernatural powers. His first name, Visoba, derived from *visne*, literally to rest or lie at ease, again points to the spontaneity and ease which was the hallmark of the Sahajiya Buddhism and its related tradition of Nath-yogis (Vaudeville 1996: 252–3).

In the dominant historiography Namdev is portrayed as an orthodox Vaishnava sant living a life of traditional bhakti. However, an objective study of Namdev and other Varakaris leaves little doubt that they were creative and colourful characters endowed with a capacity for original thinking. Namdev, for example, asks that if milk given by cows of different colours is the same, how could the caste distinction between the allegedly 'high-born' and 'low-born' stand scrutiny.

Namdev the tailor sometimes weaves his professional pride into the texture of his exquisite devotional songs. Anguished by the rigid social distinctions, the devotee in him entreats God to intervene and destroy the brahman-shudra duality. He asks God that when the brahmans insult and beat up a true devotee like himself (Namdev), does it not amount to insulting God Himself?

When I entered the temple,
they all went mad after me:
Shouting 'Shudra! Shudra!' they beat me and threw me out:
what shall I do, O my Father Vitthala?
If you grant me salvation after death,
who will know about it?
When those Brahmans called me Dhedh,[4]
was it not a blow at your Honour?
You are known as the Merciful, the Compassionate One,
all-powerful is Your arm!
Then the temple itself turned round towards Nam
and turned its back on the Brahmans! (Vaudeville 1996: 341)

Namdev pleads to God to do something about this gross injustice here and now. He mocks the theory of transmigration: 'If you grant me salvation after death, who will know?' He demands justice in this life in full public view so that it can serve as a lesson to the anti-social elements. He is even able to convince God to 'take action' against the culprits: the temple representing 'the Compassionate One' moves closer to the true devotee, Nam, and turns it back on the hypocritical pandits! The radical spirit with which sant-poets envisioned God and religion achieves this poetic justice. In their hands religion becomes a weapon against injustice.

Namdev discarded the traditional religion and its rituals, contending that religion should better concern itself with the people's misery. He gave expression to the inner and worldly agonies in his poems that stress compassion and empathy with the oppressed. Later in his life, he became itinerant, and finally settled in the Punjab where he nurtured a radical stream of devotionalism. It was perhaps Namdev who devised the *kirtan*—congregational singing—outside the precincts of the temple complexes, the doors of which were closed to the lower classes. He attracted people wherever he went, and became an inspiration for many younger sant-poets in Maharashtra and northern India. Among his admirers were renowned sant-poets such as Janabai, Gora Kumbhar, Narhari Sonar, Joga Paramananda, Savata Mali, Banka Mahar, and Chokhamela.

Chokhamela is a striking figure in the Varakari lineage. He is to the Maharashtrian dalits what Ravidas is to the dalits of northern India. He composed lyrical poems of exquisite beauty in Marathi known as *abhangas*. His verses, like other Bhakti poetry, are both devotional and subversive. The harsh and inhuman conditions in which the untouchables were forced to live made Chokhamela question God's sense of justice:

Extremely bad food to one, very good to the other; one may not get food even after demanding and another gets pleasure and the grandeur of kingly title . . . is this your sense of justice? (See Sardar 1978: 123)

Chokha can get exasperated with his dear God because in the Varakari tradition Vitthala entertains a very special love for the poor and the lowly. It is a reciprocal love which makes the deity as much dependent on his devotees as they are on him. 'It is characteristic that in the legends related to the encounters between Vitthala and Chokhamela, it is always the god who takes the initiative' (Vaudeville 1996: 226). When Chokha is abused and turned out from the temple gate by the brahmans, and even his devotion from outside is regarded as a source of pollution, the deity plays tricks on the brahmans: making a mockery of their pretensions to 'purity', the god is delighted in the company of the 'polluting' Chokha. 'It is as though He actually resented being a prisoner in His own temple, bound by the endless pretentious rituals of the priests. It is as if God Himself were sowing the seeds of social rebellion in the hearts of the downtrodden' (ibid.)

Some scholars point to Chokha's compliance with the orthodoxy and his acquiescence in his lowly Mahar identity. They argue that save a feeble criticism of untouchability, his poems are marked by the traditional devotion and piety of the devotee. In support of their claim, they cite some verses (published in his name), the authenticity of which can be questioned. Such poems seem to be spurious, since many of them bear the names of later sants. An authentic voice does come through in some of his available poems, where Chokha makes his intentions clear. On being hounded by the temple priests, Chokha cries his heart out:

O Vithu! Now run to my help! Hurry up!
The Badves (priests) are beating me (saying):
'What crime have you committed?
That garland of Vithoba, how has it come to your neck?'
They abuse me, crying: 'The mahar has polluted God!' (Vaudeville 1996: 230–1)

On the question of purity and pollution, Chokha says, 'God alone is pure; no one else is pure, everyone is impure'. It is another way of saying: either everyone is pure, or everyone impure. Humiliated by his 'low' caste, Chokha even accuses God in a poem of being 'cruel' while 'casting me away to be born'. In another *abhanga,* he narrates the suffering that he has to endure everyday because of his caste:

O God! Vile is my birth,
How then could I serve You?
People shout at me: 'Get away, get away!'
How then could I meet You?
If they happen to touch my hand
They pour water on themselves!
O my Govind! O my Gopal!
Chokhamela cries for Your mercy! (Vaudeville 1996: 230)

And then, unable to control his anger against the brahmans who have made life hell for people like him, Chokha let out a torrent of curses:

Cursed be their actions, cursed be their thinking,
Cursed be their birth and their life!
Cursed be their 'Knowledge of the Absolute'—
tis all but vain talk—
There is neither pity nor forgiveness nor peace in their hearts!
Cursed be those postures and those hair knots of theirs –
In vain did they put on an ascetic garb!
Says Chokha, cursed be the birth of such people:
In the end they'll endure the torments of hell! (Vaudeville 1996: 232)

The Varakaris reached their peak of glory and popularity with Tuka in the seventeenth century. A legend in his own time, he was the brightest star in the Varakari firmament. Born in a grocer's family, he was a poetic genius with the power to penetrate the heart of material and spiritual life. His affinity with the commoners, his outrage against injustice, and his advocacy of radical inclusiveness made him a people's poet. The growing popularity of his rebellious thinking earned him the wrath of the powerful, as we shall see shortly.

Tuka believed in *satya asatyashi man kele gwahi*—'to decide as to the nature of truth and untruth, one should go by one's own experience and reflection'. The knowledge of the world thus acquired, he reasoned, is far superior to the one contained in scripture. In a stinging attack on the sacerdotal literature, he derided scripture-quoting pandits as 'beasts of burden'. Berating the 'highly educated idiots', he rejected the caste culture that surrounded him, and demanded action against the self-seeking orthodoxies:

Compassion means good feeling towards all living things,
And also the destruction of the evil-doers. (Nemade 1997: 49)

Tuka asserts that true religiosity is not represented by the temple paraphernalia but by service to humanity:

The light is lit within;
Tukaram says, I now remain only to serve others. (Ibid.: 46)

And,

He is the true saint who embraces the oppressed and unfortunate;
God is found with him. (Ibid.: 54)

Tuka's bold utterances against caste, especially defence of or adherence to caste in the name of religion, often attracted vitriolic comments from his brahman adversaries. He would respond by laughing at the pandit's 'Vedic parrotry', hypocrisy, pride and pomposity:

Well done, O God, you made me a Kunbi,
Otherwise I would have been doomed by hypocrisy.
. . .
Tuka says, you go on with your Vedic parrotry,
Don't come in my way.
Had I been learned, it would have brought calamities on me,
I would have been subjected to pride and arrogance,
I would have taken the path of hell . . . (Ibid.: 30)

While the Bhakti sants in other regions had embraced radical monotheism eschewing all forms of idolatry, the Varakaris adopted a middle way by honouring their only deity, Vitthala. All of them, however, had similar socio-religious agenda and their common target was the entrenched orthodoxy. For example, in response to the brahmanical humiliation of the shudras, Tuka retorted, 'It is only we, the shudra devotees, that know the real meaning of the Vedas, others only carry the load of it.' In another *abhanga*, he asserts bluntly, '. . . the learned brahmans will have to become servile to us' (ibid.: 36).

The injustice and misery that Tuka saw around him anguished him so much that he even threatened his God,

I shall spoil your good name
If you continue to be indifferent. (Ibid.: 44)

As God was not showing any interest in mitigating the human misery, he did not hesitate to write,

To me God is dead;
Let him be for those who think that he is. (Ibid.)

It was in such moments of despair and desolation that Tuka the devotee cried out

I am ashamed of calling myself your servant;
You are cruel and callous
You allow your children to cry with hunger. (Ibid.)

Cymbals in hand, singing his soul-stirring lyrics that celebrated equality, Tuka became a celebrity. While his adversaries were scratching their heads debating 'can a shudra's mind perceive knowledge? can he be a spiritual leader?', people from far and near flocked to hear Tuka. Adding insult to the injured pride of the pandits were some brahmans, including women, who would attend Tuka's group singing, defying the caste injunction. One such follower was Bahinabai, a talented poet, who invited the wrath of the conservative brahmans. This is recorded in her autobiography in which she confirms stories regarding the brahmanic persecution of Tuka (Nemade 1997: 28–33).

The brahmans held Tuka guilty of many offences including belittling the value of Sanskrit learning. Their earnings were dwindling. An influential leader Mambaji, Bahinabai writes, convinced the Pune brahmans of Tuka's culpability and launched a witch-hunt against the shudra poet. The Patil of Tuka's village was persuaded to file a suit and take punitive action. The 'culprit' was thrashed, his cow was beaten to death (a shudra's cow is not that holy!), he was excommunicated, and his writings confiscated. A collection of his songs was thrown into the river.

Why were the pandits so intent on destroying Tuka's verses? The answer can be found in Tuka's own words:

We possess the wealth of words,
With weapons of words we will fight;
Words are the breath of our life,
We will distribute the wealth of words among the people. (Ibid.: 59)

All that the poet could say in his defence was that he was ordered by God to compose his songs. He continued to compose verses. The end of his life is shrouded in mystery. After being forced to throw his writings into the river in around 1645, he went into a prolonged silence and meditation, refusing food. After thirteen days of fasting, the legend goes, his papers floated up on the water. (This 'incident' is even corroborated by several of his contemporaries.) The news of the miracle spread and Tuka's followers celebrated it as their glorious triumph over their tormentors.

By all accounts, this miraculous incident seems to be a ruse to avert any popular protest against Tuka's persecution. It does not seem unlikely that the people had actually come forward to rescue their beloved poet who was being tortured. People's resistance may have forced the pandits to lift the ban on Tuka's writings. The 'miracle' might have been invented as a compromise by the chroniclers to obfuscate the bitter brahman–shudra antagonism which gave birth to this crisis in the first place.

To sum up, the Varakaris, unlike the brahman gurus, never denounced *sansar* or the worldly existence as *maya* or illusion. Tuka said, 'That the world is *maya* is a half-truth' (Nemade 1997: 12). None of the Varakaris were enamoured of renunciation and asceticism. The begging-bowl was shameful. Gora Kumbhar, Narhari Sonar, Savata Mali, and Sona Nhavi—all prominent Varakaris—led a family life and carried on their household duties. They brought about a reconciliation of worldly and spiritual life, an outstanding feature of the movement. They were confident that with the inculcation of just values and attitude, they would commit the world to happiness. They also tried to bring in the Muslims within its fold on an equal footing. With this and similar efforts caste distinctions slackened and a consciousness for human rights and dignity arose.

The Varakaris also made a major contribution to Marathi language and literature. In an initiative of far-reaching consequences, they adopted Marathi as the medium of literary and religious activity. Since their literature carried a direct appeal to the people, they consciously broke away from the Sanskritised tradition of Marathi by using colloquial idioms. They sidelined Sanskrit by producing high-quality literature in the mother-tongue. Challenging those who paraded the divinity of Sanskrit by calling it *devabhasha*, they asked if Sanskrit was the language of the gods, was Prakrit or Marathi the contribution of thieves and lowly elements?

What was the role of the occasional brahmans who joined the

movement? They found it difficult to reject caste and the scriptures that sanctified it. At the best, they made some noble noises, but within the shastric parameters. For all their greatness, Gyaneshwar and Ekanath insisted that every person must follow their caste role prescribed in the 'holy scriptures'. Gyaneshwar preached that anyone interested in making his life meaningful was duty-bound to accept the guidelines outlined in the shruti-smriti, and must discard the things condemned by the shastras (Sardar 1978). He went to the extent of suggesting that even if a brahman were to go hungry he should not eat the delicacies of a shudra. This author of *Gyaneshwari*, the popular Marathi rendition of the *Gita*, was even against speaking with the untouchables! Ekanath, relatively more liberal, also insisted on the observance of caste restrictions concerning eating and drinking. Ramdas, the brahman religious icon of the seventeenth century, was more forthright: 'Can we expect the low-born to be our guru because he is learned?' he asked.

Social Dimension of Bhakti and the Brahmanic Backlash

The defining feature of the Bhakti movement was a subversive religiosity, intimately bound up with a campaign for socio-cultural change. The transformatory zeal was at the heart of the movement. Its subaltern leaders wielded religiosity as a weapon against caste and brahmanism. The language of the protest in a vocabulary which the common people could understand was especially imperative in an era marked by the absence of modern-secular ideas and institutions. In other words, the religiosity the sant-poets employed was a decoy as it covered the whole gamut of culture.

The movement gave the much-maligned lowered castes a positive self-image as it rejected the idea of inferior status by birth. Implicit in its vision was the recognition that the people who worked hard to eke out their living were better, not worse, than the parasites—priests and princes. A society which does not accord dignity to the productive majority, its leaders emphasised in one way or another, does so at its peril. Challenging the tenets of caste-feudalism in a caste-feudal age, they demanded dignity for everyone and contended that though the world was afflicted by poverty, ignorance, and sorrow, these could be overcome by productive work and a virtuous life. This was in sharp contrast to the parasitism encouraged by leaders such as Tulsidas who did not do any physical work, as did Kabir (weaving) and Ravidas (tanning), in the smug belief that chanting mantras was the panacea for all the ills besetting the individual and society.

It seems that many flag-bearers of the institutionalised brahmanic religion joined the movement to sabotage from within the liberation struggle of the sant-poets. It is striking that against the monotheistic radicalism of *nirguna* bhakti, poet-devotees belonging to privileged castes—Chaitanya, Surdas, Vidyapati, Vallabhacharya, and Tulsidas—professed *saguna* bhakti. While the first four were besotted with their flute-playing Krishna, his *lila* (playfulness) and dalliance with damsels, Tulsi made Rama—the upholder par excellence of Varnashrama Dharma—his hero. They also celebrated love, harmony, and morality but within the hierarchical structure of Varnashrama. Anusooya's teachings to Sita in Tulsi's *Ramacharitamanasa* leaves little doubt that greater than truth, compassion, and love was adherence to socially imposed ascriptive duties. In the same 'holy book' Tulsi writes, '*Dhol ganwar shudra pashu nari/ye sab taadan ke adhikari*' (The drum, the illiterate, the lower caste, animals and women must be beaten to keep them fit). In other words, against the attempted subversion of the brahmanical order by *nirguna* stalwarts such as Kabir, Ravidas, Dadu and Nanak, the proponents of *saguna* school tried to establish the infallibility of the shastras and prescribed adherence to the caste code of conduct as necessary for good life. To them, caste was essential for social stability. Salvation was to be sought within the confines of the varna dharma. The striking absence of any significant poet-thinker from the subaltern categories within the *saguna* devotionalism is not surprising.

The brahmanical choice of *saguna* over *nirguna* was loaded with significance. *Saguna* bhakti implied worship of gods and their *avatars* whose mythology was the brain-child of the pandits, and confined in the Itihasa-Purana and Sanskritised versions of the *Ramayana* and *Mahabharata*. *Devas*, their *avatars* and *lilas* (which cunningly yet playfully explained away social divisions—disenfranchising shudras and women from education and power) was, in all likelihood, deliberate and premeditated. On the other hand, the *nirguna* preference for a formless divinity was ranged against this.

The conflict between *saguna* and *nirguna* represents unresolved strife between the caste elite and the subaltern multitude. Not for nothing in the *Uttarakanda* of *Ramacharitamanasa*, Tulsi, arguably the greatest proponent of *saguna* school, beats his breast bemoaning the emergence of shudra religious preachers as the unmistakable sign of degradation in the *Kaliyuga*. Appalled at what the shudras taught, Tulsi wrote with a vengeance against the shudra teachers.

Je baranadham teli kumhara/ Swapach kirat kol kalwara
Nari mui grihsampati nasi/ Mur murai hohin sannyasi.

(People of the lowest castes according to the varna-dharma—oilmen, potters, dog-eaters, Kirats, Kols, distillers—shave their heads and turn religious mendicants when their wives die or they lose their household goods.) [Tr. Prasad 1990: 634]

These are indirect references to lowered-caste poets like Kabir, Ravidas, and their followers. Tulsi curses the *Kaliyuga*, in which the shudras consider themselves as learned as brahmans, enter into disputations with them, and dare to give discourses on religion and society:

Sudra dvijanha upadesahin gyana
(Shudras instruct the brahmans in religious wisdom).

Badhin sudra dvijanha san ham tumh tei kachhu ghati
(Shudras dispute with brahmans, 'Are we inferior to you?')

And,

Te bipranh san aapu pujavahin/ ubhay lok nij haath nasawahin...
Sudra karahin jap tap brata nana/ Baithi barasan kahahin purana
Sab nar kalpit karhin achara/ Jai na barani aniti apara.

(The low-caste preachers allow themselves to be worshipped by the brahmans and ruin themselves in this world and the next. Shudras indulge in all sorts of prayers and penances and vows and expound the Puranas from an exalted seat. Everybody follows a course of conduct of his own imagination, and the endless perversions of morality are beyond all description.) [Ibid.: 634–5]

Tulsi's Rama is not Kabir's *nirguna* Rama but an incarnation of God, born the son of a king to maintain a kingdom of varna righteousness and brahmanical supremacy. The Sanskrit *Ramayana* of Valmiki, too, is full of caste chauvinism; this, Tulsi reworked to invigorate brahmanism and caste. The story of Shambuka, a shudra aspirant to spiritual power, narrated in the *Uttarakanda* of Tulsi's *Ramayana* is a typical example of the brahmanical attempt to institutionalise caste ideology. Shambuka, the story goes, was practising religious austerities and that resulted in the death of a brahman's son! The bereaved father reported the news to Rama, and Rama through meditation came to the conclusion that the brahman's son had died because Shambuka the shudra was practising meditation in violation of his caste duty. Rama tracked him down and killed him, and the gods showered flowers. The dead brahman boy was resurrected.

This story shows that its author had lost all sense of moral and social propriety in his eagerness to justify brahmanical self-interest. Such an unjust and barbarous act—committed by no less a person than Rama who is *Maryada Purushottam* (the embodiment of Man Supreme)—and its glorification was not surprising when education was monopolised by a particular caste which used it to keep the multitude in servitude. (Valmiki's Rama is even made to pronounce in the *Ayodhyakanda* that [the anti-caste] Buddha was a thief and that those who accept his teachings and do not believe in the deities, should be punished.) Rama is presented as an arch enemy of shudras and a blind defender of aggressive patriarchy. He forces his wife Sita to undergo a fire-ordeal to prove her chastity; later, the pregnant Sita is banished to a jungle to fend for herself.

Why did Tulsi retell the Rama story? Among other reasons, a caste chauvinist like Tulsi could not have got a more popular story and its legendary hero to propagate brahmanism. Following Manu, he sums up his objective in these words, 'Though a brahman curse you, beat you or speak cruel words—he should be worshipped, so sing the sants'. Tulsi put these words in Rama's mouth. He goes on to recommend:

Pujiye bipra sil guna hina sudra na gun-gyan pravina.

(A brahmin must be revered though he be devoid of amiability and virtue; not so a shudra, however distinguished for all virtue and learning.) [Tr. Prasad 1990: 414]

Tulsi's diatribe against shudras seems to be a brahmanic rebuff to Ravidas' rational exhortation (at about the same time when Tulsi was glorifying caste),

Brahman mat pujiye, jau howe gun-hin
Pujahin charan chandala ke, jau-howe gun-pravin.

(Don't honour a brahman who is without merit; honour instead the feet of a chandala who is virtuous and talented.)

Moreover, Tulsi spews venom against women in a foul language. Lamenting the decadence of women in the Kali age, he writes in the *Uttarakanda:*

Women have no ornament except their tresses and have enormous [sexual] appetite (are never satisfied). Though miserable for want of money, they are rich in attachment of various kinds. Though hankering after happiness, they have no regard for piety, stupid as they are. Though they are poor in wits, their minds are hardened and know no tenderness. (Ibid.: 636)

As a self-appointed guardian of the reactionary pandit community, Tulsi was, apparently, rattled by the unprecedented emergence of cultural leaders from below. They had started thinking for themselves. Tulsi's own town—Banaras—was reverberating with Kabir and Ravidas' seditious teachings, openly mocking brahmanism. By announcing *sadho, utthi gyan ki aandhi,* Kabir had triumphantly confirmed the storm (movement) of knowledge blowing across everywhere.

Summarising, the subaltern cultural leaders had surged forward to challenge the established religious and social order. (In hindsight, it seems that the presence of Muslim rule provided some fillip to the movement in the sense that the new rulers were not very enthusiastic about supporting the caste elite as the earlier Hindu kings had done.) Though weakened, the brahmanic forces retaliated, intruded the movement, and invoked the legendary king of Ayodhya. A morally questionable work like the *Ramacharitamanasa* extolling the virtues of caste and brahmanism was glorified, and transformed into a vehicle for the reimposition of caste-feudal values. No wonder Tulsi was the last major poet of the bhakti movement in the north. His celebration of brahmanism marked the end of the movement. The people's movement that started off as a protest against caste and injustice was ultimately appropriated by the caste champions who smothered its humanist spirit and subverted its egalitarian agenda.

Notes

1. According to the brahmanical propaganda, Kabir was so desperate to become a follower of Ramananda that he resorted to a cheap trick. He stretched himself across the stairs leading to the river Ganga (in Banaras) where Ramananda came for his bath in the pre-dawn darkness. As expected, Ramananda tripped over him and cried out his mantra 'Rama! Rama!' Kabir then claimed that the magical mantra had been transmitted to him, tricking the reluctant Ramananda into accepting him as a disciple.
2. Kabir, referring here to the *Purusha-sukta* of the *Rigveda,* jeers: Why do you, O! brahman, who believe in the infallibility of the Vedas, come into this world as a shudra does?
3. Phule and Ambedkar, two campaigners against caste and brahmanism in modern India, came from the Kabirpanthi background. Phule and his friends were great admirers of Kabir's poetry, which sparked the founding of the Satyashodhak Samaj (see Chapter 5). Ambedkar's parents were Kabirpanthis, and, as is well known, Ambedkar himself chose Kabir as one of his gurus. Both Phule and Ambedkar had recognised the radicalism of the Bhakti movement. Ambedkar's *Untouchables* is dedicated to Nandnar, Ravidas, and Chokhamela.
4. Dhedh is the name of an untouchable caste in Maharashtra. The word *dhedh,* like the names of all untouchable castes, is an insult—here thrown at Namdev by the brahmans.

CHAPTER 4

Colonialism and the Birth of Vedic–Brahmanic Nationalism

> The national bourgeoisie of underdeveloped countries is not engaged in production, nor in invention, nor in building, nor labour; it is completely canalised into activities of the intermediary type. Its innermost vocation seems to be to keep in the running and to be part of the [colonial] racket.
>
> FRANTZ FANON 1963: 150

The rotten state of the caste-feudal leadership of Indian society was thoroughly exposed when the East India Company gradually conquered and colonised the subcontinent, from the second half of the eighteenth century on the ruins of the Mughal empire. The feudal princes, with an exception of a Tipu here or there, were too self-indulgent and myopic to ward off the external attack. Many of them conspired against one another, colluded with the British for selfish gains, and thus helped establish the colonial rule. A backward, oppressed, impoverished, and caste-divided populace—conditioned to bear all sorts of indignities—was in no position to react to the foreign conquest of their country.[1] The caste-feudal order had for centuries been the scourge of India, responsible for social fragmentation, economic decline, cultural stagnation, and an insular outlook resulting in the neglect of science and technology. All these factors combined to facilitate the British conquest. Starting their winning streak from Plassey (1757) and Buxar (1764), the British forces in the span of a few decades established their raj throughout the subcontinent with the crucial support from many native rulers, both Hindu and Muslim. It is axiomatic that no external power can establish an enduring rule over a conquered people except with the latter's tacit toleration or active support, and the colonial conquest of India was no exception to this.[2]

The British lost no time in recognising and reciprocating friendly overtures from the Indian ruling classes. The rajas and nawabs who accepted British suzerainty were left untouched and the upper-caste gentry were rewarded with positions in the colonial dispensation, especially in the revenue administration, as born-again zamindars and rent-collectors. Striking a deal with the native elites as they were struggling to establish colonial rule, the British adopted a policy of no interference in the internal social and religious matters. The British, however, for diverse reasons, resented the Muslims and preferred and promoted the Hindu elites, giving them the status of 'natural leaders' of the majority community. Towards Muslims, there was always an undercurrent of European hostility, which went back to the days of Crusades. Historical evidence and new researches suggest that within the colonial discourse 'India' meant 'Hindu'.[3] And the colonial construction of Hinduism, as we shall see shortly, was not realistic but textual, confined within the brahmanical scriptures. Steeped in their own scripture-based religion, the British equated the shastras with Hinduism, and presumed that the shastras had a universal following among diverse Indian communities and tribes. The British patronage began to play an important role in engendering a new Hinduism from 1791 onwards when the Banaras Sanskrit College was founded. Jonathan Duncan, the British Resident at Banaras, specified its objective (in a letter to Governor-General Cornwallis) thus:

Having in view to the surplus Revenue expected to be derived from the permanent settlement . . . it appeared to me that a part of those funds could not be applied to more general advantage or with more local propriety than by the Institution of a Hindoo College or Academy for the preservation and cultivation of the Laws, Literature and Religion of this nation at this centre of their faith, and the common resort of all their tribes. (See Dalmia 2003: 32).

With this and similar moves, the British began to discover Hinduism under the tutelage of the pandits, and resurrected Manu as the 'parent of Hindoo jurisprudence'. The *Manusmriti* was flaunted—

and foisted on all 'Hindus'—as a 'system of duties, religious and civil, and of law, in all its branches, which the Hindoos firmly believe to have been promulgated in the beginning of time by Manu . . . a system so comprehensive and so minutely exact, that it may be considered as the institutes of Hindoo law' (William Jones, see L. Mani 1989: 111).

The British did not want to understand—and there was none to tell them—that the sacerdotal literature in Sanskrit represented only the brahmanical worldview. It appears that the brahmanic denigration of the masses appealed to the British as it was in keeping with their own colonial design and racist ideology. The colonialists, as Kosambi ([1962] 2000: 45) observes, 'wanted as far as possible to yield to brahmanism, as it was always a convenient tool for subjection of the natives'. Anyway, they could hardly afford to alienate the dominant native classes whose support was so vital for their survival in India. The discovery of a common Indo-European heritage with the concomitant Aryan race theory, at the very beginning of colonial rule, provided the British with a powerful vehicle to reach out to the Hindu elite. The liberals in the British regime who wanted to tinker with the brahmanic laws and practices were allowed to do so in only a few cases.

Orientalism, Aryan Race Theory, and Neo-Hinduism

Warren Hastings (1732–1818), the Company's first Governor-General who laid the foundations of British administration in India, took the momentous decision to rule India in accordance with local traditions. He enjoined that in all suits regarding inheritance, marriage, caste and other social and religious matters, the laws of shastras with respect to Hindus and those of the Koran with respect to Muslims would be strictly adhered to. Hastings also made it clear that these laws would be expounded and interpreted by the brahmans and *maulvis* for their respective communities (Kejariwal 1988: 23). As the traditional rules for Hindus, dictated by priestly-feudal whims, were often vague, contradictory, and varying from region to region, the British decided to find out exactly what these traditions were. Hence the collection and codification of traditional laws and practices.

The British ignored the existence of other Indian traditions because the brahmanical framework better suited their interests. Reviving and privileging the *Manusmriti* over other systems, both within the so-called Hinduism in the forms of non-brahman and tribal practices as well as the schools of Buddhism and Jainism and those of Islam and Sikhism, were a clear evidence of colonial patronage to the brahmanical tradition.

Nathaniel Halhed, with guidance from a group of pandits, edited Manu's laws as *A Code of Gentoo Laws: Ordination of the Pundits* in 1776. The preface to the Code states that commerce with India and the 'advantages of a territorial establishment in Bengal could be maintained only by an adoption of such original institutes of the country as do not intimately clash with the laws and interests of the conquerors' (see R.S. Sharma 1983: 3). Halhed went on to translate several Sanskrit texts such as the *Bhagavat Purana* and *Shiva Purana* into English. Soon after, an institutional endeavour to discover Indian culture and religion was made with the establishment of the Asiatic Society of Bengal in 1784 under the leadership of William Jones (1746–94). Indological studies got a further boost with the establishment of the Bombay Asiatic Society in 1804 and the Asiatic Society of Great Britain in 1823.

Hastings' academic protèges—William Jones, Charles Wilkins, H.T. Colebrooke, and James Prinsep—learnt Sanskrit and things 'Indian' from the brahman literati, and engaged in research on India, mainly through the ancient Sanskrit texts. Wilkins published a Sanskrit grammar in 1779, and rendered the *Bhagavad Gita* into English in 1785. This was the first published translation of any major Sanskrit work into a European language. Jones, a gifted linguist, soon established himself as a renowned Sanskritist and translated the *Manusmriti* and Kalidasa's *Abhijnan-Shakuntalam* into English. These were subsequently rendered into several European languages. With the publication of his three essays 'On the Hindus', 'On the Gods of Greece, Italy and India', and 'On the Chronology of Hindus' in *Asiatic Researches* (the journal of the Asiatic Society), Jones came to be regarded as an authority on Indian religion, and nicknamed 'Oriental Jones' and a 'brahmanised Briton'. Above all, Jones essayed a seminal paper *On the Origin and Families of Nations*, based on the then state of research, which brought out several features showing the striking similarity between Sanskrit, Latin, and Greek. This work is considered the starting point of 'comparative philology' and the consequent debate on the Indo-European family of languages and the migration of peoples. As comparative philology indicated a relationship between Sanskrit and the European languages, there came into currency the 'Aryan theory of race', through which the Orientalists in India and Europe asserted an ethnic kinship between the Europeans and Indian Aryans.

The affinity between Sanskrit and European languages fired the imagination of many scholars in Europe who popularised the idea of a common Indo-European homeland and heritage. The upper-caste Aryans in India came to be regarded as the lost brothers of the white Europeans. A distinction was drawn between the master race, the high-caste Aryans, and their subjects—lower-caste non-Aryans and Dravidians. The caste elites in India lapped-up and wielded this to assert their cultural superiority and antiquity of everything brahmanic. The race theory gave them an identity with the colonial rulers. Proclaiming their blood relationship with the British rulers, Keshab Chandra Sen, for example, declared at a public lecture in Calcutta in 1877, '[I]n the advent of the English nation in India we see a reunion of parted cousins, the descendants of two different families of the ancient Aryan race ' (see Hay 1988: 48). The appeal of this theory was wide and enduring. When Gandhi was working as a lawyer in South Africa, he addressed an open letter (1894) to the members of the legislature protesting against the ill-treatment of Indians, and demanded equality on the grounds of common race. Since the British and the Indians were from the same Aryan stock, Gandhi reasoned, how could the Britishers rule over their own blood brothers? It was unfair for one set of Aryans to rule over another set, he argued and then went on to describe, quoting copiously from European scholars, the accomplishments of the brahmans in various fields (Gandhi 1979: 176).

The passionate interest of European scholars such as H.H. Wilson, C. Lassen, H.T. Colebrooke, Monier-Williams, and above all,

Max Müller, in the ancient Aryan culture and Sanskrit texts gave birth to the legend of 'the wonder that was India'. They drew an idyllic picture of the Aryan Hindu civilisation and went on to create a romantic image of Indian spirituality, cultural opulence, Vedic-Upanishadic splendour, and epic heroism. The role of Monier-Williams (1819–99) is particularly important in creating the casteist-racist myth about India, Sanskrit and Hinduism, which consequently formed the ideological nucleus of brahmanic-Hindu credo that was later reinforced in the brahmanic idioms by various votaries of cultural nationalism ranging from Dayananda Saraswati to M.S. Golwalkar. In his *Hinduism and Its Sources*, Monier-Williams asserted that with the composition of Vedas Hinduism came into existence, overcoming enormous racial and social diversities, and evolved ever since then as an all-tolerant, all-assimilative, all-comprehensive religion, and what held all these together was Sanskrit and its literature. Monier-Williams, who also composed a famous Sanskrit-English Dictionary, did not have time for literatures in Prakrit and other Indian languages.

Expectedly, the glorification of their ancestors was well received by privileged-caste Indians. They found the Aryan connection especially flattering since it vindicated their 'innate' superiority over the 'lowly shudra masses' and the 'alien Muslims'. The European Orientalists and the Indian pandits saw Indian civilisation as derivative from Aryan civilisation, and the caste system was applauded as a means by which people of diverse racial and cultural backgrounds were brought together and subjected to the 'civilising' influence of the Aryans. The overall tendency of privileged-caste historians has been to uphold such racist-casteist thinking of their nineteenth-century ancestors by arguing that the 'Indians' (by which they mean the caste elites) lacked 'cultural self-confidence' during colonialism.

The belief that the white masters were not very distant cousins of their brown Aryan subjects provided a much-needed salve to the wounded ego of the dependent elite. A spate of Aryanism was unleashed. The word 'Aryan' began to feature in likely as well as unlikely places from titles of periodicals to the names of street corner shops. (Raychaudhury 1988: 8)

Colonialism and the Birth of Vedic–Brahmanic Nationalism 195

Such was the hold of the Aryan theory among the upper-caste nationalists that a scholar like R.K. Mookerji—Gandhi's favourite historian—could write as late as 1956: 'The history of India is mainly that of the Aryans of India. Its source is the *Rigveda* which is the earliest book not merely of Indians but of the entire Aryan race' (1956: 48).

In fact, the caste elites received the Oriental knowledge and Aryan race theory in a manner which can only be called racist. This, however, was in sync with the ancient racism of their ancestors, as Nirad Chaudhuri underlines with brutal frankness.

In ancient times what might be called Hindu nationalism retrospectively was based on their belief that they were 'Aryas', and as such not only different from other peoples and communities, but also superior. Anyone who is at all familiar with Sanskrit literature cannot be unaware of this, cannot remain ignorant of what the notion of being Arya meant to the Hindu of ancient times. (Chaudhuri 1974: 315–6)

Reading selective passages from the Vedic-Upanshadic texts, the Orientalists—said to be unhappy with the changes taking place in their own society in the wake of democratisation and modernisation—found an India that was the other-worldly country of esoteric philosophers, given to metaphysical speculation and a disdain for their mundane existence. In their eyes, the ancient Indians were not 'active, combative or acquisitive' but 'passive, meditative and reflective' (Max Müller [1882] 2000). However, for the Orientalists, 'the exotic East' was first and foremost a 'career' (as Benjamin Disraeli put it), and the special enthusiasm for India and the study of Sanskrit an academic as well as a racist-imperialist venture to retrieve a lost wing of the early European culture. In a set of lectures delivered in 1882 at the University of Cambridge to candidates of the Indian Civil Service—later published as *India: What Can It Teach Us?*—Max Müller, who held professorial positions at Oxford and got generous research grants from the empire, wanted the future colonial rulers of India to know

[O]ur nearest intellectual relatives, the Aryans of India, the framers of the most wonderful language, the Sanskrit, the fellow workers in the construction of our fundamental concepts, the fathers of the most natural of natural religions, the makers of the most transparent of mythologies, the inventors of the most subtle philosophy, and the givers of the most elaborate laws. ([1882] 2000: 14)

The 'Us' in the title 'What Can It [India] Teach Us', as Max Müller makes clear, is 'We sturdy Northern Aryans'. Thus, when he refers to Indians he takes into account only his racial brothers, 'not Gonds, or Bhils, or Santhals, and other non-Aryan tribes. I am speaking of the Aryan and more or less civilised inhabitants of India' (p. 46). He also debars Muslims from his notion of genuine Indians. Underlining the terrible 'atrocities committed by Mohemmadan conquerors of India' till 'England stepped in', he wonders 'how any nation could have survived such an Inferno, without being turned into devils themselves'. To him, it was the Muslims who were the ultimate cause of decadence and degeneration of India (p. 66).

Establishing his kinship with the Aryan Indians, Max Müller, who never visited India and 'politely disclaimed all interest in doing so' (Dalmia 2003: XI), took the Sanskritic name Moksha Mula. But it was not a case of unrequited romance. Vivekananda, the knight-errant of neo-Hinduism, was so besotted with Moksha Mula's championing of 'Indian spirituality' that he revered Max Müller as the incarnation of Sayana, the fourteenth-century commentator on the *Rigveda*.[4]

An impressive scholarship from the Euro-American universities as well as some academic institutes in the erstwhile colonies has established Orientalism as the dominant ideology with which the West ruled the East. Such scholarship ignores the role of indigenous elites who colluded in constructing the colonial ideology. In his acclaimed study of Orientalism and the values and motives underpinning it, Edward Said writes:

Taking the late eighteenth century as a very roughly defined starting point Orientalism can be discussed and analysed as the corporate institution for dealing with the Orient—dealing with it by making statements about it, authorising views of it, describing it, by teaching it, setting it, ruling over it: in short, Orientalism as a Western style for dominating, restructuring and having authority over the Orient. (Said 1978: 3)

This hard-hitting critique may be true in the case of Islamic world where Orientalism had become confrontationist. But in the case of India, Orientalism was seductive and collusive as it took the form of Indo-Europeanism. In the context of India, Said's brilliant polemic overlooks the nefarious role played by the native privileged groups. His theory does not take into account the complicity and culpability of caste elites who played a vital role in the making of the Oriental stereotype of Indian culture. The Aryan race theory, a key construct of Orientalism, for example, had found an effusive support among the upper-caste gentry for reasons given above. Even the greatest of nationalists—Gandhi and Nehru, as we saw in the Introduction—discovered their India, contrary to the popular myth, in the Orientalist terms. Nationalist thought in India was not merely a bundle of contradictions, as Partha Chatterjee (1986) argues but also cast in the mirror image of Orientalism. The nationalist thought, he concludes, did not respond adequately to the national question. The problem was much deeper—and more fundamental—than the brahmanic theoretician would admit.

Following the ideological framework of Said's *Orientalism*, Ronald Inden's *Imagining India* (1990) theorises the colonial construction of India—as a civilisation of caste, villages, and autocratic kings—as 'imaginary', while remaining blind to the massive injustices in pre-modern India as well as the complicity of the brahman literati whose information, interpretation, and translation of Sanskrit and other native works, became instrumental in the Oriental knowledge-construction. Even more distorted—and influential—is Nicholas Dirks' *Castes of Mind*, in which he sees caste as a modern phenomenon, almost invented by the British:

Caste (as we know it today) is a modern phenomenon, that is, specifically, the product of an historical encounter between India and Western colonial rule. By this I do not mean to imply that it was simply invented by the too clever British . . . But . . . it was under the British that 'caste' became a single term capable of expressing, organising, and above all 'systematising' India's diverse forms of social identity, community, and organisation. . . . In short, colonialism made caste what it is today . . . making caste the central symbol of Indian society. (Dirks 2002: 5)

The point is, even if colonialism transformed caste by giving it a greater institutional prominence, as stressed by Dirks, Inden, and their privileged-caste applauders, caste had to be there in some form or other to be transformed, as A. Ahmad (1992) and S. Sarkar (1996; 1997) have argued. Graded hierarchy of caste was not a construction of the colonialists; it had its pre-colonial forms; it was not simply one among many forms of identity, it was the basis of social identity. Caste had percolated every core of social and political life in India when the British established their rule. Of course, colonialism, itself built on the convergence of interests of the Indian and British elites, reinforced caste. But the process of redefining, updating, and reconstructing caste was not just a Western project; the Indian elites were active and willing collaborators in this.

The Oriental scholarship which produced the images of Aryan glory, Vedic purity and Muslim tyranny was in fact a joint and mutually beneficial project of the foreign and indigenous elites, 'with equal though different investment in such images' (Ahmad 2002: 84). Max Müller, who researched at Oxford and popularised the term Aryan, was funded by the East India Company. Let us see what he wrote about Rammohun Roy's visit to England in 1832:

For the sake of comparing notes, so to say, with his Aryan brothers, Rammohun Roy was the first who came from East to West . . . making us feel once more that ancient brotherhood which unites the whole Aryan race, inspiring us . . . and invigorating us for acts of nobler daring in the conquest of truth than any that are inscribed in the chronicles of our divided past. (Max Müller, see Kochhar 2000: 9)

Robertson (1999: 55–73) has demonstrated that Colebrook and Wilson's view of Vedanta, which eventually became identical with the standard Orientalist discourse on Indian philosophy, was heavily based on Roy's writing on the subject. Similarly, the writings of Halhed, Holwell, Wilkins and Jones provided material for Priestley's comparison of the laws of Moses and Manu. The resurrection of Manu as the Hindu law-giver was a joint endeavour of Western and Indian pandits. As Sumit Sarkar has argued, 'Colonial knowledge was not just a Western superimposition: such an interpretation gravely underestimates the extent and significance of inputs from relatively privileged Indian groups with autonomous interests and inclinations' (1997: 23).

The majority of Indians certainly suffered from colonialism, but there were also those who benefited. The alien rulers and local influential elites had worked closely together to construct Orientalism—and colonialism itself—in mutual self-interest. The colonial dispensation not only benefited the British, but also empowered and enriched their native hosts who saw colonialism as a providential fortune. Rammohun Roy frankly admitted it in the 1810s. As late as the 1890s Vivekananda (1991: 83) was saying, 'Their foreign rulers struck off their [Hindus'] fetters without knowing it.' Of course, some British scholars or administrators were compelled by the colonialist logic to mock the theories of the 'great Hindu India' or 'unparalleled national greatness of India's past', especially in the face of emerging chauvinistic nationalism. But it was the European Indologists who first invented the myth of the golden Hindu past, which was re-echoed and relayed with gusto in the works of Indian pandits.

Like the pandits, the colonial masters' intellectual preoccupation was with the Vedic-brahmanic culture and literature. While recasting the Indian past, they did not bother to correlate shastras with Buddhist and shramanic texts, or with archaeology. There was no effort whatsoever to juxtapose the sacerdotal texts with the vastly different social and cultural reality as encapsulated in alternative cultural and material sources. The fact that the Orientalist construction of ancient India was ahistorical, or at the best semi-historical, is now commonly accepted. What remains concealed in the dominant scholarship is the fact that it was the same Orientalist misrepresentation of India that was cunningly employed to 'rediscover' the greatness of brahmanic tradition by the Indian elites, including Gandhi and Nehru, in the name of nationalism.

In the process of colonial reconstruction of India's past, a new type of Hinduism, erected on the edifice of brahmanical texts and interpretations, and nurtured by colonial policy, came into existence, glimpses of which we saw in the Introduction. The pandits have always tried to monopolise knowledge and manipulate information, and seldom hesitated to sell false knowledge to promote their ideological and material interests. It was they who had provided selective information to the British on indigenous tradition and institutions, on an unprecedented scale, at an all-India level, particularly in the presidential cities of Calcutta, Bombay and Madras. This gradually generated the consciousness and dynamics for a new Hindu religion 'the likes of which India had perhaps never known before' (Frykenberg 2001). British officials became puppets in the hands of the native dominant-caste officials, secretaries, *munshis*, and *vakils*, who worked with them everyday and heavily influenced their decisions and policies:

> The hosts handled most of the paper work. They had done this before, for previous rulers. Now they did this again and did this in such a way that the rulers themselves became instruments of local and indigenous influences. Local officials, either Brahmans or Non-Brahmans who were of 'high' varna and ritually 'clean' by local standards, exercised a crucial, if not determining, role. In course of time, these very ingredients of the state rulership, both European and Native, served to bring modern Hinduism into being. (Frykenberg 2001: 89)

'Hindus' as the 'majority community' in contradistinction to the minority Muslims was created in the colonial period. The new Hinduism came about through the simultaneous interplay of various factors at work both within and outside the colonial power structure. Within the political structure of the colonial state, the process of the making of Hinduism was facilitated by the information put in by the caste elites. Outside it, reform movements emerged which were primarily aimed at the self-strengthening of the elite rather than uplift of the entire society. What this complex process—at once social and political, cultural and religious—led to was, the movement from 'Hindu' to 'Hinduism'—or, 'syndicated Hinduism', as Romila Thapar (2001) terms it. The emergent Hinduism was primarily brahmanic, ornamented at times with invocation of Buddhist-shramanic humanism, or bits and pieces of Islamic egalitarianism and Christian catholicity to enhance its universal appeal. Brahmanism, thus, got a new name—Hinduism—and flourished under the colonial regime because, as Frykenberg has argued, the British Raj was actually, for most intents and purposes, a de facto 'Hindu Raj'.

The Raj, as an imperial system of rule, was a genuinely indigenous rather than simply a foreign (or 'colonial') construct; that, hence, it was more Indian than British in inner logic, regardless of external interferences and violations of that logic by Britain (especially during the Crown period of this Raj); that, in terms of religious institutions, indigenous elites and local forces of all kinds were able to receive recognition and protection, as well as special concessions, from the State; and moreover, that they had been able to do this in direct proportion to their ability— whether by power of information control, numbers, noise, skill, or wealth—to influence local governments. (Frykenberg 2001: 90)

At the instance of pandits, shramanic religions like Buddhism, Jainism, Sikhism, and various streams of popular or folk Hinduism and egalitarian tribal culture were systematically marginalised, and brahmanic Hinduism was accorded informal status as the national religion. From many schools of philosophy—at least there were ten major schools including the Buddhist and Jain philosophies—only Veda-Vedanta was picked out and promoted as Indian philosophy. Shankara's Vedantic theory of *brahma satyam jagatmithya* (only Brahma is real; the world is an illusion), and *sahanam sarvadukhanam apratikarapurvakam* (all sorrows should be borne without the least resistance), came handy to buttress the Oriental myth of India as a society steeped in timeless resignation to the divine dispensation. The *Bhagavad Gita*, with its sanatani teaching of *nishkama karma* (work without any desire of result), *avatarvad* (ideology of incarnation), and a total trust in one's predetermined fate reinforced by the theory of *karma* and *punarjanma*, was projected as the holy book of all Hindus. Hinduism was proclaimed as assimilative, all-encompassing, and a uniquely Indian 'way of life'. This was not the handiwork of the gung-ho Europeans alone; the pandits played a very active part in this colonial construction. They concealed the all-important truth that if Hinduism was a way of life, it was a rotten caste-feudal way of life. And, then, which culture or religion is not a way of life?

Roy, Reforms, Renaissance: Facts against Fiction

The caste elites were the first to come in contact with Western culture and education, and they made the most of the new opportunities offered by colonial rule. The British patronage led to the making of the colonial middle class—'Indian in colour and blood, and British in taste, in attitudes, in intellect', to use Macaulay's words. Of course, the British needed this class to play the role of intermediaries between them and the millions they ruled. But Macaulay was naive in believing that the English-educated Indians would become the image of the British. The emergence of a colonial middle class, the spread of modern education, and the new print culture, in fact, led to a further traditionalisation—brahmanisation—of society. The lure of the newly discovered Veda-Purana proved more powerful for the English-educated *babus* than the dry humanistic knowledge of the West. They used Western education and the resources provided by colonialism to modernise their tradition based on hierarchised social authority, reinforcing their cultural and political power within the Indian society.

The more thoughtful among the Indian intermediaries, among them colonial clerks, professionals, pandits, and absentee landlords, began thinking about their deplorable social situation—manifest in rampant patriarchy, child marriage, enforced widowhood, and adherence to caste purity and impurity. Living in cities like Calcutta with modern English men and women, many of their social practices, especially the enslavement of women, appeared appalling to them, and some of them began looking for ways and means of removing them. However, while taking stock of the Indian reality, they seldom looked beyond their caste-class interests. Poverty-racked and oppressed Indians hardly figured in their thinking. For them, Indian society was confined, for all practical purposes, to the traditionally powerful groups. Though the upper-caste location of the emergent middle class is well-known, the real implication of this—in the form of the new assertions of caste hierarchy in the name of Indian tradition (as we shall see later)—has been kept hidden in the dominant narratives of modern India.

While the middle class in general was still in thrall to their Sanatana Dharma, the more enterprising among them took the lead to yoke together their brahmanical ideas and institutions with the Western concepts of liberalism and democracy. Such self-strengthening attempts at 'modernisation' were propelled by the need to get closer to the British by staking the claim of representing Indian society as well as acquiring qualifications for various jobs under the colonial government. This process of adjustment and 'reform from within' has been hailed in historiography as the 'Indian renaissance' or the 'national awakening'. Pioneered by the privileged-caste gentry, who had become wealthy at the cost of peasant pauperisation, the 'awakening' was basically an elite affair and adjustive in nature.

Rammohun Roy (1772–1833), a wannabe 'Raja' whom the colonial masters could only make a 'Rai Bahadur', was the first major architect of this modernisation. Hailing from a brahman landlord family that was relatively Persianised, having served Muslim rulers for generations, he himself was employed by the East India Company until his retirement in 1814. Fluent in English, he carefully cultivated relationships with many British officials, missionaries, and Unitarians with whom he formed a Unitarian Committee in 1821. A supporter of Western learning through English, he strongly opposed the British project of establishing a Sanskrit college in Calcutta. Notwithstanding the show of great pride in his Veda-Upanishad, he seemed to agree, like many other pandits, with what Macaulay was to notoriously call in 1835 (in his 'Minute on Education'): 'a single shelf of a good European library was worth the whole native literature of India and Arabia'.

The flashes of inquiry and rationalism that we find in the writings of Roy were largely inspired by the Enlightenment ideas brought in by his exposure to Western knowledge, but he had also inherited a mindset and cultural milieu that was dominated by the brahmanical worldview. Roy perceived colonial rule as the 'providential gift', but he also saw in it a challenge to traditional brahmanic supremacy within Indian society. The 'cultural challenge' was best embodied by the Christian missionaries whose 'propaganda' he eventually sought to defuse by claiming to find in a Vedic golden age the same values that were the cornerstone of their proselytising monotheism. He had limited knowledge of Vedic Sanskrit but this did not stop him from translating some cleverly selected portions of Upanishads, and insisting that in contrast to the pure Vedantic monotheism, Christian monotheism was hamstrung by the trinity of Father, Son and the Holy Spirit! He selected and highlighted texts that enabled him to outmanoeuvre the missionaries. As he wanted to popularise such views among the Bengali intelligentsia as well as the British rulers, he founded, in 1821, a bilingual *Brahminical Magazine* to disseminate his message.

What Roy and his followers had actually done was to assimilate some modern European thoughts with the ancient brahmanical ideas. In his study of the Bengal renaissance, David Kopf has convincingly shown that privileged-caste reformers 'used the idea of the West as a means for modernising their own traditions . . . for pouring the new wine of modern functions into the old bottles of Indian culture' (1969: 205). This marked the beginning of the neo-Hinduism and its ingenious interpretation of the tradition. The modus operandi here was to connect modern Western ideas and values to the brahmanical past and then claim modern ideas and values as part of the Hindu tradition. This process of redefining and reinterpreting brahmanical tradition in modern terms resulted in the emergence of neo-Hinduism. Writing on this phenomenon, P. Hacker explains:

More important than the fact that foreign elements have been added to the tradition, have been reinterpreted and provided with new meanings as a result of this encounter with the West. . . . The link which the Neo Hindus find to their tradition is one may say an afterthought, for they first adopt Western values and means of orientation and then attempt to find the foreign in the indigenous . . . afterwards they connect these values and claim them as part of Hindu tradition. (Cited in Basu 2002: 50)

The new Hinduism, thus, was a political construction of the westernised brahman literati during the colonial era. It is significant that Rammohun Roy used the term 'Hinduism' for the first time in 1816–17 for a faith ('practised by our brahman ancestors') that was traditionally called Varnashrama Dharma, Sanatana Dharma or simply Brahmanism (Killingley 1993: 62–3).

Oriental scholarship in the preceding years had helped Roy to project a golden image of the ancient Hinduism. The India of the past, he said, was an ideal society when men followed the 'doctrines of true religion', and enjoyed freedom under a just and competent government. Women had property rights and full independence in all respects. The government strictly followed the separation of powers—the brahmans were the legislators and kshatriyas were given executive power. The degeneration started, Roy bemoaned, with the absolute kshatriya rule when the brahmans were reduced to 'nominal legislators' under the Rajputs. The Rajputs exercised 'tyranny and oppression for a thousand years', then the Muslims 'from Ghuznee and Ghore invaded the country ... and introduced their own tyrannical system of governance' (Roy [1833] 1945, also see S.N. Mukherjee 1993: 382).

'The most obedient servant' of the British (Roy ended his every letter or petition to the colonial authorities with this appellation) paid obeisance to an 'enlightened' British rule that ended the 'rapacity and intolerance' of Muslim rule. Regarding the present, Roy stressed the need of a deep bond between the class of zamindars (that he represented) and the colonial masters. To cement such alliance, he floated the idea that a permanent colony of Englishmen should be established in India (see Mukherjee, ibid. 375).

Thus, the core ingredients of the *bhadralok* (privileged-caste) ideology that later evolved into 'cultural nationalism'—the valorisation of brahmanic values, selective modernity, and, a pro-British and anti-Muslim orientation—were all present in the embryonic form in the intellectual make-up of Roy, the alleged 'Father of Modern India'.

It can be argued that Roy and his associates donned the garb of modernisation because their own interests demanded it, and not because they set out, as argued by their admirers, to modernise Indian society. Hamstrung by the semi-slavery of their women, and the resultant all-round degeneration including an alarmingly dwindling population of the sub-caste from which Roy came, they realised that the practice of sati (widow immolation), enforced widowhood, polygamy, and purdah were obstacles to progress. These practices, which became the focus of the reformers, were primarily prevalent among the upper strata of society. Beyond the pale of strict brahmanical patriarchy, women of the lower strata enjoyed relatively greater freedom. Widow-remarriage was common among the lowered castes, partly because property was rarely an issue for them. Property was often the main reason of the privileged-caste opposition to marriage of their widows. Moreover, working-class women did not lead a secluded life as in addition to their domestic chores they also had to work in the fields alongside the men.

Championing the cause of long-suffering upper-caste women was commendable, but none of the reformers developed a realistic critique of caste and patriarchy. Occasionally, the more sensitive among them voiced a concern about caste in an abstract way, that too as an obstacle in the patriotic unity rather than as a system of discrimination and mass exploitation. None of them bothered to raise, let alone fight, the horrible injustices of caste-feudalism. The issues around which the reform movement revolved—abolition of sati, widow remarriage, polygyny (prevalent among kulina brahmans of Bengal), removal of the purdah system, and later the demand for more English schools and colleges along with better representation in the colonial administration and affairs of the state—were oriented to modernise the upper strata. The movement was confined to the brahman and allied castes.

Highly selective in their acceptance of liberal-democratic ideas from the West, the reformers' advocacy of change was not based on inclusive ethics or justice—as the cornerstone of a new society—but those of the authority taken from the brahmanical scriptures and Dharmashastras. The reformers never tried to win public opinion by showing the people the inhumanity and absurdity of the social evils sanctified by the shastric tradition. Instead they celebrated the 'wonder that was India' and tried to persuade their castemen by convincing them that the reforms were in consonance with the shastras. The tendency to misquote or misrepresent brahmanical scripture in support of reforms and progressivism was carried forward by the future reformers and can well be summed up in the words of R.G. Bhandarkar:

In ancient times girls were married after they had attained maturity, now they must be married before; widow marriage was then in practice, now it has certainly gone out . . . . Interdining among the castes was not prohibited, now the numberless castes cannot have intercommunications of that nature. (Cited in R.S. Sharma 1983: 10)

Ironically, valorisation of the past itself became the major concern of the reformers, and the issues—for which the shastras were being ransacked—were given a quiet burial. For example, Roy—whose historical fame is largely built around his campaign against sati—did not base his case against widow immolation as a crime against women but because sati had no scriptural sanction. Since he revered the *Manusmriti* as the founding text containing the 'whole sense of the Vedas', he insisted that no code be approved which contradicted it (L. Mani 1989: 109). Not surprisingly, the arguments about shastric sanction gained precedence over the subject for which the past was being invoked.

Tradition was not the ground on which the status of women was being contested. Rather the reverse was true: women in fact became the site on which tradition was debated and reformulated. What was at stake was not women but tradition. (L. Mani 1989: 118)

As the 'awakening' was taking place in this insular, past-obsessed environment, the revivalism of the supposed ancient glories became integral to reform ideology. Roy and his friends had no qualms about toeing the brahmanic line that had for centuries been the main source of obscurantism that vindicated exploitation of the masses and women of all classes on religious grounds. It is one of the tragic ironies of modern Indian history that the progressive reformers and their orthodox opponents were both ransacking the same brahmanical texts to support or oppose the reform agenda. Reactionaries (opposing even limited reforms) and the reformers both delved into the shastras to bring out examples to prove their points. Both sides tried to build their case on the past precedent to resolve current controversies. The fallacy of the reformers' approach became clear when Roy selectively quoted the 'sacred' texts in support of his campaign to ban sati. The conservatives led by Raja Radhakant Deb (1784–1867) ransacked the same texts and cited more authentic instances to prove that sati did have the sanction of the shastras. As R.S. Sharma (1983: 5) points out, 'In this particular case the enlightened opinion of William Bentinck was of more moment than the texts marshalled by Raja Rammohun Roy.'

Moreover, condemning sati through shastric invocations, Roy was bound to glorify austere widowhood. As he argued, 'Manu in plain terms enjoins a widow to *continue till death* forgiving all injuries, performing austere duties, avoiding every sensual pleasure, and cheerfully practising the incomparable rules of virtue which have been followed by such women as were devoted to only one husband' (see L. Mani 1989: 103). This created a huge headache for the later reformers who supported widow-remarriage and opposed polygamy. Toeing Roy's reform-from-within line, the later reformers would selectively quote ancient texts, especially the *Manusmriti,* for abolition of polygamy (which was prevalent among the kulins of Bengal). Challenged by the conservatives, the reformers could not prove a case for strict monogamous conjugality from any brahmanical scripture. Similarly, the campaign for widow remarriage led by Ishwarchandra Vidyasagar (1820–91) was based on the premise that the marriage of widows was permissible under the shastras. When questioned, Vidyasagar quoted from the text of Parashara showing that a woman can take a second husband under certain circumstances. Predictably, this was countered by the orthodox pandits who contended that Parashara's law-book was compiled only in about the eighth century CE. One indignant pandit wrote to Vidyasagar in 1855, 'the views of Parashara . . . have never been adopted by the Hindus, and will continue to be discarded by the people . . .' (see Bandyopadhyay 1995: 20). The reactionaries turned the tables on Vidyasagar by quoting from Manu, the pre-eminent law-giver, who permitted only the remarriage of shudra widows who had remained virgins.[5]

Obviously, the shastras represent ancient patriarchal values and as such provided more armour to the conservatives than to the 'progressives' who were taking too much liberty to conveniently interpret them to suit their reform agenda. The reformers never invoked the principles of human equality and public reason. Instead they chose to indulge in futile shadow-boxing with the scripture-quoting-conservatives with chanting mantras of their own. In discovering the 'great ideals' and 'progressivism' in the shastra-smriti, the 'progressives' surpassed even the traditionalists, invigorating brahmanical ideology and in the long run helping the hands of Hindu fundamentalism. Falling back on the obscurantist shastras meant, in actuality, the negation of an egalitarian, rational, or humanist approach to social problems.

Reform movements spearheaded by organisations like the Brahmo Samaj in Bengal, and later by Prarthana Samaj in Maharashtra, Veda Samaj in Tamil Nadu, and the Arya Samaj in Punjab and northern India were ideologically guided by (as their very names suggest) brahmanical values. The Brahmo Samaj that Roy founded in 1828 initiated a controlled attack on what was considered essentially unbrahmanical dogma, superstition, and polytheism, through ingenious but unhistorical reinterpretations of selected scriptures. In his debate with the Christian missionaries, Roy made clear that what he was defending was 'the genuine Brahmanical religion, taught by the Vedas, as interpreted by Manu, not the popular system or worship adopted by the multitude' (see I. Singh 1987: 95). His avowed aim was to purge the ancient and 'sacred' brahmanical tradition of modern-day corruption. He saw his reform movement as an attempt to preserve the pristine glories of brahmanism: 'The ground which I took in all my controversies was not that of opposition to brahmanism but to a perversion of it' (Roy [1833], see Hay 1988: 21). His chief worry was that the brahmanic society—the Brahmo Samaj—had fallen from its high standards, and the challenge was to make it rise again.

For all his alleged defiance of the caste orthodoxy, Roy took pride in his brahman identity—'my ancestors were brahmans of a high order'—and he was wary of losing caste in the eyes of his orthodox critics. To the very end, he avoided eating with anyone who belonged to any other religion or caste. Even in England (where he had later shifted) he maintained this abstinence with his English friends, of whom he had many (Kriplani 1981: 54). He never ate any food that was forbidden by the shastras for a brahman. And, when he went abroad he took his brahman cook along (see Biswas 1998: 207–8). His much-admired criticism of caste was limited to seeing it as a hurdle in the 'patriotic unity'. No

Brahmo came up with a clear criticism of caste, as Sumit Sarkar points out, until Sibnath Shastri's *Jatibheda* (1884); the 'Depressed Classes Mission for philanthropic work among Bengal's low castes and untouchables had to wait for its inauguration till 1909' (Sarkar 1996: 281).

Thus, when Roy talked of individual freedom, only the higher castes mattered. The 'lower' castes were 'superstitious' and 'fettered with prejudices'. He fully approved of social hierarchy as a natural and universal phenomenon. Such a society, he said, was implicit in the Veda-Purana, which introduced a plurality of gods and goddesses for the masses with 'limited understanding'. For the enlightened few, there had been the Vedantic doctrine of monotheism. Leaving the 'unredeemable' masses to their fate, he concerned himself exclusively with the upper classes. He pleaded that Europeans be encouraged to settle in India, but wanted only 'persons of character and capital'. He wanted only rich merchants and zamindars—'respectable and intelligible classes'—in his ideal political system (Roy, see Mukherjee 1993: 374–5). He insisted that only 'natives of respectability' should be appointed collectors 'in lieu of Europeans' (ibid.). With some clever word-play, such examples are cited in the nationalist historiography as instances of Roy's marvellous patriotism.

Roy is also lauded for his 'pioneering' advocacy of monotheism and the worship of a formless Supreme Being. Was this a novel idea? In Roy's time, millions of followers of Islam, Christianity, and Sikhism believed in monotheism and there had been a long tradition of *nirguna* even among a section of the lower strata of Hindus. Centuries before Roy, people's philosophers such as Kabir and Nanak had led far more radical and monotheistic movements (Chapter 3). Actually, there was nothing new or revolutionary in Roy's socio-religious ideas, except for the fact that he found everything good and glorious in the brahmanical tradition. Roy never supported anything that had no approval of the shastras.

Above all, Roy's monotheistic preaching did not have any impact on the ground. Dwarkanath Tagore (1794–1846), a prominent Brahmo Samaji and chief financer of Roy's movement, continued idol-worship and all priestly paraphernalia in his home.

The ineffectiveness of the 'religious radicalism' is noted even by the right-wing historian, R.C. Majumdar:

The illuminated gates of two thousand Durga Puja pandals in Calcutta whose loudspeakers and Dhak or trumpets proclaim in deafening noise, year after year, the failure of Rammohun to make the slightest impression from his point of view on 99.9 per cent of the vast Hindu samaj either in the 19th or 20th century. (Cited in Pankratz 2001: 374)

History textbooks glorify Roy's role in the making of modern India. He is seen as 'the prophet of a new age', the Renaissance figure who brilliantly led the emergent middle classes in the early nineteenth century. He is even hailed as the 'father' of modern India, but the historians who decorate him with such superlative adjectives do not elaborate who his 'children' are. The crucial questions of what social groups comprised the new middle classes, and what their aspirations and motives were in running the reform movement are pushed aside.

Roy came from a Radi Kulina brahman family, which enjoyed high status in the caste hierarchy of Bengal. This sub-caste was the most conservative and in this sense the most backward. Not for nothing did this sub-caste produce outstanding reformers such as Vidyasagar, Surendranath Banerjee and Ranglal Banerjee. Some scholars suggest that the reforms were initiated not to modernise society, but to ensure the very survival of the Radi Kulina caste:

The strict laws of endogamy, prohibition of widow remarriage and polygamy left many Radi Kulina brahmana women childless, and consequently the caste was losing in number. A 17th century Bengali poet prophesised that if the strict laws of endogamy and pollution continued, the Kulins would soon disappear. It seems that the social reforms concerning sati, widow remarriage and polygamy aimed at increasing the birth rate. (S.N. Mukherjee 1993: 367)

Most members of Roy's Atmiya Sabha, transformed into the Brahmo Samaj in 1828, were brahmans, mainly of the Radi Kulina sub-caste. On the other hand, the Dharma Sabha, the orthodox organisation founded by Radhakant Deb, was dominated by sanskritised and upwardly mobile castes such as kayasthas and subarnavaniks. Roy's outfit was committed to reforms that had become a necessity for the Kulins' survival. Not compelled by such compulsions, the Dharma Sabha members could afford to take a more hardened approach towards issues like sati and widow-remarriage. But the Dharam Sabha adopted a more liberal approach on the caste question than Roy and his Brahmo Samaj. As early as 1832, the Sabha called a special meeting on the shudra-brahman relationship (S.N. Mukherjee 1993: 365). The issue to be debated was whether the shastras permitted a shudra, if devout and righteous, to claim respect from brahmans and whether brahmans were permitted to partake of such a shudra's *prasada*. The pandits gave the verdict that a brahman should always command respect from a shudra, and under no circumstances should he eat a shudra's *prasada*. Predictably, this judgement was challenged by the non-brahmans. Bhairava Chandra Dutt, a subarnavanik, wrote a pamphlet, *Shree Shree Vaishnava Bhakti Kaumudi,* to establish that a righteous shudra could—and should—command respect from brahmans.

Thus, the caste-class contradictions fused with the political issues of the time. The old ideas and institutions, instead of dying out, had been adapted to the changed situation and actually strengthened in the process by both the Brahmo Samaj and the Dharam Sabha. The difference between Raja Rammohun Roy and Raja Radhakant Deb was very thin. Like Roy, Deb too was a Sanskritist and champion of Western education. Both wanted to settle contemporary issues through *shastrartha*. Both supported modernisation in their own way while adhering to the brahmanical tradition. Both were Rajas—one real (the British had accorded the title to Radhakant Deb) and the other wannabe (the British denied the title of 'Raja' to Roy despite a strong recommendation from the titular Mughal ruler, Akbar Shah II; however, as a consolation he was decorated with Rai Bahadur).

Above all, the reformers and conservatives, despite their conflicts, were united in their loyalty to colonialism. Also, many influential people had one foot in the Brahmo Samaj and the other in the Dharam Sabha. Dwarkanath Tagore and his younger cousin Prasanna Kumar were a kind of link between them. Dwarkanath and Deb came together in 1837 to form the Landholders' Society, which was later rechristened the British India Association. Later,

Dwarkanath's son Debendranath Tagore (1817–1905), who succeeded Roy as leader of the Brahmo Samaj, had no hesitation in becoming Secretary of the British India Association, whose President was Radhakant Deb. Debendranath would speak the language of the conservatives and use his 'rationalist-intellectual' organisation Tattvabodhini Sabha (which later merged into the Brahmo Samaj) not only to glorify the Vedas but also to offset the 'conversion threat' of Christian missionaries. With his wealth and charisma, he was able to rally many Bengali young men, most of them belonging (like himself) to brahman caste, to the cause of reviving Vedic Hinduism.

From time to time, the *bhadralok* made the right noises and invoked the ideals of liberalism and democracy. In reality, they were dedicated to 'social conservatism combined with an openness to western education'. The brahmanic and colonial loyalism, very much present in Roy's social vision, crystallised into hardcore British allegiance and anti-Muslim sentiments after 1850. The aftermath of 1857 revealed the true colours of *bhadralok* intellectuals when they vied with each other to show their colonial loyalty. The Calcutta newspaper *Hindoo Patriot* in its edition dated 11 June 1857, advised the educated class to remain pro-British because 'in three more generations they will have the best part of the property of the country in their hands . . . they have a splendid future before them, but which can be realised only by the continued existence of British rule' (see Simeon 1986). The *Sambad Prabhakar* editor Ishwar Chandra Gupta (1810–59) denounced the 1857 rebellion as a Muslim conspiracy aimed at destroying *Ram-rajya* under the British:

This [English] rule is as blissful as the rule of Ram . . . we are all getting our fulfilment in all aspects of our life as children by a mother under the aegis of the ruler of the world, the Queen of England. . . . Let the goddess of British Raj remain steady and let us enjoy the heavenly bliss of independence forever. (Cited in Simeon 1986)

Gupta in his *Bharat Bhumir Durdasa* linked the degraded status of India as 'the subject race' to the 'error and delusion' through which 'we ceased to venerate the Vedas' (see Basu 2002: 18–19).

Gupta and Bhudeb Mukhopadhyay, another reactionary in the brahmanical mould, were inspirational figures for Bankimchandra Chatterjee who took this brand of nationalism to militant heights in his creative and critical writings. It was these gentlemen and their successors who laid the foundation of communal revivalism in India. The national revival became entangled with the race and religion. The restoration of the 'Hindu culture' began to be used interchangeably with the national awakening. Nationalism became another name for the Sanatana Dharma, the orthodox Hindu religion of the past. Aurobindo's definition of nationalism (in a speech in 1909) leaves little doubt in this regard:

> Nationalism is not a mere political programme. Nationalism is a religion that has come from God. . . . If you are going to be a nationalist, if you are going to assent to this religion of nationalism, you must do it in the religious spirit. . . . It is Sanatana Dharma which for us is nationalism. . . . When it is said that India shall expand and extend itself, it is the Sanatana Dharma that shall expand and extend itself over the world. (A. Ghose 1948: 7–9, 76–80)

Dayananda's Aryan Race and Vedic Culture

A key figure of the revivalist movement that has come to be glorified as 'socio-cultural awakening' or 'cultural nationalism' was Mulshankar Tiwari, better known as Dayananda Saraswati (1824–83). His ideology was not very dissimilar from that of the bhadralok reformers of Bengal, except that he had a more fundamental vision of the Vedic golden age. A Gujarati brahman of flaming imagination, Dayananda created, rather than recalled, that heavenly era in the *Aryavarta* (abode of the 'superhuman' race of Aryans) in which the first men were born; Sanskrit, the 'mother of all tongues and the language of gods', was spoken; and, not only did 'theoretical wisdom flourish but also the practical industrial sciences'. Believing that Vedas contained all truths, including the ideas of modern science, he founded in 1875 the Arya Samaj which grew fast in urban centres of Punjab and spread its tentacles in many parts of north India. The movement brought in its wake a mythological awareness of the past permeated with an 'Aryan consciousness accompanied by its attendant baggage of associations such as virility, spirituality and highmindedness' (Chakravarti 1989: 54). Its rhetoric of the glorious Aryan civilisation became part of the Hindu consciousness of the region.

Dayananda published in 1875 his *Satyartha Prakash* (The Light of Truth). He wrote it in Hindi on the suggestion of Keshab Chandra Sen to make it accessible to the people, but in his characteristic style he linked his Hindi to Vedic Sanskrit and gave it a new name—*Aryabhasha*. Perhaps the most influential polemic of Hindu revivalism, *Satyartha Prakash* contains Dayananda's recipe for the regeneration of Hindu religion and society. He viscerally supported the *varna-vyavastha* but criticised the wrong application that bred corrupt practices. What was required was to weed out the degenerate elements that had crept into the ideal varna model. 'Go back to the Vedas' was his panacea for all the malaises afflicting India and the world.

Even though Dayananda held brahmans responsible for promoting superstitions and the decline of Hindu society, the alternative social model he proposed was based largely on the varna ideology in which the brahmans remained the ultimate mediators of religious and social truths. He denounced idolatrous and superstitious practices of 'degenerate' Hinduism, but remained loyal to orthodoxy in several basic ways—belief in the superiority of Vedic faith over all religions; allegiance to *chaturvarnya* (the order of four varnas) and *sada-darshanam* (the six philosophical schools); and faith in *karma-dharma* and transmigration of soul. The theory of *karma* and *punarjanma* justifies the status quo, however oppressive, on the ground that every being is born in a particular situation because of his or her actions in the previous births. Dayananda not only accepted all this, he even rattled off, like a veteran *karmakandi*, a list detailing what sins would lead to birth in what species (Dayananda [1875] 1960; Talwar 2001: 48–55).

Contrary to popular understanding, the 'reformer' Dayananda did not launch any campaign against caste, nor did he expect any anti-caste action from his followers. His views on shudras were self-contradictory, and his 'concern' to uplift them was full of mischief. In the first edition of the *Satyartha Prakash,* he advocates elementary education for shudra children but denies them the right to study the Vedas and other shastras. In the second edition, published in 1884 after his death, he allows worthy shudras to study the shastras but still prohibits them from reading the most sacred Mantra Samhita. In a similar vein, Dayananda grants that a shudra can study, but he is not entitled to the investiture ceremony—*yajnopavit*—which enables one to become *dvija*, the pure Aryan (Talwar 2001: 38). He enjoined the wearing of the sacred thread by the dvija as one of the 'signs of learning that distinguish the literate twice-born castes from the illiterate shudras'. At another place he advises shudras to eschew disagreement, envy, and ego, and to earn their livelihood by serving the three higher varnas (ibid.: 36). He did not have anything to say about outcastes and tribals who were beyond the pale of *chaturvarnya*—a revealing fact in itself.

Dayananda's Vedic stridency brought him in fight with 'inferior' and 'fake' religions such as Christianity, Islam, Jainism, and Sikhism. The *Satyartha Prakash* is full of venomous utterances against Jesus ('an illiterate carpenter') and Muhammad ('a hopeless debauchee'), and Kabir ('an uppity weaver').

No saint or seer or prophet escaped the brunt of Dayananda's relentless criticism. Anything that did not conform to the Vedas or deviated from a fixed trajectory of Sanskrit-based Vedic and shastric knowledge was condemned. Vedic knowledge and Sanskrit learning became the immutable orthodoxy beyond which lay a sea of ignorance and darkness. (J. Sharma 2003: 34).

Pouring scorn on other faiths and their prophets, he embarked on a programme of *shuddhi* (purification) which meant the reconversion of those people who had been 'polluted' by converting into other religions such as Islam or Christianity. The move generated more heat than light, raising the communal temperature to a dangerous level. Even among the Hindus it triggered a discord between the privileged castes and the lowered because *shuddhi* belittled all other than pure Aryans. Implicit in *shuddhi* was the concept of pure and impure, the cardinal principle which regulates caste hierarchy. This was evident from the fact that purified or reconverted persons were given the 'original' jati-varna to which they belonged before the conversion. This is revealing because their jati-varna was not determined by their individual merits and deeds, but by their ancestors' birth in a particular jati. This exposes the Arya Samaj's bluff that the original varna-vyavastha was an ideal system where one's caste was determined by one's worth, not birth.

If the Arya Samaj made any difference to the lowered castes, it was for the worse. In their study of the movement in Punjab, Pimpley and Sharma (1985) found that it did not succeed in its avowed aim of uplifting the lowered castes or removing untouchability; instead it helped the Hindu elite to consolidate their position in the region. The caste elites increased their 'political strength' by keeping the lowered castes within the Hindu fold, and stopping their conversions to Christianity or Islam, which was perhaps the real objective of this movement.

This is not surprising, given the dubious worldview of Dayananda. A reading of the *Satyartha Prakash* shows his ethics were crude in the extreme. Dayananda swears by Manu and all his barbarous laws. The people are encouraged to kill a perceived wrong-doer. The king is advised to have an adulterer burned alive on a red-hot iron bedstead, an adulteress devoured by dogs, in the presence of many men and women. In his anxiety to control women's sexuality, Dayananda drops all veneer of decency. As Uma Chakravarti points out:

> What was central to Dayananda's thinking was his understanding of the role of women in the maintenance of race, and inter alia, concern about their sexuality. Motherhood for Dayananda was the sole rationale of a woman's existence but what was crucial in his concept of motherhood was its specific role in the procreation and rearing of a special breed of men. For example, the *Satyartha Prakash* lays down a variety of rules and regulations for ideal conception. (Chakravarti 1989: 56)

Driven by his concern for a healthy and pure stock of Aryans, he advocates the appointment of (shudra) wet nurse so that the (Aryan) mother can recuperate quickly to be ready to conceive again:

> It is best therefore, for the mother not to suckle her child. Plasters should be applied to the breast that will soon dry up the milk. By following this

system the woman becomes strong again in about two months. Till then the husband should have thorough control over his passions and thus preserve the reproductive element. Those that will follow this plan will have children of a superior order, enjoy long life, and continually gain in strength and energy so that their children will be of a high mental calibre, strong, energetic and devout. (Ibid.: 56)

It was this madness with the management of female sexuality for a regenerated race of Aryans which also shaped Dayananda's ambiguity on widow remarriage. Stressing the importance of motherhood, he supported remarriage of both men and women if there were no children from the earlier marriage. As a solution to the remarriage question and the problem of sexuality, he hit upon the idea of *niyoga*, the ancient Aryan practice of sexual relationship without marriage for the purpose of procreation. In support of *niyoga*, he ransacked the ancient texts and conveniently interpreted them to uphold the practice. There was no immorality in this practice, he declared, because the rationale for both marriage and *niyoga* was to beget healthy and strong children. However, he was emphatic that a woman can *niyoga* only with a man of the same or higher varna, and not under any circumstances, with a man of lower varna (Talwar 2001: 44).

As Uma Chakravarti comments, 'This was one form of the nationalist resolution of women's sexuality; to use her biological potential for child bearing in the service of the physical regeneration of what was seen as a now weakened Aryan race' (1989: 60).

The Arya Samaj thus laid yet another stone for brahmanical revivalism. Throwing all reason and common sense to the winds, Dayananda would blithely declare that if one knew the correct way to interpret the Vedas, one could discover all modern science, engineering, and even military and non-military sciences in them. But he was not unique in arguing that 'truth, wherever it is found, it is of the Veda'. Other gladiators of Hindu nationalism revered the Vedas in the same fanatical vein. Vivekananda believed that basic principles of all sciences are to be discovered in the Vedas. He even discovered Darwin in his ancient shastras: 'The idea of evolution was to be found in the Vedas long before the Christian era; but until Darwin said it was true, it was regarded as a mere

Hindu superstition' (Vivekananda, *The Complete Works*, vol. 8: 25). Vivekananda admired Dayananda for discovering these wonders hidden in the Vedas. Similarly, Aurobindo (1872–1950) made the point that Dayananda actually underestimated the greatness of the Vedas:

> There is then nothing fantastical in Dayananda's idea that the Veda contains truths of science as well as truths of religion. I will even add my own conviction that the Veda contains other truths of a science which the modern world does not at all possess, and in that sense, Dayananda has rather understated than overstated the depth and range of the Vedic wisdom. (Aurobindo, see A. Sharma 2001: 398)

Underlining the contribution of Dayananda in the creation of a national consciousness, militant nationalist B.C. Pal (1858–1932) points out that prior to him, Hinduism suffered from an acute lack of a universal scripture that other religions like Christianity and Islam have in the Bible and Koran. It was Dayananda, he gushes, who made the Hindus militant by showing that there could *not* be a purer religion or a purer social order than the one envisioned in the Vedas. The Vedic order, Pal adds, is indeed superior even to 'the social idealism inspired by the dogma of Liberty, Equality and Fraternity of the French illumination'. It was the Vedic religious revival 'to which we owe so largely the birth of our present national consciousness' (B.C. Pal, see Biswas 1998: 218–20).

The Modernisation of Brahmanical Tradition

Why were the reformers so passionate about adjusting ancient ideas and institutions to changing socio-cultural conditions? Why were they so keen to link their patriotism to the brahmanical tradition and its obscurantist texts? Considering most of them had a critical mind, were they not aware of malignant social contents and consequences of brahmanism, and the existence of a more humane tradition, represented by the early Buddhism, Jainism, and the subaltern religiosity of the folk Hinduism?

The answer is, the reformers hailed from privileged backgrounds, and shared the ideological and political interests of their caste-class.

Rammohun Roy, Debendranath Tagore, Dayananda Saraswati, and other reformers spoke in different voices but were united in their commitment to the brahmanic culture and values. By assuming—and establishing—the brahmanical tradition as the Indian tradition, they set in motion the process of its modernisation. The construction of a particular kind of tradition was the construction of a particular kind of nationalism. This pseudo-nationalism itself came to occupy the same place that discriminatory brahmanical religion had monopolised before.

In regard to the women's question, which formed the nucleus of the reform movement, the entire focus of attention had been on the privileged-caste women (Chakravarti 1989: 78). The focus on the Hindu upper-class to the exclusion of all others—dalit-bahujans, adivasis, Muslims, etc.—was the main feature of the reformist discourse. It was evident from Dayananda's injunctions that Arya mothers should not nurse their babies, but employ wet nurses instead so that they might recover quickly and be ready to produce strong sons once more.

But what of the wet nurse? Who was she? What about her place in the system of procreation? Was she not required to produce strong sons too? Clearly Dayananda's injunctions were meant for one section at the expense of another. Vast sections of women did not exist for the nineteenth century nationalists. No one tried to read the ancient texts to see what rights the Vedic dasi and others like her had in the Vedic golden age. (Chakravarti 1989: 79)

The reformers never criticised the ancient texts for handing down terrible injustices to the lower orders and women. Some even argued that disabilities of the shudras did not reduce their happiness or well-being. Child marriage was justified on the ground that it helped a girl to know whom she had to love, before any sexual consciousness had awakened in her. Patriarchal oppression was dismissed with selective citations to prove that women were worshipped like goddesses in ancient times, and also by arguing that a woman would make herself more uncomfortable and vulnerable if she tried to step into a man's shoes by acquiring his role. Underlining the casteist and ahistorical orientation of the elitist study of the past, R.S. Sharma writes:

Colonialism and the Birth of Vedic–Brahmanic Nationalism 221

The study of the lower orders in ancient India has not only been ignored, but, strange as it may seem, in some cases they appear to have been held in the same contempt by modern writers as they were held by the members of the upper varnas in ancient times. It is stated that child marriage originated among the lower classes, while the Dharmashastra rules leave no doubt that it first began among the three upper varnas. It is said that women had a higher position among the upper classes, while the opposite seems to have been the case. The climax is reached when on the basis of his study of ancient Indian society a writer prescribes sexual self-control and abstinence for the 'Brahman' and the use of contraceptives for people of the lowest varna. (1983: 15–16)

The didactic and narrative portions of the *Ramayana, Mahabharata* and other ancient texts were often yoked together to reach favourable conclusions. The timeless character of Indian civilisation was highlighted to evade the troubled reality and the process of social development in ancient India. (Carrying this trend in the twentieth century, works of the post-Vedic period such as the Dharmashastras and Grihyasutras, were included in the Vedic period in the Bharatiya Vidya Bhawan series on *The History and Culture of the Indian People*.) All unpleasant aspects of social life were swept under the national carpet. 'Caste did not cause poverty and did not divide the city into two parts like the East End and West End of London', wrote one, while another concluded that 'in ancient India there was no concentration of the prestige of birth, influence of wealth and political office which imparts an aristocratic tinge to social organisation and sustains an aristocratic government' (see R.S. Sharma 1983: 15). Repeated joint notices of shudras and women depriving them of civil and property rights and frequent equating of woman with property in the ancient Sanskrit texts were not given any attention. It appears that the reformers' only motive was to establish somehow that all was good and glorious in the ancient period and that the degeneration set only in the medieval period under the Muslim rule.

The exaltation of caste and the patriarchal family under the cloak of patriotism, in fact, provided a potent weapon in the hands of casteist and communalist elements to block social change. No wonder the reformist movement quickly lost its steam and degenerated into revivalism.

Nationalist Vindication of Caste Ideology

The valorisation of caste became the hallmark of patriotism. Caste was praised as the adhesive, assimilative force which holds the Hindu society together and enables to withstand attacks from outside. No wonder there was a symbiosis between the rise of 'national' awakening and the resurgence of privileged-caste movements (a fact that has been conveniently erased from the history textbooks: we only hear about 'lower caste' movements which emerged later to fight the upper-caste dominance).

Along with running the reform movements, the privileged-caste landlords, professionals, and pandits also ran caste organisations. Magazines, newspapers, and pamphlets were brought out to strengthen caste consciousness. (Roy started the trend with his *Brahminical Magazine*.) Meetings and conferences were held to cement caste solidarity. Cooperatives were started on caste basis. Buildings were constructed to be rented to fellow castemen. Scholarships were awarded for carrying out studies only to the same-caste students (A.R. Desai [1948] 1991). Prominent figures took the lead in forming caste societies like the Akhil Bharatiya Brahman Sabha and the Kayastha Pathashala which had branches all over the country.

Caste—the main target of the contemporary social radicals like Phule, Iyothee Thass and Narayana Guru (see Chapters 5 and 6)—was being lauded by the caste elites as the very basis of the nation. The social reforms, ostentatiously aimed at patriotic unity, were thus oriented to invigorate the caste culture. The Arya Samaj talked about some measures for the lowered castes, with the ulterior aim to take them firmly in the brahmanic order, as we saw earlier. As the only brahmanic organisation that tried to reach out to the people, the Samaj was against any autonomous social movements among them. Evidences suggest that various initiatives of the lowered castes to organise and agitate for socio-political rights in Punjab, Uttar Pradesh, and elsewhere were strongly opposed by the Arya Samaj. Prominent dalit-subaltern leaders such as Mangoo Ram in Punjab and Acchutanand in Uttar Pradesh, who were earlier associated with the Arya Samaj, had to come out strongly against its hypocritical position on the caste question (see Chapter 6).

In an astonishing display of caste-class unity, the *bhadralok* rallied round the caste ideology, hailing it as the living testimony to India's genius. It was surmised that India would not have survived as a nation without caste. The Maharaja of Darbhanga—a Maithil brahman, a 'national reformer' and one of the major financers of the Indian National Congress in its early days—glorified caste as 'the best and surest safeguard against the spirit of unrest, against the growing bitterness between the classes and the masses, between capital and labour, which is constantly menacing civilisation' (see A.R. Desai [1948] 1991: 257). This remark, which anticipated the manifold virtues of caste in the Gandhian vein, was not his own alone.

The hierarchy of caste was glorified as 'natural', 'noble', and 'culturally uplifting'. Its lowbrow celebrants recited religious passages such as the Creation Hymn from the *Rigveda* and the karmic explanations in an Upanishadic verse.[6] The highbrow and English-speaking *bhadralok* borrowed the language of Western science and social theory to prove that caste in its true sense was not divisive or exploitative (as was argued by some missionaries and dalit-subaltern radicals like Phule), but the 'product of a free people exercising dynamic political will'. Drawing parallels with the modern concept of meritocracy, caste stratification was presented as a harmonious division of labour.

R.C. Dutt (1848–1909), a prominent nationalist scholar, in his three-volume *History of the Civilisation in Ancient India Based on Sanskrit Literature,* written in the 1880s, argued that in the ancient times caste never divided the Aryan people but rallied them as one man against the aborigines (see R.S. Sharma 1983: 9). For him, the ancient Indian history was synonymous with the Aryan Hindu history. The aborigines or non-Aryans were only a conquered and subjugated people. He fancied, in the introduction of his book, that his writing would go a long way in dispelling the superstitious worship of the past! Dutt's book quickly acquired the status of a classic and was translated into many regional languages. Other writer-scholars of the nationalist school further elaborated and illustrated his formulations. Dutt, who later emerged as a pioneering nationalist economic historian, also authored trailblazing romances about the Rajputs and Marathas, in which he portrayed Muslims as tyrannical enemies of Hindu people.

Jogendra Nath Bhattacharya was another influential writer who insisted that caste was positive, uniquely Indian, and essential to the genius of Hindu civilisation. In his *Hindu Castes and Sects* (1896), he declared that the varna scheme had been forged as 'an act of large-hearted statesmanship' which had set up ideal models of conduct and morality for a diverse and conflict-prone communities. The creation of varnas united people, taught them noble ideals, and provided the means of assimilating the 'foreign hordes' who had so often invaded the Hindu homeland. He extolled the visionary law-givers who helped transform descendants of the early Aryan-Vedic singers into 'one race under the name of Brahmans'. The fourfold varna order was a 'golden chain' which Hindus had 'willingly placed on their necks, and which has fixed them to only that which is noble and praiseworthy'. Far from being 'tyrannical' and 'cruel', he stressed, caste had endowed Indians with selfless spiritual ideals and a concept of solidarity which had long united separate 'races and clans' of India (see Bayly 2000: 163–5).

An early graduate of Calcutta University, Bhattacharya was president of the Bengal Brahman Sabha and also head of the Nadia College of Pundits, which was entitled, courtesy the colonial government, to give authoritative judgements on matters of Hindu tradition. Renowned as a nationalist scholar, his writings on caste culture—the first sociological work by an Indian—were greatly admired in the nationalist circle (Bayly, ibid.).

Close on the heels of Bhattacharya's book came Jogendrachandra Ghosh's *Brahmanism and the Sudra, or the Indian Labour Problem* (*c.* 1900). In this work, Ghosh, a prominent zamindar and a close friend of Bankimchandra, argued that self-government could be grounded in the already existing 'political dualism of British and Hindu authority', under which the former would not interfere in matters of caste governance. Locality-based Hindu and Muslim communities under firm brahman and ulema control could thus evolve into units of 'subordinate self-government'. Ghosh argued that this would be very much preferable to any attempt at importing into India Western notions of 'parliamentary-democratic' government, for there was already a 'possibility of . . . [a] dangerous upheaval from the lower depths of Hindu society'. Disruption of this kind had been avoided so far through the 'discipline effected by the Rishis and Brahmans in the heart and mind of the women and the masses', but there was urgent need now to 'repel all disturbances of Western origin . . . things like Trade Unions and Socialism . . . would be fatal to this country' (see S. Sarkar 1997: 378–9). Ghosh was desirous of the freedom 'in the regions of social and historical theory' in which there would be no place for 'rhetoric about a Sudra emancipation'.

The caste system was embraced as a divine order even by the fabled saint of Dakshineshwar, Ramakrishna Paramhans (1836–86). Vidyasagar made the saint quite angry by suggesting that God could not have been so unfair so as to give more powers to some and less to others (S. Sarkar 1997: 372). Ramakrishna retorted that big and small would always remain fundamentally different, adding variety to the world and leaving space for the *lila* of the gods (ibid.: 374). His central message was 'one of quietistic, inward-looking bhakti', and he was 'often openly scornful of socially activist, ameliorative projects, even of philanthropy' (ibid.: 201).

Vidyasagar, perhaps the most humane and rational face of the *bhadralok* reformism, 'waged a determined but losing battle against the orthodoxy'. Propounding a thesis of rational knowledge, he opposed the introduction of 'false systems of Vedanta and Sankhya' into the curriculum at Sanskrit College on the grounds that it would encourage obscurantist self-congratulation. The *bhadralok*, however, thronged to the obscurantist Ramakrishna—and later to his star disciple Vivekananda—and left the likes of Vidyasagar in the lurch to despair, 'If I had an idea of the worthlessness, dishonesty and lack of integrity of the *baralok* (high and mighty people) of our country, I might perhaps not have ventured on this movement' (see Simeon 1986: 11).

Paradoxically, as S. Bandyopadhyay has shown in a brilliant research (1995: 9–36), Vidyasagar himself failed in his avowed aim, 'as neither he nor his associates were able to offer a radically new ideology', nor did they challenge 'the power structure of Hindu society and its ideology of hierarchy'. Accepting and internalising the principle of hierarchy and patriarchy of the shastras, Vidyasagar could not see that the women's subjugation in Indian society emanated from the concept of an all encompassing hierarchy. He even went to the extent of arguing,

> No one can prove that there has been no change in our customs since the first day of creation. . . . If an example is cited, you will be able to realise more easily to what extent the customs have changed in our country. In olden times, if a Sudra sat with a Brahman, there would have been no end to his crime. Now those very Sudras take the higher seats, and the Brahmans like obliging servants sit below. (Vidyasagar, see S. Bandyapadhyay 1995: 28)

This was, in Vidyasagar's eyes, 'against the shastras', and nothing could be more reprehensible. 'There could be no clearer statement vindicating the hierarchic ethos of the traditional Hindu society. It was essentially within this discourse of hierarchy, despite occasional references to equal rights for women, that Vidyasagar situated his reform proposal' (Bandyopadhyay 1995: 29). Perhaps in vain did Ishwarchandra Sharma remove his caste surname for the momentous Vidyasagar (the sea of knowledge)!

Vivekananda's Hindu Polemics

Political expediency, the growing fear of Muslim or Christian proselytisation, and reverberations of the anti-caste movements in many parts of the country forced privileged-caste Hindus to develop a new rhetoric of Hinduism and cultural nationalism. This was especially necessitated by the emergence of non-brahman movements in the south and west India in the second half of the nineteenth century—dalit-bahujan leaders such as Jotirao Phule, Iyothee Thass, and Narayana Guru had arrived on the scene. The caste elites read the writing on the wall, and some of them came forward with their concern for the 'oppressed masses' and the enslaved Hindu nation. In sync with the earlier reformers, they located the reason for degeneration of India in the perversion of the Sanatana Dharma of their visionary ancestors. And, predictably, they found the panacea for all the maladies (of not just India but of the whole world) in a revival of the spirit of the Veda-Upanishad and Varnashram Dharma. Beginning in the upper-caste circles of Bengal—and later disseminated to various parts of the country by the likes of Dayananda Saraswati (north India) and Bal Gangadhar Tilak (Maharashtra)—this trend of (what has been labelled as) cultural nationalism gradually gathered momentum and culminated in the soft Hinduism of Gandhi on the one hand and the hardcore Hindutva of V.D. Savarkar on the other (which we shall see later).

An illustrious figure of Hindu revivalism was Narendranath Datta who renamed himself Vivekananda (1863–1902). He launched an impressive attack on the existing 'degeneration' of India but combined it, far more effectively than other cultural nationalists, with a passionate evocation of the ancient Hindu glories. His dream of a rejuvenated and vibrant India was, however, wedded, in Sumit Sarkar's words, to 'a near-total lack of clarity about socio-economic programmes, methods of mass contact, or even political objectives' (1983: 73). Jyotirmaya Sharma for his part found:

For Vivekananda, what was the life of this nation? Religion. What was the language of the nation? Religion. What was the central idea of this nation? Religion. Politics, society, poverty alleviation and social reform had to be approached only through religion. India's 'core' was not politics or social reform, but religion. It was the religion of the Aryans. (2003: 104–5)

This point is illustrated in this author's recent and most penetrating study of the man and his mission, aptly titled *Cosmic Love and Human Apathy: Swami Vivekananda's Restatement of Religion* (J. Sharma 2012).

Vivekananda appealed for identification with the *daridra-narayana* (the suffering poor), derided the sucking of the blood of the poor and the torture of the 'lower' castes, and in the same breath chastised the anti-brahman movements of the south for inciting 'fighting among the castes'. Asserting that acquiring spirituality, Sanskrit and brahmanhood was the road to freedom for the caste-oppressed, this self-proclaimed 'Vedantic socialist' said,

To the non-brahmana castes, I say, be not in a hurry. You are suffering from your own fault. Who told you to neglect spirituality and Sanskrit learning? Why do you now fret and fume because somebody else has more brains, more energy, more pluck than you? . . . Instead of wasting your energy in quarrels . . . use all your energies in acquiring the culture which the brahmana has, and the thing is done. Why do you not become Sanskrit scholars? Why do you not spend millions to bring Sanskrit education to all the castes in India? That [Sanskrit education] is the secret of power in India. Sanskrit and prestige go together in India. . . . As Manu says, all these privileges and honours were given to brahmana, because with him is the treasury of virtue. (Vivekananda 1988: 87–9)

So immersed was Vivekananda in the brahmanic culture and Aryan pride that at times he could not hide his visceral hatred of the 'lower' castes. He cursed the British for educating them and cautioned the upper castes about the threat of a looming mass awakening:

. . . And the Europeans are now educating those ignorant, illiterate low-caste people, who toil fields in their loin cloth, are of the non-Aryan race. They are none of us. This is going to weaken us and give benefit to both these Europeans and the low-caste people. (Cited in Biswas 1998: 251)

There are some references in Vivekananda's writings to the imminent shudra rule by which he meant the rise of the 'lower' castes—this is often quoted to show his revolutionary fervour—'but it is quite significant that he should also think that this represented a general lowering of culture' (A.P. Sen 1993: 331). Picking out some isolated and out-of-context utterances, his admirers project him as a champion of social justice. In reality, he was a celebrator of caste culture, as is evident from the following roll of his statements:

Caste has kept us alive as a nation, and while it has many defects, it has many more advantages. (*Complete Works of Swami Vivekananda* [henceforth *CW*], vol. II: 489)

It is in the nature of society to form itself into groups. . . . Caste is a natural order; I can perform one duty in social life, and you another; you can govern a country, and I can mend a pair of old shoes, but that is no reason why you are greater than I, for can you mend my shoes. . . . Caste is good. That is the only natural way of solving life. (*CW*, vol. III: 245–6)

Each caste has become, as it were, a separate racial element. If a man lives long enough in India, he will be able to tell from the features what caste a man belongs to. (*CW*, vol. VIII: 54)

Vivekananda denied that caste hierarchies coincided with differences in ritual status and that theories propounded in the shastras had been used to validate and perpetuate caste stratification. His faith in the varna dharma made him advocate a return to the socio-religious system of Manu and Yajnavalkya (A.P. Sen 1993: 341). The official records reveal that the Ramakrishna Math and Mission that he founded placed great importance on the 'family culture' of potential recruits. He was also strongly opposed to inter-caste marriages (ibid.: 331–2). Contradicting what many loudly proclaim as his unique socialism, Vivekananda himself admitted that he was merely aiming at religious and not social unity (ibid.).

What explains Vivekananda's occasional diatribes against the 'puritanical' and 'sectarian' brahmans? That was due to the orthodoxy's challenge to his credentials as a religious teacher, citing the reason that he was a shudra. (He came from the kayastha caste, traditionally considered low in the varna hierarchy.) After his 'triumphant' return from Euro-America in the 1890s, some jealous pandits held him 'guilty' of crossing the ocean, socialising with the *mlechchhas*, and eating 'forbidden' food. In fact, the opposition to his leadership was symbolic of a long simmering animosity between the two dominant castes of Bengal. The bone of contention was the brahmans' refusal to give high-caste status to the kayasthas. Raja Pearymohun Mukhopadhyaya, chairing a felicitation meeting in honour of Vivekananda, expressed doubt as to whether a kayastha could become a *sannyasi* (N.S. Bose 1999: 298). The members of the Reception Committee had earlier requested Sir Gurudas Bannerjee, the noted nationalist and a judge of the Calcutta Supreme Court, to preside over the felicitation meeting. Banerjee had not only refused but reprimanded the organisers saying that 'had there been a Hindu raja in the country, Vivekananda would have been hung for violating caste rules' (B.N. Datta, cited in S.K. Biswas 1998: 237). A few years later, on Vivekananda's death, the same gentleman again declined to preside at the condolence meeting. Such caste chauvinism was still practised by the brahmans, though Vivekananda's acceptance of Ramakrishna (a brahman) as his guru and Ramakrishna's affection for his star disciple had greatly helped mitigate the antipathies.

Vivekananda's humiliation for his 'low' origin, however, did not dampen his enthusiasm for caste and brahmanism. His attitude to the gender question was no different. In love with traditional asceticism, he viewed women as a 'positive impediment in spiritual life, finding womanhood best exemplified by Mother, and demanding absolute fidelity in the case of the wife. Such instincts considerably fashioned Vivekananda's social attitude towards gender relations and related issues' (A.P. Sen 1993: 330). He disapproved of women's self-assertion and aspirations of equality, mocking them as the slavish imitation of the 'outlandish' feminism of the West. Asserting that the docile Sita was our paragon of feminine virtue, he painted a 'happy picture' of Hindu women in ancient India. In a speech at Oakland, he declared that denying the child-widow the right to remarry caused no 'particular hardship' to her. A cultured and well-instructed widow, he argued, does not consider life a hardship, because she lives a life of asceticism and devotion, which elevates her to higher levels of perfection. He believed that the faithfulness of widows was the pillar on which social institutions rested. On another occasion, he made the point that upper-caste widows seldom remarried because of the relative 'scarcity of men' (ibid.: 331).

Throughout his life, Vivekananda boasted that Hinduism was the world's greatest and only complete religious as well as scientific system. As Javeed Alam (1996: 73) points out, when it comes to defining Hinduism, history evaporates, practice disappears and what one gets is a distilled, idealised version of Vedantic religion. 'If a Hindu is not spiritual,' he would say, 'I do not call him a Hindu.' But he also gave his Hindu spirituality a distinct imperialist overtone. Proclaiming India's religious superiority, he gave the call to overpower the world with Hindu spirituality.

This is the great ideal before us, and everyone must be ready for it—the conquest of the whole world by India. . . . They are waiting for it, they are eager for it. . . . We must go out, we must conquer the world through our spirituality and philosophy. There is no other alternative, we must do it or die. (Vivekananda, see Hay 1988: 76)

What was the spirituality Vivekananda was so desperate to preach to the world? He had blindly accepted every aspect of brahmanism, and was candid enough to admit that he had no religious ideology of his own. It was the same karma, dharma, incarnation, caste, and patriarchy inscribed in the brahmanical scriptures. Living more in the past than in the present, he was puffed up with pride that his vision of the future of India was based on, and inspired by, the 'glorious past'.

Nowadays everybody blames those who constantly look back to the past. It is said that so much looking back to the past is the cause of India's woes. To me, on the contrary, it seems that the opposite is true. So long as they forgot the past, the Hindu nation remained in a state of stupor and as soon as they have begun to look into this past, there is on every side a fresh manifestation of life. It is out of this past that the future has to be moulded, this past will become the future. (*CW*, vol. IV: 324)

For Vivekananda, there was no difference between Indian culture and Hindu culture. His Hindu chauvinism brought him into bitter conflict with not only Christianity and Islam, and also Buddhism. His admirers talk about his generosity and universal appeal, but he could not tolerate even the mildest criticism of his faith. When some Christian missionaries raised the issues of caste and untouchability, he questioned Christ's historicity, and asserted that early Christians may have had Hindu origins (A.P. Sen 1993: 338). But his sharpest attack was reserved for Muhammad and his religion. He portrayed Islam as irrational and violent, and depicted Muslims as mindless slaughterers. To him Muslims (in India) were not only 'foreigners' but their religion too was an unacceptable presence.

Now, the Mohammedans are the crudest in this respect, and the most sectarian. Their watchword is, 'There is one God, and Muhammad is His Prophet.' Everything beyond that, not only is bad, but must be destroyed forthwith; at a moment's notice, every man or woman who does not belong to this worship must be immediately broken; every book that teaches anything else must be burnt. From the Pacific to the Atlantic, for five hundred years blood ran all over the world. That is Mohammedanism!
(*CW*, vol. IV: 122)

Vivekananda's description of Islam and its followers borders on paranoia:

The more selfish a man, the more immoral he is. And so also with a race. That race which is bound down to itself has been the most cruel and the most wicked in the whole world. There has not been a religion that has clung to this dualism more than that founded by the Prophet of Arabia, and there has not been a religion which has shed so much blood and been so cruel to other men. In the Koran there is the doctrine that a man who does not believe these teachings should be killed; it is a mercy to kill him!
(*CW*, vol. II: 350–1)

Thus, like Bankim and other brahmanic nationalists of the time, Vivekananda had no difficulty in preferring the colonial regime to 'tyrannical' Muslim rule. India stopped progressing during Muslim rule, he said, for then it was not a question of progress but of self-preservation. 'Now that the pressure has gone, we must move forward' (*CW*, vol. IV: 318).

Vivekananda's call for the building of a new India on 'a Vedantic brain and an Islamic body', in a letter to a Muslim friend Sarfaraz Husain, has been grossly misread by many historians (including Nehru in his *Discovery of India*) as a wonderful instance of India's secular nationalism. In fact, it is a reiteration of the Hindu stereotype of Muslims congenitally endowed with physical strength but lacking in intellect. In such a synthesis, as Javeed Alam argues, Hinduism is the ideological engine and Islam is at its service as the muscled handmaiden to carry out the physical work. 'It privileges Hinduism and downgrades Islam' (Alam 1996: 74). The Vedantic-brain-and-Islamic-body is very much like the brahman-shudra harmony in which the former thinks and orders, and the latter follows and toils.

A lesser-known aspect of Vivekananda's fanaticism is his contempt for—and misrepresentation of—the Buddha and Buddhism. In this respect, too, he carries the stain of the brahmanical rubbishing of Buddhism as an unnecessary offshoot of Hinduism. The Buddha was held guilty of destroying the caste system (thus disrupting the ancient social equilibrium); committing the blunder of iconoclasm (which was later corrected by Shankara, Madhava, Ramanuja) made worse by the use of popular languages by the Buddhists in lieu of Sanskrit (thus creating a dangerous rupture from the Vedic tradition); and, bringing ruin upon India by promoting the tenet of non-killing, among other vices (Vivekananda, *CW*, vol. III: 230,

264; vol. IV: 131–2, 272–3; vol. V: 317–18; also see J. Sharma 203, 116–17). In the course of its expansion, Buddhism absorbed into its fold many different barbarous races of mankind (Vivekananda 1998: 69), and this led to the degeneration of not only Buddhism but also Hinduism. Speaking before a gathering of Orientalists in 1900 in Paris, he asserted that 'the vulgarisation of many Hindu religious symbols or objects of worship was really the result of "degenerate" Buddhism entering the mainstream of Hinduism' (A.P. Sen 1993: 335). From that time to the present, 'the whole work in India is a re-conquest of this Buddhistic degradation by the Vedanta. It is going on and is not yet finished' (Vivekananda 1998: 69).

It is notable that Vivekananda considered the arch reactionary B.G. Tilak his alter ego and for his part Tilak hailed Vivekananda as 'a person of the stature of Shankaracharya' (*Kesari*, 8 July 1902) and the real father of Indian nationalism. Their admiration for each other is understandable as both dedicated themselves to a nationalism which was inseparable from Hindu revivalism. Pride in the caste culture and confrontationist attitude towards Islam and Christianity, especially on the issue of conversion, also brought them closer to each other.

Taken in by the hagiography that has been spawned around Vivekananda, the 'Hindu secularists' now venerate him as the ultimate modern moralist, and deride fanatics for 'hijacking' and spoiling the good name of the Swami. What has come to be known as the 'Hindu Left' overlooks Vivekananda's supremacist rhetoric, his apotheosis of varnashrama and brahmanism, and his aggressive polemic against Islam, Christianity, and Buddhism. It overlooks his recipe for the salvation of the Hindus in three Bs: beef, biceps and *Bhagavad Gita*. His call to Hindu youth to acquire 'iron muscles and nerves of steel' and spread Hinduism in all corners of the world (because of its alleged superiority over other religions) were in fact a portent of the Hindu fascist ideology.

The Facade of Cultural Nationalism

By portraying brahmanical religion and philosophy as the best aspects of Indian cultural heritage, the caste elites fostered a self-glorifying obscurantism in the garb of patriotic pride. As these aspects were not common heritage of all Indians, the history became the heritage of the few. During the nineteenth century, the upper-caste values were sought to be universalised in unprecedented ways, aided and abetted by the colonial policy. The national discourse developed by the upper-caste literati had an overt or covert anti-Dravidian, anti-lower-caste, and anti-Muslim bias, with the concomitant centrality of the Aryan-brahman as the shaper of national unity. Even a sensitive reformer like M.G. Ranade saw brahmanism as the Aryan faith which had served to unite north and south in ancient India (see Chakravarti 1998: 102). Like Tilak, Ranade believed the Aryan to be the chosen race, and blamed the Aryan interaction with the 'lowly' non-Aryans for the odious aspects of Hinduism (ibid.).

The art and architecture, everyday science and technology, folk music and popular literature in which the non-elites played an important role were glossed over in nationalist history. The medieval period was portrayed as a dark age of depredation, decadence, and Islamic atrocities on the Hindus. The tendency to put all blame for India's misfortune on the subjection to Muslim rule was strong. It was customary to project the British as saviours of Hindus from the Muslim misrule and tyranny (Sarkar 1997: 19). This attitude helped create the notions of two separate and mutually antagonistic peoples, and ultimately resulted in the two-nation theory that led to the partition of the country.

The Western concepts of democracy, equality and human rights that came to India with the British rule found favour with the elite, but instead of applying the same principles to all Indians, the privileged groups appropriated the egalitarian principle only for the 'nation' of which they were the sole representatives. The question of equality, thus, became the question of equality between nations. It was selectively utilised to bolster the demand for national self-determination. The nationalist leaders, demanding self-government and independence from the British, refused to accept that the upper strata of Indian society should also give up their privileges and practise democracy in the social sphere. Cultural nationalism, in other words, was steeped in those ascriptive values that guaranteed the political domination of the few over the many within the Indian society.

In his essay 'Nabavarsha' (1902), Rabindranath Tagore, perhaps the greatest humanist of the *bhadralok* literati, argued the inevitability of inequality in human society. In another essay 'Brahman', published in the same year, he 'counterposed the entire society of gentle folk (*bhadra sampradaya*) who should be given *dwija* (twice-born) status, to those considered 'shudras', in ancient India as well as today—'Santals, Bhils, Kols, bands of sweepers'—for in a proper samaj 'neck and shoulders must not be lowered to the level of the ground' (see S. Sarkar 1997: 26). Applauding brahmans as the guardians of society, Tagore said: 'Brahmanism is a quality and it is a spiritual quality unique to the Indian nation, in contrast to Western philosophy' (see S. Basu 2002: 116). All that is sublime, all that is oriented to knowledge and wisdom, is expressed in the brahmanic qualities which are the spirit of the Indian nation. The quest of Europe-type equality and competition, he stressed, may be quietened through brahmanic prayers and pacificism. Tagore concluded that India in its quest of national identity needed to rediscover the essential brahman again. 'We do not want to be Europeans but we want to be Dwijas' (ibid.).

B.G. Tilak, lionised as the 'Father of Indian Unrest', and other militant nationalists such as B.C. Pal and Lajpat Rai attacked reform and social change as counterpoise to cultural unity and national solidarity. Grassroots movements being waged by dalit-bahujans at various levels (as we shall see in subsequent chapters) were opposed as 'divisive' as they would weaken the struggle against the colonial rule. Nationalism, thus, encouraged revivalist politics to obscure the social issues and suppress popular protest from below.

In Maharashtra, Vishnushastri Chiplunkar and Tilak took upon themselves the responsibility of defending brahmanism and its traditions. They attacked those who questioned discriminatory practices in the name of religion. Chiplunkar's essays in his magazine *Nibandhmala* (1874–81)—evocative of the lost Hindu and brahman glory—and Tilak's alliance with the Poona revivalists in the 1890s forged through opposition to the Age of Consent Bill (outlawing marriages for girls less than twelve years of age), and refusal to permit Ranade to hold the Social Conference at the Congress pavilion in 1895—Tilak and his goons violently disrupted the session and threatened to burn down the pavilion if the conference was held—were clear pointers to their reactionary politics (Keer 2000; Sarkar 1983).

Especially notable is the difference between the reformist platitudes which the caste elites sometimes had to mouth and what they practised. Addressing a conference on the depressed classes in 1918, Tilak, for example, spoke at length on why untouchability must be abolished. Soon after, asked to sign a manifesto declaring that he would not practice untouchability, Tilak refused. He also refused to acknowledge an appeal addressed to him by Bombay's untouchables for support in their temple-entry programme. In 1918, he opposed the Bill validating inter-caste marriage on the grounds that it was anti-Hindu, especially anti-brahman. He paid lip-service to protect the interests of workers and peasants, but opposed the Bombay government move in 1901 to restrict the transfer of peasant lands to moneylenders. Opposing the anti-landlord legislation, he stated: 'Just as the government has no right to rob the sowcar [moneylender] and distribute his wealth among the poor, in the same way the government has no right to deprive the khot [landlord] of his rightful income and distribute the money to the peasant. This is a question of rights and not of humanity' (see S. Sarkar 1983: 69). Such pro-rich agenda determined the politics of upper-caste nationalists before and after Tilak. The nationalism became, for all practical purposes, a smokescreen to hide the hideous reality and present the selfish interests as national interests.

The ploy to establish 'brahmanism as nationalism' took an uglier form at the turn of the new century, giving rise to the separatist Hindu-Muslim politics amidst the clamour for freedom. The frequent use of brahmanic symbols, metaphors and myths for the national cause—Tilak's Ganesh Puja and Gandhi's Rama-rajya—and the tendency of brahman literati such as Bankim to portray Muslims as enemies and foreigners created an atmosphere for the growth of communalism among both 'majority' and 'minority' communities.

The brahmanic communalism was no longer confined to Bengal and Maharashtra. In the north, especially in Uttar Pradesh, major figures of the fledgling Hindi movement followed in the footsteps of the Bengali-Marathi revivalists. The new, Sanskritised Hindi that emerged in the process was an artificial and divisive creation of vested interests. Its atavistic bonding with Sanskrit was combined with a fierce opposition to not only Urdu but also popular dialects—Avadhi, Bundelkhandi, Rajasthani, Brajbhasha, Maithili, Bhojpuri, Magadhi—of the region. The myopia of Hindi chauvinists destroyed the immense potential of a language that was earlier more earthy, dynamic, and creative (Rai 2001). Driven by the Hindu revivalist aspirations, the campaign for Hindi as the national language injected communal consciousness in the cow belt. Bhartendu Harishchandra (1850–85), regarded as the father of modern Hindi, presented the familiar admixture of colonial loyalty and Hindu patriotism. His brand of nationalism combined pleas for the observance of caste rules and the use of indigenous articles with demands for a ban on cow-slaughter and the replacement of Urdu by Hindi in courts and government offices.

The formula of 'Hindi-Hindu-Hindustan' that Bhartendu's colleague Pratap Narain Mishra invented in 1882 signalled the dangerous developments that lay ahead. Bhartendu's idea that all Indians are Hindus and Mishra's argument in his journal *Brahman* that Hindus alone are real Indians helped in moulding a literary-political discourse steeped in narrow religious identities. The campaign for a purified, homogeneous Hindi as the sole custodian of the 'equally harmonious and unified Hindu-Indian society' not only meant a rejection of the diversity of Indian culture, but also carried within it the agenda of cultural exclusions of the subaltern masses (Orsini 2002). As a top Congress leader and a champion advocate of 'official' Hindi, P.D. Tandon said, 'If you want to become national you have to forsake all attraction to other useless ideas and groups and stand under the banner of one nation, one language, one script, one culture' (see Orsini, ibid.: 381).

The ideological moorings of cultural nationalism, despite eloquent claims to the contrary, remained conservative. This nationalism, though claiming to represent all sections of society, was hopelessly divided into separate campaigns by gentlemen-representatives of Hindus and Muslims. The term Hindu became a euphemism for the upper castes who crushed any dissenting voice from the lower rungs as 'casteist', 'divisive', 'loyalist'—all in the name of social cohesion and anti-colonialism. A few appropriate noises made sporadically by a Tagore here or a Ranade there were drowned in the din of chauvinism. None of the reformer-nationalists, even when their views sometimes converged with those of the anti-caste or anti-landlord movements, were willing to forge a united front with the struggling people. For the reformer-nationalists, as Aijaz Ahmad brilliantly argues, 'the nation' was not 'the people' but

> a rhetorical category, always to be invoked but never granted any autonomous space in those projects of reform, while the reforms that were proposed or undertaken in the name of the nation always remained confined to their own class, caste and/or community. So, the line between reform and revivalism remained forever blurred, and the revivalisms as such were just so many narcissisms of those upper castes that could no longer rule in reality and therefore rule only in the imagination, not in the present but in a past that was somehow to be transformed into a future. The only thing that guaranteed the security of this fantasy was the fact of property, which they still commanded, as they had commanded in the past; here, then, was the real link between their past and their present, which they hoped to continue into the future. Colonial government was acceptable because it was now the real guarantor of that property. Those early heroes of ours were conservative, socially and politically, and not even notably anti-colonial. In this milieu, then, our nationalism was born.
>
> (Ahmad 2002: 84–5)

Notes

1. The Hindu hardliners blame the pre-modern Muslim rule for all that was wrong with the Indian society, ignoring the fact that the Muslim rule itself was made possible by inter-caste antipathies as well as the conspiracies of local (Hindu) rulers against one another. The oppressed castes, some scholars contend, had welcomed the Muslim invaders as deliverers and emancipators. M.N. Roy (1937: 96) writes that Mohammad Ibne Kassim, the first Muslim warlord who triumphantly entered India in the year

712, 'conquered Sindh with the active assistance of the Jats and other communities oppressed by the brahman rulers'.
2. It is interesting that Gandhi, while answering the question 'why was India lost?', in his *Hind Swaraj* ([1909] 1999: 18–19) frankly admitted this, 'The English have not taken India; we have given it to them.'
3. David Kopf (1969: 103) has shown in his acclaimed study of Orientalism how at Fort William College, the first college established by the British in India, the young scholars under H.T. Colebrook and William Carey 'seemed to identify India with Hinduism and regarded Muslims as intruders'.
4. Max Müller brought out in the 1870s the first printed edition of *Rigveda* with the commentary of Sayana. This made Vivekananda believe that Max Müller was a reincarnation of Sayana. 'My impression is that it is Sayana who is born again as Max Müller to revive his own commentary on the Vedas. I have had this notion for long. It became confirmed in my mind, it seems after I have seen Max Müller' (*The Complete Works of Swami Vivekananda*, vol. VI: 495).
5. The brahmanic strategy of reform 'from within' created acute problems for the intended reforms. Pointing out the contradictions in a leading reformer's advocacy against polygamy, Sumit Sarkar writes: 'Vidyasagar sought to eliminate one kind of polygamy which Manu had permitted (marrying a woman of lower caste) by emphasising that in *Kaliyuga* intercaste marriage was strictly prohibited. His polemic against Kulinism also used the argument that it often led to delayed marriages for girls in the absence of suitably high-status bridegrooms—and this, Vidyasagar emphasised, clearly contradicted the shastric command that marriage had to be consummated before the first menses. Perhaps it was this passage in his own earlier writing that contributed to Vidyasagar's surprising ambiguity on the Age of Consent issue, when his opinion was officially asked for shortly before his death' (Sarkar 1997: 269–70).
6. Upholding human hierarchy on the basis of good or bad conduct in previous births, an Upanishadic verse (*Chandyoga Upanishad*: 5. 10. 7) equates a low born person with a beast: 'Those whose conduct has been good, will quickly attain some good birth—the birth of a brahman or a kshatriya, or a vaishya. But those whose conduct has been evil will quickly attain an evil birth—the birth of a dog, or a hog or a chandala'. Chandyoga is among the Upanishads considered most important because it is derived from the *Samaveda* which has been given the most exalted place by Krishna declaring, 'I am the *Samaveda* among the Vedas' (*Bhagavad Gita* 10. 22).

APPENDIX

Parallel Fascist Thinking in East and West: Nietzsche, Nazism and the Hindu Nationalism

> The Aryans have been the prominent actors in the great drama of history and have carried to their fullest growth all the elements of active life with which our life is endowed. They have perfected society and morals . . . literature and works of art, the elements of science, the laws of art and the principles of philosophy. In continual struggle with each other and with Semitic and Turanian races these Aryan nations have become the rulers of history and it seems to be their mission to link all parts of the world together by the chains of civilisation, commerce and religion.
>
> F. Max Müller [1859] 1968: 13

Racism is at base the idea that among the three principal races—white, black, and yellow—the white is the superior. In the nineteenth century, Orientalist and Indological discourse encouraged the idea that among this chosen race the Aryan was the noblest and most powerful. All civilisation, its adherents in both Europe and India exclaimed in one way or another, flowed from the Aryan race. A parallel to the brahmanic chauvinism—the glorification of the Aryan-brahman with the concomitant debasement of the non-Aryan shudra—is to be found in the philosophy of Friedrich Nietzsche (1844–1900) whose theories of the 'master race' (*Harrenvolk*) and 'superman' (*Ubermensch*) were later appropriated by Hitler to form the Nazi *weltanschauung*. A mesmerising writer with a rare felicity of language, Nietzsche's philosophy revolved around the idea—and ideal—that power was 'godliness'. He admitted that

Colonialism and the Birth of Vedic–Brahmanic Nationalism 241

in his philosophy (of power) which became identified with 'will to power' and violence over a debased class of commoners—he was only following the scheme of Manu, the doyen of brahmanical ideology. In *The Anti-Christ,* he wrote:

> To set up a law-book of the kind of Manu means to concede to a people the right henceforth to become masterly, to become perfect—to be ambitious for the highest art of living. To that end, the law must be made unconscious: this is the purpose of every holy lie. The order of castes, the supreme, the dominating law, is only the sanctioning of a natural order, a natural law of the first rank over which no arbitrary caprice, no 'modern idea' has any power. (Nietzsche [1895] 1968a: 177)

Nietzsche was unhappy with what he termed the plebeianisation of Europe by the 'onslaughts' of democracy. For that he held Christianity responsible, despising it as embodiment of the victory of the subordinated classes over the elite. For him, Christianity was a great curse, a 'perversion' no less than the 'typical teachings of the socialists'. In his frenzied advocacy of the 'will' to subjugate the commonality, he finds inspiration in the brahmanic philosophy of power which he wields as a club to bludgeon Christianity, which represents 'the victory of Chandala values . . . the undying Chandala revenge (against the elite) as the *religion of love*' (ibid.: 58). Even the suggestion of a comparison between the *Manusmriti* with the Bible appals Nietzsche:

> . . . I read the Law-book of Manu, an incomparably spiritual and superior work, [and] it would be a sin against the spirit even to mention in the same breath the Bible. One sees immediately that it has a real philosophy behind it, in it, not merely an ill-smelling Jewish acidity compounded of rabbinism and superstition. . . . Not forgetting the main thing, the basic difference from every sort of Bible: it is the means by which the noble orders, the philosophers and the warriors, keep the mob under control; noble values everywhere, a feeling of perfection, an affirmation of life, a triumphant feeling of well-being in oneself and of goodwill towards life—the sun shines on the entire book. (Nietzsche [1895] 1968a: 175)

In his earlier work *Thus Spoke Zarathustra* (1883–5), Nietzsche announced that 'God is dead' and made a prophecy that the coming elite would rule the world and from them would spring the superman. In *The Will to Power*, he proclaims: 'A daring and ruler race is building itself up. . . . The aim should be to prepare a transvaluation of all values for a particularly strong kind of man, most highly gifted in intellect and will. This man and the elite around him will become the "lords of the earth"—yes, gods but no God, and the new gods will not spare their neighbours!' In *Thus Spoke Zarathustra*, he extols his 'superman' as the beast of prey, 'the magnificent blond brute, avidly rampant for spoil and victory', and in *The Anti-Christ* he rhapsodises about Manu's elevation of brahmans as the 'gods on earth' and his belittling of the shudras as helpless and servile. No wonder, Ambedkar—perhaps the only Indian of his time who had seriously studied Nietzsche—argued that Zarathustra was a new name for Manu and *Thus Spoke Zarathustra* was but a new edition of *Manusmriti* (Ambedkar, *BAWS*, vol. 3: 74–6).

It is interesting that in *Twilight of the Idols* (subtitled 'How to Philosophise with a Hammer') Nietzsche, like Manu, uses animal imagery to describe the 'inferior' class of humans. He describes the menial race, the shudras, as 'the non-bred human being', 'the hotchpotch human being'. He speaks glowingly of Manu's savaging of the chandala, the untouchable, who is anti-thesis of the brahman, the superman (Nietzsche [1889] 1968a: 57). Society is 'not entitled to exist for its own sake but only as a superstructure and scaffolding by means of which a select race of beings may elevate themselves to their higher duties'. This 'rearing of exceptional men' will necessarily entail, he emphasises, the drastic curtailing of man's natural rights. There is no such thing, he asserts, as a right to live, a right to work, or a right to be happy, for ordinary humans. In this respect, he is categorical that the common man, the shudra, is no different from the 'meanest worm', and stresses 'Men shall be trained for war and women for the procreation of the warrior. All else is folly'. It seems that he also inherits from Manu a vicious misogyny. In *Thus Spoke Zarathustra* he exclaims: 'Thou goest to woman? Do not forget thy whip!'

A terribly lonely man who led a wretched life, Nietzsche wrote most of his books when he was seriously sick, suffering syphilis, and wildly deluded. But this did not stop his great influence among amoral intellectuals and two of the most bloodthirsty dictators of the twentieth century. Nietzschean ideas fired the imagination of Hitler; and Mussolini regarded Nietzsche, along with Machiavelli and Mazzini, one of his ideological mentors. William Shirer, the scrupulous chronicler of the Nazi Germany, points out the connection between the Nietzschean philosophy of power and Hitler's megalomania. Though there were other eggheads who nurtured the intellectual roots of the Third Reich, Hitler was fascinated with Nietzsche and his prophecy of an elite who would replace the 'dead God' and rule the world. He appropriated not only Nietzsche's thoughts but also the latter's penchant for grotesque exaggeration: 'Lords of the earth' is a familiar expression in his autobiography *Mein Kampf*. Rantings of 'superman' and 'master race' struck a responsive cord in the Fuehrer's littered mind. 'That in the end Hitler considered himself the superman of Nietzsche's philosophy cannot be doubted' (Shirer [1961] 1991: 97–113).

Though the philosopher's admirers vehemently deny any nexus between Nietzsche and Hitler, one cannot brush aside the epistemic capability of a philosophy like Nietzsche's—and Manu's—in manufacturing mass murder. Scholars like Walter Kaufmann defend Nietzsche as a supremely disinterested philosopher, and not in any way responsible for his appropriation by the Third Reich (Kaufmann 1974). Instead of providing a serious reckoning with one of the greatest philosophers of power (as a brilliant new study points out), Kaufmann built a massive Nietzsche industry for the Anglo-American world, neutralizing his frontal attacks on democratic equality and Christian morality and erasing the darker elements of his philosophising, and presenting him as a charming and inoffensive existentialist—a 'King-Kong-in-chains . . . under heavy sedition' (Ratner-Rosenhagen 2012). But Nietzsche himself saw his work neither as philosophy nor as literature, but as 'declarations of war'. The nihilist wordsmith was in thrall to savagery and brutality without which he saw no creativity. 'The greatest evil belongs to the greatest goodness: but that is creative', he wrote in *Thus Spoke Zarathustra*.

Nietzsche's eloquence and rage against all modern conceptions of justice and equality, in fact, verge on pornography of strength. His advocacy of suppression of common people for the power of the aristocratic few carries fascist undertones. Tracing the intellectual roots of Nazism, Shirer rightly stresses that Hitler was not the originator of those megalomaniacal ideas, his monstrosity lay in the fact that he began to put those nasty thoughts into practice when he assumed power in Germany. The glorification of violence and conquest; the absolute power of the authoritarian state; the belief in the superiority of the Aryan race; the hatred for Jews and Slavs; and utter contempt for compassion and kindness—these were not original with Hitler, only the ruthless, barbaric means of employing them.

Hindutva's Fascist Connection

The fascist phenomenon has an Indian dimension and connection (that still survives in India). There was an affinity between the Nazism and the Hindu nationalism, reflected in the adoration of Hitler and his imperialistic agenda by many modern admirers of Manu. In fact, the Hindu Mahasabha and the Rashtriya Sawayamsevak Sangh (founded in 1915 and 1925, respectively) had modelled their 'Hindu nationalism' on Hitler's Nazism, extolling the Aryan race, religion, culture, and language. V.D. Savarkar—whose *Hindutva* (1923) inspired the RSS kind of 'cultural nationalism'—was in thrall to the European fascism. He coined the term Hindutva to dissociate it from the religious connotations and confines of traditional Hinduism so that he can also include all Indic religions such as Buddhism, Jainism and Sikhism in his notion of Hinduness. But it also had a strong connection with the earlier Hindu nationalisms of Dayananda, Vivekananda, Tilak, Bankim and Aurobindo, as several scholars have underlined variously (Jaffrelot 1999; Hansen 1999; Zavos 2000; A. Ahmad 2002; J. Sharma 2003).

Our nationalism was cultural well before it was political or civil or secular. In this ambience, the temptations of blood and belonging, of spiritual essence, of racial and religious particularity, of revivalism and purification were particularly strong. Religious identity was built into our canonical reform movements and into even the prehistory of Indian nationalism.
(Ahmad 2002: 83).

The RSS inherited from 'the fictions, the zealotries, the reform movements of the nineteenth century and the twentieth, from Bengal to Maharashtra to Punjab' and integrated their diverse elements into 'a singular, all-encompassing ideological position of a fascist kind and then linked, most crucially, to unique forms of organisation and mobilisation' (Ahmad 2002: 15).

Jaffrelot (1997) suggests that the rise of a particular form of Hindu nationalism in the 1920s was a cultural strategy oriented to defend brahmanic hegemony; and in this context he also un-ravels the fascination of Hindu ideologues with European fascism. In 1938, Savarkar as the president of Hindu Mahasabha, in a public meeting in Delhi, congratulated Hitler for having liberated the Sudetans who shared the 'same blood and same tongue' as the Germans. But even earlier, some Hindu Mahasabhaites had had direct contact with their fascist role models. B.S. Moonje, the president of the Hindu Mahasabha for a long time, was reported to have met both Hitler and Mussolini in 1931. Moonje came back to India and tried to transfer fascist models to the Hindu society and organise it militarily on the same pattern. So impressed was he by the military institutions of the European dictators that he established a military school at Nasik with financial support from many Indian princes (Jaffrelot 1996, 1997; Casolari 2000). At the same time, *Kesari* and *Mahratta* (journals which Tilak had launched) and *Hindu Outlook* (the mouthpiece of the Hindu Mahasabha) regularly published, between 1925 and 1935, editorials and articles in praise of Mussolini, Hitler, and Franco (ibid.).

Bhai Paramanand, who succeeded Moonje as president of the Hindu Mahasabha in 1933, saw a 'great affinity' between Hitlerism and the ideology of caste:

The message that Hitler sent on the Annexation (of Austria) in which he described himself as a tool in the hands of the Lord of Destiny for the unification of Germany reminded me of the assurance of Lord Krishna that whenever the world has need of him, He manifests Himself. Is the unity of India complete? I submit not. . . . Where is the Hitler who will bring about [Indian] unification? . . . Hitler's theory is National Socialism. . . . I find a great affinity between Hitler's National Socialism and the Varnashrama of the Hindus. (*Hindu Outlook*, 12 October 1938, see Jaffrelot 1997: 347)

Savarkar gave the call to *Hinduise all politics and militarise Hinduism*. Asserting 'We are Indians because we are Hindus and vice versa', he formulated that to a Hindu, India is not only a fatherland (*Pitribhu*) but also a holyland (*Punyabhu*), and made clear that Muslims' holyland is in Arabia and their mythology, godmen, ideas and heroes are of foreign origin. The RSS followed Savarkar's formulation as an article of faith, placing special importance on his splenetic outburst that Muslims are 'Muslims first and Muslims last and Indians never' (see Deoras 1984: 266–7). In the process, the continuous reference to the Nazi's racial policy and the comparison of the Jewish problem with the Muslim question in India reveal the evolution of the concept of 'internal enemy' along explicit fascist lines.

Showing solidarity with the Fuehrer and his Holocaust, the RSS ideologue M.S. Golwalkar, who became head of the organisation in 1940 after the death of its founder Hedgewar, writes in *We or Our Nationhood Defined*:

To keep up the purity of the race and its culture, Germany shocked the world by her purging the country of the semitic races—the Jews. National pride at its highest has been manifested here. Germany has also shown how well-nigh impossible it is for races and cultures, having differences going to the root, to be assimilated into one united whole, a good lesson for us in Hindustan to learn and profit by. (Golwalkar 1939: 35)

Golwalkar, like Savarkar, applies this logic to the Muslim minority (what Jews and Slavs were to the Nazis, the non-Hindu communities, especially Muslims, were—are—to the RSS), then spells out the local implications of what he learnt from Nazism:

[T]he non-Hindu people in Hindustan must either adopt the Hindu culture and language, must learn to respect and hold in reverence Hindu religion, must entertain no ideas but the glorification of the Hindu race and culture, i.e., of the Hindu nation and must lose their separate existence to merge in the Hindu race, or may stay in the country wholly subordinated to the Hindu nation, claiming nothing, deserving no privileges, far less any preferential treatment—not even citizen's rights. (Golwalkar 1939: 62)

The RSS' rallying cry, 'one nation, one culture, and one leader' echoes the Nazi catch-phrase 'Ein Volk, ein Reich, ein Fuehrer'. In his construction of nationalism on ethnic and cultural homogeneity, Golwalkar draws most of his inspiration from the German writers whose ideas prepared the ground for Hitler's rise to power. According to Jaffrelot,

> Golwalkar's concern with the promotion of a homogenous nation whose culture would be dominated by the Hindu Great Tradition harks back to his reading of Bluntschli and similar authors and to his admiration for their ethnic nationalism which, in Germany, prepared the ground for Nazism. Golwalkar considers cultural elements as inherent to the group, collectively inherited from its forefathers. For instance, he regards a national language—such as Sanskrit, the 'mother language' of India—as 'an expression of the Race spirit', obviously an equivalent of the German Volksgeist. (1999: 56–7)

'Upper-Caste Racism' against Dalit-Bahujans

The RSS version of 'Hindutva' or 'cultural nationalism' is based on a special kind of 'race spirit'. Its politics of exclusion, or inclusion through subordination, takes a form of 'upper-caste racism' (Pandey 1991). It takes the form of socio-cultural domination through the regulating (and time-tested) agency of caste and brahmanism, rather than being based on the rigid biological claims of the purity of blood. Jaffrelot (1999: 30–1) labels the ideology of Hindutva as a 'racism of domination [rather] than a racism of extermination'. In its discourse, the other is not excluded, but integrated to the body politic at a subordinate rank. The RSS ideologues had inherited this soft racism from their 'visionary' ancestors who had realised that this model was better suited to Indian conditions, as it was also more enduring and resilient.

It is interesting that the Hindu chauvinists who borrowed from the European Orientalists the theory of common racial origin of Europeans and Indian Aryans—and its corollary, the fabled southward migration which they interpreted to prove that the Aryans in India were the chosen race and that they had once dominated the world—did not stretch the argument beyond a point. This was necessitated by two factors. First, if the Indian Aryans insisted on racial purity they would appear to be foreigners in India; and second, the privileged castes, the core constituency of the RSS, are not more than 10 per cent of the Hindu population. Thus the RSS ideologues take recourse to the age-old fraud of 'hierarchical but holistic' Hindu society. This explains why, as Jaffrelot contends, the Hindu nationalists played down the eugenic content of European fascism and focused instead on a hierarchical corporatist organisation of society.

More recently, to cover up its hidden agenda of suppressing democratic aspirations of dalit-bahujans, the RSS tries to create an impression that something terrible is happening, that India is falling apart due to alien heterogeneity represented by the Muslims and Christians, who indulge in fissiparous politics and dance to the tune of external enemies—the Muslim Pakistan and the Christian West. In other words, the RSS makes a concerted but concealed attempt to reinforce brahmanical control of power and culture. It knows that it will have to devise new and more devious ways to tackle the traditionally subjugated people who are now demanding their rights and dignity.

It is significant that the RSS was born in the land of Phule and Ambedkar, the greatest leaders of dalit-bahujans in modern India. According to C.P. Bhiskikar, the official biographer of Hedgewar, lower-caste assertion was a danger on a par with the Muslim threat that lay behind the formation of the RSS (T. Basu et al. 1993: 14). Actually, the Muslim population (less than 10 per cent) and the supposed threat posed by it had been relatively weak in the region. But Maharashtra (as we shall see in the next chapter) had witnessed a radical movement against brahmanism from the 1870s onwards, with the establishment of Satyashodhak Samaj. Its ideas and activities were becoming popular among the dalit-bahujans. Pune, the home-turf of Tilak, was also the *karma-bhoomi* of Phule who was challenging the brahmans to bring out their Veda-Purana in the open.

By the 1920s, the dalits had started organising themselves under Ambedkar. It is notable that Nagpur, the birthplace of the RSS, was the centre of social radicalism and also the venue of the All India

Depressed Classes Conference in 1920 where Ambedkar had decisively rejected the paternalistic model of social reform advocated by V.R. Shinde and other moderates. Later, Nagpur was also to become the *deekshabhoomi* (the land of conversion) where Ambedkar led lakhs of dalits to accept Buddhism. The Phule-Ambedkar ideology is the strongest rejection of the brahmanical ideology of the RSS. Not surprisingly, the RSS targeted Phule-Ambedkarism and touted the theory that their ideology and movement emanated from a divisive 'caste mentality'.

The RSS stands by the brahmanical social order, but pretends to oppose caste. Its opposition to the emancipatory struggles of dalit-bahujans, however, leaves little doubt that its claim to fight casteism is hollow. Its idea of forging 'Hindu unity' is built on its violent politics against Muslims because, as Ambedkar once pointed out, 'a caste has no feeling that it is affiliated to other castes except when there is Hindu-Muslim riot'. Its politics serves its twin objectives of keeping the lowered castes under the brahmanical umbrella on the one hand, and fighting Muslims, Christians and other 'aliens' with the unity thus achieved, on the other.

The RSS claims that it strives for the unity of all Hindus, and that all castes and communities are equal in its eyes. It even includes adivasis and non-Hindu communities in its supremacist notion of 'Hindu', since anyone living in India is a Hindu! But the unificatory thrust of its ideology revolves around 'naturalness of the hierarchical social order', which renders autonomous dalit-bahujan assertions as divisive and anti-national. Behind its catch-phrase of *Hindu dharma, sanskriti* and *parampara* lurks visceral support for *varna vyavastha*. Golwalkar acclaims Manu as 'the first and greatest law-giver of the world' who taught everyone (without discrimination!) 'to learn their duties at the holy feet of brahmans'. In his *Bunch of Thoughts*, he rapturously repeats 'brahman is the head, king the hands, vaishyas the thighs and shudra the feet'. Thus, the RSS refutes any notion of inequality in the caste system, and exonerates upper castes from exploitation of the lowered castes (Jaffrelot 1999: 45 ff; Kanungo 2002: 141–2).

Though it hoodwinks the ignorant dalit-bahujans as foot soldiers for its dirty politics (especially during organising riots against Muslims and Christians), the RSS is basically an outfit of the privileged castes guided by a clique of brahmans. Its founder members—K.B. Hedgewar, B.S. Moonje, L.V. Paranjpe, B.B. Thalkar, and Baburao Savarkar—and all its early swayamsevaks were brahmans. In his diary, Moonje (himself a Deshastha brahman) referred to RSS cadres as 'brahman youths' and 'brahman lads' (Jaffrelot 1999: 45). Its ideological mentor was Savarkar, a Maharashtrian brahman; its founder was Hedgewar, a Telugu brahman; its organisational architect was Golwalkar, a Karhada brahman. The third chief of the RSS—after Hedgewar and Golwalkar—was Balasaheb Deoras, another Telugu brahman. Then came K.S. Sudarshan, a Tamil brahman. The present head is Mohan Bhagawat, a Maharashtrian brahman. Other modern leaders whom the RSS holds in high esteem—B.G. Tilak, S.P. Mookerjee, Deendayal Upadhyaya, and so on—were all brahman. Others have been in the RSS only to carry out the brahmanical politics.

Political commentators often speak of the RSS' hidden agenda, by which they mean things like the construction of a Ram temple at the site of the demolished mosque at Ayodhya, and the Hinduisation of all secular institutions. But the real game-plan of RSS is to keep the dalit-bahujans and Muslim masses uneducated and unempowered by raking up false issues in the name of religion. (In the 1990s, using religious symbols and slogans, the RSS and its affiliates brought the issue of temple construction at Ayodhya to the centrestage of politics in a nation where the majority of people, whether Hindu or Muslim, live in oppressive poverty.) They create a fear psychosis among dalit-bahujans against Muslims, Christians, and other 'aliens' by raising the bogey of 'Hinduism in danger' in a land where 80 per cent of the population is Hindu.

Riven as the Hindu formation is by internal divisions, this is precisely where the Muslim as full-time villain and scapegoat can serve a most useful function. Caste and communal violence have a 'symbiotic relationship'. The displacement of hatred, and the conjunction of caste/class interest with communal sentiment and indoctrination, Gujarat's anti-reservation agitation soon turned into anti-Muslim violence, and upper-caste protests against Mandal in 1990, with a little egging on by BJP, soon generated lethal attacks on Muslims throughout northern India. (S. Bose 1999: 141)

The resurgence of Islamic fundamentalism in many parts of the world, and the Congress's half-hearted secularism and dismal track-record of governance (which have over the years antagonised a large section of dalit-bahujans) come handy in the RSS design of creating religious mass hysteria. The RSS is an organisation shrouded in secrecy, it keeps even its own rank and file in the dark about its real aims and objectives, only its 'inner circle' is taken into confidence.

The discourse of [Hindutva] communalism criticises other religions for being monolithic, but aspires to build a monolithic unity. It glorifies diversity within Hinduism as a mark of its superiority over Semitic religions, but seeks to repress this diversity. It identifies aggressiveness as an evil intrinsic to other religions, but attempts to instil the same quality in all Hindus. It talks of patience and tolerance as innate virtues of Hindus, yet sees these traits as the basis of Hindu weakness. It condemns other religions for their politics of religious repression and temple destruction, but organises itself around the same politics. (N. Bhattacharya 1991: 131)

The glaring contrast between what it professes and what it practises (divide the dalit-bahujans, make them either fight each other or set them against Muslims and Christians) could teach a lesson or two to the likes of Paul Joseph Goebbels. From the very beginning, this hydra-headed organisation is fraudulent, authoritarian, and violent. (Nathuram Godse and his friends, who had close links with the RSS, shot dead Gandhi, the 'sanatani Hindu' who throughout his illustrious life resorted to all kinds of half-truths to defend and even valorise inegalitarian elements in Hinduism, only because he was a pacifist and his pacifism was seen as 'emasculating' the Hindus.) Its real politics and priorities are not made public but circulated privately among the select few. A case in point is the RSS secret circular no. 411, the sinister contents of which were exposed by a section of the print media in the 1990s. Here are some of the points of the above circular:

The RSS secret circular no. 411 has been issued to commanders and preachers. It is meant for the following actions, inter alia:

2. Scheduled Castes and other backward classes are to be recruited to the party so as to increase the volunteers to fight against the Ambedkarites and Mussalmans.
5. Hindutva should be preached with a vengeance among the physicians and pharmacists so that with their help, time-expired and spurious medicines might be distributed amongst the Scheduled Castes, Mussalmans and Scheduled Tribes.
10. Special attention should be given to the students of the Scheduled Castes and Scheduled Tribes so as to make them read the history written according to our dictates.
11. During riots the women of Mussalmans and Scheduled Castes should be gang-raped. Friends and acquaintances cannot be spared. The work should proceed on the Surat model.
15. All literature opposed to Hindus and Brahmans are to be destroyed. Dalits, Mussalmans, Christians, and Ambedkarites should be searched out. Care should be taken to see that this literature and writings do not reach public places. Hindu literature is to apply to the backward classes and Ambedkarites.
16. The demand by the Scheduled Castes and Scheduled Tribes for filling in the backlog vacancies in services shall by no means be met. Watch should be kept to see that their demands for entry into and promotion in government, non-government or semi-government institutions are rejected and their service records are destroyed with damaging reports.
18. Measures should be taken to make the prejudices amongst Scheduled Castes and backward people more deep-rooted. To this end, help must be taken from saints and ascetics.
20. Attacks should be started with vigour against equality-preaching communists, Ambedkarites, Islamic teachers, Christian missionaries and neighbours. (See O. Biswas 2001: 121–3; Shyam Chand 2002: 154–5)

The RSS, according to Shyam Chand, has not denied the existence of such a circular.

CHAPTER 5

Phule's Struggle against Brahmanical Colonialism

> Let others go where they will. We will follow the path of Jotiba [Phule]. We may or may not take Marx with us but we will certainly not abandon Jotiba's philosophy.
>
> B.R. AMBEDKAR, see Dangle 1992: 259

Jotirao Phule (1827–90) was the first in modern India to launch a movement for dalit-bahujan liberation. What Rammohun Roy, Dayananda Saraswati and Vivekananda were to the elitist cultural nationalism, Phule was to the freedom struggle of India's suppressed majority. His was an ideology and struggle against injustices in all their manifestations. Attacks on caste and brahmanism, though not unknown before, reached a turning point with him as he saw slavery of dalit-bahujans and women in the very structure of caste, and conceptualised it in a way that shifted attention from social mobility within the caste hierarchy to a rejection of the system itself. What made him a revolutionary—and the ideological-political founder of the anti-caste movement—was his ability to see the interconnections between caste, class, patriarchy, authoritarian family structure, and his multi-pronged politics to smash this oppressive matrix through a socio-cultural action based on solidarity—through a critical education—of all the oppressed.

Phule was also exceptional in seeing the close relation between knowledge and power. Underlining the crucial role of ideology in the scheme of domination, Phule delineated the knowledge–power nexus before Gramsci, Foucault, or Edward Said did (Omvedt 1994; G.P. Deshpande 2002; Chakravarti 1998, 2002; Bagade 2012). He saw brahmanism as an ideological and material system of monopolising knowledge and power by a particular class which uses these to exclude, divide and dominate other groups in society. He argued that 'even before trying to overturn the material power of the upper castes over the lower castes, and over their own women, it was necessary to step out of the ideologies of brahmanism for which access to knowledge was an essential prerequisite; that is, one had to understand a system before one could dismantle it' (Chakravarti 2002: 115). He termed this understanding of knowledge as *tritiya ratna*, the 'third eye', which was the means to end brahmanic hegemony and towards this end education, 'not mere alphabetical competence but the power to see through hegemonic ideology', was to play a crucial role (ibid.).

As he wanted to end all forms of subjugation, Phule strove to build a cultural foundation for such a transformation—a cultural transformation based on critical public education was at the centre of his struggle. Attacking the suppression of mass education as the worst form of treason, he made democratisation of education the locus of his freedom movement. The greatest injustice of caste culture, he stressed, was the relegation of all the lowered castes and women to illiteracy. It was the lack of knowledge, he bemoaned in a famous verse 'Vidya Bina Mati Geli' that turned India's toiling castes into virtual slaves.

Without education, intellect was lost; without intellect, morality was lost; without morality, dynamism was lost; without dynamism, wealth was lost; all this led to *shudras'* degradation and demoralisation: all the tragedy emanated from lack of knowledge. (Phule [1883] 1991: vol. 2: 94; slightly modified)

In 1848—the same year which saw the publication of the *Communist Manifesto*—Phule, at the age of twenty-one, dared to establish, defying the high-caste backlash, a school in Pune for untouchable women, the most oppressed and desolate segment of society. In striking contrast to the gentlemen-reformers of the time, he combined his radical ideology with radical practice. Waging struggle at all levels, he tried to develop a subversive understanding of history, culture and mythology, and communicating them to people through popular plays, songs, tracts, and organisation-building. He mocked the 'golden' ancient age, and exposed brahmanical self-interest in apotheosis of the past and maintenance of the status quo. As his intellectual biographer Rosalind O'Hanlon (1985: 150) says, 'Phule was always very much to the forefront in recognising the potential ideological importance of key symbols and concepts in nineteenth-century society, and in attempting to give them a meaning in line with his broader interpretation of history.'

Phule contended that a fragmented society could not constitute a genuine nation. Those claiming to represent the nation were actually its destroyers, he argued, since they not only ignored its exploitative divisions but actually sought to maintain them as a basis for their power. His struggle thus was very different from the priorities of organisations such as Brahmo Samaj, Prarthana Samaj and Arya Samaj, which provided the cultural bedrock to nationalism in the coming decades under the banner of the Indian National Congress.

Phule's radical ideology combined with an emancipatory grass-roots politics announced the arrival of a new factor in India's social chemistry. His understanding of the enslaving power of brahmanism was subversive. Through his popular writings and mass campaign, he unravelled the pseudo-religion and inhuman indignities that were systematically thrust upon the toiling people. Laying bare the slavery of the toiling castes and of all women, he stressed that those who did not admit of their enslavement could never be free. He made mass education the focal point of his movement, with the belief that critical knowledge would generate forces that would emancipate the subjugated.

An ideologue-activist unlike any other in India of his time, Phule grappled with all important questions facing society—caste, patriarchy, religion, history, mythology, language, literature, pedagogy, mass poverty, the state of agriculture, the lot of cultivators, contemporary politics, and colonialism. His range of concerns and ideas was broader and deeper than that of any other leader of the nineteenth century. Deshpande (2002) contends that he had 'a complete system of ideas', and that Phule was the first to identify and theorise the bipolar (*dvaivarnik*) structure of Indian society, marked by the dichotomous relationship between the oppressors (the brahmans) and the oppressed (the shudratishudras),[1] and he wanted the community of the oppressed to lead a revolution for all-round change:

Phule ... analysed the dvaivarnik structure of Indian society, and identified the shudratishudras as the leading agency of a social revolution. And the shudratishudras will lead the revolution on behalf on the whole society, to liberate the entire people from the shackles of brahmanism. What they will lead, then, is not a movement for some reform in the present structure, some tinkering here and there, but a total smashing up of the entire oppressive structure, ideological and material. Phule was the only thinker of the nineteenth century who insisted that this is both necessary and possible. (Deshpande 2002: 20–1)

To comprehend Phule, his thinking and his struggle in proper context, a quick look at the chronology of his life may be of some help. Phule was born in 1827 in a family of fruit-and-vegetable growers (Mali) in Pune. He was educated in a Marathi-medium school during 1834–8; married Savitri in 1840; continued education in an English-medium secondary school during 1841–7. In 1848, with the help of Savitri, he established a school—the first in India—for downtrodden girls; shocked and fearing a high-caste backlash, his father turned his son and daughter-in-law (who taught in the school) out in 1849. Undeterred, the husband-wife duo ran the school and set up more schools between 1848 and 1852, which admitted girls of all castes. Phule was felicitated in 1852 by the Department of Education for his educational work. In 1855, he established a night school for working people. Outraged by his activities, the reactionary elements made an abortive attempt on his life in 1856. In the 1860s, he joined the widow remarriage campaign. In 1863, he established a home for 'illegitimate' children and their mothers. Phule's father died in 1868; the same year he threw open the water-tank in his compound to the 'untouchables'. He published *Gulamgiri* (Slavery) in 1873 and followed it up with the founding of Satyashodhak Samaj (The Society of Truthseekers) on 24 September 1873. A member of the Pune Municipal Council during 1876–82, he deposed before the Hunter Commission for

Education in 1882, and gave his radical proposal for mass education. He published *Shetkaryacha Asud* ('Cultivators' Whipcord') in 1883. Honoured in a massive public meeting with the title of Mahatma on 11 May 1888; he fell seriously ill thereafter, but managed to write *Sarvajanik Satya Dharma Pustak* (The Book of True Religion) before he died on 28 November 1890.

Though impacted by Christian religious radicalism, Western rationalism and egalitarian movements of the modern West, Phule saw his anit-caste campaign as a continuation of those of the Buddha and Kabir.[2] He saw Buddha as a people's saviour, and Buddhism as antithetical to brahmanism (Phule [1873] 2002: 74). Buddhism, however, was no longer a living force in India in Phule's time. But many of his associates, including Gyanoba Krishnaji Sasane, were Kabirpanthis. Kabir's poems, especially those that presented a sharp critique of caste, played a sparkling role in shaping their radicalism. Tukaram Hanumant Pinjan, a close associate of Phule's, informs that it was Kabir's subversive verses which ignited the spark for the formation of the Satyashodhak Samaj (O'Hanlon 1985: 229–30).[3] Similarly, Tuka's radical poetry inspired them, especially his maxim *satya asatya ke man ke ne vahi, mane le nahin bahumati* (I have made my own mind with the truth and untruth; I do not accept the opinion of the gullible majority).

Power and Oppression of the Time

Born into a shudra family in Maharashtra within a decade of the collapse of brahman Peshwa rule in 1818, Phule faced many indignities commonly heaped on the lowered castes. The power of the Peshwas (who had become de facto rulers of the Maratha kingdom after Shahu's death) was gone following the British conquest, but the brahmans were still entrenched as the ruling caste. Under the Peshwai they had become very powerful, with all kinds of privileges and exemptions, which had not existed under the Maratha system founded by Shivaji. The Peshwas provided generous financial support to brahman students and scholars. The last Peshwa, Bajirao II (1796–1818), had enormously enhanced *dakshina* (gifts) for brahmans who in their turn venerated him as 'an incarnation of Krishna and Shiva' (Keer [1964] 2000: 4).

The brahmans, especially the Chitpavans, dominated the society at every level. They controlled economic, administrative, and cultural functions to such an extent that the Peshwai had come to be known as the 'Brahmanya raj' (Chakravarti 1998: 5). This raj strove to create, ideologically and materially, the ideal brahmanic kingdom. As a result, the caste system had become more rigid. Narayan Vishnu Joshi informs us that the rules of purity-pollution were strictly observed in those days. Mahars, mangs, chambhars, bhangis, dhedhs had to tie earthen pots to their waists while walking on roads. They had to sit down on noticing a brahman on the road, for their shadow was polluting. The untouchables were allowed to walk on roads only if they tied the branch of a tree to their wrist: the branch served the purpose of sweeping the earth and erasing their vile footprints! Mahars were not allowed to build their huts too close to an upper-caste location.

Renowned reformer Gopal Hari Deshmukh (1823–92), respected as Lokahitavadi, has described the horrors of the time in his *Shatapatre* (One Hundred Letters). Written in the late 1840s, it gives a graphic account of the social atrocities under the Peshwas. Himself a brahman, he viewed the oppressive situation as the by-product of centuries-old hierarchical values and held brahmans responsible for this. The social effects, he argued, of upholding ascriptive norms had been calamitous as they stifled individual merit and enterprise (see O'Hanlon 1985: 93). The verdict of the Lokahitavadi was a blunt statement of fact: 'The brahmans ruined the country' (cited in Keer [1964] 2000: 6).

The British rule brought a new system of governance, but also strengthened entrenched brahmanical dominance. As we saw in Chapter 4, collusion between the foreign and native elites was vital for the construction and survival of colonialism. This, however, was a complex process; colonialism ruined many traditionally powerful groups, but usually patronised and empowered the information-providing brahmans. It knocked off the old feudal order, but cultivated a section of the Indian elite, especially those who were able to learn and speak English, to act as intermediaries. It built an effective revenue collection system and a new administrative and legal structure to rule the subcontinent. This mammoth task involved the creation of new job opportunities, for which a certain kind of education was necessary. The brahmans who traditionally enjoyed the privilege of learning were able, despite the Peshwai's eclipse, to educate themselves (with generous colonial support) and make a smooth transition to the colonial rule by cornering almost all employment opportunities.

In the region under discussion, the colonial system elbowed out the traditional role of patil (village headman) as custodian of law and order, and empowered the brahman kulkarni (village accountant) whose help was required in the maintenance of revenue records. The introduction of private ownership of land and the gradual penetration of monetary economy in rural areas enhanced the power and prestige of the literate joshis (traditional priest-astrologers). In the new political economy, the privileged castes emerged as clear winners with their monopoly over colonial jobs. Moreover, caste-based societal rules were still strong—reinforced in many cases by the colonial policy—and worked in favour of brahmans. In a word, brahmanical dominance far from slackening its hold was in fact invigorated (Frykenberg 2001; Aloysius 1997).

Such was the social environment of Phule's time. Though education was no longer formally prohibited to the lower orders, the dominant castes did everything in their capacity to stop the dalit-bahujan children from getting an education. When Govindrao sent his son (the young Phule) to a school, Govindrao's brahman clerk ('helper') argued that learning was not the *dharma* of a shudra. (Had it not been the timely intervention of a Muslim gentleman, Gaffar Beg Munshi, and a British officer, Mr. Liggit, Joti like other children of his community would not have gone to school.) The Lokahitavadi commented on this incident in his *Shatapatre* (1850) thus:

> If a Brahmin were to come across a clerk of the Maratha caste or of a caste other than his own, he would get livid. The Brahmin would say that kaliyug was here, and learning (which had been held sacred) was being polluted by being imparted to the lower castes. Thus we see that

the Brahmins held the belief that the other castes should not be imparted education; hence, the Brahmin clerk's advice to Govindrao to withdraw Joti from school. (See Joshi 1992: 6–7)

Another incident occured in 1848 when the twenty-one-year-old Phule was humiliated for daring to join the marriage procession of a brahman friend. On learning of the caste of Phule, some incensed brahmans abused him. With tears in his eyes, Phule returned home. He narrated the incident to his father, who tried to pacify his son by suggesting that he should not take this incident to heart: 'How could we, the lowly shudras, aspire to be equal to the brahmans? Was it not very kind of them just to drive you away instead of giving you a good thrashing?' His father gave many examples of such indignities inflicted on persons of 'lowly origin', and added that he had himself seen non-brahmans humiliated and trampled under an elephant's feet for such offences.

But Phule was not like his father; he was educated in a missionary school and by now had read Thomas Paine's *The Rights of Man*; the French Revolution and the democratic upheaval in America had become part of his mental furniture. He felt through his personal humiliation and his father's pathetic response to it, the terrible enormity of social slavery. In that moment of despair and outrage, he resolved to fight and liberate the enslaved. He realised that caste slavery was the worst enemy of Indian society, and true patriotism lay in breaking the shackles of this slavery.

Grasping that his social engagement would require a great deal of time and freedom, Phule decided against taking a government job and instead stuck to his family horticultural business. This work brought him into a widening market circuit of rural-urban interlinkages. He also ventured into contracts for various construction work. Shady transactions at these sites gave him a first-hand experience of brahmanic nepotism and corruption at the intermediate and local levels of British bureaucracy. When Phule began his campaign against brahmanic privilege in the economy, the historical background of Peshwai together with his bitter personal experiences played a crucial role in the formation of his radical critique (Gavaskar 1999).

Emergence of Anti-Caste Radicalism

Despite the demise of Peshwai and advent of the British rule, the society was dominated by brahmanical forces. Phule saw that religious authority and a monopoly over education had enabled the brahmans to establish their hegemony. Living within the brahmanic political and social relationships, the dalit-bahujans mistook the upper-caste interests as common interests. Phule realised that the challenge was to create a cultural basis for revolution in people's minds, and on this basis bring about material and ideological transformation. His attack on brahmanism was thus very different from earlier attempts to fight caste discrimination.

Phule shifted attention from social mobility within the caste hierarchy to a rejection of the system itself. In 1865 he published a remarkable tract, *Jatibhed-Vivekasar* (A Critique of the Caste Divisions), written by his friend Tukaram Tatya Padwal (1839–98). It was the first modern work, in Marathi or any Indian language, to challenge the socio-religious worldview of brahmanism. It brought out the insidious nature of caste distinctions, the arbitrary notions of purity and impurity, and argued that divisions of labour or occupations should be based on the merit and aptitude of each individual. Interestingly, *Jatibhed-Vivekasar* describes attempts at upward mobility by several lowered castes claiming kshatriya or vaishya status, and the strong brahman resistance to these attempts. Padwal also lays bare the cunning of the brahman on the grant of kshatriya status to powerful social groups (O'Hanlon 1985: 42–5). Shivaji and the Marathas, earlier despised as shudras, were recognised—and co-opted—as kshatriyas after they assumed power.

Padwal's penetrative critique of caste was carried active in Phule's movement. It opposed practices such as the wearing of the 'sacred' thread, and mocked attempts at claiming higher status by adopting high-caste customs. Such moves, Phule argued, obscured the reality that all social divisions were part of the 'same engine of social oppression'. Above all, identifying with the privileged castes amounted to the acceptance of caste order and implied a distancing from castes regarded low in the hierarchy. He stressed the need to reject outright all sanskritising tendencies which led people into the trap of brahmanism and ensured the continuation of divisions among the lowered castes. Phule's target was to subvert the *bhedniti*, the policy of divide and rule. While the brahmans, he pointed out, have kept themselves united in one varna-jati, they conspired to divide the toiling masses into thousands of jatis, creating dissension and disunity among them.

Phule explained that the shastra-smritis were produced to establish cultural hegemony, distinguishing marks like the sacred thread and *Gayatri Mantra* invented to legitimise birth-based superiority, and *dharmagurus* like Shankaracharya fabricated theories to reinforce the brahmanical worldview. Phule's objective, thus, was not to make these accessible to upwardly mobile castes, but to construct an alternative culture altogether. Acutely aware of existing power relations, he made it clear that the exploitative social structure could not be dismantled without a struggle. Only then, he said, would the brahman meet the lowered castes on an equal footing.

In 1873, Phule published *Gulamgiri*—a virtual declaration of war against the slavery of caste. He included in the book a manifesto exhorting the reader to discard caste in principle and practice. *Gulamgiri* created a storm and several newspapers refused to give publicity to it because of its contents. Written in the form of dialogue, it traces the history of caste and domination and examines the motives behind inhuman laws of the Dharamashastras and other 'sacred' texts. The main objective of framing these falsehoods under the cloak of religion, Phule argued, was to dupe the mind of the ignorant masses and chain them to a system of perpetual bondage. Putting the upper-caste version of Aryan race theory upside down, Phule depicts Aryan-brahmans as perfidious outsiders who gradually usurped everything belonging to the original inhabitants. Justifying his attack on brahmanism, he insisted that 'no language could be too harsh by which to characterise the selfish heartlessness and consummate cunning of the brahmanic ideology by which India has been governed so far'. What he had described in his book was 'not one hundredth part of the rogueries' that were practised on his 'poor, illiterate and ignorant shudra brethren'. Though written in Marathi, Phule's eloquent Preface is written in English, proving that he could write in English powerfully when he needed to. The famous Dedication that celebrates the American abolition of slavery in 1863, too, is in English.

Satyashodhak Samaj: The Vision of a New Society

Phule and his associates believed that the dalit-bahujans should not align with brahmanic organisations but strike out autonomously to form a just and casteless society. With this objective, they founded the Satyashodhak Samaj in 1873. At the core of its activities was the idea of social reconstruction. Members were exhorted to encourage truth and right-thinking among common people, and make them aware about their human rights and obligations. Social evils of all kinds were to be identified and eliminated. Public education was accorded the highest importance. Members were urged to make every effort to spread education by teaching women and children, and by helping those who wanted to go to school and college. Betterment of cultivators' life through introduction of improved techniques in agriculture was among the priorities. Membership was extended to all communities including brahmans, mangs and mahars, and even some Jews and Muslims were its members in its early phase (Keer [1964] 2000: 128). Weekly meetings of the Samaj were held in Pune where issues like mass education, promotion of self-reliance, women's freedom, widow-remarriage, freeing people from superstitions and beliefs in astrology, and the encouragement to simple marriage ceremony at minimum expense were passionately discussed.

With its avowed aim to save the people from the 'hypocritical brahmans and their opportunistic scriptures', the Samaj insisted that performance of any religious ceremony by a brahman priest for a member of another caste validates the ritual purity of the brahman (that he alone has the power to mediate between the human world and that of the gods). This implies that it is the brahmans who control the entry of divine power into the world—the belief which provides the basis for Hindu religious and social hierarchy and the notions of purity and impurity. Therefore, Phule activated the Samaj to organise and conduct religious and marriage ceremonies in people's language without brahman priests and their 'mumbo-jumbo in Sanskrit' (Keer [1964] 2000: 126–42; O'Hanlon 1985: 220–50).

The reactionary backlash was swift in coming. The orthodox brahmans launched a vilification campaign against the Samaj. They brought psychological pressures upon its simple adherents to leave the organisation. How would your prayers reach God if they were said in Marathi and not Sanskrit? (Phule had to pacify the people by making them grasp that God understood the yearnings and prayers in every language.) The reactionaries also tried to intimidate the people that their association with the Samaj would destroy their family and fortunes on account of the curses of brahmans and their gods. Many Satyashodhaks were harassed, and some were even forced, on flimsy charges, to leave their jobs in government by their superior officers, mostly brahmans (Keer [1964] 2000: 128). Such dirty tricks, however, failed to dampen the spirit of most Satyashodhaks.

The most daunting challenge was to forge unity among the oppressed communities. Phule made some brilliant moves in that direction. He explained that the disabilities suffered by the untouchables and the exploitation of the cultivators are the result of the same phenomenon. He placed both 'clean' shudras and 'untouchable' atishudras in the community of the oppressed, and gave mahars and mangs 'the central place in the fused group of the oppressed'. His community of the oppressed consisted of all those who were at the receiving end of the oppressive system. Arguing that all those who produce society's wealth were shudratishudras, he strove to bring all women, kunbis, malis, dhangars, Muslims, bhils, kolis, mahars and mangs under one umbrella. O'Hanlon has noted that one of the aims of his 1855 play, *Tritiya Ratna,* was to convince his audience that the heterogeneous collections of social groups that fell within the category of exploited did, in fact, share common interests and a common social position:

This was to be done by the ideological construction of a social grouping that would be both socially credible and attractive. The latter was particularly important, so that elite non-brahman castes might not feel that they were losing by their association with traditionally low castes.

This new social construct was to be the community of the oppressed itself, with its explanation of social evils in terms of the exploitation of all by one group, and its atmosphere of hope and striving for change. (O' Hanlon 1985: 131)

This clear-headed understanding had radical implications. First, it meant that Phule was rejecting the system of graded hierarchy which engineers divisions among the oppressed. And second, while rejecting the hierarchies, the main thrust of his attack was on the inhuman and oppressive nature of brahmanism (Deshpande 2002: 8). The community of the oppressed, thus, was based on the idea of unity among all those who suffer and believe in equality and justice. This solidarity transcended all arbitrary divisions of caste, class, gender, language, religion, and nationality. That is why Phule felt closer to a democratic foreigner than to a casteist Indian. It was for this reason that he was branded by his opponents as a semi-Christian and a hater of Hinduism. Indeed, he admired the egalitarian aspects of Christianity and Islam, but he made it clear that he did not believe in the idea of revealed truth, and as such had nothing to do with the fundamentalism of any creed or religion.[4]

For Phule, the subversion of brahmanical culture was the starting point of an alternative reconstruction. He felt that this could not be done without replacing the caste-bound religion with a new universal religion. The individual and society, he thought, needed a religion by which he meant an ethical conscience and fairness in human relationships. His *Sarvajanik Satya Dharma Pustak*, written on his death-bed, is like his final testament, containing his proposal for an inclusive and compassionate religion. Though Phule preferred Christianity and Islam (for their broad egalitarian spirit) to caste Hinduism, he did not believe in the God and prophets as propounded by organised religions nor did he believe in theories of hell and heaven, incarnation and pre-destination. His own mind and conscience, to paraphrase his favourite writer Thomas Paine's maxim, was his temple.

Though he coined the word *Nirmik* (Creator) for God, he believed that *Nirmik* has no role to play in a human's life after creating him; so individuals have to take full responsibility of their lives. The social world, devoid of supernatural intervention, was left open to investigation by secular reason in all its empirical implications. Blind beliefs and superstitions have no place in Phule's religion. The brahmanical religion claimed the caste hierarchy to be divinely-ordained and eternal. Phule rejected this pseudo-religion and its false gods and dismissed its scriptures as unethical and fraudulent.

His *Nirmik* is *sarvajanik*—equally accessible to all without the mediation of priesthood. Giving a central place to the 'great sacred sentence'—'Do unto others as you would have others do unto you'—he believed that man could never be happy in the world unless his conduct was humane and righteous towards one another. He exhorted people to 'hug brotherly Christians, Muslims, Mangs, Brahmans'. Ethics to him was nothing but truthful human conduct. It did not matter, then, whether the one who practised it was a Christian, a Muslim, or a Satyashodhak.

Phule set a personal example by his impeccable integrity. He threw open the well in his courtyard to the 'untouchables' in the teeth of resistance from his caste fellows. It was rumoured that he had converted to Christianity, since only Christian missionaries were not supposed to believe in being polluted by the untouchables. Earlier, some conservatives had forced his father to banish him and his wife for setting up a school for untouchable girls. The Phule couple left the home but did not close down the school. Another example: Phule and Savitri were childless and he was being pressurised even by his father-in-law to remarry; he rejected the suggestion with disdain, and instead adopted with his wife the 'illegitimate' child of a brahman widow. Similarly, on the death of his father, he performed the last rites differently—by feeding orphans and the physically challenged. On his father's death anniversary, he would distribute books among needy students and give food to the poor.

Phule's congruity of principle and practice stands in sharp contrast to the dubious track-record of the top leaders from the other spectrum. In 1873, M.G. Ranade, a scholar and a champion reformer, then aged thirty-two, lost his wife and immediately married a girl of eleven. This appalled Phule. He wrote a scathing article in *Vividhadnyan Vistar* in which he asked Ranade not to preach what he himself could not practice (Keer [1964] 2000: 136). Earlier, in

1871, when Ranade's young sister was widowed, he said that if she remarried, his father would be devastated and the Pune brahmans would ostracise him. To which Phule replied, 'Then, don't parade yourself as a reformer and a champion of widow-remarriage' (ibid.). Later, Ranade in his capacity as a judge passed a verdict against the Satyashodhak marriage ceremonies without brahman priests. In his 'enlightened' opinion, even if the priest had not been invited to the wedding, he should still be given the traditional gifts. Phule had to challenge the verdict—the lower court rejected his case but the higher court ruled in his favour.

The Lokahitavadi was another brahman reformer, widely respected for his progressive ideas. His impressive reforming career, however, came to an inglorious end when he accepted to undergo an expiation for having sent his son to England for education in defiance of the scriptural ban imposed on crossing the seas. Later, he himself caved in to the caste prohibition to cross the 'black waters' when he was required to go to England. Worse, the Lokahitavadi married his two grandchildren when they were barely six and eight years old (Keer [1964] 2000: 136–7). Phule, who admired the reformer, was aghast at the betrayal.

Rewriting of History and Mythology

For Phule's intended social revolution, the entrenched brahmanic mindset presented the biggest obstacle. The hegemony of brahmanical power lay in the ancient religious literature. Over the centuries, the people had been mentally enslaved through extensive integration of the Dharmashastras and Itihasa-Purana into the popular culture and oral traditions. Since the brahmans paraded their shastras as divinely ordained and sacred, Phule thought, it was necessary to expose their anti-social contents. The battle for the mind could not be won without launching a counter-cultural movement. With this thinking, Phule strove to develop contestatory accounts of sacerdotal literature and myth-histories. Most ingenious was his attempt to link the subversive reading of the past with symbols and stories from the contemporary local milieu. This became possible because he tried to understand the present by understanding the past and vice versa—which some contemporary professional historians rightly suggest is needed to know our real history but seldom practice it themselves.

Phule's reconstruction was based on the vision of uniting the enslaved people, both men and women, hierarchically divided into hundreds of castes and sub-castes. During the four decades of his public life, Phule brought out various prose and poetic works that presented a broad paradigm of a myth-history from the viewpoint of the oppressed. Through tracts, plays, and leaflets, aided by attempts at organisation-building, Phule launched a cultural broadside against the monopolisation of education and power. With rare imagination and insight, he linked the present oppression with past atrocities and depicted the history of India as a longstanding struggle between the brahmans and the shudratishudras. In this process, he analysed the genesis and growth of caste system in a historical-materialist perspective. Prior to this, scholars, both Indian and foreign, had portrayed caste as a social institution that existed from time immemorial. In a paradigm shift, Phule presented caste and brahmanism as symbiotic and historical. They represented for him an organised system of oppression that had to be critically grasped, fought and crushed.

For this, Phule produced many subversive tracts against brahmanism, contesting its basic philosophical and metaphysical formulations. He rejected the doctrine of karma which traces everything including individual suffering and one's caste and gender status to the karma of previous births. Repudiating such fatalism, he accused the brahman of imprisoning the gullible people by indoctrinating notions like *daiva* (fate), *sanchit* (accumulated merits-demerits of previous births), and *prarabdha* (predestination) which have made them lose their dialectical relationship with the world. In the same vein, he dismissed the theory of avatar which postulates that Vishnu took many incarnations at different times to save the society from anarchy. This thesis is at the heart of brahmanic religious system as it dissolves the contradiction between polytheistic religious practices and monotheistic Vedantist metaphysics (Deshpande 2002). In a radical departure from traditional meaning, Phule interpreted the various incarnations of Vishnu as different stages of Aryan onslaught on the original inhabitants of India, and unmasked the atrocities of various godheads. By rejecting the doctrines of karma and avatar, Phule tried to uproot the very foundation on which brahmanism was founded and sustained.

Phule's best-known work *Gulamgiri* (Slavery [1873] 1991, vol. I; 2002: 22-99) is an attempt at such deconstruction and reconstruction of history. Blazing a new trail, in sharp contrast to the dominant historiography which traced the first colonial encounter to the Muslims and then the British, Phule portrayed the Vedic-Aryan as the original coloniser of the indigenous people. He argued that the upper strata of Indian society were descendants of the savage aliens who cruelly subordinated the peace-loving aborigines by usurping their land and property. The invaders imposed inhuman social and religious practices on the local populace in order to keep them in permanent subjugation. The introduction of caste system, he underlined, was a critical instrument by which the brahmans concealed their original act of usurpation and ensured the perpetuation of their privileged position.

Rewriting many of the central episodes of brahmancial mythology—the incarnations of Vishnu; the story of King Bali and the dwarf Vaman; the legend of Parashuram's extirpation of the kshatriyas, etc.—Phule argued that these symbolised the real history of ancient India, deliberately garbled by later brahman writers, in order to conceal their misdeeds and consolidate their power over the lowered castes. He also illustrated this by reinterpreting core elements in the social milieu and popular culture of contemporary Maharashtra, presenting them as survivals from the remote past. Towards the end of the book, Phule tries to show how the brahmans shifted their position in recent times and kept intact, even enhanced, their power during the British rule which allowed real power to slip from its hands into those of the high-caste professional elite which served the empire.

Before *Gulamgiri*, Phule wrote a ballad on Shivaji—*Shivaji Pavada* ([1869] 1991, vol. II). In it he depicted Shivaji as a shudra king and a rebel against caste whose descendants were robbed of their power by the treacherous Peshwas.⁵ As if anticipating the brahmanical appropriation of Shivaji in the 1890s as an orthodox anti-Muslim and saviour of the brahmanic culture—*gau-brahman-pratipalak* (protector of cows and brahmans)—Phule placed Shivaji within the anti-brahmanical tradition of Maharashtrian history. The ballad portrays lowered castes and untouchables as the descendants of the original kshatriyas, who were led by the legendary King Bali. Phule argues that the kshatriyas had been destroyed at the time of the Aryan invasions, and they remained in pitiable conditions ever since. He supported his thesis by explaining that the term kshatriya was derived from the word *kshetra,* which means a field or land; all those who lived or worked on their land were kshatriyas. Using Shivaji's 'low' caste status to his advantage, he portrayed Shivaji as leader of all shudratishudras, the descendants of the forgotten kshatriyas. He draws a parallel between Shivaji and King Bali as the brave and just leaders of their communities who fought against the alien oppressors.

Predictably, vitriolic comments and reviews greeted the 'unknown' author who dared to venture into history-writing. Drunk on the 'glorious past' and oblivious of the social evils of their time, the learned custodians of Indian culture lambasted the audacity of a 'semi-literate' shudra to contradict their cherished understanding of Indian history. Leading the pack of such pandits was Tilak's soulmate Vishnushastri Chiplunkar who derisively dismissed Phule as a 'Shudra Religious Teacher' and a 'Shudra World-Teacher' (Keer [1964] 2000: 146). Phule's associates decided to join the issue, and *Deenbandhu,* the journal of Satyashodhak Samaj, carried a sustained campaign against Tilak and Chiplunkar. Later, Phule's fellow Satyashodhaks wrote two polemical books—Dinkarrao Javalkar's *Deshache Dushman* (Enemies of the Nation) targeted Tilak and Chiplunkar, while *Marathyanche Dasiputra* (Maratha's Bastards), written by R. N. Lad, mounted a frontal attack on the Chitpavan Peshwa dynasty that fraudulently wrested all power from Shivaji's descendants and headed the Maratha confederacy in the eighteenth and early nineteenth centuries. (Peshwas, it may be noted, were the inspirational icons for Chiplunkar, Tilak and other revivalists in Maharashtra.)

Education as Emancipation and Empowerment

Phule's reconstruction of history and linking it to the oppressive present was one aspect of the attempt to fight the system. He felt that a complementary and more effective way to change the existing power structure was education. That is why he laid the greatest emphasis on education—not conservative education but the one that was rational and modern, and which could work as a catalyst for social change. He opposed the obscurantist attempts of his elitist contemporaries to yoke together modern science with Vedic knowledge. For him, education was a resource to bring about an attitudinal change and a cultural revolution. He was a pioneering system builder, and his pedagogy was animated by an emancipatory understanding of knowledge and power.

Phule was the first Indian 'system builder'. . . (the) first to attempt at transforming plural categories of history into singular or universal. Phule talked about knowledge and power much before Foucault did. In fact, Foucault's post-modernist analysis came at a time when Europe has literally seen an 'end of history' whereas Phule's efforts were to change the world/society with the weapon of knowledge. (G.P. Deshpande, see Omvedt 1994: 23)

Phule's 1855 play *Tritiya Ratna*—The Third Eye (a metaphor for education)— argues that by denying knowledge to the shudratishudras, the brahmans might be held responsible for the backwardness of not just the lowered castes but Indian society itself. His differences with his brahman colleagues, working with him in the early 1850s, who stressed the common backwardness of Hindu society as the cause of the sufferings of the lowered castes, rather than attributing these to any particular social group, were precisely on this point. The matter came to a head when the brahman activists insisted that it was enough to give the basic skills of reading and writing to the 'lower' caste people, while Phule maintained that they must be given a critical education which should enable them to read the world and distinguish between good and bad.

The high expectation Phule had from public education was not unrealistic. The 'potential explosiveness' of education was evident when Muktabai, an eleven-year-old Mang girl in Phule's school, wrote the essay *Mang Maharachya Dukha Visaiyi* (About the Grief of the Mangs and Mahars) in 1855.[6] In this she presented a heart rending description of the untouchables, and lambasted the brahmanical social and religious order for their plight. Analysing the essay, Uma Chakravarti writes:

> Muktabai presents the best example of Phule's belief that a special vision, a tritiya ratna, would be the outcome of education and would have the means to strip the falsity of Brahmanic ideology. It enabled her to proclaim, 'Let that religion where only one person is privileged and the rest deprived, perish from the earth, and let it never enter our minds to be proud of such a religion'.... Muktabai's essay ends abruptly, 'Oh God! What agony is this! I will burst into tears if I write more about this injustice.' Even so, the anguished Muktabai understood and rejected the existing social order and provided a scathing critique of Brahmanical power in nineteenth century Maharashtra. The newly acquired skills of literacy for this untouchable woman had made it possible to question, in print, the most 'sacred' person in the social hierarchy, and reject unequivocally his 'knowledge' and his authority. (1998: 74-5)

Phule and his associates spearheaded an intense campaign for mass education. But they knew that their efforts were not enough. Phule wanted the government to spend the people's money, collected through taxes, on developing an infrastructure for universal education. He asked, advised and (in exasperation) warned the government to shoulder more responsibility in this regard. He was very critical of the British policy on education because, as he put it, it grossly neglected primary education in its eagerness to promote higher education (in order to produce a class of professional and administrative allies) which only benefited the elite. In a petition in 1882 to the Education Commission, headed by William Hunter, Phule lambasted the government for ignoring the education of the lower classes by toeing a trickle-down theory ([1882] 2002: 101-12). The government, he said, was under the illusion that people from the higher classes would spread education among the lower classes. It squandered the taxes it earned from poor farmers on educating the upper classes. But the children of the rich who availed free education and achieved material success on its strength, did nothing to uplift their poor countrymen. The British policy ensured 'monopoly of education by the brahmans' and as a result 'all the senior government posts are monopolised by them'. He suggested that primary education must be made compulsory up to the age of twelve. Higher education, to which the government had already devoted generous resources, might be better left to the efforts of private individuals.

Phule wanted the Commission to meet the poor and the unlettered, and then frame an appropriate education policy. But this was not to be, and an embittered Phule was left to remark: 'The Hunter Commission did not interview farmers. It relied solely on the discussions it had with Parsis, Christians and Brahmins and accepted their word as final. Hence, the report of this Commission will not benefit the illiterate and the poor.'

In his ballad *Vidyakhatyatil Brahman Pantoji* (Brahman Teachers in the Educational Department) and in his introduction to *Gulamgiri*, Phule attempted to show how the caste elites had appropriated all positions in administrative and educational institutions under the British regime. Explaining the conditions that had kept the lowered castes illiterate, and why the brahmans were unwilling to impart education to the other castes, he demanded education for all and recruitment of teachers from other castes as well (O'Hanlon 1985: 215).

Phule could see the formation of a class of English-educated native administrators who were continuing the traditional policy of exclusion of the lowered castes by convincing the British that these people had no liking and aptitude for learning. His repeated exhortation to the British to democratise education was based on the anxiety that the accumulated educational deficit of the dalit-bahujans was being reinforced by the colonial power structure. His concern for public education was of course not shared by the powers that be, whether foreign or Indian. Deploring the system, Phule gave vent to his frustrations by depicting the 'drain of wealth' within the country wherein the taxes paid by the working class go into educating the scions of the rich and powerful:

He who owns goods suffers the most
goes the Pathan saying,
children of queer people study;
Mali, kunbi slog in the fields to pay taxes,
don't have enough to clothe. (Phule, see Gavaskar 1999)

Phule did not let go any opportunity to promote the cause of public education. As a member of the Pune Municipality in the 1880s, he opposed a proposal of its president to spend money on decorating the city on the visit of the Governor-General, arguing that the money would be better spent on the education of the poor. In another instance, the Prince of Wales was greeted on his visit to Pune in 1889 by the boys and girls of Phule's school with a jingle:

Tell Grandma we are a happy nation,
But 19 crores are without education. (Keer [1964] 2000: 245)

Against Patriarchy and Women's Subordination

In the nineteenth century, Rammohun Roy was followed by many reformers who engaged with the women's problems. They took up issues like sati, widow remarriage, child marriage, women's education, etc. But their approach was paternalistic and brahmanic. Their high-caste prejudice was apparent in much of their thinking and activities, as we saw in Chapter 4. Phule's position was very different from such gentlemen-reformers. Phule attacked what Uma Chakravarti (1993; 1998; 2003) has aptly called 'brahmanical patriarchy', arguing that it treats all women as inferior creatures. The Dharmashastras put them together with dasas or shudras. On this basis, he included all women in the community of the oppressed, and pointed out that denial of education to women and toiling castes was the main cause of the backwardness of Indian society.

Like the elitist reformers, Phule was a forerunner of female education and women's rights, but he was unique in asserting equality between the sexes. As he saw subjugation of women as a part of the larger dominance inherent in the caste structure, his critique implied the view that the end of the brahmanical system would ensure the end of patriarchy as well. Critiquing caste as a system, Phule emerges as a rare critic of brahmanical patriarchy.

He alone, among nineteenth century social reformers, was able to stand outside Brahmanical patriarchy and, although gender was not a central factor in his analysis of caste and the reproduction of inequality, his rejection of the caste system and of brahmanic Hinduism enabled him to adopt a more radical approach to gender inequality than any of his contemporaries. (Chakravarti 1998: 65)

Phule believed in radical gender equality. In the context of widowhood, he said that when a husband dies, it is the woman who leads a life of suffering, burdened by widowhood for the rest of her life. Earlier they even burnt themselves and became sati. But 'has anyone ever heard of a man burning himself alive in the event of his wife's death and become a *sata*?' (Phule [1889] 2002: 231). *Sata* was an ironical coinage by Phule to suggest a male sati. He wanted that the traditional family and marriage system be changed in the light of reason and gender justice. His *Sarvajanik Satya Dharma Pustak* suggested new marriage rites laying stress on man–woman equality. He was the first to draw attention to the fact that the labour of the young bride is used as bonded labour by the family the girl marries into.

Since exclusion from knowledge was the main cause behind women's subordination, education was to be his main resource to liberate them. As we saw earlier, the first school Jotirao and Savitribai Phule established in 1848 was for girls. Despite economic hardships and fierce social opposition, the Phules set up 18 schools between 1848 and 1852. Out of these six were in Pune town, six in rural areas of Pune district, three in Satara and three in other places. Their educational campaign was causing consternation among the conservatives. Savitribai was often greeted with insults and threats while going to teach in these schools. Also, an attempt was made on Phule's life in 1856.

The 1860s saw Phule campaigning for widow remarriage and banning the practice of child marriage. He arranged the remarriage of a brahman widow in 1864. He made a more daring move when, moved by the plight of widows, he set up a sanctuary in his own home compound in Pune for pregnant brahman widows, which was boldly advertised by means of notices pasted up in the brahman locality. It is to be noted that enforced widowhood was a problem largely of brahman and allied castes; the remarriage of lowered caste widows was quite common in Maharashtra and elsewhere.

The material and sexual consequences of enforced widowhood were responsible for a large number of young brahman women becoming pregnant. Abortion or desertion of newly-born baby was common, but if the matter became public, murdering the 'fallen women' to uphold family honour was also common within the cloisters of high-caste homes. Phule's decision to establish a foundling home to save the widows and prevent infanticide picked on 'one of the most vulnerable spots in brahmanism, the linchpin of upper-caste gender codes, enforced widowhood and its consequences' (Chakravarti 1998: 76). The Phule couple gave protection to frightened pregnant widows and assured them that the orphanage would take care of their infants. It was in this orphanage that a brahman widow gave birth to a baby boy Yashwant in 1873 whom Phule and Savitri adopted as their son.

Besides other humiliations, the widows were forced to shave their heads. Against this Phule organised a successful barbers' strike where the barbers refused to perform the customary tonsure of widows. He devised similar ingenious ways of highlighting women's issues in a provocative manner. Quoting one of Phule's friends, O'Hanlon (1994: 19) recounts how he employed a brahman woman, Gangubai, as a domestic help on very high wages, as a way of helping the deserted woman and mocking the wealthy brahmans who usually employed poor women from other castes to do their domestic chores. He seemed to have succeeded in this case, for Gangubai's relatives came and took her away.

While Phule was sensitive to common gender problems faced by all women, he was also conscious of acute caste differences among women and their place in the system of production. In *Shetkaryacha Asud*, Phule has shown how the women of toiling castes have to labour at home and in the fields, whereas the brahman women work only at home and lead a relatively comfortable life. Thus 'the brahman women are subject only to the power of the brahman men, while the labouring women are doubly crushed as they are dominated by both the upper-caste men and the men of their own families'. He has brought this out vividly in his poem *Kulambin*,

'The Peasant Woman' (see Phule 1991, vol. II, pp. 111-14). Here, Phule compares the hardships of a shudra woman—clad in a tattered sari, balancing her tiny child on her back, slogging from early morning to late evening both at home and then in the fields with the men; she has no time to comb her hair or bathe—with the cosy life of the 'bejewelled *bhatin*', the brahman woman. The latter does not have to work as a labourer, to tend to the cattle, to collect cow-dung, to carry the sheaves of corn to the threshing floor. A shudra woman works as a dasi in a brahman's home but the brahman woman 'does not grind the corn in the shudra's house nor does she sprinkle water in the courtyard of the shudra, to earn her livelihood'. While the kulambin's labour nourishes and sustains the whole society, including the 'brahman beggar', the bhatin 'does not look after shudra children, does not kiss them'. Phule is aghast that the brahman woman, like her menfolk, despises the toiling woman as an inferior being and addresses her by various disparaging names.

Phule clearly perceived the interdependence of caste and gender hierarchies. He saw how the safeguarding of the caste structure was achieved through enforced seclusion and silence of women. This understanding was expressed when he defended feminist pioneers Pandita Ramabai and Tarabai Shinde against attacks from the male orthodoxies. 'In Ramabai's case he mounted an attack on brahmanism, in which much of the high-caste woman's oppression was located. In Tarabai's case he went further, as he was critical of his own compatriots in the non-Brahman movement with regard to recognising women's subordination' (Chakravarti 1998: 77).

Pandita Ramabai (1858–1922) was an outstanding activist and a scholar of Sanskrit. In 1882, she founded the Arya Mahila Samaj to promote the women's cause. She was the first woman to declare, on the basis of her close study of the shastras, that the 'Sanskritic core of Hinduism was irrevocably and essentially anti-women'. Later, she embraced Christianity, denouncing the Hindu scriptures and preachers for portraying women as 'bad, very bad, worse than demons, and unholy as untruth, and that they could not get *moksha* as man (could)'. Her conversion to Christianity and increasingly bold espousal of women's issues had made her a pariah. Accused of betraying her Hindu society, she was damned and deserted not only by her conservative friends and relatives but also by the reformers and nationalists. Among Ramabai's detractors were Tilak (P. Rao 2010: 130 ff.), Ramakrishna and Vivekananda (Chakravarti 1998: 319–20).[7]

Ramabai's renouncement of Hinduism was seen by the caste elites as an attack on the Hindu tradition within which they had comfortably pitched their tents of social reforms and cultural nationalism. Chakravarti (1998) has pointed out that after her conversion Ramabai represented not the supposed glory of the Hindu women but a discordant voice who spoke for the subjugated women of the nineteenth-century India. She became a thorn in the flesh of the upper-caste nationalists since her standpoint on women and religion could not be accommodated in their construction of the nation which was exclusivist—Hindu, patriarchal and upper-casteist—in orientation.

Phule was the only person who came forward to support Ramabai's struggle. He applauded her efforts for education among high-caste women. In his booklet *Satsar* (The Essence of Truth [1885] 2002: 203-13), he argued that Ramabai, as a truly educated woman, had seen for herself the discrimination of shastras against women and lowered castes. The brahmans, he argued, had prevented women from acquiring education because the educated ones like Ramabai would 'throw away the scriptures' and revolt against the male authority.

Phule also pointed out that Ramabai was not the first to defend women's rights and dignity; before her, Tarabai Shinde of Buldhana (Berar) wrote a book against the patriarchal order. Tarabai's 1882 tract *Stri-Purush Tulana* (A Comparison between Women and Men, tr. O'Hanlon 1994) was indeed the first feminist work in India. Written in a biting language, it presented a searing criticism of patriarchy, describing the way men devalued women and excluded them from power. Tarabai came from the Satyashodhak background and shared much of its radicalism. But her rebellion against patriarchy among non-brahman castes was not taken kindly by many Satyashodhaks. Phule intervened and presented a stirring defence of Tarabai, arguing that women of non-elite castes suffered doubly from discrimination and as such they were far more victimised than the caste-oppressed men. He referred to Tarabai as *chiranjivi*, 'our dear daughter', and lauded her work.

Engagement with Agriculture, Peasantry and Labour

In Phule's time, India was predominantly an agrarian society. It was natural for someone like Phule, born and brought up among cultivators, to be involved in the issues of agriculture and peasantry. Cultivators were the producers and sustainers of society who themselves led a wretched life due to an exploitative system made worse by abysmally low productivity in agriculture. 'A cultivator is one who is born in debt and dies in debt' was not just a saying, but a fact. In his later years, Phule worked intensively among the poor peasantry. He used the terms 'shudra cultivators' and 'shudra labour' who formed the bulwark of the community of the oppressed. He dealt with issues like frequent drought, lack of irrigation facilities, primitive tools, ignorance about new agricultural equipment and techniques, excessive taxation, and the callous negligence of the rural sector by the state.

The last quarter of the nineteenth century witnessed severe agrarian crisis and unrest in western Maharashtra. In 1875, the peasantry in Deccan, particularly in the districts of Ahmadnagar, Pune, Satara, and Sholapur, rose in revolt against the moneylenders. In 1877, the region faced a devastating drought, but there was hardly any state or community-level support for the famine-stricken. No one among the reformers or nationalists bothered about the peasantry and agrarian crisis. Phule was the first social activist who made agriculture and the lot of cultivators one of his central concerns (O' Hanlon 1985; Deshpande 2002). During the uprising of 1875 he came out in support of the peasantry, and during the 1877 famine he led the Satyashodhaks to set up an orphanage for the destitute and deserted children. His engagement with rural life and labour intensified after 1880. With a team of Satyashodhaks, he extensively toured in rural areas, addressing large gatherings of peasants, and helped organise a boycott of the exploitative brahmans and moneylenders. During this period he wrote and delivered a series of speeches. His writings constitute one of the most elaborate and minutely observed pieces of social reporting of the contemporary rural society (O'Hanlon 1985). In 1883, Phule reworked them into a single volume entitled *Shetkaryacha Asud*.

In *Shetkaryacha Asud* (Cultivator's Whipcord [1883] 2002: 113-89), Phule not only details the material life of cultivators but also raises important social and political questions in the larger context. Comparing the cultivators of India with the farmers of other countries, he notes that the former's lot is far worse. For their plight, he holds the ruling British and brahmans responsible. He points to the nexus that exists between the local exploiters—brahmans and moneylenders—and the distant one, the British officials, who get exorbitant salaries 'for listening to the subordinate brahman officials' and doing nothing.

Because the white government officers are mostly engrossed with luxury, they do not have time enough to enquire into the real conditions of the farmers and because of this negligence most government departments are dominated by brahman employees. Both these causes have the effect that the farmers are looted, and are without enough to fill their bellies or cover their bodies. (Phule [1883] 2002: 131)

Being fleeced thus, the cultivator is in no position to send his children to school. Even if some lucky cultivator, Phule adds, has the necessary means he is dissuaded by the brahmans from sending his little ones to school.

Phule puts forward several suggestions for structural change in rural society. He proposes a productive partnership between the community and the state. Though he wants the government to play a more responsible role, his rural reconstruction rests, more than anything else, on educating the public. Cultivators must get basic education about better agricultural operations and production, but greater emphasis, he insists, should be given to their children's proper education in new agriculture techniques. Their teachers should be selected from their own community, and such teachers must have first-hand experience of agricultural activities and operations. Phule suggests that children should get professional training in trades like iron-smithery and carpentry, and those who excel in these areas should be sent abroad to good agricultural schools. Talented boys from these schools, who also show good leadership qualities, should be made the patils or village heads. He hopes that the non-hereditary and well-qualified patils will also help in breaking down divisions along caste lines and in stopping infighting and expensive legal wranglings among the ignorant farmers (generally created by the village elites for selfish ends). He also wants the government to give employment to cultivators' educated children in different departments, particularly those concerned in any way with rural and agricultural sector. He demands a representation of all communities in proportion to their number in all government offices, as the privileged few who have monopolised jobs are solely interested in feathering their nests.

Besides public campaigns and writings to highlight the cultivators' cause, Phule made use of his talent for symbols to identify Satyashodhak Samaj as the authentic voice of the peasantry. Here is an example. The Duke of Connaught visited Pune in 1888 and the city dignitaries hosted a dinner in his honour, to which Phule was also invited. He arrived after all the other guests, who were startled to see a poor, ragged farmer in their midst. Phule was dressed as a typical Maharashtrian cultivator—a torn turban on his head, a tattered blanket round his shoulders, a rustic dhoti, a scythe at his waist, and battered old sandals tied with string on his feet. After dinner, he created a stir by delivering an impassioned speech in fluent English. He contrasted the poverty of the peasantry with the affluence of the rich invitees, and pointed out to the British guests that the people gathered here did not represent India: the real people of India were to be found in villages and city slums inhabited by the poor. He told the visiting dignitaries to go home and inform the people-in-power that they had met a real villager, a representative of millions of Indians, whose protection and advancement were the first duties of the government (O'Hanlon 1985: 272–3).

Deenbandhu, the weekly published by the Samaj, regularly highlighted the plight of workers and peasants. N.M. Lokhande and Krishnarao Bhalekar, Phule's close associates, were among the first to build an organisation of workers in India (Keer [1964] 2000). From 1880 onwards, Phule and Lokhande addressed several meetings of the textile workers in Bombay. They started a trade union movement for the redressal of the workers' grievances (ibid.).

Phule was also the one to invest labour with dignity and positive value. His thinking on this evolved over the years in a significant way. While earlier he saw people's labour as a tool of upper-caste oppression, later he attached aesthetic value to productive work, contrasting it with the idle life of the rich. As we saw, his poem *Kulambin* pays a touching tribute to a poor peasant woman who works tirelessly near the hearth and in the fields. By showering praise on the untidy labouring woman and speaking derisively of the bejewelled woman, who idles away her time on titivating herself, Phule appears to be crying for a radical change in the traditional criteria of value, beauty and aesthetics.

Phule was eager to bring about an attitudinal change towards labour. O'Hanlon has recorded an incident which shows his respect for labour. Once Phule was with the workers on his orchard outside Pune. He got up and started to drive the well-bucket, singing cheerfully as he worked. When the workers laughed, he stopped to explain that he was proud to be a cultivator and all cultivators had to make their music as they worked—it was only those who did not toil had the leisure to sit with musical instruments. Another incident is narrated by his biographer Keer, describing how on finding a little snotty-nosed poor boy crying for food, Phule lifted him, washed him, and purchased some food for him. A person passing-by recognised Phule and asked him how could he bear to fondle the dirty child. Phule replied that poverty of the parents was the reason why such children were dirty. It was not their fault, it was the responsibility of society to provide all children with basic things like water, soap and clothes. He reminded the gentleman that the boy's body wanted washing, but your (the questioner's) mind needed thorough cleaning.

Critique of Nation and Nationalism

To discern Phule's views on nation and nationalism, it is important to discern the elitist orientation of reform movements which sowed the seeds of nationalism in India. The reformer-nationalists (as we saw in Chapter 4) concentrated only on those customs which were concerned with the privileged groups. The oppressed majority seldom figured in their reformist and national discourse. It was this continued exclusion that forced the dalit-bahujans to rise in revolt against upper-caste dominance in many parts of the country. This is known as the non-brahman or anti-caste movement. At the root of the movement lay the centuries-old social injustice which was being replenished under the seductive rhetoric of 'nationalism'. Phule was the pioneering leader of this movement which not only denounced the basic tenets of brahmanic culture but also challenged the elite-based nationalist project that glorified that regressive tradition.

Phule was scathing in his criticism of the so-called nationalists, because as he saw it, they were actually constructing a neo-brahmanism under the cloak of nationalism. Their glorification of caste and brahmanic tradition represented for him an outright treachery to the nation and its subjugated people. The basic postulate of these nationalists was that their earlier domination by the Muslims and more recent conquest by the British had been the result of weakness caused by the corruption or degeneration of the classical caste system and religion of the Aryans (Chapter 4). The remedy for this degeneration was for all castes to unite—through faithful adherence to their respective caste duty—and return to the purity of their ancestors. The unity thus achieved, they urged, would make Hindu society strong enough to drive away the foreigners and establish swaraj.

Phule was utterly dismissive of this brand of patriotism, seeing in it the elite attempts to preserve traditional hierarchies from the modern influences that accompanied the British rule. For him, the mass exploitation inherent in caste and brahmanism was far more sinister than the one in the British rule. His persistent insistence was on equality or universal justice, which he held up as the criterion to unite not only the community of the oppressed but society as a whole for any larger political projects (O'Hanlon 1985: 202–3). The image of universal brotherhood which he presented as the standard by which contemporary expressions of patriotism were to be judged necessitated a decisive break from the conventional hierarchies of Hinduism, which the upper-caste 'patriots' wanted to strengthen in order to achieve 'harmonious unity' of the past.

In a far-sighted insight and anticipation, Phule spoke sharply of a few 'half-baked shudra scholars' and some 'belly-filling clerks from amongst the shudras' who might be duped into entering a false national alliance with the brahmans. Such fraudulent unity, he warned, would neither be fruitful nor long-lasting.

... If the brahmans really wish to unite the people of this country and take the nation ahead, then first they must drown their cruel religion, which is customary amongst both the victors (brahmans) and the vanquished (shudras), and they, publicly and clearly, must cease using any artifice in their relationship with the shudras, who have been demeaned by that religion, and trample on inequality and the Vedanta opinion, and till a true unity is established, there will be no progress in this country. If by chance, in their inherited and customary cunning the Arya brahmans join hands with a few half-baked shudra scholars and manage some progress, that improvement will not last for too long. (Phule [1883] 2002: 178)

Through his challenging renditions of history, politics, education, religion and ethics, Phule tried to politicise-radicalise diverse arenas of public discourse. Asserting that the brahmanic tradition was part of, not the solution to, the national problem, he challenged the 'nationalists' to bring their Vedas out in the open—*Brahmananache Veda maidani aana na*. To those who sang the glories of the past and cited European scholars' rhapsodies about the Aryan-Vedic religion, he asked why the Orientalists like Max Müller were not embracing Hinduism if they were so enamoured of its grandeur.

Thus, in contrast to the elite reformers, Phule's agenda was to smash up the whole material and ideological edifice which supported the base and superstructure of the hierarchical order. That is why he was very critical of Brahmo Samaj, Arya Samaj and Bombay-based Prarthana Samaj, and had derisively dismissed them as *Aryan-Brahman Samajes* (Keer [1964] 2000: 119, 129–31; O'Hanlon 1985: 268–9). Arguing that the notions of 'Brahma' and 'Arya' were essentially anti-shudra, he termed elite organisations like Sarvajanik Sabha[8] as 'Naradachi Sabha' (Narad being the fabled mischief-maker who was emissary between men and gods).

Phule was unique in establishing—through historical and contemporary facts and their reinterpretation—the interconnectedness of many forms of brahman power in modern times:

> The different areas of Brahman activity—in the religious and economic life of the village, in the new local and provincial political institutions, in the religious reform societies and the social reform movement amongst Brahmans—were but varying manifestations of an essentially unitary force. This force waged a hidden war on these different fronts to maintain the power of Brahmans as against other social groups, and appeared in different guises the better to confuse and mislead its victims. (O'Hanlon 1985: 206)

The selfish agenda of the caste elites who were in the forefront of the newly-formed Indian National Congress provoked Phule to question their 'nationalist' credentials. He argued that the Congress did not represent the nation, because it did not represent the interests of the majority of Indian people. His point was that it could not become national until it engaged itself with wider social issues and emancipation of the oppressed within Indian society.

The Congress indeed did not take up the question of caste and untouchability for a long time (see Chapter 7). Some reformer-nationalists led by Ranade had, however, organised since 1887 a Social Conference after the annual session of the Congress under the same pavilion. The idea was to discuss social issues but even this slender connection between the Congress and social concerns was opposed by top leaders such as Dadabhai Naoroji, S.N. Banerjee, and above all, Tilak, with the logic that mixing up social issues with political matters would divide society and weaken the Congress. The matter came to a head in the 1895 Congress session in Pune when Tilak, on his home turf, threatened to burn down the Congress pavilion if such a meet was held after the session. The reformists beat a hasty retreat; the reactionaries won the day; the Congress snapped its ties with the Social Conference.

Phule, on the other hand, wanted to orient politics to engineer social change. The politics divorced from the burning social issues was to him the politics of vested interests. He bluntly branded the elites anti-national loudmouths who pretended to represent the nation without bothering to resolve the main contradiction in Indian society by which he meant the challenge of bringing the suppressed majority into the socio-political mainstream. For him, a nation had to be built on abolition of social hierarchies and establishment of equality which would allow the feeling of commonness to develop. This commonality—for which he uses the term *ekmey lok*—is an essential and integral element of the nation-building. His own politics was driven by this democratic ambition. Nowhere was this more clear than in his response to an invitation by Ranade to participate in the plenary session of the Conference of Marathi Authors in 1885. In his reply, Phule expressed his inability to participate since his taking part in such conferences—'where the people with their heads in the clouds have no idea of the oppressive reality on the ground'—would not benefit the downtrodden classes:

> The conferences and the books of those who refuse to think of human rights generally, who do not concede them to others and going by their behaviour are unlikely to concede them in future, cannot make sense to us, they cannot concur with what we are trying to say in our books. These upper-caste authors who are forever miles away from reality and who can only make ceremonial and meaningless speeches in big meetings can never understand what we the shudras and atishudras have to suffer and what calamities we have to undergo. . . . If these leaders of men are genuinely interested in unifying all people they must address themselves to the discovery of the root of the eternal love of all human beings. Let them discover it and may be formulate and publish it as a text. Otherwise to turn a blind eye to the divisions among the human beings at this hour is simply futile. (Phule [1885] 2002: 200–1)

Phule's castigation of ivory-tower intellectualism and advocacy for a new kind of engaged literature was emblematic of his vision of politics, nation and nationalism. For him, nation was nothing if it was not a democratic society. The birth of a nation required the growth of a civil society, the celebration of citizenship, and beginning of the process of education and empowerment of all people. Change from a hierarchical to an egalitarian type of society was integral to his concept of nation and nationalism. No wonder Phule dismissed the Congress brand of brahmanic nationalism:

> There cannot be a 'nation' worth the name until and unless all the people of the land of King Bali—such as Shudras and Ati-shudras, Bhils (tribals) and fishermen etc., become truly educated, and are able to think independently

for themselves and are uniformly unified and emotionally integrated. If a tiny section of the population like the upstart Aryan Brahmins alone were to found the 'National Congress' who will take any notice of it? (Phule [1890] 1991: vol. II: 29)

Phule did not miss the collusive nature of brahmanical (internal) colonialism and British imperialism. As he wrote in *Satsar*, 'Our wise rulers have until now spent crores of rupees from the royal and local fund on educating the brahmans. Then they appointed them on responsible posts and made them happy in every way. The reason must be that the scholar brahmans would come to the aid of the government in times of crisis' ([1885] 2002: 212). His writings, *Shetkaryacha Asud* in particular, were interspersed with trenchant criticism of colonialism. He bitterly criticised the British for adopting anti-poor and pro-rich policies. He tried to explain how feudalism and big business in India were fused into a caste-class mode of brahmanism. And since brahmanism and colonialism fed on and fattened each other, the thrust of his argument was that without fighting brahmanism the so-called anti-imperialist nationalism would only strengthen the oppressive forces in Indian society.

With this thinking, he was the first to challenge the elitist domination of the Congress. The Satyashodhaks had built an effigy of a poor, emaciated farmer near the venue of the third session of the Congress in Bombay to drive home this point (Keer [1964] 2000: 246). Phule's charge against organisations like Congress was that despite their declared policies of public welfare, the larger people, peasants and 'untouchables' were not members of these bodies. Criticising the kinds of demands made by the Congress, he argued that Indianisation and brahmanisation were not the same thing. He vehemently contested Ranade's 'shallow advice' that caste distinctions did not hinder the social goal and national advancement. In his opinion as long as traditional restrictions on meeting, dining and marrying outside the caste remained, it was not possible to create a sense of nationality among the people. In brief, he argued in many ways that social equality and massification of education were necessary prerequisites of nation-building.

There is a tendency in the elitist historiography to portray Phule as a British loyalist. This criticism is based on some laudatory references to the British rule in his writings. But these were also interspersed with severe criticism of colonialism as he saw it as anti-people and pro-elite. For example, he refuted Ranade's claim that the condition of the cultivators was fairly good during the British period. Ranade had also shown his fondness for feudalism by showering praises on the hereditary land-owning class 'as they served a useful purpose in society'. Phule wrote a booklet in 1885, appropriately titled *A Warning,* to rubbish all such claims, and to highlight the plight of the toiling people who were leading a hand to mouth existence in the caste-feudal order patronised by the colonial power (Phule [1885] 1991: vol. II: 48–63). He consistently opposed the exploitative nature of the state, marked by excessive taxation, cesses, and takeover of farmer's lands reducing them to servility. His *Gulamgiri* begins with an epigraph in which colonialism is seen as 'an extension of the demoralising brahmanism'. We saw earlier, in his own words, his uncanny understanding of collusion between colonialism and brahmanism. But he also knew, unlike the upper-caste nationalists, that brahmanism would outlive colonialism in India—and his ideological and political struggle was animated by this understanding. Anyway, Phule died in 1890, but up to 1912, every annual Congress session would begin with the ceremonial hoisting of the Union Jack. Yet in the nationalist historiography Phule is portrayed as pro-British, and the Congress and its leaders as the flawless fighters against imperialism.

Summarising, though the common people recognised him as Mahatma in his life-time for his liberation struggle, he remained an insignificant 'low caste' leader in the eyes of the nationalist elites. Phule was the 'trouble-maker' who saw caste as the divider and degrader of the productive majority into hundreds of mutually antagonistic castes in a hierarchical order that allowed the upper castes to live off the labour of the former. In his biting language, he called this the 'drain of wealth'—from the productive majority to the parasitic few—within the country. Seeing the relationship between the so-called high castes and the rest as the relationship of the coloniser and colonised, he saw the internal colonialism (brahmanism) as the lynchpin of a vicious slavery, equally, if not more, sinister than the external colonialism.

Notes

1. Shudratishudra is shudra and atishudra. Literally, atishudra means 'shudra in the extreme', or those beyond the shudra. In contemporary language, shudras and atishudras would be 'other backward classes' (OBCs) and dalits respectively. But Phule also included women, adivasis, Muslims and all others who are at the receiving end of the brahmanical order in his notion of shudratishudra. In other words, it was his expression for what we call today dalit-bahujans.
2. Later, Ambedkar, too, identified his struggle with this tradition. He considered Phule one of his three masters, along with Buddha and Kabir (Keer [1964] 2000: VII; 139). In fact, Ambedkar saw his own work as the continuation of the struggle started by Phule. Dedicating his book *Who were the Shudras?* (1946) to Phule, he underlined Phule's revolutionary contribution. In his last days, Ambedkar was keen to write a biography of Phule which he could not do due to his deteriorating health (Keer, ibid.).
3. Quoting Pinjan's letter to M. Patil, O'Hanlon underlines the strong influence of Kabir's ideas on Phule and his colleagues which led to the formation of Satyashodhak Samaj (1985: 229–30). See also (in Hindi) Sadanand More's *Mahatma Phule Ka Vicharatmak Gathan* (Ideological Formation of Mahatma Phule) in Hari Narke, ed., *Mahatma Phule: Sahitya Aur Vichar* (1993: 53).
4. Phule admired Jesus and Muhammad for their egalitarianism. Jesus figures in his writing as a champion of justice, a sort of Western alter-ego of his Bali Raja, the mythical king renowned for his benevolence. And he wrote a laudatory poem hailing Muhammad as a prophet of brotherhood.
5. Contrary to the popular myth, Shivaji was humiliated by the custodians of Hinduism. The story of Shivaji's coronation as *Chhatrapati* after his brilliant military exploits, documented by Jadunath Sarkar and G.S. Sardesai, shows how a man who saw such spectacular success had to hunt down a brahman priest from Banaras, Gagabhata, to perform the 'purification' and thread ceremony that could lend legitimacy to his coronation. As the local brahmans were strongly opposed to the grant of kshatriya status to him, Shivaji had to engage Gagabhata who declared after receiving huge monetary largesse and gifts that the Bhosale's family (to which Shivaji belonged) could claim a direct line of descent from the Sisodia Rajput kings of Udaipur. The local pandits boycotted the coronation ceremony, and those who attended demanded—and got—enormous sums of money which emptied Shivaji's coffer. Jadunath Sarkar (1973) informs that though Shivaji was installed as *Chhatrapati*, he was not allowed to recite the *Gayatri Mantra,* the holiest of the Vedic mantra. The ambiguity over the caste status

of Shivaji and his descendants was to give birth in later years to the bitter conflicts between the brahman Peshwas and Shivaji's successors.
6. The full essay is available in English in my translation, see Braj Ranjan Mani, 'The Revolt of a Dalit Girl: An Essay by a Student of Phule's School', in B.R. Mani and P. Sardar, eds., *A Forgotten Liberator: The Life and Struggle of Savitribai Phule*, pp. 70–5 (Delhi: Mountain Peak, 2008).
7. Regarding the position of women, particularly widows, in Hindu society, Ramabai and Vivekananda had diametrically different views, and as Uma Chakravarti (1998: 333–7) has shown, they clashed over the issue, though without referring to each other directly, in the USA in the 1890s. Ramabai had gone to the US in 1886 and stayed there for two years during which she travelled a lot and addressed hundreds of meetings. She also authored a bestseller, *The High Caste Hindu Woman,* as part of her effort to collect money for the suffering women in India. She was the first public figure from India to seek financial assistance for social work back home. In the following decade, after his fabled pyrotechnics on Hindu spirituality at Chicago (1893), Vivekananda did the same but used a very different strategy. While Ramabai appealed to American women to help the oppressed widows in India, Vivekananda, in his ardour to romanticise India as a uniquely spiritual country, painted Hindu women as chaste, self-sacrificing goddesses. Regarding the question of widows, he argued that they voluntarily chose to lead an austere life in deference of their dead husbands. In a lecture on womanhood, he asserted that though Hindu women disdained material aspects of life, they had enjoyed, unlike their American counterparts, property rights for thousands of years. This was challenged by Ramabai's American friends, while the Swami's followers attacked Ramabai whose 'unpatriotic' position on the women's issues, they alleged, was spoiling India's image abroad. Being a widow herself and having travelled to Banaras, Mathura and Brindavan, Ramabai knew how the widows were oppressed and sexually exploited without any 'Mahatma championing their cause'. In a letter from India, she appealed to the 'learned brothers and comfortable sisters' of America to take a good look, beyond the poetry, into the prose of women's lives and decide for themselves the nature of the fruits of the 'sublime philosophies' (ibid.: 336).
8. The Sarvajanik Sabha, founded in Pune in 1870, was a public association of brahman reformers and liberals. Its members set themselves up as middlemen between the government and the people.

CHAPTER 6

Guru, Iyothee, Periyar, Achhutanand
Different Strategies, One Goal

> India is a strange place which collects all sorts of social groups, divided by different religions, thoughts, practices and understandings. But broadly speaking, they can be categorised into two—the majority low castes who have been devoid of humanity for centuries and a handful who take their pleasure, call themselves superior and live at the cost of the majority. One's welfare is another's misery; that is their connection.
>
> MUKUNDRAO PATIL [1913], see Omvedt 1976: 157

The upper-caste nationalist leadership never took into consideration institutionalised discrimination against dalit-bahujans nor did it recognise the existence of multiple traditions and faiths within and without the larger 'Hindu' fold. Barring the rhetoric, the monolithic-supremacist nationalism they espoused was propelled by two objectives: first, to wrest the state power from the British, and, second, to maintain their dominance within the traditional caste-class structure (Omvedt 1994; Aloysius 1997). The construction of brahmanic Hinduism as the cultural basis of nationalism was in essence the reformulation of upper-caste hegemony. If we set aside the semantic quibbling between the so-called progressives/secularists and the conservatives/revivalists, the foundational basis of Indian nationalism in both its secular and communal versions was the same—the sanskritic culture and ideology. While many openly valorised caste as the fundamental basis of Hindu or national unity, the 'progressive' nationalists fine-tuned the art of either keeping silent about it or spouting platitudes on social harmony and unity in diversity.

Such a strategy gave the caste elites a double-edged sword: it enabled them to assume national leadership in the name of anti-colonial struggle, and provided them with an attractive polemic to dismiss dalit-bahujan protests as divisive and anti-national. Phule, Periyar, and Ambedkar who demanded socio-economic reconstruction as an indivisible part of patriotism were branded as enemies of the nation. The anti-caste movements which aimed at people's liberation from the native ruling classes were disdained as casteist and anti-national assertion of the illiterate lower classes. Baburao Bagul saw this perfidious nationalism thus:

> The intelligentsia, that is the Indian national leadership, divided the national liberation movement . . . into two warring factions: a political movement and a social movement. They also declared those who organised social movements, those who theorised on agriculture and industry, to be stooges of the British and traitors. The national movement was turned into a form of historical, mythological movement and ancestor worship. . . . Those who propounded inequality and did not wish society to be democratic, started eulogising history, mythology and ages gone by because, in those mythological and historical ages, they were the supreme victors and leaders. (See Omvedt 1994: 88)

The emergence of social movements from below, from non-brahmanical traditions, was a slow and tortuous process. Colonial rule had accepted the traditional caste and community relations, which meant further exploitation of the toiling castes who were now burdened with additional 'caste duties' for new forms of surplus production. As colonial exploitation operated through the implementation of caste relations, the British had no option but to depend on the Indian elite as valuable partners. Colonial rule, thus, rested on collusion between the imperial and indigenous elites. On the whole, colonialism enlarged, elevated and even *nationalised* the upper strata of society, and thus further marginalised the lower strata.

Colonialism, however, unwittingly opened some unprecedented channels of mobility for the lowered castes, with far-reaching consequences. To avail itself of a cheap supply of labour for various projects, the colonial administration encouraged migration. Now the suppressed castes could escape the stranglehold of local oppressors by migrating to distant places, including overseas colonies, to become plantation, factory, or mine workers. The doors of the British armies and factories were open for them. The advent of industrialisation and the railways helped the caste-oppressed escape village tyrannies. The British had also brought with them a proselytising religion which held promises of equality, dignity, and economic freedom. The poor and the despised now had the option to convert to Christianity. The changed times had also opened for them a small window of educational opportunity, especially in towns and cities. A few educated and semi-educated individuals from the lower orders acquired a consciousness of their degraded status, and some even rose in revolt (as we saw in Chapter 5).

The stirrings of awakening among the dalit-bahujans manifested in the emergence of multiple forms of activities and protests. Varying from place to place, community to community, issue to issue, both in intensity and spread, the struggles took different forms in different places, depending on the circumstances. There was, however, a common thread running through these struggles as the oppressed attempted to throw out civic-religious-educational-economic-administrative disabilities imposed on them by the caste elites. As oppression rested on traditional caste order and 'because colonial exploitation involved the extraction of surpluses mediated through caste and community relations, very often caste and community became . . . issues and weapons of resistance for the exploited' (Omvedt 1994: 93). The scattered and uneven movements of the toiling castes—Shanar-Nadars and Parayars in Tamil Nadu; Ezhavas and Pulayas in Kerala; Mahars, Malis, and Kunbis in Maharashtra; Malas and Madigas in Andhra Pradesh; Chamars, Ahirs, Koeris, and Kurmis in Bihar and Uttar Pradesh; Kaibarta, Rajbansi and Namashudras in Bengal; Dheds and Bhangis in Rajasthan; Chamar-turned-Adi-Dharmis in Punjab, etc., along with similar struggles among Muslim and other communities across the subcontinent—were economic-political as well as civil and human rights movements (Aloysius 1997).

Dynamics and Dimension of Egalitarian Emergence

Citizenship rights formed the core of the issues the dalit-bahujans raised and agitated for. While the upper-caste nationalists were organising themselves first to demand a greater share in colonial power structure and then to launch a movement for transfer of power, the lower orders had to agitate to ensure their right of access to public places (roads, markets, schools and offices); the right of their women (like in Tamil Nadu and Kerala) to cover themselves; the right of access to religious places and educational centres; the right to give up agricultural bondage and hereditary occupations and the liberty to choose any other. These struggles had to be waged not against the imperialists of the West, but against the internal colonisers—brahmans and allied groups of zamindars and money-lenders. In many localities the agitating people had to seek state protection from the local oppressors who would unleash murderous attacks by their henchmen. The 'middle class' nationalist leaders of various persuasions were also upper-caste gentlemen, overwhelmingly brahmans, and most of them had a connection with the land. 'Thus power-holders in the Congress up to the very end tended to oppose anti-landlord legislation and the efforts to protect peasants and tenants' (Omvedt 1994: 89). The 'nationalists' would vehemently denounce anti-zamindar and anti-caste movements as 'anti-national' attacks on Indian custom and tradition.

Education, monopolised for centuries by the fraudulent few, was now an empowering agency capable of liberating the enslaved majority. As early as 1848, Jotirao and Savitribai Phule had set up a school for untouchable women, making it clear that education would be their main weapon to effect change. Later, Narayana Guru, the architect of modern Kerala, advised the people: 'Educate that you may be free and organise that you may be strong'. *Mitavadi*, a journal brought out by his supporters, adopted this maxim above its masthead. Ambedkar's clarion call to the depressed classes at the time of founding his first organisation, Bahishkrit Hitkarani Sabha, in the early 1920s, was: 'Educate, Organise, and Agitate'.

Following Gellner (1983), Aloysius argues that mass education is at the heart of the transition to nationhood.

> The significance of the battles fought all over the length and breadth of this country during colonial times by the shudras and untouchables to gain entry into schools and other educational institutions, much against the resistance, atrocities and oppressions of the powerful high caste, could be better grasped if they are seen as the birth pangs of a modern India.
> (Aloysius 1997: 82)

The non-brahman movements, insofar as they promoted egalitarianism as a social ethos and citizenship rights as the basis of the new polity, were actually aiding the process of the birth of the nation (ibid.: 80–1).

The colonial period actually saw two nationalisms, two struggles: one for freedom in the form of transfer of power from the British to the Indian elite; and the other for freedom from both external and internal domination. It was the latter that necessitated a structural change in society. It had a bigger agenda and was a more authentic nationalism in the sense that it incorporated people's struggles for education, employment, social mobility, and political democracy, besides tenancy rights, land, and water which alone could give meaning to freedom to the dalit-bahujans. This nationalism was grounded in the local struggles and anti-caste movements which erupted in multiple forms across the subcontinent during the colonial rule. The struggles revolving around the issues of oppression and emancipation reflected the birth pangs of a civil society.

As early as 1800, a defiant group of Ezhavas, the toddy-tappers of Kerala, claiming equality, tried to enter the famous Vaikkom temple. For violating the 'sacred tradition', they were killed and their bodies buried in a corner of the temple compound (M.S.A. Rao 1979: 58–9). This is the first recorded instance in modern India of an agitation against civil and religious disabilities.[1]

In the early nineteenth century, Ezhavas in Kerala and their Tamil counterparts, Shanars or Nadars, had a running battle with the aggressive castes for asserting their women's right to wear blouse. Known as the breast-cloth controversy, the struggle against the degrading custom of partial nakedness of their women as a mark of respect to the dominant castes sparked off a determined fight to throw off the yoke of caste slavery (Hardgrave 1968; 1969).

In the 1850s, a Mahar boy from Dharwar was refused admission in a government school due to his 'untouchable' status. He took the matter to the Education Department of the Bombay Province, and later to the Government of India at Calcutta. Under strong pressure and influence of the caste elites, his petition was thrown out (Ambedkar, *BAWS*, vol. 2: 339; Nurullah and Naik 1951: 421–2).

Balak Das, son of Guru Ghasi Das (1756–1836), who transformed the much-despised Chamars of Chhattisgarh into Satnamis, a sect preaching monotheism and human equality, was killed in 1860 for daring to wear the sacred thread. A half century later (1917) the Satnamis again ventured to organise a thread-wearing ceremony. This again invited upper-caste wrath: the sacred threads were branded on the Satnamis' chests and backs with red hot iron, and some of them were beheaded. In the teeth of such atrocities, a Satnami Mahasabha was founded which demanded a new identity, dignity and their democratic representation in socio-political sphere (Fuchs 1965; Aloysius 1997).

In 1872–3, a 'Chandala movement' erupted against social and civil disabilities in Faridpur and Bakarganj districts of eastern Bengal. The toiling castes refused to serve their tormentors, the upper-caste landholders. After a few months, the agitation petered out as their poverty forced them to return to work. But during the 1880s they rallied around the Matua cult, an egalitarian, non-brahmanic form of Vaishnavism, and renamed themselves Namashudras. The man who led the movement was Guru Chanda. He emphasised the need of education for social emancipation and economic betterment. The Namashudras claimed equality, set up schools for their children, and sought new job opportunities in defiance of upper- caste resistance (Bandyopadhyay 1990; 2004).

With emancipatory aspirations, the tribal people in Orissa revived an earlier Mahima or Alekha Dharma under the stewardship of Bhima Bhoi (*c*.1855–94). The poet-prophet Bhima faced insults and threats for his radical monotheism and his opposition to idolatry and the caste system. These did not stop him to lead a march (1881) to the seat of brahmanical power—Puri—to reclaim the supposedly hidden Buddha image beneath the statue of Jagannath from brahmanic clutches. The villagers from nearby areas who tried to enter the Puri temple were detained, tortured, and some of them killed (Narasu [1922] 2003; Senapati 1975).

At the turn of the twentieth century the Moamaris and other lowered castes in Assam organised themselves into political bodies to overcome various civil disabilities and promote education among their children. Several despised castes discarded their traditional names and identities and demanded education, equality and diversification of occupation (V. Rao 1976).

The early twentieth century witnessed spontaneous as well as organised protests from lower orders in Bihar and Uttar Pradesh. The Triveni Sangh, an association of Koeri-Kurmi-Yadav castes in Bihar, and similar organisations in Uttar Pradesh were fighting against *begar* (forced labour) and defying prohibitions against wearing the sacred thread, footwear and the use of horses and palanquins. In village after village they refused to perform free or forced labour for zamindars, and refused to pay *nazrana* (gifts) and the increased taxes (Choudhary and Shrikant 2001).

Anger against caste-feudalism and human bondage was building up among the oppressed across the country from the early nineteenth century. Protest found expression in myriad ways—sometimes in a religious garb, at other times directly with a secular agenda. In region after region, the tenants and landless workers were rising in revolt against 'free labour, rent-farming, arbitrary evictions, cheating, juggling of accounts, and all forms of physical maltreatment including not too rarely murder' (Aloysius 1997). The oppressive situation gave birth to a series of peasant revolts—the Deccan grain riots, the Pabna agrarian agitation, the Mapilla revolts, the tribal revolts of the Santhals and Mundas, and the cultivators' agitations in the plains of Bihar and Uttar Pradesh. These movements invited the combined wrath of colonial and Indian rulers and exposed the collusive and collaborative nature of colonial rule.

Thus, the late nineteenth and early twentieth century—the period of the spectacular rise of nationalism and movement for transfer of power—also witnessed a widespread awakening of political consciousness among the lowered castes and communities.

Their egalitarian aspirations produced several streams of movement against the stranglehold of ascriptive hierarchy, caste slavery, and feudal exploitation. These struggles threw up several leaders who were unrelenting critics of caste and its consequences. They confronted the hypocritical nationalist leadership for keeping pro-equality social movements out of the national agenda. Phule, Shahu Maharaj, and Ambedkar in Maharashtra; Iyothee Thass and Periyar in Tamil Nadu; Narayana Guru, Dr. Palpu, Kumaran Asan, K. Ayyappan and Ayyankali in Kerala; Bhagyareddy Varma in Andhra; Mangoo Ram and Chhotu Ram in Punjab; Achhutanand and Ram Charan in Uttar Pradesh; Hari Chanda Thakur, Guru Chanda and Jogendranath Mandal in Bengal; Sonadhar Senapathy in Assam; and many lesser-known social crusaders mocked the patriotic pretensions of elites, and attacked the system of exploitation at every level. They rejected the high-caste cultural tradition and tried to create socio-religious practices embedded in the non-brahmanic cultures of the land. It is striking that all of them variously underlined Phule's basic contention that 'just as India went through a phase of British colonisation, it had previously passed at various stages of its history through brahmanical colonialism'. Linking the oppressive present with the historical past, they pointed out that the internal colonialism has its roots in a false philosophy and a pseudo-religion which sanctify caste-based discrimination and domination. They tried to underscore the existence of traditions which were more conducive to the development of a new, democratic and egalitarian culture.

Narayana Guru and Kerala's Liberation Movement

Kerala is recognised now as a model state for its 100 per cent literacy and remarkable socio-economic progress. But not long ago, this state on the coast of south-west India was a hotbed of oppression where the lower classes were subjected to the most degrading practices. The notorious practice of *theendal* or 'distance pollution' was reflective of the subhuman status of the lowered castes who suffered the worst kinds of atrocities at the hands of Nambudiri brahmans and Nayars.[2] The populous Ezhava community—regarded today as an affluent OBC—was despised, like the 'untouchables', as a source of pollution and suffered several social disabilities. They were not allowed to use public tanks and wells, or roads and bridges that ran near upper-caste homes and temples. They were not allowed to wear footwear or carry an umbrella. Their women were not permitted to wear upper garments. Forced to render free services to the dominant castes, they were denied admission to public schools, and were kept away from the administrative services (Rao 1979: 24). The prevailing belief among the dominant castes, who enjoyed privileges and on that strength had monopolised access to English education and government jobs, was that the Ezhavas should confine themselves to their traditional occupations of farming, toddy-tapping, and weaving.

Resentment was simmering against the oppressive situation that obtained in Travancore, Cochin and Malabar. In 1885 Dr. Palpu (1863–1950), the first Ezhava graduate who could not get a government job due to his caste, demanded the removal of civil disabilities against the lower orders. He led a popular campaign on these issues. A memorandum signed by 13,176 Ezhavas was given in 1896 to the ruler of Travancore, asking that government schools and the public service be opened up to them. This demand was turned down on the grounds that the Ezhavas did not require to aspire for education or government jobs!

Kerala society was in ferment—the new forces were surging ahead for change, while the old order was refusing to die down. It was at about this time that Narayana Guru (c.1854–1928), an ascetic belonging to Ezhava caste, through his imaginative public activities emerged as a liberator. The movement he led released forces that not only challenged the material aspect of upper-caste domination, but also subverted the hegemonic social hierarchy.

A deeply spiritual person, what Narayana Guru saw around him—widespread misery, ignorance, and the negation of basic human rights to a vast majority of people in the name of dharma—appalled him. Shudras like him were debarred from entering the sacred domain of religion. He had no right to become a religious teacher or leader. Narayana Guru challenged this and created history by establishing scores of debrahmanised temples and ashramas. At the time of the first consecration (10 February 1888) at Aruvipuram in south Travancore, he picked up a stone from a nearby stream and installed it as a Shiva shrine. The brahmans reacted strongly: an Ezhava, they said, had no right to consecrate an idol of Shiva. Guru silenced the incensed brahmans with the minimum fuss: 'I consecrated the Ezhava Shiva, not the Brahman Shiva, and I did it for the untouchable Ezhavas.' Similarly, when the purists accused him of committing a grave mistake by not consulting astrologers for ascertaining the auspicious time for consecrating the idol, Guru made this reply: 'We cast a horoscope only after a child is born, and not the other way about, don't we? The idol has been sanctified. Now you may please cast the horoscope' (Kunhappa 1988: 25–6). Guru went on establishing a chain of temples in different parts of the state where everyone was welcome, including the lowest-of-the-low Pulayas and other 'untouchables'. When a memorial temple was built at the site of his first consecration at Aruvipuram, Guru had the following message engraved there:

Here is a model abode
Where men live like brothers:
Bereft of the prejudice of caste
Or the rancour of religious differences. (Kunhappa 1988: 23)

Guru was born and brought up in a conservative milieu. The ordinary people of that era had enormous faith in established religious practices. His brilliance lay in the fact that he filled the traditional symbols with humane and inclusive values. His initiative to set up people's temples was integral to his universal vision, manifested in his famous slogan 'One Caste, One Religion and One God for Man'. On one occasion, he spelt out the purposes of pilgrimage as general education, human understanding, organising the followers of his faith, besides devotion to God.

The temples Narayana Guru established were harbingers of social change as the officiating priests in all these temples were the ones considered impure in the Varnashrama Dharma. In fact, he envisioned these temples as hubs of productive activities and educational opportunities for the deprived. He insisted that the temple buildings and premises must be used as schools, libraries, meeting halls, or even weaving sheds. The money received as offerings was to be utilised for public good and setting up schools as well as vocational and technical centres.

Guru stressed the need of modern education in both English and Malayalam with a view to promote development and employment opportunities in new fields. The motto he gave to his followers was: 'Educate that you may be free, and organise that you may be strong'. In a speech in 1910 to the Vijnana Vardhini Sabha at Cherai, he underlined the need for women's education, and for technical training to establish industries. He was unhappy that the temples did not play the desired role of bringing people together; instead, he noted with concern, they deepened the caste divides. This made him declare in a message in 1917 that he regarded educational institutions to be the real temples which would educate people into sinking caste differences:

> People are likely to regret the spending of money on construction of temples.... The major temples should be educational institutions.... It was thought that through temples, all people could be brought together without caste distinctions. But the experience doesn't justify the hope. Temples increase caste barriers. Now we must try to educate the people. Let them have more knowledge; that is the only way of improving them. (See George 1991: 17)

Beneath his religious garb Guru was a social revolutionary. Some scholars see his movement within the parameter of orthodox Hinduism because of his love of Sanskrit and Vedanta philosophy. It is notable, however, that his system of thought and activities, oriented as it was towards social transformation, militated against the culture of caste. Unlike Gandhi, he was sensitive to the cultural implications of the co-option of the caste-oppressed into brahmanical modes of worship. So he sought to create new places of worship rather than initiate a campaign for the entry of lowered castes into the brahmanical temples. Through debrahmanisation of religion, democratisation of education, diversification of occupations, and the adoption of a generally rational approach to society and culture, Narayana Guru strove to build an enlightened society. As such Guru carried forward the legacy of the counter-culture which had challenged caste and brahmanism since the Buddha's time.

Guru's ambition was to resurrect a demoralised and divided society through cultural–educational empowerment of the people. For this, he was willing to embrace anyone, irrespective of ideological difference. An ever-evolving saintly person, he respected democratic dissent and divergence of opinions which enabled him to carry along a wide variety of thinker-activists. His leading associates whose talents and hard work took the movement to glorious heights included Dr. Palpu, a scholar-activist and an impassioned campaigner for education; Kumaran Asan (1873–1924), Kerala's leading poet and a Buddhist enthusiast; C.V. Cunhuraman (1871–1949), a rationalist par excellence; K. Ayyappan (1889–1969), an agnostic and a thorough-going radical who changed Guru's slogan of 'One Caste, One Religion and One God for Man' to 'No Caste, No Religion, and No God for Mankind'; and T.K. Madhavan (1886–1930), a moderate who resorted to satyagraha for the rights and dignity of the 'untouchables'.

Guru felt the need for an open-ended network to reach out to the masses, and encouraged some of his closest allies to set up an organisation. A society called the Sree Narayana Dharma Paripalana Yogam, popularly known as SNDP, was founded in 1903 for the dissemination of Guru's dharma and empowerment of the oppressed. The SNDP soon became a movement whose annual gatherings attracted thousands of volunteers. Palpu and Kumaran Asan played a leading role in making it a platform for social change. Palpu organised a women's conference which became a regular feature at the annual meetings. A votary of science and technology, he also organised an industrial exhibition in 1905 as part of the SNDP conference.

Palpu and Asan led an agitation to secure the admission of Ezhava boys and girls to public schools. This resulted in a series of violent clashes between Ezhavas and the high-caste Nayars. When a school at Haripat was thrown open to Ezhavas by the then Dewan of Travancore in 1903, the Nayars went on a rampage, robbing the Ezhava houses and attacking the school boys (Rao 1979: 49). The right to enter the educational domain was thus won in a protracted struggle waged by the SNDP. The Ezhava agitation inspired other deprived communities to launch similar struggles. New schools were set up and pressure for the admission of depressed classes to state-run schools mounted. The spread of education among the deprived did not wait for sarkari action, much of it came through peoples' own efforts.

Traditionally, Ezhavas were divided into Thiyyas, Chovans, Thendans, and other sub-castes, who did not intermarry. There were several superstitions and unsavoury practices. The SNDP helped mould them into one community and made them shed ugly customs and rites. It led them to forgo alcoholism and traditional jobs like toddy-tapping, and instead seek employment in new industries or crafts. It organised industrial exhibitions, and conducted several vocational training programmes.

The SNDP's concerns and activities were not confined to Ezhavas; it made a concerted effort to break barriers among castes. The society's temples and hostels were open to all, including the Pulayas, Parayas and Cherumas. And as Guru's biographer Murkot Kumaran has puckishly put it, 'Even brahmans were permitted temple entry!' The movement had a cascading effect on all castes, including the Nambudiris and Nayars, by making them realise the need to discard the old and the ugly and replace them with better values and institutions. In other words, it launched a decisive campaign against social injustice by rousing public consciousness and warning the oppressors to change their ways. Poet Asan put the high-and-mighty on notice with the prophetic call: '*Change you the laws yourselves, or else/The laws will change you indeed*' (see George 1991: 66).

Kumaran Asan, the executive secretary of the SNDP for a long time, used his creative talent to a give a cultural base to the movement. Reckoned as one of the three greats of modern Malayalam poetry—the other two being Vallathola and Parameswara Iyer—Asan blazed a new trail in the literary arena with his innovative techniques and radical content. Many of his poems were inspired by a passion for social reconstruction. Wielding his pen to arouse patriotic feelings and revulsion against caste, he wrote in 1908:

Your slavery is your destiny, O Mother!
Your sons, blinded by caste, clash among themselves
And get killed; what for is freedom then? (See S. Sarkar 1983)

In his poem 'Duravastha' (The Deplorable Condition), Asan shows how the Mappillas, converts to Islam from outcastes, had embraced the new religion to escape the atrocities of the Hindu upper-castes. He weaves a narrative to yoke together in matrimony a Nambudiri woman and a Pulaya man. The marriage between the highest and the lowest in the caste hierarchy invited the venom of many savarna critics. Asan responded that the poem was inspired by the ideal of a casteless society.

Asan saw the Buddha as a historical role-model against caste and brahmanism (Awaya 1999). Some of his most celebrated poems, 'Chandalabhikshuki' (The Untouchable Nun) and 'Karuna' (The Compassion) are anchored in the Buddhist legends. His enthusiasm for Buddhism made him translate Edwin Arnold's *The Light of Asia* into Malayalam under the title *Sri Buddha Charitam*.

The urge to embrace Buddhism among Kerala's lowered-caste intelligentsia was strong, and manifested itself in various forms throughout the movement. Linking their present condition to the history of Buddhism in the region, they asserted that because of their ancestors' attachment to Buddhism even after the spread of brahmanism in Kerala, their social position was pushed down to the lowest rung of caste hierarchy. In this light, their social marginalisation, they argued, could be interpreted as a result of their historic resistance against the onslaught of brahmanism (Awaya 1999).

Many intellectuals associated with the SNDP presented Buddhism as the anti-thesis to brahmanic Hinduism. They opposed the fight-from-within-Hinduism line adopted by Guru. In line with outstanding subaltern theoreticians elsewhere (Phule, Iyothee Thass, Periyar, Ambedkar et al.), they believed that so long as they remained within Hinduism they would not attain dignity and equality. One Sivaprasada Swami wrote an article in *Mitavadi* (February 1917) in which reflecting on the SNDP activities, he deplored its strategy of remaining within Hinduism: 'So far as we remained within Hinduism, we who were born to a depressed class would remain depressed.' He also dashed off a letter to Narayana Guru in which he stressed the fact that the more Guru spread Vedic teaching, the more caste consciousness was strengthened. His plea to Guru was to start a new religion, preferably a religion like Buddhism which denied caste. His was not a solitary voice. Leaders such as K. Ayyappan and C. Krishnan, and other radical Ezhavas held the same view (ibid.).

Enthusiasm for revival of Buddhism was considerable, but there was no unanimity on the issue. There were people like Cunhuraman who preferred Christianity, while a few others like T.K. Madhavan were against any conversion. But the decisive factor that tilted the scale against mass conversion to Buddhism was Guru's own reluctance. He pacified the Buddhist enthusiasts by arguing that 'whatever one's religion, it is sufficient that man be good'. Nevertheless, many in the movement remained committed to Buddhism, and some of them—C. Krishnan and R. Sugatan are two prominent examples—actually converted. In his book *The Light of Buddhist Teaching* (1929), Krishnan laid emphasis on its rational and ethical aspects. He contended that Buddhism, unlike Hinduism, only gives the principle of a meaningful life, not dogmas, rituals, or practices like offering money and food to deities and priests. A similar view was expressed by R. Sugatan, who later became an outstanding leader of the trade union and communist movement in the state. Sugatan and his friends established an organisation called the Buddha Mission in their native Alleppey to spread Buddhism.

A significant fallout of the quest for an emancipatory religion was the socio-political radicalisation in the 1920s and 1930s that led to the growth of rationalism and socialism in the state. The rationalists held a meeting in 1925 at the Advait Ashram established by Guru in Alwaye, and started a Malayalam magazine called *Yuktivadi* (The Rationalist) with K. Ayyappan as its editor. Another important development in the 1930s was the Swatantra Samudayam (Independent Community) movement that rejected all religions and stressed the need to restructure society and culture on egalitarian values. Its leaders held the view that the Ezhava and other lowered castes should declare that they were an independent community, not Hindus, and that without converting to any religion they should opt for an enlightened atheism. They attacked institutionalised religions, especially caste-ridden Hinduism, for promoting injustice and obscurantism. E. Madhavan wrote *Swatantra Samudayam* in 1934 in which he held religion responsible for chaining man to the regressive ideas that stopped his progress. He saw organised religion as a threat to advancement of science and education, freedom of expression, and peaceful co-existence. Hinduism, he argued, had promoted additional evils like caste discrimination. The temple down the ages had been a hotbed of segregation and superstition, stunting the growth of social and ethical values, Madhavan contended. He also took Gandhi to task for supporting varna ideology and promoting temple-entry as the panacea for the caste-oppressed (Awaya 1999: 155).

K. Ayyappan was the most radical face of the movement. His organisation Sahodara Sangham (The Association of Brotherhood) celebrated its first anniversary by burning the effigy of a monster symbolising caste. He identified with the plight of the untouchables, and wanted all the lowered castes to interdine, intermarry, and move forward together. His mingling with the much-despised Pulayas incurred the wrath of the conservatives of his own caste, who excommunicated him, accusing him of taking too much liberty with Guru's teachings. Jeered as 'Pulayam Ayyappan', he was made to suffer so much that he had to approach Narayana Guru for advice. Guru, however, was very pleased with Ayyappan's activities. Showing solidarity with him, he even gave his support in writing: 'Whatever be the religion, language, custom, caste or dress of individuals, since they are all human beings, there can be no objection to their interdining or intermarrying' (Kunhappa 1988: 56). This silenced Ayyappan's critics.

The SNDP movement preceded the Congress-led national movement by a few years in Kerala. When the Congress gained some ground in the state in the early 1920s, its elitist orientation alienated the dalit-bahujan leadership. They attacked the Congress for neglecting social issues and caste discrimination. Ayyappan pointedly asked Gandhi why he did not call such Indians devilish who were treating Pulayas, Parayas and other lowly castes as subhumans, though he fulminated against the British and called them 'satanic' for their oppression of Indians. Ayyappan gave voice to the general anguish of the dalit-subalterns when he bitterly remarked that neither Gandhi nor other leaders of the national movement had understood the evil of caste and cultural oppression.

However, the SNDP leadership was quick to seize Gandhi's distinctive use of satyagraha as a weapon against caste discrimination. As early as 1918, the Passive Resistance League was established in Kozhikode to fight social evils like *theendal*. The Congress' temple satyagrahas in the 1920s, particularly at Vaikkom and Guruvayur, were not only inspired by the SNDP movement but the bulwork of mass support also came from its cadre. T.K. Madhavan, the organising secretary of the SNDP during the 1920s, was the proponent for passing the temple entry resolution at the 1923 Kakinada Congress Conference. He was also the main organiser of the Vaikkom satyagraha. Earlier, Madhavan and Ayyappan had themselves entered the prohibited area, defying the exclusion of lowered castes from the temple and surrounding areas. For the Congress, temple-entry was little more than a political ploy to win mass support for its transfer of power agenda, while the SNDP leaders viewed it as a step towards a bigger social movement. Revolutionaries like Ayyappan soon tired of the temple-entry matter, and went on to criticise the Congress and Madhavan for exhausting people's energies on a side issue.

Even Narayana Guru was dissatisfied with the Vaikkom satyagraha as he wanted the agitationists to 'scale the barricades' and not only walk along the prohibited roads but enter all temples (S. Sarkar 1983: 244). The Congress remained brahmanical on caste while paying lip-service to issues like temple-entry. Nowhere was this more evident than Gandhi's famous conversation with Narayana Guru in which the former shamelessly defended the caste order by insisting that all leaves of the same tree are not identical in shape and texture. To this, Narayana Guru pointed out that the difference is only superficial: the juice of all leaves of a particular tree would be the same in content. But Gandhi's faith in Varnashrama Dharma remained unshakeable to the last.

The SNDP movement galvanised the 'untouchables' into collective action to throw off the yoke of slavery. The Pulayas came forward to assert their civil rights, walking on main roads, entering market places, attending schools, and claiming right to own land. In a dramatic fashion, Ayyankali (1863–1941) led Pulayas, driving their bullock carts through the thoroughfares of town after town, defying the tradition that denied them access to public roads.

Under his leadership, Pulaya women gathered in several places to publicly assert their right to cover themselves fully and cast away the *kallumalai* (the garland of stone), the symbol of their slavery, that was their only sanctioned covering above the waist (Saradamoni 1980: 152–3). In 1907, Ayyankali organised the Sadhu Jana Paripalan Sangham, the membership of which was not confined to the Pulayas. Though himself illiterate, he led a movement for modern education and vocational training for all communities, particularly among the Cherumas, Parayas, and Pulayas. He set up several schools for 'untouchable' girls in the teeth of resistance from the caste elites. He created history in 1915 by organising the first-ever landless workers' strike in the subcontinent, which was not for any economic demand but to insist on the right of 'untouchable' children to go to school (ibid.: 149).

Later, the Ezhava–Pulaya struggle expanded to include Christians and Muslims in a bigger alliance, and together they formed the Civil Rights League in 1919, which demanded, among other things, universal franchise and equality of citizenship. Thus the SNDP movement 'effectively laid the first foundation stones for the new civil society in Kerala through promotion of education both literary and technical, diversification of occupations and vertical social mobility' (Aloysius 1997). Narayana Guru's middle-of-the-road approach, as against the more radical course advocated by firebrand leaders like Ayyappan, did not raise much dust, but shifted the pyramid of social hierarchy. It started a social process which gave a body blow to the old order.

Dravidian Upsurgence: Iyothee Thass and the Justice Party

In the Tamil land, the nineteenth century witnessed sporadic yet determined attempts by lowered castes to break free from the brahmanic prisonhouse and revive their Dravidian culture. Some radicals began to see caste, priesthood, and Sanskrit scripture as destroyers of the native civilisation. The recovery of their supposed egalitarian past thus became entwined with the struggle for civil rights in the present. Here, it was easy to develop a distinct linguistic–ethnic identity for the non-brahmans who had a language with non-Sanskrit origin, recognised as Dravidian or Tamil.[3] The oppressive present and distorted past were attributed to the invasion of the Aryan-brahmans. Such understanding was buttressed by the situation that obtained in the region, strengthening the suspicion that the brahmans were still conspiring to suppress the Dravidian people and their culture. Surviving Dravidian religio-cultural practices were testimony to the alienness of the brahmanic culture.

In a sense the most striking indication that high religion never aquired a dominance over the autonomy of local belief and worship in South India was provided by the history of religious practice in the nineteenth and twentieth centuries. To some extent Brahmans were always outsiders in Tamil and Malayali society as became clear with the growth of political non-Brahmanism in the early twentieth century. (S. Bayly 1992: 463)

The revival of Tamil customs coalesced into the political battle for equality. Several Tamil Sangams were formed in cities like Madurai and Madras. The awakening of interest in ancient Tamil classics spurred the publication of tracts that attacked the alien and oppressive brahmanic culture. The *Ramayana* was turned on its head by glorifying Ravana and depicting Rama as the villain. (In oral tradition, this anti-Aryan view was entrenched in the Dravidian psyche before the nineteenth century.) The killing of Shambuka by Rama because of his caste was roundly condemned. The Dravidar Kazhagam of 1882 raised and debated the ideological matrix of Dravidianism. At the turn of the century, the stage was set for the emergence of a powerful non-brahman movement in the region.

Iyothee Thass (1845–1914), a dalit by birth and a Buddhist by conviction, was an outstanding figure in the socio-cultural awakening which preceded the rise of the non-brahman movement in the Tamil land (Geetha and Rajadurai 1998; Aloysius 1998). A Tamil scholar and Siddha medical practitioner, he was a cultural radical whose ideas and activities broke new ground in the dalit-subaltern struggle for identity, dignity, and justice.[4] Grasping the liberating potential of Buddhist tradition and drawing on the Tamil-Buddhist connection in the past, he was the first to interpret Tamil history and literature from the viewpoint of a Buddhist presence in the region. His writings taken together with the work of some of his associates like Masilamani comprise a corpus which represents a Buddhist vision of the Indian past. Part history and part polemic, they anticipated, in many ways, the historiographical writings of Ambedkar (Geetha and Rajadurai 1998).

More important, they prefigured and, to an extent, overlapped with an emergent Dravidianism which ... provided a wholly new historiographical tradition. Directed against the Aryan version of history, this latter came to articulate a historical sensibility that was assertive in its Tamilness and scornful of what it considered the Aryan element in India's culture. (Ibid.: 92)

Iyothee Thass was the pioneer of the engaged Buddhism in modern India. Based in Madras, he founded the South Indian Buddhist Association which by 1910 had many branches in India and abroad (Aloysius 1998). Tamil Buddhism was constructed on the matrix of castelessness since the caste system in the region was perceived as a crucial factor in the 'discriminatory distinction in public life, both secular as well as sacred'. What was remarkable about the Tamil Buddhism was its ability to evolve and articulate the concerns of all the marginalised into a universal vision of emancipation.

Subaltern concerns—such as welfare measures for the upliftment of the poor, removal of civil disabilities of the 'outcaste', etc. are, here, seen as being inseparable from those of the social whole; and sectional emancipation is unthinkable without simultaneously effecting an overall structural change. And this was done through subtle shifts in emphasis: from ascriptive groups to organising principles and from sectarian obsession to universal vision. The emancipatory strategies of a religion of the oppressed are necessarily the opposite of those of the oppressors. (Aloysius 1998: 153–4)

Iyothee Thass' concerns and activities encompassed a range of subjects. He spearheaded a campaign for education among the dalit-subalterns, setting up with his colleagues several schools in slum enclaves in the urban centres. He ran a popular weekly, *Tamizhan*, for years. He published pamphlets and tracts and widely circulated them among Tamils everywhere. The articles he wrote for *Tamizhan* give an idea of the range of his concerns: caste domination, untouchability, indigenous medicine, agricultural rituals, folk deities, issues involved in a census and conversions, Buddhism and Jainism in the Tamil land, etc. His writings are remarkable not only for their insight into the nature of society, but also for espousing the cause of social emancipation, Buddhism, rationalism, and the new egalitarian Dravidian identity.

Iyothee Thass was among the earliest Adi-Dravida intellectuals who presented a sharp critique of brahmanical power, its role in modern society and polity, and its espousal of a problematic nationalism (Geetha and Rajadurai 1998). He drew attention to rampant civil injustices and acts of social and ritual discrimination that ensured brahman exclusivity. He cited instances of prejudice and discrimination practised by not only the brahman nationalists, but also by the largely brahman-owned press which mediated and manufactured public opinion. It is striking that he located the power of the modern–secular brahman in the control he excercised over the construction of public opinion (ibid.: 63). He pointed out the caste bias and rancour prevalent in the presentation of events or opinions in the nationalist press. Appalled by the brahman's proclivity to fortify their caste status and promote their castemen whenever in position of power, he asserted that a caste so obsessed with its interests and expropriation of the interests and concerns of others, could hardly be considered national or representative (ibid.).

Iyothee Thass linked the exclusive nature and content of the brahman-piloted swaraj and swadeshi projects to 'a flawed epistemology and a jaundiced worldview' (Geetha and Rajadurai 1998: 66). Probing this worldview and its deleterious implications, he saw the brahmanical learning to be unproductive and passive because it induced laziness and reduced knowledge to a concern with the superficial. The brahman's contemplative knowledge, Thass argued, deters him from aligning his knowledge to action. Divorced from the creative realm, his intellectual energy is expended on gratuitous tasks such as defining the notions of defilement. Moreover, his age-old indulgence in the art of religious inquiry keeps breeding new creeds, each advancing its own claims on truth and wisdom through endless hair-splitting and convoluted arguments. This deeply flawed knowledge-system, he stressed, has not changed with the brahman's acquisition of modern education: he is more interested in flaunting his mastery over the English grammar than expressing an original or useful idea. Not surprisingly, the new political ideal produced by the insular knowledge-system of the brahman seemed to Thass to be as deficient as the tradition which informed it (ibid.: 66–7). He was categorical that unless nationalism heeded the concerns and anxieties of the producing masses and until it learnt to express itself in people's language, it could neither be representative nor effective.

Led by social critics like Iyothee Thass, the intellectual ferment thus generated unleashed forces that facilitated the emergence of a political radicalism in the then Madras Presidency consisting of Tamil Nadu, Karnataka, Andhra, and Malabar Kerala. The South Indian Liberal Federation, commonly known as the Justice Party, was formed in 1916, on an anti-Congress, anti-brahmanical plank with the objective of radical redistribution of socio-political power. Thyagaraya Chetty and T.M. Nair played a pivotal role in the emergent 'shudra movement'. They issued in December 1916 the Non-Brahman Manifesto against the preponderance of brahmans in the fields of education, public service, and politics. Brahman domination in the public sphere was clearly reflected in statistics. While 80 per cent of the brahman populace was literate, barely four per cent of the rest had learnt the alphabet. According to the 1901 census, brahmans accounted for only three per cent of the Presidency population, but between 1897 and 1904 they had secured 94 per cent of positions in the Provincial Civil Service. In 1914, 450 out of the 650 registered graduates of the Madras University were brahmans. In 1914, out of 16 individuals elected as delegates of the Congress from the region 14 were brahmans. Up to 1901, there was not a single non-brahman representative in the Madras Legislative Council (Irschick 1969).

The Justicites hammered home the point that the brahmans had usurped all power, while the toiling masses, cultivators, and others who constitute 97 per cent of the population remained deprived. Demanding democratic representation for non-brahmans in the fields of education, administration and legislation, the Justice leaders lashed out at the brahman-dominated Congress nationalism, and claimed that the Justice movement cherished very different ideas about nation-building and freedom. This implied that nationalistic imperative to free the country from colonial rule should not subsume the vital question of internal discrimination and subordination. The Justicites insisted that if democratic ideals were to be realised, mere affirmation of equality without any change on the ground would make little difference. The non-brahmans who constituted the 'producing communities', they asserted, would have to come forward to wrest power from the entrenched interests of a tiny minority. Declaring caste as antithetical to the national unity, M.V. Naidu, a prominent Justicite, underlined that caste hierarchy had thwarted the growth of mutual sympathy and the spirit of co-operation which bound people together into a political community. Efforts to blend different communities into a homogeneous whole had not succeeded, he argued, because of systematic opposition by orthodox Hindus (Geetha and Rajadurai 1998: 127–8).

Presenting the Justice road-map, Thyagaraya Chetty and Nair exuded confidence that the non-brahmans could attain a unity and wholeness, both in their resistance to the brahman power and through assertion and practice of an alternative culture with their own values and conventions. Justice leaders suggested four lines of action for putting democratic principles into practice. First, non-brahmans were to educate themselves in large numbers. Second, they were to work for their and the country's economic development. Third, they were to come together and work to ensure proportional representation for all communities in administration and in the legislative bodies. Last, they were to make efforts, through their unified interaction, to build a casteless fraternity that abided by modern values (Geetha and Rajadurai 1998: 128–9).

This was a tall order. While it was relatively easy to work, through both legislation and action, on issues like public education and proportional representation, no purposive action on the question of socio-economic transformation was possible without a programme of structural change. Given the formidable socio-historical circumstances and very limited power under the dyarchy under which the Justice Party was constrained to operate (after its electoral victory), it could not bring in structural changes. Moreover, the city-based and English-educated Justice leaders, notwithstanding their claim to represent the entire spectrum of peasants, workers, and artisans were not in a position to galvanise the dalit-subalterns living in remote villages or towns. However, in respect of education and affirmative action in government jobs, the Justice Party indeed played a historic role. It was able to address—and bring together—the common people, all of whom were sensitive to the historical wrongs. Even in this instance, Justice leaders had to face a hostile brahman press and a brahman-dominated public sphere. 'They literally had to unmake public opinion with respect to caste and the question of representation, and their successes in this regard, constituted no mean achievement. For, they amounted to nothing less than a redrawing of the limits of civil society in the Tamil country' (Geetha and Rajadurai 1998: 129).

In 1920, the Justice Party won a remarkable mandate in the elections to run a diarchic government in the Madras Presidency. On assuming office, it passed a Government Order (16 September 1921) directing an increase in the proportion of posts in government offices held by non-brahmans. This was the expansion of the 1851 Standing Order (No. 128, Clause 2) of the Revenue Board of Madras instructing all district collectors to be careful to see that subordinate appointments in their districts were not monopolised by a few influential families (Irschick 1969). Standing Order 128 was the first recorded attempt to remove the upper-caste monopolisation of government jobs. The order however was hardly implemented at any stage: half-hearted efforts to enforce it proved futile in the face of dogged opposition by the caste elites who stood to lose by the order. The brahmans projected the move as an attempt by the British to 'divide and rule'.

Predictably, the new move to ensure representation of all communities in public appointments was derided by the brahman lobby as divisive and dangerous. Opinion-makers like C.P. Ramaswamy Iyer organised protest meetings which resolved that such reservation was 'detrimental to the best interests of the country' and as regards the Hindus, 'such divisive move would prove highly injurious to the integrity of Hindu society' (Geetha and Rajadurai 1998: 158). The Justice government, however, refused to be deterred by such outbursts and brought a new order on 22 August 1922 to ensure that representation from below was extended both to initial recruitment and at every point in promotion. This move, though hamstrung by the British ambivalence on the issue and strong brahmanic opposition, laid the foundation of affirmative action in India.

During its tenure the Justice Party also brought in progressive legislation pertaining to intermarriage, franchise for the common man, abolition of the devadasi system, throwing open temples to depressed classes, regulating temple administration and bringing it under the control of the state, and educational facilities and reduction of fees for weaker sections. Above all, it did a splendid job in promoting primary education, women's education and a more viable technical, industrial and agricultural education. For instance, by 1925, in about 18 out of 25 municipalities, free and compulsory school education was introduced. The Education Act of 1920 was amended with a view to offset high drop-out rate and keep poor children in school. The Justice Party also introduced a scheme to feed deprived children in schools. It was held that children, once in school, could not be taken out within the period of their school age and parents who attempted to do so were liable to pay a penalty. It also paid special attention to the spread of education among Adi-Dravidas and insisted that all public schools admit them, failing which the managements would forfeit grants-in-aid. Adi-Dravida students were also given concessions in fees, besides other facilities (Geetha and Rajadurai 1998: 133–4).

The Justice's legislation regarding social and educational reforms was bold and imaginative, even if its implementation left much to be desired. One reason was an acute financial crunch, aggravated by the fact that, though elected, the government under dyarchy could not resolve problems of finance. Secondly, the brahman-dominated bureaucracy was biased against implementation. This was compounded by the Justice Party's own inability to link its progressive legislation to a sustained ideological and social struggle against brahmanism. Not only did it fail to build a credible ideological alternative to brahmanism, some of its leaders also showed an elitist tilt, which prevented them from taking the movement to the grassroots. The task of mass mobilisation for a radical politics was left to social revolutionaries like Periyar.

Periyar and the Self-Respect Movement

E.V. Ramaswami Naicker (1879–1973), better known as Periyar (a title meaning 'great man' that was conferred on him by the people during his heroic struggle), was a relentless critic and campaigner against brahmanic culture and ideology. His public life and politics bring out the hidden—and sordid—history of Congress nationalism. Joining the Congress in 1919, he rose quickly to become a major figure of the Tamil Nadu Congress, but soon became disillusioned with what he dubbed its hyprocritical politics. He left the 'brahmanic Congress' to organise a 'Self-Respect' movement which represented not only the radical phase of the non-brahman movement but also a response to the 'politics of piety' as espoused by Gandhi (Geetha and Rajadurai 1998). The Self-Respect League that he formed in 1926 bore a striking similarity in its objectives to that of Phule's Satyashodhak Samaj, calling for the annihilation of caste, opposing brahmanical hegemony, and championing the liberation of dalit-bahujans and women. A trenchant critic of caste hierarchy, ritualism, and idolatry, Periyar, like Phule and Ambedkar, conflated Hinduism with brahmanism, and lambasted Hindu laws and institutions as instruments of 'brahmanic', 'male' and 'Aryan' exploitation. His militant, mass-oriented movement attacked the Congress nationalism as the political front of brahmanism that set aside vital issues such as power, difference and discrimination within the country.

The Self-Respect movement was 'fundamentally opposed to the holy alliance of religion, caste and nationalism, an alliance which it understood as embodying a social and political order that was inherently inegalitarian' (Geetha and Rajadurai 1998: 303–4). Periyar was critical of the way the brahmans continued to 'conflate ritual scruple with national principle', and felt acutely the slights brahmans routinely handed out to non-brahmans in the emergent public spheres. The turning point was his clash with the Congress leadership over the question of separate dining for brahman and non-brahman students in a Congress-sponsored residential school (*gurukulam*) near Madras. It was a galling—and eye-opening—experience for Periyar that the school, set up with the aim of inculcating social service and patriotism in students, was practising untouchability by arranging separate dining for non-brahman boys. Congress nationalists including Gandhi were supportive of this practice under the pretext of maintaining traditional harmony. Periyar tried to reason with the 'nationalists' that 'the gurukulam must stand for an ideal—for Indian nationalism—and there should be no invidious distinction between man and man' (Viswanathan 1983: 49). Nationalism, he argued, should be nurtured by citizens without bargaining their dignity and conscience on a common agenda which must include 'all round growth of knowledge; spread of education; the cultivation of rational thought, work, industry, equality, unity, initiative and honesty and the abolition of poverty, injustice and untouchability' (Geetha and Rajadurai 1998: 472). Before all else, the nation, he insisted, required the abolition of Varnashrama Dharma and its birth-based discrimination.

Periyar's relationship with the Congress was stormy and short-lived. In 1920, he had presided over a separate session of non-brahmans at the 26th provincial session of the Congress at Tirunelveli. In this meeting, resolutions were adopted demanding the reservation of constituencies and government jobs for non-brahmans. Srinivasa Iyengar, the Congress president, however, did not allow these resolutions to be taken up in the open session, vetoing them in the 'public interest'. Again, in the 1924 provincial Congress session at Thiruvannamalai, Periyar in his presidential address emphasised that he was for the abolition of caste system, but unless that was done members of all castes and communities should get representation in every field. He attempted to convince the Congress leadership that until the evolution into castelessness, the only way out should be to balance the wrongs of history in a democratic manner to empower the caste-oppressed. Reservation, he said, was one of the ways to redistribute existing power.

Periyar again piloted a resolution demanding representation to all communities at the Kanchipuram Congress session in 1925. He was informed that his resolution would be considered if it had the approval of 30 delegates. Periyar enlisted the support of 50 delegates, yet it was not allowed to be taken up in the open session. This led to pandemonium, and amidst the babel of angry exchanges, Periyar walked out of the Congress with his supporters. Before leaving he said:

> We are talking of sacrificing all for swaraj. If we attain swaraj, it must be a swaraj for all the people. Today, there is a growing fear in the minds of the people that swaraj would be brahman raj in toto. We must create confidence in people. Every community should be cordial to others. We must ensure that every community is safe and prosperous. Today, crores of people are in a pitiable state. They are dumb. The only way is to give legitimate representation to all the communities. (See Sunil 1991: 17)

Periyar unmasked the Congress hypocrisy again in 1928, when the Justice Party-supported S. Muthiah Muddaliar cabinet issued a government order (GO) giving representation to all communities in public employment. The Congress leaders were furious at this 'divisive' move 'taken at the behest of the British'. Periyar responded that non-brahmans would be ready to forgo the benefits of the GO if brahmans came forward to give up all caste distinctions. The 'nationalists' did not reply; Periyar's poser exposed them thoroughly. The GO was finalised and passed on 27 December 1929, paving the way for the reservation policy that exists in various forms till today.

Here, let us digress a little to know the story of how Periyar had to wage a harder battle for reservation after Independence. When the Constitution was adopted on 26 January 1950, it did not have the category we know today as 'other backward classes'; there were only scheduled castes and scheduled tribes. On this ground, the Nehru-led government at the Centre called for the abrogation of the reservation for the backward classes. The reservation was also challenged in the Madras High Court which ruled in August 1950 that it was unconstitutional. The Supreme Court, too, took the 'unconstitutional' line, upholding the high court decision. Spontaneous protests erupted everywhere in Tamil Nadu. The people were furious and tempers ran high. Giving voice to the mass anger, Periyar deplored the Constitution as the hand-maiden of brahmans. He pointed out that though Ambedkar was the chairperson of the drafting committee, he was the lone representative of dalit-bahujans and had to capitulate before the four brahman members of the panel—three of them (A. Krishnasamy Iyer, T.T. Krishnamachari and Gopalasamy Iyengar) hailing from Tamil Nadu itself. The agitation intensified. Wave after wave of people took to the streets; dharnas and strikes became the order of the day. At Periyar's call, 14 August was observed as GO Day which brought the state to a complete standstill (Sunil 1991). Periyar threatened to separate from the Indian Union 'ruled by the brahmanical elite'. The unrelenting protests forced the Union government into the very first amendment of the Constitution to incorporate Article 15(4) which enabled the state to make any special provisions, notwithstanding Articles 15(1) and 29(2), for the advancement of the socially and educationally backward classes as well as the scheduled castes and tribes. It was under this provision that the reservation policy was reintroduced in Tamil Nadu and also adopted at the Centre and in different states in subsequent years in different forms.

But Periyar's movement was not confined to the reservation and political non-brahmanism. The Self-Respect movement aimed at bringing about a cultural revolution on the bedrock of castelessness and rationalism. Periyar visualised the term 'non-brahman' as a grand fraternity comprising all those whom the brahman and brahmanism held to be low, despised, and less than human.

Even Christians, Mohammedans, Anglo-Indians and other non-Hindus are non-brahmins. Amongst the Hindus all those, excepting those of the brahmin caste . . . are non-brahmins. Those referred to as untouchables and who therefore are marginalised as unseeable and unapprochable are also non-brahmins. If all those communities are to escape ensnarement by the magic web of Brahminism, and live in self-respect, they have to transcend minor sectarian differences, shed their self-interest and cease to be the brahmin's spies. . . . They need to trust in universal progress and unite to achieve this objective and meanwhile should eschew prejudice and falsehood. (Periyar, see Geetha and Rajadurai 1998: 290)

The basic thrust of the movement was to free the shudras from their shudrahood and prepare them to come together with the atishudras and others to reconstruct a society in which caste distinctions would have no place. To Periyar, much like Phule and Ambedkar, the abolition of untouchability required the abolition of caste. Not only was the progress of non-brahmans, he stressed, linked to the progress achieved by the 'untouchables', but the sorrows of the latter were a matter of concern and feeling to all non-brahmans. He deemed reservation more necessary for the 'untouchables' since the latter had to endure more ignominies than other non-brahmans. Assuming positions of authority would enable the untouchables to prevent atrocities and civil disabilities inflicted upon them (Geetha and Rajadurai 1998: 288–90).

Stressing egalitarian social relations across caste, community, and gender lines, Periyar advocated the overthrow of caste and patriarchy. He instituted non-brahmanic forms of marriage celebrating the equality of women and their right to choose their life-partners. Alongside existing religious beliefs and practices, he wanted to demolish the whole brahmanic structure of society, the root cause of subordination of women and the non-brahmans. In contrast to the Justice Party, which could not mobilise the people at the grassroots, Periyar's movement attracted thousands of youth, both men and women, in urban and rural localities, who were mostly poor and first-generation learners. The movement's central agenda, the restoration of self-worth, pride, and dignity to long-humiliated men and women, had obviously caught the people's imagination. From time to time, Periyar resorted to strident rhetoric to draw attention to important issues. At various points, the movement organised dramatic assaults on brahmanic symbols. The members burnt texts such as the *Manusmriti*, or showered discriminatory gods and priests with shoes, or marched defiantly into the prohibited temples in mass demonstrations.

In reaction to brahmanic nationalism and the reactionary role the caste elites were playing through the so-called nationalist press such as *The Hindu,* Periyar founded his own journals and newspapers. Through mouthpieces like *Kudi Arasu* written in racy Tamil, he reached new audiences well beyond the elite-based Justice constituencies. Periyar developed the Self-Respecter's style of social activism and distinctive acts of social protests as a counterforce to Gandhi's 'politics of piety' in the cultural and political domains.

Initially impressed by Gandhi's espousal of constructive programmes and social reform, Periyar soon saw through the latter's position on caste, culture, and nationalism, and his respect for the Mahatma turned into a bitter resentment. In 1924, he had participated in the Vaikkom temple agitation, and clashed with Gandhi, questioning the latter's ambiguous approach to socio-religious oppression. Despite his avowed atheism, Periyar supported temple entry for the untouchables with the understanding that the 'temple was a civil sphere as well as a religious one'. But as Gandhi and the Congress embraced the cause to subsume the larger question of caste exploitation (as we will see in Chapter 7)—after the showdown with Ambedkar on the question of separate electorates for depressed classes (in which Periyar stood firmly with Ambedkar)—the Dravidian leader lost all interest in the movement for temple-entry, dismissing it as 'hankering after a worthless dream' which would only strengthen the brahmanical order.

Periyar's final break with Gandhi came earlier, when during a tour of the south in 1927 Gandhi glorified Varnashrama Dharma and praised the brahmans as worthy custodians of 'holy' Hindu life. Rubbing salt into the wounds of anti-caste radicals, Gandhi also maintained that a ban on intermarriage or interdining was essential to the ideal Hindu system. Even earlier, in April 1921, addressing a public meeting in Madras, Gandhi had lauded the tradition established by the brahmans and in an obvious reference to the anti-caste movement, reprimanded the non-brahmans on the attempt to 'rise upon the ashes of brahmanism'. Coinciding with Gandhi's visit to the south, a 'Brahman Sammelan' organised at Tuvar in the district of Thanjavur approved the continued validity of varna-dharma, observing that at present there were only two varnas—the brahman and the shudra—and it behoved both to stick to their varna vocation with sincerity (Geetha and Rajadurai 1998: 299).

Periyar responded angrily: if shudras were to follow Gandhi's advice, he said at a public meeting in Tinnevelly, they would end up only serving the brahmans. He reiterated the same in an editorial, cautioning the public that Gandhi's politics would only help the brahmans, and stressing that his obscurantist ideas on caste and culture need to be exposed and countered:

Though the public believes that Mahatma Gandhi wishes to abolish untouchability and reform religion and society, the Mahatma's utterances and thought reveal him to hold exactly the opposite views on this matter ... if we are to follow the Mahatma's untouchability creed, we will slip into the very abyss of that untouchability we are attempting to abolish. We have been patient, very patient, and tight-lipped but today in the interests of abolition and self-respect we are, sadly enough, forced to confront and oppose the Mahatma. (See Geetha and Rajadurai 1998: 299)

The editorial analysed Gandhi's views on caste and varna, and found them indistinguishable from the standard brahmanic position on the issue. This ruffled the feathers of caste elites who vented their ire on Periyar's 'distortion' of Gandhian views. Periyar, in his inimitable style, pitied such carpers, holding their protests in ridicule: 'He meant this, not that' or 'He did not intend to be understood thus'. Periyar and his associates asserted that they could easily see Gandhi for what he was: 'a crucial player in the construction and deployment of Congress-brahmin hegemony' (ibid.: 300).

At Gandhi's assassination in 1948, Periyar wrote a unique obituary, condemning his killing but also noting that 'Godse [the killer] was not an isolated bigot or madman but rather an expression of the very forms of Hindu nationalism that Gandhi himself had done so much to cultivate, and that had become pervasive in India at large' (see Dirks 2002: 263). Gandhi was struck down by a 'cancer within', a scourge that the Dravidian leader saw as fundamentally about a cloying connection of brahman privilege to Hindu ideology (ibid.).

Periyar's radicalism galvanised not only ordinary people, but also many creative talents. Among them was Bharati Dasan whose poems presented the Self-Respect idealism as an inspiration for socialist modernity that shatters the darkness of regressive tradition:

Is it greatness to refuse the right of women?
Or is it great to be happy with the progress of women?
... Is it right to believe in the Vedas, in God, in all this decay?
Or is it right to establish socialism on earth?
Will we live continuing the divisions which surround us?
Or will we live rising up through self-respect?
(Cited in Omvedt 1995: 56–7)

Dasan's socialism reflected a new politics and a short-lived alliance of anti-caste–class themes in the early 1930s. In 1932, Periyar visited the Soviet Union, and was enthused by what he saw there. He started speaking against the Indian elite and British imperialists as agents of world capitalism. This resulted in a close monitoring of his activities by the British government. M. Singaravelu, a Buddhist scholar and a pioneering labour leader with the reputation of being the 'first communist of south India', encouraged Periyar's growing fondness for socialism. He wrote a series of articles in *Kudi Arasu*, expounding socialism and a materialistic interpretation of history (Omvedt 1995: 57). Periyar joined hands with Singaravelu, and the Self-Respect Samadharma Party was launched in December 1932.

For the Self-Respecters, the term *samadharma* was not merely the Tamil equivalent of socialism, it assumed equality between men and men and between men and women as a given. Moreover, it required that this equality be realised through an affirmation of each individual's self-worth and self-respect. As such, the principle of samadharma stood not only for a new age of economic justice but also the realisation of a millenarian dream whereby caste society in its entirety and in all its complex ways of being would be transformed (Geetha and Rajadurai 1998: 420–1).

M. Singaravelu and Lakshmi Narasu, both Buddhist scholars of distinction, used and interpreted *samadharma* in a different light, though with the same objective. They sought out its Buddhist origins as an expression and as an ideal, stressing the revival of the socialistic spirit of Buddhism that had long been the moral–spiritual counter to discriminatory Hinduism (ibid.: 421–2). Adi-Dravida thinker-activists simply identified a caste-free society as a samadharmic society. The ideal of samadharma was not yet clearly enunciated, it was left theoretically open-ended though Self-Respecters at different times and in different contexts identified its ideal with a set of clearly defined material attributes necessary for building a socialist society (ibid.). But it certainly marked an upsurge in the radicalisation of the non-brahman struggle. Socialism now began to be advocated from its platforms, and several anti-capitalist and anti-landlord conferences were held by the Self-Respecters.

However, this coming together of the anti-caste struggle and the leftist movement did not last long. The conservatives in the movement remained unenthusiastic about socialism, but more than that, the communists opposed the anti-caste movement as a casteist dilution of the class war. Singaravelu's type of indigenous socialism was found to be dangerous by the communist bosses in Bombay.

The real split came on a straightforward political issue. On the eve of the 1934 elections, the Self-Respect movement was faced with the choice of supporting either the Justice Party or the Congress, as there was no socialist party at the time. While Periyar saw the Self-Respecters' future in a revival and radicalisation of the Justice Party, the left could see it only in the Congress, which by the mid 1930s they identified as the 'anti-imperialist united front'. In 1936, the upper-caste Marxist leaders ordered Singaravelu and his comrades to dissociate from Periyar's movement and instead join the Congress Socialist Party, part of the Congress within which the communists were working (Omvedt 1995: 58).

The result of the split proved disastrous for both Periyar and the left. Hereafter Periyar hardened his attitude towards the 'brahmanic' left and Congress nationalism, and increasingly identified with a linguistic–regional nationalism. In 1936, Periyar assumed the leadership of the fading Justice Party and strove to make it not only a movement of social change but also a vehicle of Dravidian language, culture and nationalism in opposition to what he termed the Aryan-brahmanic-and-north-dominated nationalism. He led a militant agitation against the imposition of Hindi in government schools by the Congress in 1937, citing it as yet another instance of the oppressive character of 'Aryan nationalism'. Seeing it as a part of the bigger Hindi-Hindu-Hindustan conspiracy of the brahmans, he now demanded the creation of a separate state for the Tamil, Telugu, Kannada, and Malayalam speaking people of the south.

In the 1940s, Periyar's politics came to be dominated by the demand for an autonomous casteless federation of Dravida Nadu. In 1944, he established the Dravida Kazhagam, which had as its objective the establishment of a Dravidian state. It must be noted, however, that it was his zeal to build a truly casteless community that propelled him to raise such a demand. The new community was to be 'distinguished from the brahmanic caste order by its civilisational and cultural differences' (Geetha and Rajadurai 1998: 327). Dravidian ethos signified the acceptance within its fold of all those who consented to the rejection of caste culture. Thus, when Ambedkar met Periyar in 1944 to discuss joint initiatives, the former claimed that the idea of Dravidasthan was in reality applicable to all of India, since brahmanism was a problem which afflicted the entire subcontinent (ibid.).

The non-brahman movement of Tamil Nadu spread to neighbouring regions. In the princely state of Mysore, brahman dominance in the fields of education, public service, and politics began to be contested by the deprived communities. The major ethnic groups of the region, the Lingayats and Vokkaligas, along with the Muslims took the lead in challenging the brahman monopoly of the public sphere. The Vokkaliga Association was formed in 1906, and the Virashaiva Mahasabha (representing the interests of Lingayats) in 1909. Other organisations founded during this period included the Adi-Dravida Abhi-Vruddhi Sangha, the Kuruba Association, and the Central Muslim Association. By 1917 various ethnic groups formed an alliance called the Praja Mitra Mandali. In 1918 they submitted a memorandum to the government asking for adequate representation of non-brahmans in public service, educational institutions, and legislature. The Miller Commission appointed to examine the demands issued a report—recommending representation to the backward castes—which was accepted by the government in 1919. This enabled the non-brahmans, particularly the Vokkaligas and Lingyayats, to enter the domains of education, governance and politics.

Non-brahmans raised the banner of revolt in Andhra too. Unlike Mysore, where the anti-brahman ideology did not take the form of Dravidianism, Andhra, especially in the coastal areas, was influenced by the militant Dravidianism of Tamil Nadu. While the dalits of Tamil Nadu and Karnataka constructed their cultural identity as Adi-Dravidians and Adi-Karnatakas respectively, Telugu-speaking Malas and Madigas proclaimed themselves as Adi-Andhra, claiming, like the former, that they were the original inhabitants of the soil and rulers of the region (Omvedt 1994: 117). They argued that Hinduism was not the ancestral religion of the aborigines who abhorred discriminatory scriptures like the Vedas and *Manusmriti*. The Vedic religion, its beliefs and prejudices, the dalits contended, had been thrust upon their ancestors by the invading outsiders.

A conference of dalits in Vijayawada in 1917, sponsored by the reformist Hindus, tentatively labelled as the First Provincial Panchama Maharaja Sabha, changed its name to the Adi-Andhra Maharaja Sabha at the insistence of the radicals. The dalit delegates had trouble getting accommodation in the town, and the major temples there, fearing an attempted entry, were closed down for three days (Omvedt 1994: 118). Subsequently, the Adi-Andhra conferences were held every year in different parts of the region. The movement had a mass base, and as the 1931 census indicated nearly a third of the Malas and Madigas of the Madras Presidency claimed identity as Adi-Andhra (ibid.).

Bhagyareddy Varma (1888–1939), a Hyderabadi dalit originally named Madari Bhagaiah, played a major role in organising the dalits and building a protest movement. Having organised Adi-Hindu conferences since 1912, Varma used the term Adi-Hindus for the natives who had been crushed and pushed down to the south by the Aryan invaders. A strong votary of dalit autonomy, he was opposed to the temple-entry campaigns: at one instance, when the delegates of Adi-Andhra conference (1938) in East Godavari were debating this issue, Varma refused to preside until all agreed not to support a bill for temple-entry then being introduced in the Madras provincial council by the dalit reformer M.C. Rajah. Varma also had a profound interest in Buddhism. From his early life he admired Buddha for his struggle against caste and brahmanic injustice. He organised a function on the occasion of the Buddha's birth anniversary in 1913, and again in 1937, two years before his death. During his last days when he became somewhat inactive, he extended his support to a new generation of radical Ambedkarites (Omvedt 1994: 124).

A common theme running through the non-brahman movements, especially the dalit liberation struggles, was linkages between the oppressive present and the past history of the Aryan conquest and brahman exploitation through a pseudo-religion. Nowhere was this subversive construction as visible as in Maharashtra, the land of Phule and Ambedkar. We have studied Phule's anti-caste movement in the previous chapter, and shall delve into Ambedkar's liberation struggle in the next one. Suffice it to say here that Phule's social radicalism was carried forward by many pre-Ambedkar dalit leaders of the region. One such leader, Kisan Faguji Bansode (1870–1946), gave expression to the growing dalit militancy in a 1909 article:

The Aryans—your ancestors—conquered us and gave us unbearable harassment. At that time we were your conquest, you treated us even worse than slaves and subjected us to any torture you wanted. But now we are no longer your subjects, we have no service relationship with you, we are not your slaves or serfs.... If you don't give us the rights of humanity and independence, then we will have to take our own rights on the basis of our own strength and courage, and that we will do. (See Omvedt 1994: 110)

The Battle in the North: Achhutanand and Mangoo Ram

In Uttar Pradesh, a marginalised existence and low occupational experience, especially in urban centres, created among dalits a context for revival of the radical tradition of Kabir and Ravidas, and the assertion of autochthonous equality (Gooptu 1993). The dalits began their liberation struggle at the turn of the new century under the leadership of Swami Achhutanand (1879–1933) and Ram Charan (1888–1939). Their own humiliating experiences estranged them from the brahmanical society, and became a driving force behind the construction of an emancipatory identity. Like other dalit-subaltern leaders in the subcontinent, they demanded social justice and repudiated the brahmanic trajectories on caste, culture and society.

Achhutanand, an ascetic from Mainpuri district, was the main ideologue of the dalit liberation movement in Uttar Pradesh. He had flirted for a while with the Arya Samaj, but soon he and his associates left it after they realised that it aimed to 'make all Hindus slaves of the Vedas and the brahmans' (Gooptu 1993). To them, its emphasis on the Vedas implied the divine sanction of caste hierarchy and a further fortification of caste distinctions. Alarmed by the 'army of high-caste Hindus' being raised by the Arya Samaj, the dalits thought that its only intention was to rally the Hindu community against the Muslims, and that its attempt to uplift the lower castes was merely a part of this strategy. They argued that the Samaj did not aim to abolish untouchability and that *shuddhi* was a cunning ploy to perpetuate the hold of the higher castes over the untouchables. 'Its professions of purification', declared Acchutanand, 'are a clever fraud and a clever verbal gimmick of the varna system.' He termed the programme of intercaste marriage led by the Samaj as an eye-wash, challenging its leaders to arrange such marriages between twice born and low born to vindicate their position (ibid.).

The dalit thinkers opposed birth-based division of labour and labourers, arguing that this prevented occupational diversification resulting in the continued poverty, illiteracy, and fragmentation of the suppressed groups. The anti-caste sentiment being spread by leaders like Achhutanand and Ram Charan evolved into a movement spread across the state, especially in urban centres such as Kanpur, Lucknow, Allahabad, and Banaras (ibid.). The movement was animated by the cultural radicalism of Kabir and Ravidas, and an assertion of a supposed pre-Vedic egalitarian religion of the original inhabitants, whom they called Adi Hindus, the ancestors of the dalit communities. Achhutanand argued that the Aryans conquered the Adi Hindus—Dasas and Dravidians—not by valour but by 'deceit' and 'manipulation', reducing the aborigines to poverty and slavery. 'Those who ardently believed in equality were ranked, and ranked lowest. The Hindus and untouchables have since always remained poles apart' (see Khare 1984: 85).

Importantly, the dalit thinkers emphasised the need to build their own knowledge-system to understand the past and present— 'from Manu down to Gandhi'—in order to regain their freedom. Instead of toeing the reformist approach, they advocated a complete overhaul of the cultural system that bred social injustice and discrimination. Quoting their words, Khare (1984: 85) has summed up their formulations thus:

The cobweb of Hindu scriptures, deities, incarnations, temples and Brahman priests is so intricate and pervasive that it has imprisoned the Hindu within his family and jatis, and consigned the Untouchable to the bottom. Since there have been no truths in this cobweb—from Manu down to Gandhi, the Untouchable has to take the lead on his own.

And this means that he has to examine the Hindu social tactics very closely to get his freedom. The Hindus have suppressed and destroyed all critical literature produced by the Untouchable intellectuals from ancient times until recently. Hence, the Untouchable must start rebuilding his knowledge, moving carefully from the recent to the remote past. At present, one knows little about anything other than the Hindu's side of the story. . . . Marriage, commensality, occupation, Gita-Ramayana, and extended family are the five most important sacred domains where the Untouchables encounter maximum discrimination and resistance. The radical solution must therefore reject totally and exactly those reasons the Hindus accept and value.

Asserting the separate identity of dalits which became the fulcrum of their protest movement, Achhutanand formed the Adi Hindu Sabha in the 1920s. The Sabha spread its activities in the region through a network of articulate volunteers culled from the literate segments of town-based dalits (Gooptu 1993). Its leaders were regularly invited to address meetings of local caste panchayats and socio-religious congregations. The Ravidasis and sweepers of Kanpur hailed Achhutanand as their leader and invited him to address their meetings. In Allahabad and Lucknow, the Ravidasis proclaimed their support for the movement and held public meetings to celebrate their 'separation from upper-caste Hindus' (ibid.). The Kumbh Mela of 1928–9 at Allahabad witnessed the strident proclamation of Adi Hinduism. At the mela, a *mahotsav* of all Adi-Hindu devotional sects was held, in which Kabirpanthi, Ravidasi, and Shivnarayani groups participated.

A key aspect of the Adi-Hindu ideology of emancipation was mass education. Its leaders stressed the role of education in social and cultural liberation and in the improvement of economic conditions (Gooptu 1993). They argued that illiteracy was the root cause of dalits' domination by the upper castes and the former's exclusion from economic opportunities and better jobs. Education was also necessary for thinking-for-oneself and developing an autonomous worldview, independent of brahmanical notions about life, religion, and culture. Critical thinking and introspection were roads to *atmagyan* (self-realisation) and *sadgyan* (true knowledge) that 'would enable one to discern the difference between truth and falsity, which in turn would reveal the irrelevance and falsity of one's low role in society'. Interacting with fellow dalits, Achhutanand observed:

> Real knowledge is the knowledge gained through introspection and which you have understood and realised on your own. For this reason, you will have to discern between good and evil, virtue and vice, auspicious and inauspicious, through your own introspection. . . . Self-realisation is the only touchstone against which you can test truth and falsity, high and low. (See Gooptu 1993: 291)

Underpinning this thinking was an anti-caste worldview that *varna* and *jati* divisions were neither divinely ordained, nor natural, nor grounded in truth. There was no justifiable basis, they asserted, for the low and menial jobs that the dalits were expected to perform as the servants of the upper castes. They argued that the shudras were forced to do dirty and menial jobs, and then, on the logic of ritual impurity, were accorded a servile status. Underlining this in a speech in 1927, Ram Charan, the Adi-Hindu leader of Lucknow, said:

> The untouchables were made to do the most insulting and demeaning jobs, such as cleaning excreta and dirty clothes. They were repeatedly told that you are shudras and your work is to serve (gulami). Those who were thus made to serve (gulam or das) were then called untouchables. (See Gooptu 1993: 291)

The Adi-Hindu ideologues created a counter-myth, an egalitarian golden past of their own, anchored in the Indus Valley civilisation, to debunk the myth of the Vedic golden age. There had been Adi-Hindu kingdom, capital cities, forts, and a thriving civilisation, they claimed, which were destroyed by the invading Aryans through treachery and brute force. The creation of caste and repressive social laws embodied in the Vedas and codified in the *Dharmashastras*, they contended, were intended to relegate the original inhabitants to untouchable status, and strip them of their civil and economic rights. The caste system was an expression of the Aryan political manipulation. In the words of Ram Charan, 'The rule of making shudra was not a religious rule. It was naked politics' (ibid.: 292). By arguing that caste was a lethal political weapon to enslave the shudras, the dalit leaders exhorted their people not to tolerate the oppressive system which condemned them to a life of deprivation and illiteracy. They also attempted to build a positive self-image by presenting themselves as hard-working and honest people, inheritors of a glorious egalitarian tradition (ibid.: 293–4). They said they had been treated as slaves for centuries after their capitulation to the barbaric Aryans, but now they would reclaim their dignity and their rights to education and power.

In Punjab, too, the movement against untouchability and injustice took the form of an autochthonous radicalism. Here, dalit leader Mangoo Ram, also a disillusioned Arya Samaji, founded Adi Dharma in 1925, and declared untouchables a separate *qaum*, an independent religious community similar to those of the Hindu, Muslim, and Sikh communities. They claimed that their *qaum* had existed long before the Aryan invasion:

> We are the original people of this country and our religion is Adi-Dharma. The Hindu qaum came from outside and enslaved us. When the original sound from the conch was sounded all the brothers came together—Chamar, Chuhra, Sainsi, Bhanjre, Bhil all the untouchables—to make their problems known. Brothers, there are seventy millions of us listed as Hindus, separate us and make us free. (See Juergensmeyer 1982: 46)

The first item on the agenda of Mangoo Ram was to get the dalits' new identity as the Adi Dharma community officially accepted. At his instance, more than four lakh dalits identified themselves as Adi-Dharmis in the 1931 census. With an emancipatory vision and the might of numbers, the Adi-Dharmis entered the political fray. Like dalit organisations elsewhere, the Adi-Dharmis opposed the brahmanical Congress and Gandhi, and 'wanted no part of independence if independence meant government by upper-caste Hindus'. The movement demanded dignity and a representative share in economic and political spheres for the hitherto excluded communities as a necessary pre-condition for broader social integration. Invoking democratic principles, the Adi-Dharmis appealed to the upper castes to forgo their oppression and accept the egalitarian change with grace. Juergensmeyer, who has studied this movement in depth, observes: 'Movements like Adi-Dharma have been separatist only to the extent that they have insisted on separating their followers from old ideas of social integration. They have tried to provide new visions of society in which the upper castes are also invited to play a role, albeit a more humble one than at present' (ibid.: 275). The Adi Dharma campaign petered out in the years to come and was gradually absorbed into Ambedkar's movement in the late 1930s and 1940s.

Movements from Below Signal the End of Colonialism

The brahmanic nationalists targeted only colonial exploitation—after colluding and collaborating with, and fattening themselves on, colonial rule for a century and a half. Nationalism provided them a powerful rhetoric to subsume all issues related to caste-feudal and capitalist exploitation within the Indian society. Their aim was not solely to wrest power from the British, but also to keep the traditional caste–class structure intact. The dalit-bahujan leadership was left with no option but to challenge the 'official' nationalism and chart a different course for a new India where the suppressed majority would play a leading role in nation-building. Their movements became a thorn in the sides of the upper-class nationalists. The Congress under Gandhi and Nehru later sought to appropriate in some measure both elite-based and mass-oriented nationalisms, but their 'democracy' and 'humanity' had no problem with caste. They visualised either the self-sufficient village communities, or science, technology, or state in the ways that never challenged caste inequality and exploitation. On the other hand, the dalit-bahujan struggles for an inclusive society reflected the birth-pangs of the nation. Based on the values of equality, liberty, and fraternity, the movements from below were, in Omvedt's words, 'a crucial expression of the democratic revolution in India'.

The main figures of this larger anti-caste movement . . . attacked the system of exploitation at all levels, culturally, economically and politically. They challenged the 'Hindu-nationalism' which was emerging as a consequence of the elite organising from the nineteenth century onward to define Indian society, and the majority of Indian people, as essentially 'Hindu': not only did they criticise distortions and 'excrescences', they attacked Hinduism itself by arguing that it was in essence Brahmanical, caste-bound and irrational. They asserted that Hinduism had not been the religion and culture of the majority but rather was an imposed religion; and that escaping exploitation today required the low castes to reject this imposition, to define themselves as 'non-Hindu' and take a new religious identity. Phule tried to formulate a new, theistic religion; Periyar promoted atheism; Ambedkar turned to Buddhism; others in the Tamil Nadu nonbrahman movement tried to claim Saivism as an independent religion, Narayanswami Guru formulated 'one religion, one caste, one God' while his more radical follower Ayyappan proclaimed 'no religion, no caste, and no God for mankind'. Whatever the specificities, the rejection of Hinduism remained a feature differentiating the anti-caste radicals from the reformers. (Omvedt 1994: 12)

The anti-caste movements had a radical agenda of economic and political emancipation of the masses:

They were also economic radicals, though from different points of view, identifying themselves not simply with low castes but with peasants and workers as such. Phule strongly attacked the exploitation of peasants by the bureaucracy; Ambedkar and Periyar both supported and helped organise movements of peasants against landlords and workers against capitalists; and Ambedkar unambiguously identified himself as a socialist. Politically they opposed the Indian National Congress as controlled by upper castes and capitalists ... and sought for an alternative political front that would represent a kind of left–Dalit unity with a core base of workers and peasants. They (particularly Ambedkar) also insisted that this had to lead to the empowerment of Dalits and other exploited sections. In the language of the Dalit Panther's manifesto, 'We don't want a little place in Brahman alley; we want the rule of the whole country.' (ibid.: 12–13)

Thus, contrary to the brahmanic position that the anti-caste movements were instigated and supported by the colonial rulers to divide and weaken the national unity, the beginning of equality-driven mass resistance signalled a democratic revolution and marked the beginning of the end of colonialism, both external and internal. In a ground-breaking study Aloysius (1997: 90-1) contends:

The struggles of the hitherto excluded communities bear the special significance of signalling democratic revolution, however uneven and irregular, against the vested interests of the dominant, both native as well as foreign. The pact between the native and foreign dominant groups on which colonialism itself was founded, was indeed based on the premise that the status quo of power, resource and leadership distribution within the colonised country was to be maintained and that rule itself was to be indirect, through the medium of local dominance. The British imperialist policy of non-interference was not based on any goodwill or appreciation of Indian culture, but on compulsion, and they had no choice in the matter. In this situation, the lower class/caste struggles did have the unfortunate effect of upsetting the precariously balanced applecart of colonial power struggle and ideology. The British were certainly aware of this: the colonial educational policy, for example, was dictated by the realisation that if education descended from the higher to the inferior classes, it 'would lead to a general convulsion of which foreigners would be the first victim'.

The colonial rulers and Indian elite were both aware of the implications of mass emergence. Both feared its cascading—democratic—effect. Both tried to prevent it in their pursuit of monopoly power. As their interests complemented each other, they often united to suppress peasant and tribal struggles during colonial rule. On socio-religious questions, the British adhered to the no-interference policy, thus upholding the oppressive brahmanical tradition. However, towards the end of the Raj, when the British were compelled to concede some demands for representation in employment, education, and legislative bodies from the lowered castes/classes, the upper castes and classes turned nationalist, clamouring for total transfer of power. They accused the British of pursuing a nefarious policy of divide-and-rule and tarred the movements from below with the same brush, as anti-national or pro-colonial.

This was the hypocrisy of the nationalist leadership, and Gandhi, Nehru, and brahmanic socialists were an integral part of this nationalist farce. The attempts of the lowered castes and classes to get their share of the educational-social-political spheres 'cannot but have the same application as those of the attempts of the upper castes, for instance, the aspiration to become civil servants under the Raj'. Pointing this out, a non-brahman leader of the south wryly remarked: 'If we ask for a ministry, it is job-hunting, but if a Congressman asks for it, it is patriotism' (see Baker 1976: 360).

As a matter of fact, the dalit-bahujan struggles were not only against the caste-feudal forces but also against the colonial regime. The appearance of compromise with the colonial rulers—to get some social and economic concessions—was a tactical move necessitated by the highly antagonistic attitude of Indian elites. But why did these widespread though scattered struggles fail to transform themselves into a pan-Indian form and upstage the elitist national movement? Aloysius (1997: 92) has given a credible explanation:

The reasons for this are crucial—economic, cultural and ideological, the inherent difficulties of a generally traditional, subaltern and colonially dispossessed social position, particularly in the absence of widespread economic change, was the first. Secondly, these struggles were well-rooted in the vernacular, regional cultures and were a continuity of the alternate subcontinental tradition not only of power as resistance but also power as diversity which the colonial impact did much to damage. In this sense, the diversified, vernacularised and hence the rootedness of these movements were indeed an asset that could have led to a federal and de-centralised modern India. Thirdly, the antagonistic pan-Indianism of the nationalists towards this process of internal democratisation articulated from a traditional as well as colonially empowered social position is the ideological reason why mass emergence as the nation could not but be stopped from formally and verbally articulating the anti-colonial nationalist ideology.

Notes

1. Rao's source is a Malayalam article (1968) by K.R. Narayanan. This rebellion against religion-based discrimination, as Aloysius (1997) points out, took place 125 years before the Gandhi-led Congress was reluctantly drawn into the temple-entry agitation. The same temple at Vaikkom became the site of tussle in 1925 in which Narayana Guru's followers and Periyar (who had come all the way from Tamil Nadu) defiantly entered the temple, while Gandhi kept appealing for a compromise formula. The 'nationalist' historians, however, tend to present the agitation as a Congress-Gandhi affair.
2. In pre-modern Kerala society, the rules of purity–pollution (which included not only untouchability but also the distance pollution) were maintained with utmost severity. The Nambudiri brahmans, at the top of caste hierarchy, were considered purity personified, while other castes and their worth were measured in terms of their distance from the Nambudiris.

'The Ezhavas had to keep between 20 to 36 feet away from the Nambudiris, the Cherumas and the Pulayas 64 feet; and the Nayadis 72 feet. There were also some tribes whose mere sight polluted the Nambudiris; but only a touch of a Nayar polluted them. The Nayars were the bridge between the Nambudiris and the category of castes that polluted from a distance' (Rao 1979: 24).

3. The antiquity of Dravidian culture and literature was discovered in the nineteenth century by some Indian researchers and British Indologists. P. Sundaram Pillai (1855–97) and Robert Caldwell were among the earliest scholars who revealed that the Dravidian language had originated independent of Aryan-Sanskrit influence, and that the former was more ancient than Sanskrit. Pillai was also among the first who extolled the virtues of the 'native' Ravana and portrayed Rama as a leader of the invading Aryans.

4. It is only recently that Iyothee Thass' pioneering work has caught the attention of some scholars. Geetha and Rajadurai's outstanding work on the Dravidian movement, *Towards a Non-Brahmin Millennium: From Iyothee Thass to Periyar* (1998) explores the writings of Iyothee Thass and the rise of dalit consciousness in colonial Tamil Nadu. G. Aloysius' *Religion as Emancipatory Identity: A Buddhist Movement Among the Tamils Under Colonialism* (1998) is a penetrating study of the socio-religious movement in which Iyothee Thass played a leading role. See also Aloysius' *Iyothee Thassar Sinthanaigaal* (The Thoughts of Iyothee Thassar), two-volume collection of Iyothee's original writings in Tamil, published by Folklore Resources and Research Centre, Polayamco-Hai, Tamil Nadu.

CHAPTER 7

Nationalist Power Politics, Excluded Masses, and the Gandhi–Ambedkar Debate

> Patriotism in its simplest, clearest, and most indubitable signification is nothing but a means of obtaining for the rulers their ambitions and covetous desires, and for the ruled the abdication of human dignity, reason, and conscience, and a slavish enthralment to those in power.
>
> Leo Tolstoy [1894] 1987: 103

Historians subscribing to the nationalist discourse and Gandhian politics tend to portray Ambedkar as an unpatriotic reactionary for his 'politicisation of caste' and his insistence that the untouchables were a separate social category, a subordinated one, and not part of brahmanic Hinduism. Ambedkar was indeed vocal on this point, as he wanted dignity and justice for the caste-oppressed and not the condescension and charity that was being offered by the Gandhian nationalism. However, as we have seen in the previous chapters, even before Ambedkar's emergence on the scene there had been considerable dalit-bahujan alienation and antagonism against the elitist nationalism. From the days of Phule, it was seen as an upper-caste mobilisation for monopoly power in the name of patriotic unity and freedom. The censuses of 1901 and 1911 and the Congress leadership's opportunistic move to incorporate the untouchables in the Hindu fold to bolster their majoritarian claims are significant in this context.

Census Commissioner H.H. Risley's attempt in 1901 to classify castes in each region according to notions of 'social grade and precedence' had generated strident status claims and counter-claims.

The imperative to prove one's higher pedigree in the caste hierarchy for census operations was the result of collusive acceptance and reinforcement (by the British and Indian elites) of the brahmanical social order. Livening up of the 'caste-spirit' was heightened by the brahmanic orientation of nationalism, which had excluded, except for the rhetoric, a vast majority of dalit-bahujans from the national domain. Parallel to the nationalist power politics, the dalit-bahujans were trying to organise themselves locally and regionally across the subcontinent into a multiplicity of movements against the oppressive forces. The limited yet significant spread of education and political awareness had awakened a section of the dalit-bahujans. Caste-based as well as anti-caste agitations had been building up in many parts of India well before the colonial design to conduct censuses on caste identities. The nationalist leadership, however, tended to deride such movements as 'divisive' and, hence, not in the 'national' interest. To safeguard their entrenched interests, the caste elites retained their brahmanic dogmas under the garb of nationalism, repudiating the people's grievances and democratic aspirations as unpatriotic and anti-national.

With democratic representation being conceded in principle under the Morley–Minto reforms of 1909, the 1911 Census Commissioner, E.A. Gait, sought to estimate the population of different religions amidst the controversy over inclusion of the untouchables within the Hindu fold. He formulated a questionnaire—known as the Gait circular—which spelt out the criteria for ascertaining the validity of a subject's statement of religious affinity. Gait defined the meaning of the term Hindu by suggesting omission from that category of those excluded from temples and priestly services or considered to be untouchable.[1] This invited strong protest from the Hindu elite as it underlined the fact that the Hindu population included millions who were denied entry into places of worship. Several dalit-subaltern communities, whom the upper-caste census enumerators of 1901 and 1891 did not acknowledge as Hindu, were now being vehemently claimed as 'our Hindu brothers'. But there were many who did not consider themselves Hindu, and many 'objected to being so classed' (Gupta 1985: 36–70; Mendelsohn and

Vicziany 2000: 26–9). Given the complexities of the exercise, it was promptly abandoned. Gait decided that the question of social precedence would not be reopened and ordered a return to an alphabetic classification. Yet this had created for a while a turbulence in the ranks of Hindu nationalists.

The importance attached to numbers in the political and administrative calculations of the British jolted the upper-caste (barely 15 per cent of the Hindu population) leaders out of their stupor. Adding to their consternation was the Muslim League, formed in 1906 to represent the Muslim interests, which sought to argue that the Hindu population was being artificially inflated by the inclusion of the untouchables. Compelled by the arithmetic of parliamentary representation, the custodians of Hinduism now woke up to the misery of their 'untouchable brethren'. Lajpat Rai, a prominent Hindu and Congress leader, noted with anxiety: 'They [the untouchables] are with us . . . but they are not of us, their fidelity is being put to a severe strain and unless we recognise the justice and humanity of their cause and recognise it in time, no blame could attach to them if they were to separate themselves from us and join the ranks of those who are neither with us nor of us' (see Gupta 1985: 39). Rai's apprehensions grew with time. In 1915, he wrote: 'Indications are not wanting that many of them (the depressed classes) have already become conscious of the wretched position they hold in Hindu society. . . . It will be no wonder if a large number of them leave Hindu society with thoughts of retaliation and revenge.'

The Hindu nationalist anxieties were not misplaced: some dalit groups were showing signs of rebellious restlessness. Besides contemplating conversion to more egalitarian religions like Christianity, Islam, or Buddhism, they were getting politically organised in many parts of the country. Gopal Baba Walangkar and Shivram Janba Kamble represented the early stirrings among the Mahars of Maharashtra, the caste from which Ambedkar came. In 1904, a memorandum was sent to the Governor of Bombay on behalf of 15,000 Mahars, requesting the removal of restrictions in public schools, permission to join the police and the army, and admission to lower grades of public services. A similar and better-written petition was sent in 1910 by the Conference of Deccan Mahars to the then Secretary of State for India. Such democratic assertions were being made by dalit leaders across the country. In this process, in the early 1917, the Depressed Classes of Bombay had expressly asked the Congress to take on its agenda the issue of caste oppression and untouchability in exchange for their support. The dalit demand was made in the same vein as the Muslim one a year earlier that had resulted in the famous Lucknow Pact of 1916 between the Congress and Muslim League. The writing on the wall was clear: if the Congress leadership wanted to establish its national credentials it could no longer afford to ignore the aspirations of the caste-oppressed.

It was this compulsion—the census exercise, the pressure of representative politics, the upper-caste Hindu fear of losing the untouchables, and a slow yet steady political awakening among the latter—that forced the Congress in 1917 to adopt a resolution underlining its commitment to remove various caste disabilities. This forced resolution, however, did not bring about any actual change in the Congress attitude towards the caste question. Annie Besant, the British racist activist who had made the 'Aryan India' her home and was openly praising the laws of Manu and the system of caste, and asking the brahmans to revive their ancient nationalism (Besant 1913; 1917), was made the president of the Congress in the same year (1917). Tilak, the top Congress leader of the time, made caste and sex-based discrimination the foundation of his nationalism, as a brilliant work (Parimala Rao 2010) has unearthed. He was vehemently opposed to the education and empowerment of women and dalit-bahujans. 'Rakmabais, Saraswatibais [that is, the educated women]', he demanded, 'should be punished for the same reason as there is punishment for thieves, adulteresses and murderers' (Tilak, see Rao, ibid.: 96). In the same vein, opposing the entry of dalit-bahujans in the parliamentary politics, he jeered, 'Will the kunbis [peasants] plough the field and shimpis [the tailors] sew clothes in the legislative assembly?' Like Tilak, many Congress leaders of the time continued to conflate their brahmanism with nationalism, and kept chanting the mantra that 'reform is revival and revival is reform'. The show of solidarity with the caste-oppressed was a stage-managed affair, a matter of sheer political expediency, as a historian rightly points out:

The interest that the Congress showed after 32 years of neglect in social reform was intrinsically political in the worse sense of the term and its espousal of the cause of the depressed classes an expedient which was not seriously implemented. It is worth noting that from this half-hearted manoeuvre sprang the painful process by which the depressed classes passed into a mood of distrust. (S. Natarajan 1959: 145)

It was under such circumstances that Gandhi entered national politics and addressed the question of untouchability, cleverly separating it from the original varna order in which he showed his absolute faith. While making some politically correct noises on untouchability, Gandhi was consistently emphatic that an individual's caste was ascribed at the moment of birth, and not to live by one's caste was 'to disregard the law of heredity' because 'varnashrama is inherent in human nature and Hinduism (had) simply reduced it to a science.' It is notable that Gandhi was initially opposed even to the temple-entry demand from the depressed classes,[2] and even after his 'change of heart' on this issue, his position remained ambiguous.

In sync with the upper-caste politics, Gandhi's 'politics of piety' was driven by the political expediency to include the untouchables in the Hindu fold to form a Hindu majority. It becomes obvious when one sees Gandhi's over-anxiety to present the untouchability problem as an exclusively Hindu affair, and not a national one. Intervening during the Vaikkom temple agitation of the 1920s, where the social activists including some local Syrian Christians were fighting for the untouchables' right to temple-entry, Gandhi took pains to stress that the movement was a Hindu affair and that 'Hindus (alone should) do the work' (Menon 1994: 81). Gandhi insisted, reiterating the Congress resolution at Nagpur, that only Hindus should be involved in this intra-Hindu affair, but tried to present the issue as part of the national, not Hindu, reconstruction, thus making it clear that despite his occasional evocation of Hindu-Muslim unity as basis of Indian nationalism, he equated the latter with Hindu nationalism.

The Myth of the Mahatma

A great panegyric, academic as well as popular, has been created around Gandhi and his nationalist politics. So much so that much of what passes off as modern Indian historiography is but a hagiography of Gandhi and Gandhism. This has been done with missionary zeal because Gandhi was the one who, more than anyone else, defended—and validated—brahmanism when its legitimacy was seriously challenged and its existence seemed precarious. Behind the facade of unique patriotism and selfless service, Gandhi's politics, as we will see, was tethered to Varnashrama Dharma and the whole socio-cultural structure of caste and brahmanism. At the very beginning of his autobiography ([1927] 1996), while identifying himself as a bania, Gandhi hastens to add that for three generations his forefathers had not practised the caste occupation—groceries—but had served as prime ministers (traditionally, such jobs had been the preserve of the brahmans) in several princely states in Kathiawad region of Gujarat. The region was a bastion of orthodoxy dominated by the wealthy merchant caste and its puritanical conservatism. Gandhi was an outstanding product of this milieu: he was a bania more brahmanised than brahmans. It is notable that Gandhi recollects (in his autobiography) his mother telling him when he was a child that the shortest cut to purification after touching an untouchable was to cancel the touch by an even dirtier one—by touching any Muslim passing by. The dutiful son grew up to become a legendary reformer, but he always kept a safe distance from dalits and Muslims, despite all the stage-managed shows to the contrary. While winning friends and influencing people through his seductive rhetoric of truth, non-violence, God, sin and punishment, he never gave up his belief in the brahmanic fundamentalism which is evident from his constant evocation of Varnashrama, Ram-rajya and Trusteeship—the three unmistakable status quoist concepts embedded in the traditional structure of hierarchy—that represent his social, political and economic philosophies.

Gandhi was pious and self-sacrificing but a victim of naïve self-delusion who personified austerity but on whom wealthy caste fellows showered comforts, who personified self-effacement but was turned into a veritable god by the wily pandits. Minus his 'half-naked' holiness and demonstrative religiosity (something he and his upper-caste constituency knew well), he would be much easier to dismiss. As a sympathetic critic points out, 'Gandhi's approach to politics was based on emotion and religious faith, and he seldom reasoned out his course of action' (Gill 2001: 182). The best defence one can present for Gandhi, as his sophisticated apologists do, is that in his philosophy

> equality has been seen not in terms of political or social relations, but as related to the perfecting of the self. . . . On this view, the primary challenge of equality is not about our relationship with others, it is primarily about crafting the right relationship with one's own self. The root of inequality, in some form or the other, always lies in an exaltation of materialism, which compels us to seek domination over others. (Mehta 2012)

Even this apologist accepts that 'as a means of achieving equality, it proved counter-productive, for it immediately tied the politics of equality to an idiom [and politics] of renunciation . . .' (ibid.). Arguments like this are basically obfuscatory and indulgent since Gandhi, behind the veil of self-denial and moralising mysticism, had actively supported caste, brahmanism, and trusteeship, taking the side of the exploiting classes, and sidestepping in most sinister ways the question of workers, peasants and the dalit-bahujans. Gandhi created many waves for freedom and social reform, but he did not lead a single movement for peasants and workers. He shed copious tears to improve their lot, but did not consider them mature enough to take any autonomous initiative to throw off their slavery. He could trust only upper-caste notables to spearhead his movement, and dreaded the prospect of mass awakening and mass militancy. 'I know that the only thing that the government dreads is this huge majority I seem to command. They little know that I dread it even more than they.' He disapproved of peasant agitations for rent-reduction or non-payment of interest as well as workers' strike for better payment, arguing 'faithful servants serve their masters even without pay'. Workers 'resort to strike on flimsy grounds. . . . I am distressed to see strikes going on in coal mines and other establishments engaged in producing consumer goods.' Workers are resorting to strikes because 'life here as elsewhere is today uprooted from its basis, the basis of religion, and . . . cash nexus has taken place.' And then he adds, 'But when labour comes to fully realise its strength, I know it can become more tyrannical than capital'. A conscientious critic takes note of these troubling statements of Gandhi and 'his ingrained respect for property', and observes, 'These observances are not only unsympathetic to the workers, but based on wrong premise. There is no counter-advice to the industrialists to become more humane employers. It is doubtful if Gandhi had ever seen the working conditions in coal mines' (Gill 2001: 163–4).

Gill surveys the history of Gandhi's politics and ideology as sympathetically as possible, but cannot help coming to the sad conclusion that the Congress and Gandhi's own national politics 'was always dominated by conservative elements rooted in propertied interests' at the cost of the vast majority of the poor peasantry and the labour, the untouchables and tribals, the bulk of Muslims and other minorities. Only a small segment of the propertied classes for whom Gandhi deflected the course of the national movement 'supported the national movement, and even this support . . . was opportunistic. In fact the landed gentry was the class that the British had bolstered up, and it was closely allied to the imperialist system. It was a bulwark of reaction, and opposed to even the mildest of land reforms' (Gill 2001: 165–6).

In other words, the authorised—hagiographical—version of Mohandas Gandhi is very different from the real one. Gandhi found enlightenment in Varnashrama Dharma while he was leading the anti-colonial struggle. He reiterated brahmanic myths about caste, Hinduism, and Indian society in the garb of great Indian truths, totally suppressing the material and cultural dimensions of indigenous oppression and resistance. The upper casteist abstraction and fondness with which he saw the culture of caste made him ignore its exploitation and violence and sing its praises as an embodiment of social harmony—a fact that the upper-caste controlled intellectual establishment in India has totally suppressed. In the actual socio-political context, the discourses of the finest neo-Gandhians such as Bhikhu Parekh (1989) and Ashis Nandy (1980; 1983)—and their numerous Euro-American imitators whose expertise on India is based on a few brahmanic books they have read—are nothing but an academic subterfuge to defend and glorify a hardcore conservative. Their caste–class interests make the elites blind to the fact that Gandhi was 'gripped by a set of regressive personal fixations and phobias, had a very limited intellectual formation, was impervious to rational argument, and entirely unaware of the damage he was doing to the national movement by suffusing it with Hindu pietism as he reconceived it' (Anderson 2012b).

Gandhi's synthesis of varna dharma, Indian culture, and nationalism was highly successful but achieved at the cost of the dalit-bahujan interests. The essence of *swaraj* (self-government or freedom)—each time Gandhi spoke on the subject he gave a different definition of the word—was kept 'delightfully vague' (Nehru [1936] 1999: 76). It meant almost everything to everybody, without changing anything or disturbing anybody. The nationalism that the Congress under Gandhi established was the same, perhaps a bit more evolved as per exigencies of time, as visualised by the nineteenth-century proponents of Vedic-brahmanic nationalism. Since the past model of caste-based 'organic' and 'harmonious' society was Gandhi's ideal, he was for strengthening, not weakening, the established order. Awash with religious symbolism, his nationalism was sharply opposed to the mass struggle for social and material change; whatever changes were to be effected had to come from above. The net result, of the real nature and impact of Gandhian nationalism, as Aloysius (1997: 170–213) has shown, was to 'deflect the course of political awakening from the hard world of the economic and political to that of the nebulous and mysterious'.

Criss-crossing the subcontinent and conquering the masses with the mesmeric straddling of religion and politics—made possible by material support from his wealthy castemen (Bombay industrialists and Ahmedabad millowners) and the unquestioned leadership accorded by the grateful upper castes—Gandhi gave a body blow to the secular political agendas of the dalit-bahujan and Muslim masses, which till now were gaining momentum across the subcontinent, and instead established an abstract, vacuous nationalism embedded in a conformist religiosity that negated the emergence of the masses into a newly aware political community. In short, the

Gandhian synthesis meant little more than *religion for the lowered castes and politics for the upper castes*, which in essence degraded both religion and politics.

Before Gandhi's arrival on the scene, as Aloysius argues, political mobilisation was not only interest-based, but also a reflection of the horizontal divide between the upper castes and the masses in general, a divide that had widened as a result of colonial policies and practices.

While this social disjunction, in the absence of large-scale industrialisation and social mobility, did not come anywhere near the Marxian concept of class, it did unambiguously point out the direction in which economy and politics were moving. Propertied classes in the subcontinent came to be perceived as upper casteist (with a handful of the Muslim elite thrown in, of course), and the shudra, Ati-shudras, tribals and Muslim masses represented the dispossessed. The class-like formation was clearly horizontal, cutting across so-called religious unities. Particularly remarkable was the fact that the Muslim masses, most of whom were converts from the lower castes, stood within the social structure as near equals to their Hindu counterparts exhibiting unmistakable signs of unity of interest with them. Together they were antagonistically poised towards the upper castes/classes. (Aloysius 1997: 182–3)

Gandhi, a champion of the presumed *organic* and *inclusive* nature of Hindu society where the lowered castes have for centuries been living in harmony with the upper castes, was alarmed by this subversive trend. The Hindu-Indian ethos, he insisted, toeing the line of early Hindu chauvinists like Dayananda and Vivekananda, was eternally spiritual and harmonious, unlike the materialist and decadent West. Those who were clamouring for social and material change, Gandhi claimed, did not know the 'eternal India'. This basic Gandhian refrain was elaborated into an attractive patriotic ideology by an impressive array of brahmanic scholar-activists. This was tailor-made for the political needs of the dominant groups who lost no time in recognising their messiah, and happily handed over the reins of nationalist leadership to him. Gandhi's insistence on adherence to what he called passive resistance and non-violence proved very effective in disciplining the peasants and workers. The caste elites wanted the masses to be roused only against British rule; they restrained, with Gandhi's crucial help, the masses from their fight against internal exploitation.

Gandhi's first agitation against the British—the Non-Cooperation movement—was a case in point. Based on Khilafat, cow protection, and anti-untouchability, it was not directed only against the British but also aimed at arresting and reversing the secular political movement of the lower classes. Gandhi gave the mass of 'Hindu' workers and peasants who aspired for material change, the issues of cow-protection and anti-untouchability, while his prescription for the Muslim masses (who, like the Hindu lower classes, were agitating for education, social betterment, diversification of occupations, and such issues) was Khilafat (to restore the Caliphate in Turkey as the global Islamic head, when the Arabs and Turks themselves had turned their back on the Caliphate in favour of modern political establishment). The Khilafat, however, met the political aspirations of the Muslim elite who were looking for a separate constituency.

In this project of the setting up of a vertical pan-Indian Muslim political community, under the leadership of the Ali brothers, Gandhian Khilafat and Non-Co-operation played a major, if not a decisive role. In several senses this coming into being of a pan-Indian Muslim political consciousness is a logical sequel and a necessity to the previous rise of pan-Indian Hindu political consciousness. (Aloysius 1997: 183)

Though aimed at bringing Hindu–Muslim unity, what Khilafat actually achieved was a cosmetic and transitory unity of Hindu and Muslim elites in terms of symbolic religious categories. The first wave of Gandhian nationalist politics—using the idioms of religious categories—succeeded in rupturing the ongoing process of unity of the lower Hindu classes with the Muslim masses, and effectively brought them back under the traditional upper-class leadership of their respective communities. 'This shift from the secular to the spiritual, politics to religion, was presumed to be in accordance with the Eastern genius and a part and parcel of the erection of the nationalist moral response to imperialism' (Aloysius 1997: 184). In this nationalist paradigm the advocates of Hindu–Muslim unity (the so-called secularists) as well as the practitioners of communal Hindu and Muslim politics 'both had a remarkable identity of function: to prevent the nation from emerging. The autonomy of the lower caste masses was to be denied at all costs and their differential and modern political agenda to be submerged'. In the nationalist version, the nation was now 'composed of two vertical communities presumably run on the basis of the pre-modern social order, of course with the necessary expansion of power and a political role for the upper-caste elite' (ibid.: 185).

The Hindu and Muslim elite grabbed the opportunity that Gandhi provided to reassert their leadership on 'religious' lines, which helped them thwart the egalitarian aspirations of dalit-bahujans. Both sides dreaded the socio-economic ramifications that the democratic–secular politics would necessarily entail. The Gandhian politics of religion gave them the unique opportunity to conjure up an external threat—the 'Hindu threat' to Muslims and the 'Muslim threat' to Hindus—to divert attention from public pressure for socio-economic changes. Such politics necessarily led to polarisation on communal lines and was shamelessly exploited by the elites not only to corner many colonial benefits and jobs in the name of representing their communities, but also in building their 'nationalist' credentials among their respective masses. Of course, it was in the British interest to fan suspicion between Hindus and Muslims, but the policy of divide and rule was also in the interest of the vested interests of both communities. So the Hindu–Muslim elite actively helped the British to succeed in the divisive design. In his autobiography, written in the 1930s, Nehru could see the sinister and quintessentially anti-national face of this politics:

It is nevertheless extraordinary how the bourgeois classes, both among the Hindus and the Muslims, succeeded, in the sacred name of religion, in getting a measure of mass sympathy and support for programmes and demands which had absolutely nothing to do with the masses, or even the lower middle class. Everyone of the communal demands put forward by any communal group is, in the final analysis, a demand for jobs, and these jobs could only go to a handful of the upper middle class.... These narrow political demands, benefiting at the most a small number of the upper middle classes, and often creating barriers in the way of national unity and progress, were cleverly made to appear the demands of the masses of that particular religious group. (Nehru [1936] 1999: 138)

What Nehru could not see was the fact that he himself was an integral part of the Congress' brand of vacuous 'secularism' which kept the masses out of the politico-economic mainstream. He also could not see that communalism or pseudo-nationalism (that he was rightly castigating) was deeply linked to the brahmanic politics of Gandhi. By overlapping nationalism with brahmanic Hinduism, the Gandhi-led Congress of which Nehru was an integral part only carried this tradition forward to its logical conclusion—Hindu–Muslim polarisation, religion-based violence, and the ultimate partition of the country. The bloody vivisection of the country, in which millions lost their lives in riots that accompanied the truncated freedom, was a disaster waiting to happen—the result of mixing religion with politics in which the Congress was as complicit as the Muslim League.

Ambedkar's Revolt

In the 1920s when Gandhi was established as the supreme leader of the national movement, B.R. Ambedkar (1891–1956)—an erudite, astute, articulate, and audacious dalit, later to emerge as the leader of what he termed *Bahishkrit Bharat* (the excluded India)—entered public life. The people for whom he was to wage a life-long struggle were not only socially and economically subservient and culturally suppressed, but also regionally dispersed and divided into hundreds of castes and sub-castes. He thus had only two alternatives—either to offer himself in a spirit of resignation to the reformist patronage of brahmanic Hinduism led by Gandhi, or to strike out on his own to liberate his long-suffering people. While the first option offered a rosy personal prospect, the second was hugely daunting, requiring him to fight, without any material or moral support, the immensely powerful forces of oppression. He chose the path strewn with thorns.

Ambedkar's struggle was an extension and evolution of the traditions of counter-culture with which he consciously attached himself. He was emphatic about his ideological kinship with Buddha, Kabir, and Phule. The changing strategies of his struggle in the face of extremely hostile circumstances notwithstanding, he never wavered from the broader vision and objectives of his movement which he enunciated in the very beginning of his public life. 'Self-esteem, liberation, and the opportunity to develop one's potential was the goal. Politics and law were the means. Organisation and unity were necessary for success in political conflict. Education was important in itself, but also as a means to gain economic opportunity and administrative office' (Gore 1993: 214). All of this was enshrined in his call to 'Educate, Agitate and Organise' which he subsequently elaborated in different ways and with newer emphasis throughout his life.

From his early public life in the 1920s to his conversion to Buddhism, the establishment of the Republican Party, and his death—all in 1956—Ambedkar's life is a story of ceaseless struggle to liberate the dalit-subalterns. To understand Ambedkar is to understand that one is not born but becomes a dalit—oppressed, broken, brutalised. His genius lay in the fact that he lost no time in grasping that the ignorance, humiliation and inaction of the oppressed had been symbiotically linked to the whole situation of their domination—social, religious, and political. Forcibly kept away from education for centuries, the depressed classes had not been allowed to know or respond to the situation that submerged them in a state of subjugation and slavery.

Ambedkar had himself suffered the humiliation of caste and untouchability that was routinely heaped on dalits. Beverley Nichols, author of the controversial *Verdict on India,* who considered him one of the six best brains in the India of the mid-twentieth century, has sketched the upper-caste treatment to the dalit Ambedkar:

...a creature from whose touch the extreme orthodox must fly as though he were a leper, a monster whose slightest contact compels them to precipitate themselves into the nearest bath-tub, to soap and pray, and pray and soap, so that the filth of Dr. Ambedkar—(M.A. London)—the shame of Dr. Ambedkar—(high honours at Columbia University)—the plague and scourge of Dr. Ambedkar—(special distinction at Heidelberg)—should be washed for ever from their immaculate and immortal souls.
(Nichols 1946: 30)

As if to give credence to this dramatic description, Nichols adds chillingly: 'We are not talking of the past, but of the year 1944.

These are not legends, fairy tales, gypsy songs; they are news paragraphs, stop-press' (ibid.). As India was bracing itself to kick out the external colonialists, untouchability—'history's most flagrant example of man's inhumanity to man'—was still deeply rooted in the Hindu social order. Thanks to the internal colonisers, nearly all attempts to abolish it had met with failure.

Ambedkar, who was often greeted with casteist slurs and insults and who had to leave rental accommodation and jobs where upper-caste peons flung files at him, considered caste as anathema to the nation and nationalism. He argued—through a series of incisive writings such as *Annihilation of Caste* (1936)—that caste and brahmanism have together been responsible for horrifying forms of deprivation, ignorance and servitude of shudras and (especially) ati-shudras. As he wanted to liberate the caste-oppressed, he wanted to annihilate caste. He wanted dignity and equality, not patronage and charity. He wanted social reconstruction backed by constitutional measures and legal safeguards, not Gandhian trusteeship. Ambedkar's endless clash with the Congress and Gandhi along with the kind of nationalism the latter envisioned and practised was precisely on these issues.

A visionary yet incorrigibly objective, Ambedkar's reading of the Indian reality proved to be frighteningly true. When he launched a peaceful campaign to ensure to dalits the right to draw water from a public tank at Mahad (Maharashtra) in 1927, brutal retaliation from the local upper-castes was swift in coming. But more invidious—and revealing—was the reaction of the nationalist luminaries. When Ambedkar was burning the *Manusmriti* for prescribing servitude to shudras and women during the Mahad struggle, Gandhi was glorifying the varna order and trying to prove that Hindu scriptures do not sanction any social discrimination. At about the same time, S. Radhakrishnan, symbolising the mindset of brahman literati, was waxing eloquent on the harmonious Hinduism at Oxford, seeing unparalleled unity of humanity in the varnashrama philosophy. And Jawaharlal Nehru, the high priest of airy-fairy socialism, was learning the precious lessons about Varnashrama Dharma and Indian philosophy from the likes of Gandhi and Radhakrishnan. Ambedkar had reason to suspect that Nehru's pride in his Pandit title and his deafening silence on caste was not that innocent.[3] As we saw in the Introduction, Nehru 'discovered' India through a brahmanical eye, effectively covering up flaws, frauds and failures of the caste system. Not for nothing does he confess in his *Autobiography*: 'A Brahmin I was born, and a Brahmin I seem to remain whatever I might say or do in regard to religion or social custom' (Nehru [1936] 1999: 118). Obviously, a beneficiary of the ideology and practice of caste could only become the most interested party for its reproduction, and the upper-caste nationalists were no exception to this.

It was under such circumstances that Ambedkar in his Mahad speech of 25 December 1927 declared that the issue at stake was not merely to enable the untouchables to drink water from the prohibited lake (that water was not nectar that would make us immortal, he jibed) but 'to assert that we too are human beings like others'. The real reason why the upper castes prevented the untouchables from drawing water, he stressed, was not because they would pollute it, but to show that castes declared inferior by the sacred tradition of shastras were not their equals. The struggle, therefore, was to set up the norm of equality. This could not be done unless the edifice that supported the hierarchical mindset was brought down. Comparing the struggle with the French Revolution, he said the issue was not merely to remove untouchability but to restructure Indian society on the principles of equality, fraternity, and liberty. 'We need to pull away the nails which hold the framework of caste-bound Hindu society together, such as those of the prohibition of intermarriage down to the prohibition of social intercourse so that Hindu society becomes all of one caste. Otherwise untouchability cannot be removed nor can equality be established' (Ambedkar, see Dangle 1992: 223–33).

For Ambedkar, Hindu or any other identity was subordinate to human dignity. 'We want equal rights in society. We will achieve them as far as possible while remaining within the Hindu fold, or if necessary, by kicking away this worthless Hindu identity' (see Gore 1993: 91). He was also emphatic that the task of removing untouchability and establishing equality would be carried out not by others but by the sufferers themselves. Putting the Mahad struggle in a wider perspective, a mainstream sociologist equates its significance with that of Gandhi's Dandi march:

The burning of a copy of the Manusmriti at Mahad was one way of symbolically rejecting the rules that it specified and the doctrine of inequality at birth on which the caste system was based. As a method of communicating a message to an illiterate following, this had the same significance as the making of salt at Dandi by Gandhi. They both symbolised a rejection of the premise on which authority was based and they both helped to break down the mystique of 'divine' dispensation.
(Gore 1993: 199)

Ambedkar's argument that 'the freedom which the governing class in India was struggling for is freedom that rules the servile classes in India' was not an endorsement of colonial rule but a devastating—and justifiable—denunciation of the self-serving nationalists. In the plenary session of the First Round Table Conference, he clarified his political stance *vis-à-vis* the British government and the Hindu society. In his speech on 20 November 1930, Ambedkar stated that the 'bureaucratic form of Government of India should be replaced by a government of the people, by the people and for the people'. He demanded a unitary state and adult suffrage with reserved seats and legal safeguards for the depressed classes. He stressed that the British government had not done anything about social evils as it had 'accepted the social arrangements as it found them'. The British, he said, had not been interested in removing exploitation of farm and industrial labour by landlords and capitalists. Asserting that the goodwill of the British was irrelevant, he also pointed out the danger from within:

We feel that nobody can remove our grievances as well as we can . . . It is only in a Swaraj constitution that we stand any chance of getting the political power in our own hands, without which we cannot bring salvation to our people. . . . We know that political power is passing from the British into the hands of those who wield such tremendous economic, social and religious sway over our existence. We are willing that it may happen, though the idea of Swaraj recalls to the mind of many the tyrannies, oppressions and injustices practised upon us in the past. (*BAWS*, vol. 2: 505–6)

Ambedkar was for freedom, but he held the view that as no country was good enough to rule over another, no class or caste was good enough to rule over another. For this reason, his concepts of freedom, nation, and nationalism were very different from the ones held by the high-caste nationalists who represented the power politics mainly of landlords, capitalists, and moneylenders but as leaders of all sections of Indian society. He resented the fact that the masses were drawn into the Congress-led nationalism only to be camp followers, with no say in policy.

Ambedkar argued that the governing classes in India—driven by the discriminatory philosophy of brahmanism—were hostile to those outside the fold and, therefore, did not sympathise with the masses, their wants, pains, or aspirations. The Congress did not favour the idea that the deprived masses should be educated and appointed to high office, and it opposed their movement for self-respect (*BAWS*, vol. 9: 235–6). The ancient tradition and its social ideology on which the brahman-bania[4] prided themselves, he elucidated with facts and compelling arguments, were grossly unjust and barbaric. He spelt out six 'lawless laws' of the brahmanic law-books.

1. Graded inequality between the different classes;
2. Complete disarmament of the shudras and the untouchables;
3. Complete prohibition of the education of the shudras and the untouchables;
4. Ban on the shudras and the untouchables occupying places of power and authority;
5. Ban on the shudras and the untouchables acquiring property; and,
6. Complete subjugation and suppression of women. (*BAWS*, vol. 9: 215)

Ambedkar summarises that inequality was the official doctrine of brahmanism which sanctified the suppression of the lower classes by the upper classes. India was the only country where the intellectual class not only made education its monopoly but declared that acquisition of knowledge by the lower classes was a punishable crime. Exposing the double standards of the high-caste nationalists who took pride in the tradition of suppression of majority of their own countrymen but flailed the British—from a high moral pedestal—for outraging the dignity and human rights of Indians, he argued:

> The record of the Brahmins as law-givers for the Shudras, for the Untouchables and for women is the blackest as compared with the record of the intellectual classes in other parts of the world. For, no intellectual class has prostituted its intelligence to invent a philosophy to keep his uneducated countrymen in a perpetual state of ignorance and poverty as the Brahmins have done in India. (*BAWS*, vol. 9: 215–16)

In Ambedkar's view, the elite nationalism was constructed and nurtured on such immoral tradition. He argued that most nationalist leaders, including Tilak, Patel, and Nehru, were quite conscious that they belonged to the governing class and were destined to rule. Citing examples from contemporary life and politics, he showed that the oppressive tradition was kept alive in both ideology and practice by the 'nationalists'. He gave the instance of anti-social attitude of Tilak:

> In 1918, when the Non-Brahmins and the Backward Classes had started an agitation for separate representation in the Legislature, Mr. Tilak in a public meeting held in Sholapur said he did not understand why the oil pressers, tobacco shopkeepers, washermen, etc.—that was his description of the Non-Brahmins and the Backward Classes – should want to go into the Legislature. In his opinion, their business was to obey the laws and not to aspire for power to make laws. (*BAWS*, vol. 9: 209)

Similarly, in 1942, when the Viceroy invited many Indians, including some members of the depressed classes, to support the war effort, Patel commented maliciously that the Viceroy sent for even Ghanchis (oil pressers) and Mochis (cobblers) (ibid.). Citing such examples, Ambedkar reveals how the means adopted by the Congress in its politics of boycott also reeked of contempt for the lower classes. The Congress in its attempt to dissuade others from contesting elections took out processions in various states carrying placards,

Who will go to the Legislatures?
Only barbers, cobblers, potters and sweepers.

When the Congress found that this was not enough to deter many 'respectable' persons from standing for the elections, it went to the extent of putting up illiterate barbers, potters, and sweepers, and got them elected in order to make the legislatures the object of derision:

> While on the one hand Congressmen were engaged in fighting for Swaraj which they said they wanted to win . . . for the masses, on the other hand . . . they were committing the worst outrages upon the very masses by exhibiting them publicly as objects of contempt to be shunned and avoided. (*BAWS*, vol. 9: 211)

The mentality of these nationalists towards their unprivileged countrymen, he remonstrated, was as odious as that of the British for the colonised. In the name of Indian people and nationalism, they wanted to establish their monopoly power. What is to be the fate of the masses under this governing class, he asked despairingly. The governing class, he warned, would not disappear by the magic wand of Swaraj, it would remain as it was and having been freed from the incubus of British imperialism, it would acquire greater vigour and capture power—as the governing classes in every country do—to serve its own interests (*BAWS*, vol. 9: 212).

The True Story of the Poona Pact

The Second Round Table Conference (1931) and the MacDonald Award for separate electorates set the stage for a frontal confrontation between Gandhi and Ambedkar on the question of the depressed classes. Let us examine what was at stake, and what led to the fight. While giving shape to a proposed constitution, the first conference had agreed upon two disturbing things from the nationalist viewpoint—the powers left to the princely states or its 'federal' structure, and the provision of separate electorates for the minorities. Ambedkar's stand during the first conference—espousing universal adult suffrage and special provisions for empowerment of the weaker sections—should have been closest to the nationalist perspective. The Congress could have seized this opportunity to give a nationalist direction to the future constitution by forging an alliance with Ambedkar and other social democrats. However, for reasons best known to Gandhi and his followers, the Congress did not oppose either the 'federal' structure or separate electorates for Muslim and Sikh minorities. Not only did the Congress capitulate before the powerful Muslim lobby, it did not show any resolve to press for democracy in the princely states either (Omvedt 1994: 169).

This situation amidst the Congress' growing impatience for the transfer of power forced Ambedkar to demand special protection (in the form of a separate electorate) for the untouchables, the most exploited and vulnerable section of society. However, their special protection was not possible unless the untouchables established their separate identity. Ambedkar wanted a freedom in which power would not be monopolised by the privileged Hindu and Muslim. But the Congress was quick to cry foul at his demand of special measures for the untouchables. Gandhi opposed any form of special representation to the untouchables, insisting that what they needed the most was social and religious acceptance by the upper castes, not legal and political rights or safeguards. Gandhi's strategy was to deny the untouchables a special identity and a separate electorate with the intent that once their demand for special representation was rejected there would be no discussion of special protective measures, except in so far as the upper castes wished to concede them of their own free will (Gore 1993: 135).

Not unexpectedly, Gandhi and Ambedkar clashed at the Second Round Table Conference. Before the conference, Ambedkar had met Gandhi in London in August 1931 in a surcharged atmosphere. According to B.C. Kamble's description, Gandhi treated Ambedkar with a lack of even normal politeness, while Ambedkar responded with a condemnation of the Congress, walking out after a scathing speech ending with the famous statement, 'Mahatmaji, I have no country.' This was not dialogue, but confrontation. They confronted each other again at the conference, each speaking with emotion and eloquence, with the self-assurance of leaders who can gather masses behind them. Each claimed to speak on behalf of untouchables. There was a vast difference in point of view, with Ambedkar stressing the need for political power for the Dalits, and with Gandhi arguing for reform and protection from above: 'What these people need more than election to the legislatures is protection from social and religious persecution.' But the emotional quality of the debate indicates an ever deeper clash. (Omvedt 1994: 170)

The conference ended inconclusively, and the Indian delegates, including Gandhi, left the matter of separate electorates to be decided by the British Prime Minister. Finally, in August 1932, Prime Minister Ramsey McDonald announced the policy on the issue. There would be special seats for the depressed classes to be filled by election from special constituencies in which only the members of the depressed classes, electorally qualified, would be entitled to vote. The depressed classes would also be entitled to vote in the general constituencies. Reserved constituencies were to be formed in areas where the depressed classes were most numerous and, except in Madras, they should not cover the whole area of the province. The arrangement was limited to twenty years. MacDonald also clarified in a letter to Gandhi that the number of special seats thus created 'will be seen to be small' and was just not intended to 'provide a quota numerically appropriate for the total representation of the whole of the depressed class population'. He made it clear that this proposal was different from the idea of a 'communal electorate for the depressed classes', as it was primarily intended to 'place them in a position to pick for themselves'. The method of creating legislative reservation of seats, he further clarified, was not considered helpful since it was unlikely to produce representatives who could genuinely represent the depressed classes 'because in practically all cases such members would be elected by a majority consisting of higher-caste Hindus' (see Baxi 2000).

Gandhi thought this reasonable proposal to be dangerous—'calculated to destroy Hinduism'—and decided to oppose it with the threat of self-immolation. He began his fast unto death in Yeravada prison 'as a man of religion' and also as a leader of 'numberless men and women who have childlike faith in his wisdom'. Gandhi did not give any reasons against the separate electorate for the depressed classes, except declaring that for him the matter was purely a religious one. 'For me the question of those classes is predominantly moral and religious. The political aspect, important though it is, dwindles into insignificance compared to the moral and religious one.'

Gandhi, however, revealed his real motive a day after he began his fast in a conversation with Sardar Patel. Mahadev Desai, Gandhi's secretary, has recorded what he said to justify his threat of self-immolation:

> The possible consequences of separate electorates fill me with horror. Separate electorates for all other communities will still leave room for me to deal with them, but I have no other means to deal with 'untouchables'. ... It will create division among Hindus so much so that it will lead to blood-shed. Untouchable hooligans will make common cause with Muslim hooligans and kill caste Hindus. (See Zelliot 1998: 167)

After the Gandhi-Ambedkar clash in London, a dirty political game ensued in which the upper-caste leaders, in league with the 'nationalist' press, sought to hijack leadership of the depressed classes by organising meetings and producing untouchable spokespersons to sing praises of Gandhi and lambaste Ambedkar (Keer [1954] 1971; Omvedt 1994). By the time of Gandhi's fast, Ambedkar was isolated and reviled for 'putting the Mahatma's life in danger'. Keeping his cool under most trying circumstances, Ambedkar rose to the occasion.

> It has fallen to my lot to be the villain of the piece. But I tell you I shall not deter from my pious duty, and betray the just and legitimate interests of my people even if you hang me on the nearest lamp-post in the street.
> (Ambedkar, see Keer [1954] 1971: 209)

On the eve of Gandhi's fast, to begin on 20 September 1932, Ambedkar issued a long statement (*BAWS*, vol. 9: 311–17), clarifying his position on the issue and requesting Gandhi to reconsider his decision to immolate himself and avert 'terrorism by his followers against the depressed classes'. Gandhi's arguments, he said, were 'strange and incomprehensible', and if given a choice 'between Hindu faith and the possession of political power', the depressed classes would choose the latter, and thus end Gandhi's agony and fast. Remonstrating that 'he has staked his life in order to deprive the depressed classes of little they have got', he counselled Gandhi that his 'determination to fast unto death was worthy of a far better cause'. Responding to Gandhi's claim that the proposed electoral separation would arrest the 'marvellous work' of generations of Hindu reformers and give a jolt to the campaign for removal of untouchability, Ambedkar said:

> There have been many Mahatmas in India whose sole object was to remove Untouchability and to elevate and absorb the Depressed Classes, but every one of them has failed in his mission. Mahatmas have come and Mahatmas have gone. But the Untouchables have remained as Untouchables. (*BAWS*, vol. 9: 315)

Ambedkar argued that if separate electorates of Muslims and Sikhs would not split up the nation, there was no reason why a separate electorate for the depressed classes, who were more in need of protection, should threaten national unity. Referring to the 'manufactured' opposition from some 'untouchable' Congressmen (supporting joint electorates) who were being projected as the voice of dalits, he made it clear that they could vote in general constituencies and contest from them; it was not compulsory for these or any members of the depressed classes to enrol in separate electoral rolls or to contest from separate constituencies if they so desired. He asked Gandhi that the latter should not force him to go against his helpless people:

> I desire to assure the public that although I am entitled to say that I regard the matter as closed, I am prepared to consider the proposals of the Mahatma. I however trust the Mahatma would not drive me to the necessity of making a choice between his life and the rights of my people. For I can never consent to deliver my people bound hand and foot to the caste Hindus for generations to come. (*BAWS*, vol. 9: 317)

Meanwhile, many prominent politicians gathered in Bombay and tried to break the deadlock by arranging a one-to-one talk between Gandhi and Ambedkar. After hard bargaining, the conflict ended in an uneasy compromise known as the Poona Pact. Gandhi accepted reserved seats; Ambedkar acceded to a joint electorate with a provision for primary elections in which the depressed class vote would decide who would stand for the election. Ambedkar secured 148 seats—he wanted 197—in the Provincial Assemblies for the depressed classes out of a total of 780, and 10 per cent of seats in the Central Assembly. However, his insistent demand for a referendum after twenty-five years and not before was set aside when a 'critically ill' Gandhi said with a tone of finality, 'Five years or my life' (Keer 1971: 214).

The pact gave dalits some reserved seats but robbed them of the opportunity to elect their own leaders. Under the scheme, the non-dalit choice became crucial in selecting and electing dalit representatives in the reserved constituencies since there was no constituency in any state where dalits were more than 25–30 per cent of the electorate. In order to win, dalit candidates were, necessarily, to enter into an acquiescent relationship with non-dalit voters, making the emergence of an assertive dalit leadership impossible. This was the real implication of the Poona Pact and that is why Ambedkar had been adamant about a separate electorate.

Not surprisingly, the militant dalits derided the Poona Pact as a defeat, and so did Ambedkar soon after the compromise. The sense of betrayal was to deepen in subsequent years as the Congress leadership would not nominate able, educated dalit candidates for reserved constituencies. In an incisive analysis of the 1937 elections, Ambedkar was to show how and why the Congress selected the best educated candidates from the high castes, and preferred to field the least educated SC nominees for the reserved seats (*BAWS*, vol. 9: 217–24). (Since then all mainstream parties, making a mockery of Ambedkar's dream, have practised the duplicity of nominating weak and pliable SC/ST candidates. This nefarious pattern was also applied in the case of other backward classes—and continues still.)

Dalits still debate the issue and curse Gandhi for falsely claiming to represent their 'cause' and their 'vital interests'. Gandhi feared a political division and violence in the villages, but as Omvedt (1994: 172) points out, he 'ignored the division that already existed; in his warning against the spread of violence, he ignored the violence already existing in the lives of the dalits'. Claiming to speak in the name of dalits, Gandhi did not play the part of a national leader; he played the role of a typical upper-caste charlatan. In the words of Ambedkar's biographer Dhananjay Keer:

. . . [T]he politician in Gandhi became successful and the Mahatma was defeated! So effective and crushing was the victory of Gandhi that he deprived Ambedkar of all his life-saving weapons and made him a powerless man as did Indra in the case of Karna. ([1954] 1971: 216)

Ambedkar himself saw the fast a 'moral blackmail' since Gandhi's self-immolation would have provoked a bloody retaliation against dalits from upper castes. Pointing out that initially Gandhi was opposed to even the idea of reserved seats for dalits, Ambedkar saw in Gandhi a politician whose politics was oriented to safeguard the vested interests. 'There was nothing noble in the fast. It was against the untouchables and was the worst form of coercion against a helpless people. . . . It was a vile and wicked act' (*BAWS*, vol. 9: 259).

Today, there is a consensus among dalit thinkers that the rejection of the demand for separate electorates gave a body blow to the idea of independent political participation by dalit-subalterns. The brahmanical forces led by Gandhi orchestrated the whole affair in a manner that ensured that only dalit stooges could have come out of it. In Kanshi Ram's words, the Poona Pact heralded *the chamcha age* (the age of stooges):

Poona Pact made dalits helpless. By rejecting separate electorate, dalits were deprived of their genuine representation in legislatures. Several and various kind of *chamchas* were born in the last fifty years. As and when India's high-caste Hindu rulers felt the need of *chamchas* and when the authority of the upper castes got endangered by real and genuine dalit leaders, *chamchas* were brought to the fore in all other fields. (Kanshi Ram, see Dubey 2001: 295)

On the other hand, elite historians have portrayed the hard power politics that underpinned the conflict between Ambedkar and Gandhi as a unique moral instance of Gandhi's ability to win over his opponent's heart! A brahmanic mythification has been created to erase the sordid reality:

Gandhi had thus achieved what as a true Satyagrahi he always strove for: He had won his opponent's heart! . . . The differences between the two leaders, one an untouchable by birth, the other an untouchable by volition, were thus healed. . . . The agreement between the Mahatma and Ambedkar saved a society from turning into itself and committing collective suicide. Indeed, the Poona Pact was a victory won by Gandhi in the course of a struggle seeking to liberate Hindu society from a dangerous malformation lodged in the very core of its social being. It was, perhaps, the Mahatma's finest hour. (Ravinder Kumar 1987: 98–9)

Such 'scholarly' perception appears to be formed on information provided by Gandhi's 'propaganda friends' whose sense of 'sacrifice for the country' was synonymous with beating the Mahatma's drum. What one such Gandhian, Rai Bahadur Mehrchand Khanna, said at a meeting of the untouchables at Peshawar on 12 April 1945, under the auspices of the Depressed Classes League, captures the sum and substance of the upper-caste chorus on the issue:

> Your best friend is Mahatma Gandhi, who even resorted to a fast for your sake and brought about the Poona Pact under which you have been enfranchised and given representation on local bodies and legislatures. Some of you, I know, have been running after Dr. Ambedkar, who is just a creation of the British Imperialists and who uses you to strengthen the hands of the British Government in order that India may be divided and the Britishers continue to retain power. I appeal to you in your interests, to distinguish between self-styled leaders and your real friends. (Cited in *BAWS*, vol. 9: 239)

The dalit-subaltern and the brahmanic interpretations of the Poona Pact is a classic example of how masses and classes—and their representative scholars—view the same event with vastly different perspectives. Contrary to the Vedic dictum *ekam sat vipra bahudha vadanti* (the truth is one and the pandits spell it out in different ways), truths in general, and historical truths in particular, are not absolute; they are relative and hold different meanings for different strata of society. What was the truth for Gandhi was a travesty of the truth for Ambedkar.[5] Indian historiography, like the nation and nationalism, has been a victim to the corrupt tendency to perpetrate only that truth that serves the entrenched interests of the privileged groups and helps maintain their monopoly over knowledge and power.

Anatomy of Gandhian Paternalism

In an exposé of the Gandhian bluff on caste and untouchability, Ambedkar showed that as an exploitative system untouchability was even worse than slavery. In slavery, the master had the responsibility to look after the slave and keep him in good condition lest his market value fall. But the Hindu takes no responsibility for the maintenance of the untouchable. As an economic system, it permits unbridled exploitation without obligation:

> The system of Untouchability is a gold mine to the Hindus.... In it the 240 millions of Hindus have 60 millions of Untouchables to be used as forced labourers and because of their state of complete destitution and helplessness can be compelled to work on a mere pittance or sometimes on nothing at all. In it the 240 millions of Hindus have 60 millions of Untouchables to do the dirty work of scavengers and sweepers which the Hindu is debarred by his religion to do and which must be done by non-Hindus who could be no others than Untouchables. In it the 240 millions of Hindus have 60 millions of Untouchables who can be kept to lower jobs.... In it the 240 millions of Hindus have the 60 millions of Untouchables who can be used as shock-absorbers in slumps and dead-weights in booms, for in slumps it is the Untouchable who is fired first and the Hindu is fired last and in booms the Hindu is employed first and the Untouchable is employed last. (*BAWS*, vol. 9: 196)

Gandhi, on the other hand, flatly refused to see the untouchability problem in socio-economic terms, arguing that the issue is 'predominantly moral and religious' and he would deal with it as such. As he also contested Ambedkar's claim to understand and represent the dalits, the onus was on Gandhi to prove his bona fides as their real leader. He accepted the challenge with the confidence of a mass leader and started a campaign that he called *achhutoddhar* (uplift of the untouchables). Renaming the untouchables Harijans (the children of God) which was the functional equivalent of their position as the helpless beings, he formed the Anti-Untouchability League. In his Harijan campaign, Harijans themselves were not to take any part since it was intended as 'an expiation of upper-castes' sin' (of practising untouchability). They were to be passive objects for the penance and practice of virtue by the upper castes. As Gandhi put it, 'We have to obtain not the salvation of the untouchables but ours by treating them as equals.' Besides temple entry, Gandhi's Harijan campaign consisted of a series of symbolic actions which centred on upper-caste reformers working among untouchables to inculcate in them temperance and discipline, and reforming their unhygienic ways, meat-eating and alcoholism, which were seen as main reasons for their degradation. Gandhi made it clear that he did not have any agenda of civil rights, political power, or economic opportunity for them. His approach was the 'change of heart' and the creation of an 'ideal bhangi', who would continue to clean the excreta of others with the status of a brahman.

Gandhi did not bother to enter into a dialogue with Ambedkar and other dalits, concentrating instead on courting the upper-caste Congressmen, who found his anti-untouchability campaign a political necessity, a fact Gandhi knew better than anyone else. Swami Shraddhanand has reported that many high-caste reformers who put the show of mixing with the untouchables in Gandhi's presence went and took a bath later, with their clothes on! The real point, however, was lost on Shraddhanand: Was Gandhi himself very different from the upper-caste charlatans?

In a letter to A.V. Thakkar, General Secretary of the Anti-Untouchability League (later renamed Harijan Sevak Sangh), Ambedkar suggested that rather than dissipating its energies on symbolic gestures like temple entry, temperance, and discipline, the League should concentrate on campaigns to secure civil rights, equality of opportunity, and active social intercourse. His letter did not evoke any response—it was not even acknowledged. Ambedkar refers to another incident. To a deputation who waited on Gandhi requesting him to appoint untouchables on the managing committee of the Harijan Sevak Sangh, Gandhi was reported to have said:

> The welfare work for the Untouchables is a penance which the Hindus have to do for the sin of Untouchability. The money that has been collected has been contributed by the Hindus. From both points of view, the Hindus alone must run the Sangh. Neither ethics nor right would justify the Untouchables in claiming a seat on the Board of the Sangh.
> (*BAWS*, vol. 9: 142)

Gandhi was against the untouchables giving up their traditional degrading occupations like latrine-cleaning, tanning, flaying, etc. One born a scavenger, Gandhi insisted, must earn his livelihood by being a scavenger. And then to give an aura of morality to this sinister suggestion, he added, 'For, a scavenger is as worthy of his hire as a lawyer or your President. That, according to me, is Hinduism' (*Harijan*, 6 March 1937). He was also against the sweepers going on strike to demand better wages and working conditions. Chastising the sweepers of Bombay who went on strike in 1946, Gandhi wrote:

> My opinion against sweepers' strike dates back to about 1897 when I was in Durban. A general strike was mooted there and the question arose as to whether scavengers should join it. My vote was registered against the (strike) proposal.... In spite of my close attachment to sweepers ... I must denounce the coercive methods they are said to have employed. They will thereby be losers in the long run. City folk will not always be cowed down.... A Bhangi may not give up his work even for a day. (*Harijan*, 21 April 1946)

This statement is from a man who is eulogised for his supreme love—and sacrifice—for the scavengers. His acolytes never tire of citing his declaration: 'I may not be born again, but if it happens I will like to be born in a family of scavengers, so that I may relieve them of the inhuman, unhealthy, and hateful practice of carrying nightsoil' (*Young India*, 27 April 1921). The irony of the statement is lost on his admirers: had he been born in a family of scavengers, Gandhi of course would have struggled to relieve them of the subhuman task; but in his present avatar as an upper-caste Hindu he was willing to do no more than keep them in their (birth-based) place.

It is not difficult to see why Ambedkar detested Gandhi's humbug on caste and untouchability. He found Gandhi's moralising that poverty was soul-uplifting, and that all castes were equal and 'a scavenger has the same status as a brahman', as 'an outrage and a cruel joke on the helpless classes':

> If Gandhism preached the rule of poverty for all and not merely for the Shudra the worst that could be said about it is that it is a mistaken idea. But why preach it as good for one class only? ... If Gandhism preached that scavenging is a noble profession, with the objective of inducing those who refuse to engage in it, one could understand it. But why appeal to the scavenger's pride and vanity in order to induce him and him only to keep on to scavenging by telling him that scavenging is a noble profession

and that he need not be ashamed of it? ... To preach that poverty is good for the Shudra and for none else, to preach that scavenging is good for the Untouchables and for none else and to make them accept these onerous impositions as voluntary purposes of life, by appeal to their failings is an outrage and a cruel joke on the helpless classes which none but Mr. Gandhi can perpetuate with equanimity and impunity. (*BAWS*, vol. 9: 292–3)

Gandhi's image and reality are vastly different. Take the example of Gandhi's promotion of the spinning wheel and khadi, symbolising self-reliance. He and his minions spoke of it as a historic initiative that would provide mass employment and affordable clothing to the people. But khadi self-reliance, ironically, always survived on subsidies provided first by his rich friends and later by the governments of free India. In reality, he cunningly used it for political mobilisation. At one point he was seriously considering spinning to be imposed as a pre-condition for Congress membership. But Gandhi never thought of adopting a similar approach for the removal of caste disabilities. Between the transfer of power and the eradication of social discrimination, Gandhi gave priority to the former and was in no mood to concede the depressed classes anything more than pious assurances. He resorted to direct action against British rule because it was founded on injustice, but was opposed to any such action against the upper castes which perpetrated worst kinds of crimes against millions of their own countrymen. Gandhi was in the habit of going to fast on everything, but did not ever go on a fast against the social oppression.

The Harijan campaign was a political charity, intended to integrate the depressed classes into the Hindu fold, not as partners but as poor relations. Gandhi had once even asked a Christian missionary to pray for the Harijans but not to try to convert them as 'they did not have the mind and intelligence to understand what you talked. ...Would you preach the Gospel to a cow?' (*Harijan*, 19 December 1936). This provoked even Jagjivan Ram, the rising Harijan mascot of the Congress, who registered a strong protest and described the Harijan Sevak Sangh as being 'erroneous in conception, faulty in emphasis, and halting in execution'. Ram had to be pacified with Gandhi clarifying that no ill-will was intended, for him the cow was 'a symbol of gentleness and patient suffering' (Zelliot 1996: 170).

Above all, Gandhi extracted a very heavy price from the dalits for his symbolic opposition to untouchability. The temple-entry drive, the fulcrum of his anti-untouchability campaign, cleverly shifted attention from the question of socio-economic rights. Ambedkar, who initially supported the temple-entry programme as a way of restoring religious rights to the untouchables, saw through the game and eventually came out strongly against this 'side issue', asserting that the real issues were education, employment and economic development. Even on this side issue Gandhi remained hypocritical. He led a much-glorified campaign of temple entry for the untouchables in 1933, but had no hesitation to say in the *Harijan* of 23 February 1934:

I have absolutely no desire that the temple should be opened to Harijans, until caste Hindu opinion is ripe for the opening. It is not a question of Harijans asserting their right of temple entry or claiming it. They may or may not want to enter that temple even when it is declared open to them. But it is the bounden duty of every caste Hindu to secure that opening for Harijans.

Criticising such politics with the disdain it deserved, Ambedkar described the temple entry as 'strange game of political acrobatics':

Mr. Gandhi begins as an opponent of Temple Entry. When the Untouchables put forth a demand for political rights, he changes his position and becomes a supporter of Temple Entry. When the Hindus threaten to defeat the Congress in the election, if it pursues the matter to a conclusion, Mr. Gandhi, in order to preserve political power in the hands of the Congress, gives up Temple Entry! Is this sincerity? Does this show conviction? Was the 'agony of soul' which Mr. Gandhi spoke of more than a phrase? (*BAWS*, vol. 9: 125)

Tethering his Harijan politics to Varnashrama Dharma, Gandhi was defending caste under the fig-leaf of varna system at a time when caste discrimination dominated social life, and due to it millions of people were deprived of their basic human rights. Writing in *Navjivan,* Gandhi saw the seeds of Swaraj in caste and argued that the Hindu society had been able to survive because it was founded on the caste system.

> The seeds of Swaraj are to be found in the caste system.... A community which can create the caste system must be said to possess unique power of organisation.... The caste system is a natural order of society. In India it has been given a religious coating. Other countries not having understood the utility of the caste system ... have not derived ... the same degree of advantage as India has derived. (Reprinted in the vol. II of the series called Gandhi Sikshan, cited in *BAWS*, vol. 9: 275–6)

Rebuffing those who advocated social democracy and wanted to do away with the principle of hereditary occupation, Gandhi asserted:

> To destroy the caste system and adopt the western European social system means that Hindus must give up the principle of hereditary occupation which is the soul of the caste system. Hereditary principle is an eternal principle. To change it is to create disorder. I have no use for a Brahman if I cannot call him a Brahman for my life. It will be a chaos if everyday a Brahman is to be changed into a Shudra and a Shudra is to be changed into a Brahman. (See *BAWS*, vol. 9: 275–6)

In his essay 'Varna Vyavastha' Gandhi insists that varna is not a human invention but an immutable law of nature which 'reveals the law of one's being and thus the duty one has to perform, it confers no right, and the idea of inferiority or superiority is wholly repugnant to it' ([1934] 1993: 218). After this, he orders: 'What is essential is that one must seek one's livelihood, and no more, from following the vocation to which one is born' (ibid.: 221). This from a person who himself quit the *tarajoo* (the scale) of the grocery shop, his ancestral calling, in favour of the brahmanic profession of preaching the dharma.

What is Gandhi's construction of the ideal shudra? The shudra who serves the higher castes as a matter of religious duty and who will never own any property, who indeed has not even the ambition to own anything, Gandhi writes in *Varna-Vyavastha*. Such a shudra is 'worthy of the world's homage.... The gods will shower their choicest blessings on him. One may not say this of the proletariat of the present day. They certainly own nothing, but I expect they covet ownership' (ibid.: 220). It was this sinister mindset which occasionally made Gandhi oppose the education of the masses which, he feared, might ignite their mind about the wretched conditions in which they lived:

> What do you propose to do by giving literacy to the children of the peasants? What comfort are you going to add to their life by educating them? Do you want to ignite discontent in his mind for his thatched hut and pathetic condition? ...We are going to do excess when some preach for imparting education for all, without considering its pros and cons.
> (Gandhi, cited in Biswas 1998: 267)

Such ideas came naturally to Gandhi since he considered the caste system the natural order, perfected religiously in India. For him 'the caste system has a scientific basis. Reason does not revolt against it.... I can find no reason for its abolition. To abolish caste is to demolish Hinduism.'

Social scientists have variously interpreted or rather explained away Gandhi's support for the caste order. Some have argued that his views were not that simple; they were 'richly ambivalent'! Prostituting their intellect, some pandits even portray him as a crusader against caste. There are others who cook up the excuse that Gandhi as a mass national leader had to make compromises with the upper-caste forces. This, too, is a lame argument: in reality, Gandhi's views on caste, as we saw, mingled and converged with the upper-caste views. Those who cite the homilies of Gandhi and try to glorify him by recording his 'soul's agony' and lamentation against untouchability tend to turn a blind eye to the fast-changing scenario of the time. It was no longer possible for brahmanical forces to openly justify the outrageous social practices as instances of protests were on the rise in many parts of the country.

Varna Swaraj and an Obscurantist Critique of Modernity

Using religious and homespun idioms, Gandhi often spoke of the India of his dreams that would become a reality after Swaraj, through Ram-rajya, trusteeship, and self-sufficient village republics. All these and similar half-baked ideas have been coherently crafted by a long line of hagiographer-historians into what is known as

Gandhism. His ideology has been interpreted as an indigenous recipe for a peaceful revolution, 'a clarion call for a new social order and a blueprint for New India'. What is left unsaid by the pandits is the fact that Gandhi's worldview, his social ideology, and his vague and vacuous swaraj were all embedded in Varnashrama Dharma. Gandhi called himself a 'sanatani Hindu' who believed in the sacerdotal literature of Sanskrit, the concepts of avatar and rebirth, idol-worship, cow-protection, and above all, varna-vyavastha (*Young India*, 6 October 1921). Like other Hindu supremacists before and after him, he blithely equated sanatani Hinduism with all Indian faiths and traditions, including Buddhism and Jainism.[6] He carried forward the dogma of the early nationalists that Hinduism, founded on the varna ideology, had produced in the past a uniquely spiritual and harmonious culture which made India superior to the materialist West. Speaking in the obscurantist language of a fundamentalist, Gandhi declared: 'What of substance is contained in any other religion is always to be found in Hinduism. And what is not contained in it is insubstantial or unnecessary' (*Young India*, 17 September 1925). Thus, far from a call for a new egalitarian order, Gandhism was based on an appeal for a reversal to the status quo ante.

Gandhi's varna order was built on the consensus of all concerned. Seeing no inequality or exploitation in varna, he argued that a 'stricter fulfilment of the law would make life livable, would spread peace and content, end all clashes and conflicts, put an end to starvation and pauperisation, solve the problem of population and even end disease and suffering' (Gandhi [1934] 1993: 218). There was harmony between the brahman and the shudra: his bhangi loved to clean excreta of others just as a bania loved to amass wealth and a brahman loved to acquire knowledge. He found the varna model of society worthy of export to the whole world. 'Though the law of varna is a special discovery of some Hindu seer, it has universal application. The world may ignore it today but it will have to accept it in the time to come' (ibid.: 219). Warning of the dangers of 'class wars and civil strife' unleashed by the ongoing process of modernisation, he gave the call to return to the varna purity to end 'the conflicting inequalities':

These wars and strife could not be ended except by the observance of the law of varna. For it ordains that everyone shall fulfil the law of one's being by doing it in a spirit of duty and service that to which one is born. Its due observance by a large part of mankind will end the conflicting inequalities and give place to an equality in diversity. (Gandhi [1934] 1993: 219)

The Gandhian way to meet the modern challenges was to hark back to the purity of varna order. His reconstruction of tradition not only denies a conflict-ridden past but also makes a mockery of the radical heterodoxy and egalitarian aspirations of the suppressed classes. In the words of Aloysius (1997), 'Gandhi's construction of the ideal–typical tradition is composed of the worst elements of the subcontinental history, elements that kept the masses under social and cultural tyranny.' Laying emphasis only on the unifying and uniformising aspects of Indian culture, Gandhi conveniently cast aside diversification as an aberration. But unity and diversity in the context of the historical-cultural development of the subcontinent are highly dialectical terms loaded with socio-political significance.

Unity represents the dominant and uniformising culturo-ideological and mythical Brahminic factors and is thus oppressive: Vedic-Brahminic Hinduism as the only acceptable form of Hinduism, Sanskrit as the basis of all languages, Brahmins as the caste to be found all over the subcontinent, and Varnashrama Dharma as the traditional order, representing the dominant and oppressive, ideal social order of the ruling and vested interests. Diversity on the other hand, stands for the movement away from these uniformising factors, the tendencies of resistance of the subaltern and the locally rooted castes and communities in general; the growth of the vernaculars and their cultural communities, and the scores of attempts of creating culturally specific non-Brahminic myths and popular religions, are, in a sense, the defiance of the commoners against the imposition from above. Finally, the actual and attenuated realisation of the Varnashrama Dharmic ideal in the different regions of the subcontinent represent a history of resistance and uneven success. (Aloysius 1997: 186–7)

Viewed in this perspective, 'India's history, culture and inheritance are composed of both these distinct yet often dialectically united streams.' However, Gandhism as a particular mutant of the broader brahmanic construct of the Indian culture, and the nationalism based on it, 'elevated only one trend and that too the oppressive one', thus sabotaging 'the political emergence of the social forces that historically represented the subaltern and the suppressed'. An essential component of Gandhian reconstruction of Indian tradition is to regard equalitarianism, or any form of protest against the ascriptive establishment as alien, foreign inspired, Western, and hence to be rejected in the 'national' interest (ibid.).

Gandhi's call to return to the old order to get rid of the modern maladies represents the perspective of the traditionally powerful. Ideologies of dominant classes in India and elsewhere have always viewed transformative politics as dangerous and counter-productive, while lower classes everywhere have aspired for change and revolution. What was remarkable about the Gandhi phenomenon was its phenomenal success. While earlier champions of brahmanic nationalism in India had failed in their endeavour to weld together diverse social forces, Gandhi created a cocktail of history, myth, and religion, and used his carefully crafted saintly persona to win over or at least neutralise the masses. Behind his trademark simplicity lay a sanatani mind of extraordinary shrewdness that could pursue its course with single-minded devotion. His goal was to expel the British, but freedom had to be won without any social upheaval. He was well aware of the veneration that saintly figures receive from the Indian masses. Clad in the loincloth, and using cultural symbols associated with the life of a holy man—austere living, fasts, the observance of days of silence, the demonstrative use of celibacy, holy books, and prayer meetings—gave him the image of a saint. His deft use of religious language to communicate with the masses absolved him of the need to lay out his plans in concrete terms. He and his brahman-bania associates exploited to the hilt his saintly image while indulging in worst kind of power politics.

The symbol of Ram-rajya, steeped in supposed inclusiveness and the harmony of varna society, was to offset the growing protest and stridence of the lower classes in the new political structure and emerging civil society. Gandhi and his upper-class followers were deeply disturbed by the intensifying rivalries between the landlords and tenants, capital and labour, privileged castes and the lowered, all of which they attributed to modernity. Gandhi's advice to the masses was to accept the traditional leadership in order to make a broad-based unity against the British. Sermonising to the tenants of the United Province who had risen against their landlords, he wrote in *Young India* of 18 May 1921:

> While we will not hesitate to advise the kisans (cultivators) when the moment comes, to suspend payment of taxes to government, it is not contemplated that at any stage of Non-Co-operation we would seek to deprive the zamindars of their rent. . . . The kisans must be advised scrupulously to abide by the terms of their agreement with the zamindar, whether such is written or inferred from custom.

Similarly, Gandhi told workers to fall in line with their employers/capitalists and not to resort to strike to improve their economic conditions because, as he wrote in *Young India* of 23 February 1922, 'India's history is not one of strained relations between capital and labour.'

For Gandhi Western modernity was the biggest obstacle in realising the 'purity and simplicity' of the old order. This made him a trenchant critic of modern civilisation and all that it represented—science, technology, railways, representative democracy, new secular institutions, judiciary, and modern medicine. He articulated these views in his *Hind Swaraj* or Indian Home Rule (1909). This anti-modernity manifesto is perhaps the most important tract to understand Gandhi as it represents his muddled worldview at its coherent best.

In *Hind Swaraj* Gandhi unravels his vision of Indian utopia, and launches a polemic against Western modernity, seeing in it nothing but spectre of dangerous developments (Gandhi [1909] 1993: 3–66). He equates the West with the immoral materialism (which modernity promoted), and India with its timeless spirituality. 'The tendency of Indian civilisation is to elevate the moral being, that of Western civilisation is to propagate immorality. The latter is godless, the former is based on the belief in God' (ibid.: 36–7). Vividly reminiscent of the images of *Kaliyuga* conjured up by the brahmanic minds against the backdrop of challenges mounted by the caste-oppressed from time to time, Gandhi here brands modern civilisation 'satanic' and a 'disease' that must be shunned. He refuses to see that all traditional societies had been more or less religious and there was nothing exceptional about India in this regard. Neither does he recognise that Indian culture as other cultures had been open to, and considerably shaped by, influences from outside. The fact that Eastern as well as Western civilisations have evolved through the process of give-and-take by which cultures blend and form fresh ones was beyond Gandhi's understanding.

For Gandhi, machinery, the 'chief symbol of modern civilisation', guarantees nothing but a 'great sin'. In the new world, 'Women, who should be the queens of households, wander in the streets or they slave away in factories.' The British Parliament 'which you consider to be the Mother of Parliaments' is a 'sterile woman' and a 'prostitute', and democracy is an 'emblem of slavery' (Gandhi [1909] 1993: 13–18). 'Hospitals are institutions for propagating sins' because their existence encourages 'men (to) take less care of their bodies and immorality increases' (ibid.: 33–4). Railways, the services of which Gandhi frequently availed both in India and abroad, also attracted his wrath. Seeing them as the villainous facilitator of disease and disaster, he holds them responsible for the British hold on India and for spreading plague and famines (ibid.: 23–4).

On the other side, Gandhi's heart beats for economic primordium, educational orthodoxy, and cultural insularity, along with religiously sanctioned social hierarchy. True civilisation, he insists, can flower only in the traditional mode of living, in the absence of technological change and life-corroding competition.

> We have managed with the same kind of plough as existed thousands of years ago. We have retained the same kind of cottages that we have had in former times and our indigenous education remains the same as before. We have had no system of life-corroding competition. Each followed his own occupation or trade and charged a regulation wage. It was not that we did not know how to invent machinery, but our forefathers knew that if we set our hearts after such things, we would become slaves and lose our moral fibre. (Gandhi [1909] 1993: 35)

Therefore,

> India's salvation consists in unlearning what she has learnt during the last fifty years. The railways, telegraphs, hospitals, lawyers, doctors and such like have all to go. . . .

When Gandhi's guru Gopal Krishna Gokhale saw the book he was horrified and pronounced it 'the work of a fool', and consoled himself with the thought that his disciple would destroy it sooner than later (Payne 1997: 224). After Gokhale, many assumed that Gandhi's thinking underwent a sea change after the *Hind Swaraj* phase and that he outgrew most of the obscurantist ideas contained therein. Gandhi himself dispelled such misgivings from time to time. This is what he wrote in the 1920s: 'The booklet [*Hind Swaraj*] is a severe condemnation of modern civilisation. My conviction is deeper today than ever. I feel that, if India would discard modern civilisation she can only gain by doing so' (*Young India*, 26 January 1921). He held fast to his dogmas till the very end. In the 1940s, he would solemnly present *Hind Swaraj* to his appointed heir, Jawaharlal Nehru, saying that it contained the blueprint for the Indian Republic. When Nehru dismissed the book as being hopelessly out of date (Payne 1997: 220–1), Gandhi wrote to Nehru on 5 October 1945:

I have said I still stand by the system of Government envisaged in *Hind Swaraj*. These are not mere words. All the experience gained by me since 1908 when I wrote the booklet has confirmed the truth of my belief. (See Austin 2001: 39)

In Gandhi's fantasy, the priests and princes had always been kindly to the poor. He probably knew all this was untrue, and in the 'highest degree reactionary' (Payne 1997: 222), but Gandhi permitted no change in the relationship between the feudal lord and his peasant servants, or the rich and the poor. His denunciation of technology, industry, allopathic medicine, newspapers, and his so-called anti-capitalism were strange and full of irony. He often rode in railway trains and motor cars, and was a willing victim to what he termed 'medical tyranny'. He gave his consent to an operation for his appendicitis in 1924, and was at all times an ideal patient under the safe care of allopathic physicians. He railed against newspapers for prompting capricious and partisan information, and yet he relied on them to circulate his own brahmanic half-truths about India and things Indian. Through these contradictions, he himself showed that a return to 'tradition' was neither possible nor advisable. Likewise, his 'constructive' projects and *ashram-vyavastha* at Sabarmati and Wardha were financed by the captains of industry such as Ghanshyam Das Birla and Jamnalal Bajaj. All expenditure incurred on him and his large following was borne by his rich friends (as Gandhi himself admitted).[7] Should a man so dependent on the generosity of the rich—which must have spurred him to come up with his 'trusteeship' thesis—have fancied himself as the saviour of the poor? And did the Birlas and the Bajajs (who financed the Gandhian politics and went on to become India's top industrialists after Independence under a friendly Congress regime) share his anti-capitalist and anti-machine enthusiasm? Playing the double role of saint of the masses and champion of the propertied classes, Gandhi's hypocrisy was indeed staggering.

Within the Gandhi-Event a running discourse on renunciation and moral regeneration is carried on with another, of ruthless pursuit of monopoly, political power. The elaborate agenda of wresting moral authority from the British is but a prelude to investing the same on a set of power-driven politicians. The different Ashrams as part of constructive programmes, though intended for moral regeneration of Hindu society at large, were also propaganda centres for Congress politics. (Aloysius 1997: 176)

Gandhi carried many serious contradictions. His trademark poverty, as Sarojini Naidu once quipped pointing to the money that moved the Mahatma and his politics, cost a fortune: 'It costs a great deal of money to keep Gandhiji in poverty.' Gandhi never grasped that living like a poor man was very different from being one. Similarly, his discourse on the spiritual equality of all people was anchored in his faith in the discriminatory Varnashram Dharma. And he preached renunciation and virtue of powerlessness, but treated Congress as his personal fiefdom brooking no rivals in leaderships. His self-effacement was coupled with claims to exclusive access to the truth, and the careful cultivation of a large army of followers who took his every word like an article of faith.

Tagore, Nehru, Roy, and Ambedkar on Gandhism

Even some conscientious supporters found it embarrassing to align with the frustrating paradox that was Gandhi. Rabindranath Tagore, though he maintained a cordial relationship with Gandhi, was very critical of the core aspects of his politics, which the poet found to be chauvinistic and dangerous. Tagore was 'apprehensive that an isolationist obscurantism might develop if India, obsessed with the sin and shortcomings of Western civilisation, failed to take a broader view of humanity as a whole' (see Bhattacharya 1997: 8). A brahman aristocrat, Tagore himself celebrated a sophisticated version of brahmanism, but even he was horrified at times by Gandhi's gross glorification of varna order, as can be seen in Tagore's brilliant 1927 essay 'The Shudra Habit'. Unlike Gandhi, Tagore saw no moral, mental, or national nobility in maintaining hereditary occupations, assigning some to lowly occupations and others to superior ones by birth. If anything, the 'fixed external observations' and rituals of varna, he argued, restrict human freedom. The 'perpetuation of the dharma of caste' is nothing but a means to engender 'shudra habits' not only in shudras but in everyone imprisoned in the beliefs and rituals of caste.

Tagore was also critical of Gandhi's 'constructive' programme being symbolised by the *charkha* (hand-spinning) and the burning of foreign cloth as the panacea for India's problems. When Gandhi advised him to use the spinning wheel for half-an-hour a day, Tagore retorted, 'Why not eight and a half hours if it will help the country?' (see Edwards 1986: 204). In his essay 'The Cult of the Charkha' ([1925] 1997: 99–112), Tagore suggests that the root cause of India's poverty lies in our rotten social system and personal corruption, and gimmickry like the *charkha* only stops us from engaging with our deeper failures.

> The charkha is doing harm because of the undue prominence, which it has thus used whereby it only adds fuel to the smouldering weakness that is eating into our vitals. . . . [T]he blind suppression of intellect which guards our poverty in its dark dungeon will remain inviolate. This narrow activity will shed light only upon one detached piece of fact keeping its great background of truth densely dark. (Tagore, ibid.: 110–11)

Another person who saw through the Gandhian humbug was Jawaharlal Nehru, who posed in public as a Gandhi's disciple but almost wholly disagreed with his master's 'narrowly moralist' politics based on a muddled understanding of history and society. Although in his pursuit of power Nehru staked a claim to the Gandhian legacy, he has in his autobiography summarily written off the ideas contained in Gandhi's *Hind Swaraj* as 'utterly wrong ... and impossible of achievement'. To Nehru, this was true of Gandhism in general. This is what he writes in his *Discovery of India*:

> Even some of Gandhiji's phrases sometimes jarred upon me—thus his frequent reference to Rama Raj as a golden age which was to return. ... He was a very difficult person to understand, sometimes his language was almost incomprehensible to an average modern. But we felt that we knew him well enough to realise he was a great and unique man and a glorious leader, and having put our faith in him we gave him an almost blank cheque, for the time being at least. Often we discussed his fads and peculiarities among ourselves and said, half-humouredly, that when Swaraj came these fads must not be encouraged. (Nehru [1946] 1996)

Questioning Gandhian ideas of trusteeship, change of heart, and making moral men in an immoral society, Nehru argued that individuals and groups could be allowed to interpret ethics in accordance with their own interests only at the cost of democratic principles and procedure (Nehru [1936] 1999: 543). 'Is it reasonable to believe in the theory of trusteeship—to give unchecked power to an individual and expect him to use it entirely for the public good? Are the best of us so perfect as to be trusted in this way?' (ibid.: 528). Nehru added that this would only perpetuate 'the snobbery of birth, position, and economic power' and the consequences would be 'disastrous'. He rejected Gandhi's preaching that socio-economic justice could be ensured by ethical persuasion alone.

> If there is one thing that history shows it is this: that economic interests shape the political views of groups and classes. Neither reason nor moral considerations override these interests. Individuals may be converted, they may surrender their special privileges, although this is rare enough, but classes and groups do not do so. The attempt to convert a governing and privileged class into forsaking power and giving up its unjust privileges has therefore always so far failed, and there seems to be no reason whatever to hold that it will succeed in the future. (Nehru [1936] 1999: 544)

Nehru thus had fundamental problems with Gandhi's 'muddled humanitarianism'. The evocation of justice and non-violence notwithstanding, Gandhi's opposition to any suggestion of structural change, Nehru feared, would not only reinforce the status quo but also exacerbate the violence of the powerful:

> For years I have puzzled over this problem: why with all his love and solicitude for the underdog he yet supports a system which inevitably produces it and crushes it; why with all his passion for non-violence he is in favour of a political and social structure which is wholly based on violence and coercion? Perhaps it is not correct to say that he is in favour of such a system but ... he accepts the present order. (Nehru [1936] 1999: 515)

Unlike Gandhi, Nehru clearly grasped that British imperialism had forged strong links with the Indian feudal and business classes, and the success of the national movement depended on breaking the stranglehold of internal exploiting classes along with overthrowing colonialism. In an apparent reference to Gandhi's fantasy that in his swaraj the prince and the pauper would enjoy equal protection, Nehru said:

> [T]he Congress, it is said, must hold the balance between capital and labour, and zamindar and peasant. But the balance has been and is terribly weighted on one side and to maintain the status quo is to maintain injustice and exploitation. The only way to right it is to do away with the domination of any one class over the other. (Nehru 1929)

It is another matter altogether that Nehru's own actions, when in power, were not consistent with this understanding. But he was indeed dismayed at times to find that Gandhi not only lacked reasonable intellect and insight into social reality, but also 'perhaps an ethical attitude'.

> In spite of the closet association with him [Gandhi] for many years, I am not clear in my own mind about his objective. I doubt if he is clear himself. ... Be good in your personal individual lives, and all else will follow. That is not a political or scientific attitude, nor is it perhaps an ethical attitude. It is narrowly moralist, and it begs the question: What is goodness? Is it merely an individual affair or a social affair? Gandhiji lays all stress on character and attaches little importance to intellectual training and development.

Intellect without character is likely to be dangerous, but what is character without intellect? How, indeed, does character develop? (Nehru, see H. Mukherjee 1991: 208)

After making such candid comments about Gandhism, Nehru would bend over backwards to praise the great man. Personal dividends, caste–class interests, or whatever the reason, Gandhi and Nehru, despite all their differences, remained united in safeguarding entrenched interests.

Another important critic of Gandhi was M.N. Roy. A Marxist who later became a proponent of 'radical humanism', Roy presented a brilliant assessment of Gandhi and his ideology in a series of articles in the 1920s and 1930s. First, he pointed out that Gandhi's economic reconstruction would solve none of India's rural misery. Second, he argued that Gandhi's stress on social harmony in a grossly unequal society would reinforce existing inequalities. Third, he analysed Gandhi's reactionary view of history as rooted in nostalgia for an imaginary past that had never existed (Roy 1950; also see Dalton [1983] 2012; Kohn and Mcbride 2011: 152).

Later, Roy reworked these arguments and published them as *India's Message* (1950). The title essay is a perceptive critique of Gandhi's cultural nationalism and its disastrous consequences for the common Indians. Roy debunks the myth that India is more spiritual than the West by pointing out the rich tradition of religious mysticism and idealist philosophy in Europe. He argues that metaphysical speculation may take different forms but is not the exclusive possession of any particular culture. In both India and Europe, 'love, truth, goodness, etc.' are affirmed in theory and ignored in practice (p. 219). Gandhi's insistence that Indians have remained more faithful to truth and justice, he underlined, is wishful thinking, or more accurately, a dogmatic assertion. Even a cursory glance at history shows that rather than love and renunciation, Indian history is full of caste violence, the subordination of women, and oppression of the peasantry.

Roy concludes, 'The Gandhian utopia is a static society' (p. 217). The consequence of this static is to naturalise hierarchy and injustice. Moreover, the Gandhian nonviolence entails an acceptance of indirect forms of coercion that guarantee and perpetuate exploitation (p. 215). Elsewhere, Roy wrote that Gandhi served to hungry people 'spiritual moonshine', and the cult of non-violence was in fact 'the clever stratagem of the upper class to head off a revolutionary convulsion'. This was, it may be noted, the standard Marxist reading of Gandhi: Congress was frankly seen as the party of the bourgeois-landlords, and Gandhi as the leading representative of the capitalists and landlords (R.P. Dutt [1940] 1989: 621 ff.). Subsequently, however, the upper-caste Marxists, who never took any serious note of caste and brahmanism, gradually changed track and started singing hosannas of Gandhi as the liberator of India and 'classical modern figure' (Namboodiripad [1958] 2010) alongside other brahmanic intelligentsia.

The greatest critics of Gandhi and Gandhism were of course dalit-bahujan thinkers such as Periyar and Ambedkar. We saw Periyar's trenchant critique of the Congress and Gandhi in Chapter 6. Here, we shall see Ambedkar's. *What Congress and Gandhi Have Done to the Untouchables?* (1945, reprinted in *BAWS*, vol. 9) is a classic deconstruction of almost every aspect of Gandhian ideology and politics. In Ambedkar's eyes, barring Gandhi's 'illusory campaign' against untouchability, Gandhism is just another form of sanatanism, the ancient name for militant orthodox Hinduism (*BAWS*, vol. 9: 295–6). All Gandhism has done, he argues, is to find deceptive arguments to justify Hinduism and its dogmas. Hinduism is merely a set of rules, which gives it the appearance of a crude and cruel system, and Gandhism supplies a philosophy to smooth its surface and give it the appearance of decency and respectability. It says that 'All that is in Hinduism is well, all that is in Hinduism is necessary for public good.' Gandhian Hinduism suits the privileged and accords with their interest, but what does Gandhism mean, Ambedkar asks, to the caste-oppressed? Referring to Gandhi's differentiation between caste and varna, he asserts that this is an eyewash of an arch reactionary who beguiles the unthinking Hindu with arguments which make no distinction between fair and foul. All the oppressive instruments—the sanctity of the shastras, the iron law of caste and karma, the senseless law of the status of birth—which have mutilated and blighted the life of the lower orders are to be found intact and untarnished in the bosom of Gandhism (ibid.: 296–7).

Ambedkar also analyses the Gandhian critique of modernity and machinery and finds them fundamentally fallacious. He finds nothing original in the Gandhian diagnosis of economic ills either, insofar as it attributes them to science and technology. The arguments that modernisation caused monopolisation of wealth and resources in a few hands, as well as environmental decay, have merit, but they are all old theses propounded first by the likes of Rousseau, Ruskin, Carlyle, and Tolstoy.[8] Ambedkar concedes that excessive and indiscriminate mechanisation produces evils, but these were not due to machinery but to 'wrong social organisation which has made private property and pursuit of personal gain matters of absolute sanctity'. If science and technology have not benefited everybody, the remedy is not to condemn them but 'to alter the organisation of society so that the benefits will not be usurped by the few but will accrue to all' (ibid.: 283). (This point was made eloquently as early as 1930 by a Latin American radical Jose Mariategui ([1930] 1996), 'The spinning wheel is powerless to resolve the social question of any people', that is, a myth that romanticises a regressive socio-economic vision will ultimately prove disastrous.)

Arguing that throughout history human faculties have devised ways to make life easier through inventions, Ambedkar stresses that the machine, by lessening human toil, produces the much-needed leisure and makes a life of culture possible. This, he adds, is especially necessary in a democratic society which must assure leisure and culture to every citizen, not only to the privileged few. An undemocratic, class-divided society, however, can afford to do away with machinery by subjecting the majority to a life of toil and drudgery for the leisure and pleasure of the few. Caste-class cleavages are still with us, but Gandhism, he argues, makes social and economic hierarchy sacrosanct, with the consequent distinctions of rich and poor, high and low as permanent parts of social organisation. Social consequences of such rigid social structure, he argues, are pernicious as the class division sets in motion material and psychological influences harmful to the entire society. As there is no common place where the privileged and commoner meet, there is no social interaction between them, and such segregation not only dehumanises the lower order into slaves but also, though less perceptibly, brutalises the higher class:

> The isolation and exclusiveness following upon the class structure creates in the privileged classes the anti-social spirit of a gang. It feels it has interests 'of its own' which it makes its prevailing purpose to protect against everybody even against the interests of the State. It makes their culture sterile, their art showy, their wealth luminous and their manners fastidious. Practically speaking in a class structure there is, on the one hand, tyranny, vanity, pride, arrogance, greed, selfishness and on the other, insecurity, poverty, degradation, loss of liberty, self-reliance, independence, dignity and self-respect. (*BAWS*, vol. 9: 285)

The consequences of hierarchies are disastrous for a democratic society and nation, but Gandhism, Ambedkar said, wants caste–class structure to function as a living faith. The Gandhian idea of trusteeship of the rich for the poor is ridiculous, because in the conflict between ethics and economics the latter has always overpowered the former. Vested interests have never been known to have willingly divested themselves unless there was sufficient social and material force to compel them. Trusteeship, he argued, was a silly attempt to deceive the masses into believing that 'a little dose of moral rearmament to the propertied classes . . . will recondition them to such an extent that they will be able to withstand the temptation to misuse the tremendous powers that the class structure gives them over servile classes' (ibid.: 286).

Regarding Gandhi's advocacy of *Gram Swaraj* (village democracy), in which the traditional caste society is invested for discharging functions such as the spread of primary education or the settlement of disputes, Ambedkar points out that caste is the worst possible instrument for such tasks. The Gandhian theory of 'harmonious' rural culture (as against the ugliness of urban life) holds no water. Ambedkar dismisses the antagonism between village and city as simplistic.

Cautioning against the Gandhian utopia of a free India based on the 'beauty' and 'harmony' of the timeless village, Ambedkar underlined the gross injustices of village life in a speech at the Constituent Assembly. The love of the intellectual for the village community, he said, was based on Metcalfe's romanticism of it as 'idyllic self-sufficient little republics' that have survived the vicissitudes of many eras. Survived it has, he conceded, but on a low and selfish level. Far from the hub of freedom and creativity it was made out to be, the village was 'a sink of localism, a den of ignorance, narrow-mindedness and communalism'. Ambedkar emphasised the need of speedy industrialisation along with development of the agricultural sector.

The Nation as Social Democracy

Ambedkar wrote as early as 1920 in his journal *Mook Nayak* (Voice of the Voiceless) that it was not enough to be a free country, India must become a secular and social democracy, offering every citizen an opportunity to rise in life and creating favourable conditions to their advancement. A swaraj wherein the depressed classes were not given opportunities to pursue careers of their choice and to lead a dignified life would not be swaraj. In the same article he argued that 'if the Brahmins were justified in their attack upon and opposition to the unjust power of the British Government, the Depressed Classes were justified a hundred times more so in their opposition to the rulership of the Brahmins in case the transfer of power took place' (Keer [1954] 1971: 41).

While most historians depict Ambedkar as a spokesman of the depressed classes, they do not present the Congress, Gandhi and Nehru as flag-bearers of the upper classes. Ambedkar made this point repeatedly, underpinning the contradictory views of (governing) class and (servile) mass and observing that far from sacrificing their privileges for nationalism, the higher castes were exploiting nationalism to preserve them. Whenever the depressed classes asked for representation in the legislatures or the public services, the governing class raised the bogey of 'nationalism in danger'. They claimed that such measures were inimical to national unity. They gave the impression that by insisting that every place of power and authority should be filled by none but the best person available, they were strengthening the nation built on meritocracy. Exposing this merit mythology, he asserted that 'the argument completely fails to carry conviction when in practice one finds that having regard to the historical circumstances of India every time the best man is chosen he turns out to be a man from the governing class'. He asked who determined the criteria of merit. Had not education been monopolised for centuries by the governing class? Had not all strategic posts in the past been reserved for a particular class as per the injunctions of the Dharmashastras? Above all, could the 'best man' from the viewpoint of the governing class be necessarily regarded the 'best man' from the perspective of the oppressed?

Nobody will have any quarrel with the abstract principle that nothing should be done whereby the best shall be superseded by one who is only better and the better by one who is merely good and the good by one who is bad.... But man is not a mere machine. He is a human being with feelings of sympathy for some and antipathy for others. This is even true of the best man. He too is charged with the feelings of class sympathies and class antipathies. Having regard to these considerations the 'best' man from the governing class may well turn out to be the worst from the point of view of the servile classes. The difference between the governing classes and the servile classes in the matter of their attitudes towards each other is the same as the attitude a person of one nation has for that of another nation. (*BAWS*, vol. 9: 229–30)

Thus, nationalism to Ambedkar was not merely protest against and eventual expulsion of the alien domination but also the termination of internal oppression. The point was: for whose freedom the Congress was fighting.

... [W]ords such as society, nation and country are just amorphous, if not ambiguous, terms.... Nation though one word means many classes. Philosophically it may be possible to consider a nation as a unit but sociologically it cannot but be regarded as consisting of many classes and the freedom of the nation if it is to be a reality must vouchsafe the freedom of the different classes comprised in it, particularly those who are treated as the servile classes. (Ibid.: 201–2)

For the privileged, swaraj meant reinforcement of the traditional brahmanical order, whereas for the oppressed, swaraj meant the destruction of that order. For this reason the nationalism of the oppressed stood in direct contrast to the upper-class nationalism:

Speaking for the servile classes, I have no doubt that what they expect to happen in a sovereign and free India is a complete destruction of Brahmanism as a philosophy of life and as a social order. If I may say so, the servile classes do not care for social amelioration. The want and poverty which has been their lot is nothing to them as compared to the insult and indignity which they have to bear as a result of the vicious social order. (Ibid.: 212–13)

Ambedkar's nationalism, thus, rested on questioning and ultimately destroying the traditional social order so as to build a new democratic society, while Gandhi's project was to preserve the hierarchical social structure. Going by the form and substance of Congress politics, Ambedkar knew that once India got freedom, the dalit-bahujan would once again be subjected to discrimination, albeit in a vastly different and modernised garb.

Compelled to stand apart from the national movement, Ambedkar exposed the nationalists, most of whom were openly lauding caste as a superior form of social organisation, while others were supporting and practising it in private and the remaining few were pretending as though the problem did not exist. His criticism was denounced in nationalist circles as anti-patriotic, any attack on caste and brahmanism being seen as an attack on Indian culture.

To the dalit-bahujans who were trying through both individual and organisational efforts to break free from caste-based occupational, religio-cultural and educational restrictions or liabilities, the political plank and banner of the upper classes—protection of ancient culture and tradition in the name of nationalism—seemed to be plainly a call to reinforce the old caste order (Aloysius 2002). Not surprisingly, the domain of the national came to be increasingly identified with the privileged-caste exclusivism. The Congress-led nationalism and Ambedkar's nationalism have to be analysed within this broader framework where the upper and lower classes were locked in an irreconcilable conflict of interests.

Ambedkar's nationalism was founded on egalitarianism and fellow feeling between citizens. 'Nationality is a social feeling. It is a feeling of corporate sentiment of oneness which makes those who are charged with it feel that they are kith and kin' (*BAWS*, vol. 8: 31). Nationality is a 'consciousness of kind' which binds together those who have it. In other words, for Ambedkar nationalism was nothing if not a social democracy. 'Democracy is not merely a form of government. It is primarily a mode of associated living, of conjoint, communicated experience. It is essentially an attitude of respect and reverence towards fellowmen' (*BAWS*, vol. 1: 57). The anti-social spirit of caste, however, makes common activity and associated living impossible. Castes have an innate tendency to develop their own interests and do injustice or mischief to others. Caste creates a breeding ground for mutual distrust and animosity. It is hard for separate groups to recognise the equal rights of the others. The caste system is not only an assortment of castes, but also a congregate of several warring groups living for themselves in an insular environment with their selfish ideals (*BAWS*, vol. 1: 52). As he argues elsewhere, there cannot be just one caste. Caste can exist only in the plural. 'The genius of caste is to divide and disintegrate' (*BAWS*, vol. 5: 211). Caste-consciousness has also served to keep the memory of past feuds alive. Pinpointing caste-mindset as the mother of communalism, he argues that nationalism necessarily implies a negation of the caste spirit. 'Caste has killed public spirit. Caste has destroyed the sense of public charity. Caste has made public opinion impossible. Virtue has become caste-ridden, and morality has become caste-bound' (*BAWS*, vol. 1: 56).

In short, Ambedkar enunciates that casteless equality is the prerequisite for the nation to emerge. He strongly negates the notion that equality as a political theory is peculiar to the Western world. It is not Western or Eastern, but to be found everywhere as aspirations of the lower classes.

Ambedkar thus had basic differences with the Congress, but it was based on a principled politics which he carried from the beginning of his public life to the end, except for short periods of issue-based collaboration with the Congress. As he made clear in 1930 during the First Round Table Conference, he stood for freedom but wanted an honest debate about internal exploitation, with a view to develop a cultural and political vision to overcome caste, class, and gender discrimination. It is notable that those who attacked Ambedkar for his advocacy of affirmative action for the weaker sections were silent on the nomination of princes and landlords in the legislatures in the British India. Only Ambedkar opposed the nominations of *raja-maharajas* and demanded the representation of dalit-subalterns.

When the Constituent Assembly formally abolished untouchablity (for which Ambedkar had contributed more than anybody else) the privileged-caste members paid homage only to Gandhi with cries of *Mahatma Gandhi ki jai!* Referring to his humiliating marginalisation, Ambedkar said, 'I am not one of your national leaders. The utmost rank to which I have risen is that of a leader of the untouchables. I find even that rank has been denied to me. Thakkar Bapa very recently said that I was only the leader of the Mahars' (*BAWS*, vol. 8: 346).

Ambedkar suspected, not without reason, that a conspiracy was hatched by the Congress to divide the dalits along caste and sub-caste lines. Besides promoting incompetent and corrupt Harijan leaders with the lure of offices, 'silver bullets' through the nationalist press were freely used for creating divisions in the ranks of the dalit-subalterns. It must have been under such provocation that Ambedkar had asserted that his loyalty to the dalits came first and to India next. In 1935, he made it clear that he wanted a total break with oppressive Hinduism. In 1936, he founded the Independent Labour Party with radical socio-economic objectives. In 1942, he established the Scheduled Castes Federation, and three years later he set up People's Education Society dedicated to the spread of higher education.

Radical Realism Amidst the Euphoria of Freedom: The Constitution and the Hindu Code Bill

Ambedkar's radicalism in the 1930s as a political agitator-organiser who demanded swaraj was replaced in the first half of 1940s by his tactical co-operation with the British. His decision to join the Viceroy's Executive Council as Labour Member appears to be in retaliation to the utter indifference of the privileged-caste nationalists to burning social issues. Apparently the mutual antagonism between Ambedkar and the Congress leadership had by then become irreconcilable. Ambedkar was impatient for structural change and annihilation of caste while all Gandhi could offer was assurances of a 'change of heart' within the parameters of Varnashrama Dharma. That is why even at the height of the Quit India movement, Ambedkar remained aloof from the agitation and concentrated his efforts on benefits for the dalit-subalterns. As the Labour Member of the Viceroy's Council he authored a labour legislation which became the model on the subject for much that followed after Independence. He constituted a Labour Conference to consider matters like the formation of a Joint Labour Management Committee and an Employment Exchange, and initiated measures to institute social security for industrial workers. Similarly, his pioneering work on water resources development proved to be far-sighted and had a powerful bearing on the water management policy in independent India.

However, the rapidly changing political situation in the 1940s and imminent independence from the British forced Ambedkar to change his strategy and co-operate with the Congress for a brief while. This co-operation was issue-based, and even in this hour of bonhomie he did not succumb to the nationalist rhetoric. His main concern was to ensure the best possible deal for the dalit-subalterns in the wake of Independence. To safeguard their rights, at least in the theoretical framework, he joined the Nehru cabinet as Minister of Law. On the strength of his constitutional expertise, his brilliant work at the Round Table Conference, his membership of the Joint Committee on Indian Constitutional Reform, and his participation in the Constituent Assembly, he was elected Chairman of the Drafting Committee for the new Constitution.

Ambedkar's interest in Constitution-making was not only due to his commitment to get the depressed classes essential safeguards in the Constitution which his participation made possible. He took up this backbreaking job which required a rare degree of legal expertise also because 'he had a wider vision of the kind of society and polity that should be brought into existence in India' (Gore 1993: 183). It is significant that he wanted nationalisation of land and industries, and a time-bound scheme for social and economic empowerment of the poor. He wanted insurance to be a state monopoly and every adult Indian to be compelled to have life insurance. When such schemes and provisions were set aside, he tried to make the Directive Principles of State for social welfare as rigorous as possible. However, he was aware that a constitution is like a pledge one makes to oneself. Its accomplishment lies in one's sincerity and ability to live up to it. He said the problem was not the laws but the lack of their implementation due to 'bad administration' by the classes who practised 'tyranny and oppression' against the weak. The remedy, he argued, was to make members of the suppressed communities part of the various organs of governance and civil services.

Summing up his arguments in the Constituent Assembly on 25 November 1949, just before the Draft Constitution was adopted for the Republic of India, Ambedkar said many prophetic things in a forceful manner. He warned—even in that hour of euphoria—of the dangers both to India's independence and her democratic constitution. First, he advocated holding fast to constitutional and democratic methods of achieving the social and economic objective (*BAWS*, vol. 13: 1215). Second, to make democracy strong, he felt the need for vigilance against hero-worship which leads to people's servitude and subversion of institutions. 'There is nothing wrong in being grateful to great men . . . but there are limits to gratefulness. . . . Bhakti in religion may be a road to salvation of the soul. But in politics, bhakti or hero-worship is a sure road to degradation and to eventual dictatorship' (ibid.).

Third, Ambedkar advocated the conscious fostering of social and economic equality so that the democracy that the country has embraced after centuries of wilderness could become real social democracy.

We must make our political democracy a social democracy as well. Political democracy cannot last unless there lies at the base of it social democracy. Social democracy . . . means a way of life which recognises liberty, equality and fraternity as the principles of life. These principles . . . form a union of trinity in the sense that to divorce one from the other is to defeat the very purpose of democracy. Liberty cannot be divorced from equality, equality cannot be divorced from liberty. Nor can liberty and equality be divorced from fraternity. Without equality, liberty would produce the supremacy of the few over the many. Equality without liberty would kill individual initiative. Without fraternity, liberty and equality could not become a natural course of things. (Ibid.: 1216)

Pointing out the institutionalised inequality of caste, he said that Indian society had not recognised the values of equality and fraternity and 'on the economic plane, there are some who have immense wealth as against many who live in abject poverty'. Equality in principle and widespread inequality in practice, he stressed, would create a dangerous situation for the new democracy.

On the 26th of January 1950, we are going to enter into a life of contradictions. In politics we will have equality and in social and economic life we will have inequality. In politics we will be recognising the principle of one man one vote and one vote one value. In our social and economic life, we shall, by reason of our social and economic structure, continue to deny the principle of one man one value. How long shall we continue to live this life of contradictions? (Ibid.)

Ambedkar also cautioned against the 'delusion' that India was already a nation. It was fragmented into thousands of castes, which was a menace to the emerging nation. 'The sooner we realise that we are not as yet a nation in the social and psychological sense of the word, the better for us. For then only we shall realise the necessity of becoming a nation and seriously think of ways and means of realising the goal' (ibid.: 1217). The remedies, he said, may not be very pleasant to some as in this country political power had for far too long been the monopoly of a few, but the long-suppressed people were tired of being governed, they were impatient to govern themselves.

If we wish to preserve the Constitution in which we have sought to enshrine the principle of Government of the people, for the people and by the people, let us resolve not to be so tardy in the recognition of the evils that lie across our path ... nor to be weak in our initiative to remove them. This is the only way to serve the country. I know of no better. (Ibid.: 1218)

Ambedkar's role as a member of the Union cabinet was secondary during the Constitution-making period. After that, his differences with the Congress over several policy matters cropped up. He saw that there was an upper-caste caucus in the Congress that took decisions on important issues before they were placed before the Cabinet. The Congress politics and priorities upset him but he somehow continued in the Cabinet until September 1951. As Law Minister, he introduced and steered through Parliament the Representation of People Bill. But his heart was set on the Hindu Code Bill, which he regarded as an indispensable part of his struggle for social change. The Bill included Hindu women's rights to inheritance and property. Conservative Hindu elements, including many top Congress leaders, raised a stiff opposition and put spokes in the passage of the Bill. Nehru too, who was seen as favouring the Bill, could not do much as the Congress refused to issue a whip in favour of the Bill. A vicious campaign was orchestrated against the Bill and Ambedkar was targeted. Jere Shastri, one of the Shankaracharyas, was not the only one to abuse Ambedkar as 'an untouchable who dared to interfere with our Hindu practices'.

Ambedkar was also aggrieved that despite Nehru's promise to give him charge of an administrative portfolio in addition to law, he had not only been denied this but even shut out from the policy-making Cabinet Committees. This was a serious thing because the Cabinet worked mostly in committees and these committees 'worked behind an iron curtain' so that 'others who are not members have only to take joint responsibility without any opportunity of taking part in the shaping of policy'. Ambedkar resigned from the Cabinet. He was not allowed even to read out his resignation statement in the Parliament and he had to issue a Press brief in which he spelt out his reasons for leaving. The Government's decision to drop the Hindu Code Bill; the betrayal of the dalits; a ruinous Kashmir policy; and the fiction of Cabinet responsibility were the reasons he gave for his resignation. As a person dedicated to the uplift of dalit-subalterns, he was distressed over the non-serious approach of the Nehru government to this issue. He challenged Nehru to issue a public statement detailing what the government had done or intended to do for the downtrodden.

Unlike Nehru, Ambedkar was deeply aware that 'democracy in [the caste-obsessed] India is only top dressing on an Indian soil which is essentially undemocratic'. He argued that the contradictions and inequalities in Indian society were not just economic, but also religious and cultural. The outcastes and those lowered in the caste hierarchy, he stressed, needed a new imaginary and a new emancipatory identity along with vibrant participation in democratic politics to overcome their centuries-old subordination.

Ambedkar's alignment with Buddhism in his last years, glimpses of which we saw in Chapter 2, was animated with the vision of a casteless and enlightened India. As he put it, the purpose of Buddha's dhamma was to reconstruct the world. With Buddhism as an alternative to Varnashrama Dharma, he wanted to give a cultural and moral foundation to the struggle for social renewal and personal transformation. Accordingly, he strove to construct a new Buddhism in the mould of an open-ended and secular humanism, shorn of traditional rituals and orthodoxies, that he termed Navayana (New Vehicle). Any consciously built identity presupposes the existence of the other, and the Ambedkarite Buddhist identity was clearly in contention against the caste-bound Hinduism which was aligned with the 'Indian' identity in the elitist nationalist discourse. 'Ambedkar ultimately undertook a formal religious conversion not as merely a personal act, living his conversion not as a personal salvation but as militant repudiation of caste society and as an invitation to mass repudiation of the same' (Ahmad 2002: 85).

Summarising, Ambedkar was not merely a champion of the dalits or scheduled castes—which he definitely was—but a representative voice for all marginalised classes, with an alternative vision of society, culture, and nation. His ideology and struggle—which have been either obscured or distorted in the academia like that of the people he represented—was not only remarkably creative, but also national and democratic in the best sense.

Notes

1. Gait issued a preparatory circulation—detailing exact criteria—to his provincial commissioners on the question of drawing the border between Hindus and those communities/tribes who could be regarded as such. The circular contained six questions to resolve the issue:
    a. Do the members of the caste or tribe worship the great Hindu Gods?
    b. Are they allowed to enter Hindu temples or to make offerings at the shrine?
    c. Will good brahmans act as their priests?

d. Will degraded brahmans do so? In that case, are they recognised as brahmans by persons outside the caste, or are they brahmans only in name?
   e. Will clean castes take water from them?
   f. Do they cause pollution, (a) by touch; (b) by proximity?
   (*The Tribune,* 12 November 1910, see Mendelsohn and Vicziany 2000: 28)
2. For a long while Gandhi himself was opposed to the untouchables entering temples, saying, 'How is it possible that the Antyajas [untouchables] should have the right to enter the existing temples? As long as the law of caste and ashram has the chief place in Hindu Religion, to say that every Hindu can enter every temple is a thing that is not possible today' (*Gandhi Shikshan*, vol. II: 132; cited in Ambedkar, *BAWS*, vol. 9: 107).
3. Many are 'under the impression that Pandit Nehru is a socialist and does not believe in caste', Ambedkar writes and quotes Pattabhi Sitaramayya from the latter's Introduction to the *Life of Pandit Jawaharlal Nehru* (written by Y.G. Krishnamurti), 'Pandit Nehru is very conscious of the fact that he is a Brahmin.' Nehru's sister, Vijaya Laxmi Pandit, was equally proud of her caste identity. 'At the All-India Women's Conference held in Delhi in December 1940, the question of not declaring one's caste in the Census Return was discussed. Ms. Pandit disapproved of the idea and said she did not see any reason why she should not be proud of her Brahmin blood and declare herself as a Brahmin at the Census.' He quotes this from J.E. Sanjana's *Sense and Nonsense in Politics* (see Ambedkar, *BAWS*, vol. 9: 208–9). Also worth recalling is what Nehru's brother-in-law Ranjit Pandit (Vijaya Laxmi's husband) said to Romain Rolland in 1926 in presence of Nehru:
   He [Ranjit Pandit] professes a theory that between the Aryans of India (he says 'Brahmins'—he is one of them, like his wife and Nehru himself) and the Europeans, there is only a difference of language and climate, but no difference whatsoever of temperament or civilisation. An Indian Brahmin in England, in France, etc., within a vey short time assimilates perfectly all the ideas, and recognises them as closely similar to his own. They come of the same stock. (Rolland 1951: 145, see Deleury 2005: 317–18)
4. Ambedkar argues that the brahman is the principal governing class in India on the basis of (a) his most elevated, even sacred, position in the caste society, and (b) preponderance in administration. The brahman has always cultivated others as his allies provided they are prepared to work with him in subordinate position. In ancient and medieval times, the brahman made such an alliance with the sword-wielding kshatriya, and together as ruling classes they controlled and exploited the masses. However, in the modern age, dominated more by money than the sword, the brahman, he contends, has left the kshatriya and bonded with the class with money, the bania. Huge money required to run political machinery could come only from

the bania who for his part has 'realised that money invested in politics gives large dividends'. This class, led by the Ahmedabad millowners and Bombay businessmen, was financing the Congress largely because Gandhi, who hailed from this caste, could be trusted to represent its interests. Ambedkar quotes Gandhi who himself admitted—in an interview with Louis Fisher on 6 June 1942—that the Congress was almost totally financed by 'rich friends'. As Fisher writes in *A Week with Gandhi*:

I said I had several questions to ask him about the Congress Party. Very highly placed Britishers, I recalled, had told me that Congress was in the hands of big business and that Gandhi was supported by the Bombay millowners who gave him as much money as he wanted. 'What truth is there in these assertions', I asked.

'Unfortunately, they are true', he declared simply, 'Congress hasn't enough money to conduct its work. We thought in the beginning to collect four annas (about eight cents) from each member per year and operate on that. But it hasn't worked'.

'What proportion of the Congress budget', I asked, 'is covered by rich Indians?'

'Practically all of it', he stated. 'In this ashram, for instance, we could live much more poorly than we do and spend less money. But we do not and the money comes from our rich friends.' (See *BAWS*, vol. 9: 208)

5. Jabbar Patel, the author of a remarkable cinematic biography of Ambedkar, who intensely researched the Gandhi–Ambedkar tussle to ensure that everything filmed was historically accurate (as the film was funded by the Gandhi-deifying government) holds that Gandhi behaved like 'a cunning, selfish politician always anxious to outwit Ambedkar. . . . That is why Ambedkar felt so slighted. Ambedkar tried his best to explain his point of view but Gandhi was not ready to listen. Gandhi pushed him to the edge by refusing to listen to him. That comes out clearly if you look at the historical evidence.' (Interview with Pritish Nandy, *The Times of India*, New Delhi, 29 June 2000).

6. 'I do not regard Jainism or Buddhism as separate from Hinduism', Gandhi wrote in *Young India* of 20 October 1927.

7. See note no. 4 above.

8. The neo-Gandhians like Ashis Nandy (1983) and Bhikhu Parekh (1989) who regard Gandhi's critique of modernity as strikingly original and portray it as 'critical traditionalism'—a uniquely Eastern rejection of the colonialist West and its oppressive science, fail to recognise this simple truth. Gandhi himself concedes that his critique of modernity draws 'freely, explicitly and enthusiastically from Western sources' (Kohn and Mcbride 2011: 148). In the appendix to *Hind Swaraj* he suggests that readers who want to explore his arguments in depth should read Tolstoy, Thoreau, Mazzini, Plato, Maine, and Ruskin. He especially refers to Edward Carpenter's *Civilisation: Its Causes and Cures* ([1889] 1921) in the text, and in fact much of his criticism of civilisation and science are simply brahmanised reiteration of Carpenter's work.

Epilogue

Institutionalised Discrimination from the Past to the 'Democratic' Present

> He who would confine his thought to present time will not understand present reality.
>
> JULES MICHELET (1846)

> The Indian State can deliver a nuclear bomb and launch satellites but not universal primary education and decent public health. This is not an accident. It is a choice made by the elite who have been in power for 60 years and reflects their values. . . . The Indian State has been mainly manned by upper caste elites and they do not consider the lower orders deserving of education and health.
>
> MEGHNAD DESAI (2013)

Today, India (after China and the US) has the world's third largest middle class (250–300 million); 72 enlisted dollar billionaires (black-market economy and overseas banks allow some crooks to remain unlisted); and the single largest concentration of the world's poor (800 million), mostly illiterate or semi-literate. Before the liberalisation (1991), India was a socialist state which actually worked to empower and educate the privileged castes. Now, the same groups, hiding behind a middle-class identity, are reaping the benefits of free-market bonanza while the poor are fully exposed to the relentless inequalities of crony capitalism. As India is producing thousands of millionaires, it has one-half of the world's malnourished children and one-third of the world's most poor. India produces 100,000 students a year in global top 10 per cent and also churns out millions with zero skills. Millions of children, despite the recently introduced Right to Education legislation, are unable to go to school. And those who do continue to be trapped in underfunded, brutal, and ineffective state schools which are among the worst in the world.

Despite the remarkable economic growth of recent years, India continues to rank at the bottom of the world tables on literacy and public health. In 2010, 43 per cent of children below the age of 5 years were underweight, 48 per cent were stunted. Half of the population did not have toilets and defecated in the open. Today, illiteracy smothers one in every three in India whose elites pride themselves on its glorious intellectual tradition. One out of every three persons in the world lacking safe drinking water is an Indian; every fourth person on the planet dying of water-borne diseases is an Indian. India has the highest numbers of people suffering from blindness, hepatitis-B, tuberculosis, leprosy and AIDS. It has the highest number of occupational casualties. It shares with the sub-Saharan countries the highest infant mortality rates. There is one doctor (mostly unavailable) for 25-odd villages (containing over 25,000 people) in parts of the country while a large chunk of the health budget goes to urban hospitals. All this in a 65-year old republic whose Constitution (Article 47) declares, 'The State shall regard the raising of the level of nutrition and the improvement of public health as among its primary duties.'

Who are the inhabitants of this suppressed India? Around 45 per cent of the Indian poor are rural or urban labourers. Another 45 per cent are marginal farmers. The remaining 10 per cent are artisans. Millions of these poor are migrating to urban centres in search of employment. Save a few thousands, almost all these 'disenfranchised' people are dalit-bahujans, including the Muslim masses. What do the privileged strata which made most out of the modern Indian state think about the 'other India'? Rajni Kothari observed (in the so-called socialist phase itself) that the other, non-modern and 'vernacular' India was 'not just getting marginalised and pushed to the peripheries of socio-economic and political systems', they were also 'pushed to the peripheries of our consciousness'.

As I talk to my friends, my relatives, my professional colleagues today, I get a feeling of total ignorance of the other India. When in fact they are forced to take note, such as when they walk through the pavements on which people are sleeping, there is a feeling of revulsion, of rejection, of contempt, not of compassion, empathy and least of all of any sense of guilt. (Kothari 1986)

The policies and priorities of the ruling elite have been widening the gulf between the two Indias. The logic of economic liberalisation and modernisation in essentially technological terms have not only widened all-round inequalities but also driven the marginalised out of the policy framework of the state. The privileged class nurtures the illusion that what is good for it is also good for the country as a whole.

Under aggressive privatization, with an exploding population and capital-intensive, technology-driven development, the number of the jobless or semi-employed is rising. Private and public enterprises, known as the formal sector, are able to absorb only 10 per cent of the employable people; the rest (the 90 per cent) still work in the informal sector. The worst sufferers are the traditionally oppressed groups—the people with combined and cumulative disadvantages of low social status, low education, and little access to bureaucracy and political power. On the other hand, traditionally privileged castes, with generations of education, wealth, and power behind them, are making use of their social capital and systematic networking, cornering all opportunities of development, and preaching the virtues of economic trickle down. It is no gainsaying that the state is not a neutral observer of things even in the era of free market: its policies and actions affect the distribution of income, wealth and power in a major way. Contrary to its professed goal, the state is not keen to help the poor but those who are already capable of helping themselves.

Amidst the claims of great changes sweeping India, its upper and middle classes are still composed of former brahman, bania, and kshatriya groups. This caste cluster—the heavy preponderance of upper castes in key domains and modern professions—holds true for the social composition of capitalist class and the intelligentsia. According to a recent survey, not even one of the 315 editors and senior leaders of the print and electronic media was a dalit or adivasi (Dreze and Sen 2011). Perhaps there were two or three OBCs, who generally hide their humiliating shudra identity for sheer survival. The situation is no different in academia. During 2010–11, nearly half the teaching positions reserved for dalits and adivasis in twenty-four central universities remained unfilled. The situation of the OBCs was much worse. As on 31 March 2011, of the 5,876 faculty members in the central universities the faculty representation of dalit-bahujan categories was as follows: dalit 513 (8.73 per cent), adivasi 203 (3.45 per cent) and OBC 195 (3.31 per cent). The proportion of representation of these groups diminishes drastically as one moves up the faculty hierarchy (Oommen 2013). According to a newspaper editorial, 'The situation is unlikely to be very different in other educational institutions.' The editorial makes the point that 'a loosely defined concept of merit is conveniently used to keep out eligible candidates. Laws and rules are often undermined by systemic bias' (*The Hindu*, 6 July 2012).

Though rendered invisible by the elite-controlled media and academia, low-caste status still spells disadvantage and disaster. People working as agricultural labourers, scavengers, leather workers, fishermen and the like are almost wholly culled from the toiling castes. Almost all labour-intensive, low-paid work continues to be 'almost wholly shudra-manned. The class position of the shudra communities is thus obvious. It is possible to come across a rich shudra but the reality is that much more frequently it is the poor shudra that we come by' (Chatterjee 2010). The vast majority of those in menial and despised occupations—in the farm, factory and households—belong to the lowered castes, while the overwhelming majority of those in the highest or most coveted professions—industry, business, medicine, engineering, the media, and academia—are from the upper castes (Panini 1996: 32–6). In a sociological study of contemporary India, Satish Deshpande (2004: 120) demonstrates, in every field that offers a promising career, 'the upper castes dominate and the middle and lower castes are more or less severely under-represented. . . . It is no longer possible to evade these realities as being the by-product of historical inequities. We have to face up to the uncomfortable truth that caste inequality has been and is being reproduced in independent India.'

Contrary to the refrain that economic growth and expansion of middle class alongside new opportunities of individual mobility have made caste irrelevant (as 'its hierarchy is replaced by competing equalities'), the ground surveys and statistics show the reality of huge reproduction of inequalities in caste terms. Two outstanding studies of existing data on caste and occupation and standard of living confirm this reality (Thorat and Newman 2010; A. Deshpande 2011). As the author of *The Grammar of Caste* puts it,

> [D]ata point more towards continuation of traditional hierarchies rather than towards their dissolution, with upper castes at the top, Scheduled Castes-Scheduled Tribes at the bottom, and Other Backward Classes (OBCs) somewhere in between. . . . What is very revealing is that lip-service to merit notwithstanding, contemporary, formal, urban sector labour markets show a deep awareness of caste, religious, gender, and class cleavages, and that discrimination is very much a modern sector phenomenon, perpetuated in the present. So it is neither a thing of the past nor confined to the rural areas. (A. Deshpande 2011: xiv-xv)

Another scholar who has studied caste over the years makes a point which helps us better grasp why things are as they are: 'There can be no denying that for centuries [dalits and other lowered castes] have been at the receiving end of all communication—information (nay, disinformation), sermons, commands and the like, and compelled into a position of powerlessness. Not surprisingly, the legacy persists' (Chatterjee 2010: 285). Yet another social analyst more than affirms this, arguing with compelling examples how caste is the main culprit that makes India undemocratic, notwithstanding constitutional laws to the contrary: 'Democracy in India is reduced to that of a few privileged castes who manage individuals to control all institutions. Therefore, it has become in practice only an oligarchy of castes, and not a truly representative form of government. As a result, the spirit of democracy to ensure social justice is lost' (Chalam 2007).

It is the kind of horror that haunted Ambedkar both before and after Independence. Unmasking the ugly, hypocritical universe that existed behind that soul-stirring phrase 'Freedom Struggle', he had pointed out that the kind of freedom the elite nationalism was striving for was the freedom to perpetuate the discrimination and exploitation. It is futile to argue that Ambedkar's agenda was less patriotic, less relevant in the colonial period than Gandhi's. The real point is a contemporary one: the Ambedkarite agenda for dignity, education, healthcare, and equality of opportunity remain largely unrealised, though the major Gandhian objective was accomplished in 1947 with the attainment of freedom. Ambedkar's insight into Indian reality, especially his critique of caste and its consequences, can help us better grasp why the judiciary, bureaucracy, the army, and higher education remain so unrepresentative? Why do the dalit-bahujans continue to be excluded from the portals of knowledge and power despite the 'deepening' democracy? And why their presence in the booming market economy, industries, print and electronic media, television, film and music industries is so small?

Is it simply the triumph of merit or does systemic discrimination still exist in India? Are the people who slog in fields and factories, who interact with instruments of production and services, still not treated as 'inferior beings'? Is there no link between the political extremism, religious terrorism and the growing rich–poor divide? Is an egalitarian change in India possible without a cultural reconstruction? Had Phule and Ambedkar been alive today, would they have chosen to bask in the 'glory' of their elitist cooption into the pantheon of great Indians? Or would they have stepped off their pedestals, shrugged off the empty adulation and walked out onto the streets, in villages and towns, to rally their people once more?

Behind the smokescreen of 'national development', the privileged sections get many kinds of direct or hidden support from the government. To give one telling example, contrary to popular perception, the state subsidises the higher education of the rich and the resourceful at the cost of primary education of the poor.

A large number of schools in India are privately owned. Their funds, though, come from the public. As much as 60 per cent of government expenses on schools goes in grants to privately owned institutions. In fourteen major Indian states, education claims 32 per cent of all subsidies on social services. Much less than half of this is spent on primary education.

Paucity of funds does not seem to cripple institutes of higher learning run by and for the elite. (Sainath 1996: 52)

Such dubious policy has resulted in a few Indians doing exceedingly well, while for the majority, education only means identifying letters; in fact, in the villages, the illiterate as well as the 'literate' don't even manage that. India's literacy rates are no better than those of the sub-Saharan Africa, the most undeveloped region of the world (Dreze and Sen 1998: 114). Why India is doing no better than sub-Saharan Africa in the field of basic education appals Professors Sen and Dreze because, as they point out, unlike many countries of sub-Saharan Africa, India since Independence has been relatively protected from the calamities of political instability, military rule, civil war, and recurring famine. The persistence of endemic illiteracy appears odious also in view of its impressive record in higher education and scientific research. Enormous educational disparities, in fact, have roots in enormous social and economic inequalities.

The Indian elites still seem to hold that their knowledge, power and prosperity have to be based on ignorance, powerlessness and poverty of the lower orders. The mindset of hierarchy has always valorised and buttressed this tradition. Despite all the changes, old attitudes still persist and affect children of dalit-bahujan families—*education is not for you*. Ascriptive attitudes, protected from above, produce active discrimination, and hierarchical attitudes internalised within the family make it difficult for the children of the lowered castes to see themselves as people who can excel in intellectual pursuits. Such attitudes, unfortunately, have been strengthened by no less a person that the 'Father of the Nation'. Gandhi praised 'the shudra who only serves the higher castes as a matter of religious charity, who has nothing to call his own and who has no desire for ownership.' One wonders had Gandhi not toed the brahmanical line, and not equated the discriminatory Varnashrama Dharma with the national dharma, would he have been made the 'Mahatma' and deified as the 'Father of the Nation'?

Modernisation and technological advance without attitudinal change towards egalitarianism have, in fact, heralded a neo-brahmanic dominance. Obviously, technology and electronic gadgets cannot become an instrument of people's empowerment without a change of mentality. The need is to thoroughly debrahmanise values that still pervade all aspects of life, culture and economy. To show how poverty is being perpetuated by the coexistence of caste distinction with modern technology, Kancha Ilaiah cites a specific example: billions of rupees that circulate in the name of temple economy do not benefit a single dalit family at a time when Hindu religion has been operating in an inter-connected manner with advanced technology. 'Today more computers are being used to modernise the images of Hindu deities than for computing the nature of caste-class inequalities and the number of atrocities taking place on dalits and women' (Ilaiah 2004: 175).

Caste and corruption are symbiotic and tend to feed and prosper each other. To take but one example, the judiciary, the supposed citadel of justice, is also the citadel of caste elites and their vested interests. It remains most unrepresentative, and has in its own way contributed to subvert the egalitarian goal enshrined in the Constitution. A Parliamentary Committee on the Welfare of Scheduled Castes and Scheduled Tribes headed by Karia Munda in its second report in September 2000 shows how the judiciary and the bar in the higher courts is 'neither sympathetic nor unbiased to the cause of backward classes'. It points out that the members of the judiciary have so far been drawn from the very section of society which is 'infected by ancient prejudices and is dominated by notions of gradations in life.... The internal limitation of class interests of such judges does not allow them full play of their intellectual honesty and integrity in their decisions. These judges very often betray a mindset more useful to the governing class than the servile class' (Munda 2000). Lamenting that there were only 15 SC and 5 ST judges among the 481 High Court judges in the country and there was no judge from this social group in the Supreme Court as on 1 May 1998, the Committee reports: 'Judges take oath that they (will) uphold the Constitution and the laws. But the Supreme Court and a few high courts by claiming power over the Constitution, practise untouchability and are disobeying the Constitution with regard to Articles 16(4) and 16(4a)' (ibid.)

The Committee scoffs at the notion that the judiciary is a 'super speciality' service with 'merit' as its bedrock. 'To argue that only

those with merit have found a berth in the judiciary is specious...
. This presupposes that those from the weaker sections do not have enough merit.' Citing the observation of Justice P.B. Sawant in a landmark judgement in the early 1990s, in which he had argued how in the name of merit and national interests 'all aspects of life are controlled, directed and regulated mostly to suit the sectional interests of a small section of society which does not exceed a tenth of the total population', the panel contends:

> How can 10 per cent of the population represent the 'national interest' and is not the so-called merit the result of the cumulative advantages on social, educational and economic fronts enjoyed by a select social group? The Supreme Court which is the nation's last court of appeal, cannot afford to appear unjust in its own domain. But unfortunately that seems to have happened over the years. Judges have, of course, the power, though not the right, to ignore the mandate of a statute and render judgments despite it. (Munda 2000)

If this is the state of affairs in the judiciary, one can imagine the plight of dalit-bahujans in other areas of national life. The classical pattern of excluding the commoners from knowledge and power is embedded in the unwritten codes of the state and its institutions. Various facets of modernisation—industrial and technological developments, liberal-democratic laws enshrined in the Constitution, modern educational institutions, etc.—have not been able to offset the dominance of caste in newer and subtler forms. The caste structure has taken technological breakthroughs in its stride, and 'this transition, not transformation, has been quite smooth in as much as the skilled human resources with education, training and experience (as a result of monopolies of the high castes over them since the beginning of Indian society) have taken control of the new developments and as such only they have been the beneficiaries' (Chatterji 1998: 36). The various elements of the brahmanical social order, are still functional as instruments of distribution of power excluding the many.

Sita and Shambuka, Karna and Ekalavya are still clamouring for their rightful place in Indian society.

Bibliography

Acharya, Poromesh. 1996. 'Indigenous Education and Brahminical Hegemony in Bengal.' In *The Transmission of Knowledge in South Asia*, ed. Nigel Crook, pp. 98–118. Delhi: Oxford University Press.

Ahmad, Aijaz. 1992. *In Theory: Classes, Nations, Literatures*. London and New York: Verso.

———. 2002. *On Communalism and Globalisation: Offensives of the Far Right*. Delhi: Three Essays.

Ahmad, Imtiaz, ed. 1973. *Caste and Social Stratification among the Muslims of India*. Delhi: Manohar.

Aktor, Mikael. 1999. 'Smritis and Jatis: The Ritualization of Time and the Continuity of the Past.' In *Invoking the Past: The Uses of History in South Asia*, ed. Daud Ali, pp. 258–79. Delhi: Oxford University Press.

Alam, Javeed. 1996. 'Tradition in India Under Interpretative Stress: Notes on Its Growing Social Irrelevance.' In Indu Banga and Jaidev, eds., *Cultural Reorientation in Modern India*, pp. 66–79. Shimla: Indian Institute of Advanced Study.

———. [2004] 2012. *Who Wants Democracy?* Delhi: Orient BlackSwan.

Ali, Daud, ed. 1999. *Invoking the Past: The Uses of History in South Asia*. Delhi: Oxford University Press.

Allen, Charles. 2002. *The Buddha and the Sahibs: The Men Who Discovered India's Lost Religion*. London: John Murray.

Aloysius, G. 1997. *Nationalism without a Nation in India*. Delhi: Oxford University Press.

———. 1998. *Religion as Emancipatory Identity: A Buddhist Movement among the Tamils under Colonialism*. Delhi: New Age International Publishers.

———. 2000. 'Caste In and Above History.' In S.L. Sharma and T.K. Oommen, eds., *Nation and National Identity in South Asia*, pp. 151–73. Delhi: Orient Longman.

———. 2002. 'Caste Against Nation in Ambedkar', *The Radical Humanist*, February and March.

———. 2010. *The Brahminical Inscribed in Body-politic*. Delhi: Critical Quest.

Altekar, A.S. 1956. 'Buddhism and Indian Culture', *The Journal of the Bihar Research Society,* Buddha Jayanti spl. issue, vol. 2.

Althusser, Louis. 1971. 'Ideology and Ideological State Apparatuses.' In idem, *Lenin and Philosophy and Other Essays,* pp. 121–73. London: New Left Books.

Ambedkar, B.R. 1987–2003. *Dr Babasaheb Ambedkar: Writings and Speeches (BAWS),* vols. 1–17, ed. Vasant Moon et al. Bombay: The Education Department, Govt. of Maharashtra. 'Castes in India' (1916) and 'Annihilation of Caste' (1936), vol. 1; *The Revolution and Counter-Revolution in Ancient India,* unfinished work (1956), vol. 3; *The Problem of the Rupee* (1923) and *The Evolution of Provincial Finance in British India* (1925) vol. 6; *Who were the Shudras?* (1946) and *The Untouchables* (1948), vol. 7; *Pakistan or the Partition of India* (1940), vol. 8; *What Congress and Gandhi Have Done to the Untouchables* (1945), vol. 9; *The Buddha and His Dhamma* (1957), vol. 11.

———. 2002. *The Essential Writings of B.R. Ambedkar,* ed. Valerian Rodrigues. Delhi: Oxford University Press.

Amin, Shahid. 1996. 'Gandhi as Mahatma.' In Ranajit Guha, ed., *Subaltern Studies III, Writings on South Asian History and Society.* Delhi: Oxford University Press.

Anderson, Benedict. 1983. *Imagined Communities: Reflections on the Origin and Spread of Nationalism.* London: Verso.

Anderson, Perry. 2012a. *The Indian Ideology.* Gurgaon: Three Essays Collective.

———. 2012b. 'Respect Gandhi If You Will, Don't Sentimentalize Him', *Outlook,* see www.outlookindia.com/article.aspx?282832

Angar Ee, HaBir. 1994. *Pali is the Mother of Sanskrit.* Nagpur: Tarachand Chavhan.

Armstrong, Karen. 2000. *Buddha.* London: Phoenix.

Ashton, Stephen. 1987. *The British in India: From Trade to Empire.* London: Batsford.

Ashvaghosha [*c.* 100 CE] [1936] 1992. *Buddhacarita or Acts of the Buddha,* tr. E.H. Johnston. Delhi: Motilal Banarsidass.

Austin, Granville. [1964] 2001. *The Indian Constitution: Cornerstone of a Nation.* Delhi: Oxford University Press.

Awaya, Toshie. 1999. 'Some Aspects of the Tiyyas' Caste Movement.' In H. Kotani, ed., *Caste System, Untouchability and the Depressed,* pp. 139–68. Delhi: Manohar.

Baber, Zaheer. 2006. *Secularism, Communalism and the Intellectuals.* Gurgaon: Three Essays.

Bagade, Umesh. 2012. 'Probing Alternative Paths of Knowledge: Mahatma Phule's Encounter with History and Anthropology.' In Ajit Danda and Rajat Das, eds., *Alternative Voices of Anthropology*, pp. 441–64. Kolkata: Indian Anthropological Society.

Baird, Robert D., ed. 2001. *Religion in Modern India*, 4th revised edn. Delhi: Manohar.

Baker, C.J. 1976. *The Politics of South India 1920–37*. Delhi: Vikas.

Bali, Arun P. 1978. 'The Virasaiva Movement.' In S.C. Malik, ed., *Indian Movements*, pp. 67–100. Shimla: Indian Institute of Advanced Study.

Ball, Terence and Richard Dagger. 2004. *Political Ideologies and the Democratic Ideal*, 5th edn. New York: Pearson Longman.

Bandyopadhyay, Sekhar. 1990. *Caste, Politics and the Raj: Bengal 1872–1937*. Calcutta: K.P. Bagchi & Co.

———. 1995. 'Caste, Widow-remarriage and the Reform of Popular Culture in Cononial Bengal.' In Bharati Ray, ed., *From the Seams of History*, pp. 8–36, Delhi: Oxford University Press.

———. 2004. *Caste, Culture and Hegemony: Social Dominance in Colonial Bengal*. Delhi: Sage.

Banerjee-Dube, Ishita, ed. 2008. *Caste in History*. Delhi: Oxford University Press.

Banga, Indu and Jaidev, eds. 1996. *Cultural Reorientation in Modern India*. Shimla: Indian Institute of Advanced Study.

Bapat, P.V., ed. [1956] 1997. *2500 Years of Buddhism*. Delhi: Publications Division, Govt. of India.

Bardhan, Pranab. 1999. 'The State Against Society: The Great Divide in Indian Social Science Discourse.' In Sugata Bose and Ayesha Jalal, eds., *Nationalism, Democracy & Development*, pp. 184–95. Delhi: Oxford University Press.

Barua, B.M. [1921] 1970. *Pre-Buddhist Indian Philosophy*. Delhi: Motilal Banarsidass.

Basham, A.L. [1954] 1991. *The Wonder That Was India*. Delhi: Rupa.

———, ed. [1975] 1985. *A Cultural History of India*. Delhi: Oxford University Press.

Basu, Shamita. 2002. *Religious Revivalism as Nationalist Discourse: Swami Vivekananda and New Hinduism in Nineteenth-Century Bengal*. Delhi: Oxford University Press.

Basu, Tapan et al. 1993. *Khaki Shorts and Saffron Flags: A Critique of the Hindu Right*. Delhi: Orient Longman.

Basu, Tapan, ed. 2002. *Translating Caste: Stories, Essays, Criticism*. Delhi: Katha.

Batchelor, M. and K. Brown, eds. 1994. *Buddhism and Ecology*. Delhi: Motilal Banarsidass.

Baxi, Upendra. 2000. 'Emancipation as Justice: Legacy and Vision of Dr. Ambedkar.' In K. C. Yadav, ed., *From Periphery to Centre Stage: Ambedkar, Ambedkarism and Dalit Future*, pp. 49–74. Delhi: Manohar.

Bayly, C.A. 2001. *Origins of Nationalism in South Asia*. Delhi: Oxford University Press.

Bayly, Susan. 1992. *Saints, Goddesses and Kings*. Cambridge: Cambridge University Press.

———. 2000. *Caste, Society and Politics in India: From the Eighteenth Century to the Modern Age*. Cambridge: Cambridge University Press.

Bazaz, Premnath. 2002. 'The Role of the Bhagavad Gita in Indian History', *The Radical Humanist*, August issue.

Bergunder, Michael. 2004. 'Contested Past: Anti-Brahmanical and Hindu Nationalist Reconstructions of Indian Prehistory', *Historiographia Linguistica* XXXI: 1, pp. 59–104.

Berlin, Isaiah. 2003. *The Crooked Timber of Humanity: Chapters in the History of Ideas*. London: Pimlico.

Berreman, Gerard D. 1979. *Caste and Other Inequities: Essays on Inequality*. Meerut: Folklore Institute.

———. 1991. 'The Brahmanical View of Caste.' In Dipankar Gupta, ed., *Social Stratification*, pp. 84–92. Delhi: Oxford University Press.

Besant, Annie. 1913. *Wake Up India*. Madras: Theosophical Society of India.

———. 1917. *Birth of New India*. Madras: Theosophical Society of India.

Beteille, Andre. 1997. 'Caste in Contemporary India.' In C.J. Fuller, ed., *Caste Today*, pp. 150–79. Delhi: Oxford University Press.

Bhagavad Gita. Translations of S. Radhakrishnan (Delhi: Oxford University Press, 1992) and Purohit Swami (London: Faber & Faber, 1965).

Bhattacharya, Neeladri. 1991. 'Myth, History and the Politics of Ramjanambhoomi'. In S. Gopal, ed., *Anatomy of a Confrontation: The Ramjanambhoomi-Babri Masjid Dispute*. Delhi: Penguin.

Bhattacharya, Sabyasachi, ed. 1997. *The Mahatma and the Poet: Letters and Debates between Gandhi and Tagore 1915–1941*. Delhi: National Book Trust.

Bilgrami, Akeel. 1994. 'Two Concepts of Secularism', *Yale Journal of Criticism*, vol. 7.

Bipan Chandra et al. 1989. *India's Struggle for Independence*. Delhi: Penguin.

Biswas, Oneil. 2001. *Dalits after Partition*. Delhi: Blumoon Books.

Biswas, Swapan K. 1998. *Gods, False Gods and the Untouchables*. Delhi: Orion.

Bloch, Marc. 1953. *The Historian's Craft*, tr. Peter Putnam. New York: Vintage Books.
Bose, N.K. 1953. 'The Hindu Method of Tribal Absorption.' In idem, *Cultural Anthopology and Other Essays*. Calcutta: Indian Associated Publishing Co.
Bose, Nemai Sadhan. 1999. 'Swami Vivekananda and Challenge to Fundamentalism.' In William Radice, ed., *Swami Vivekananda and the Modernisation of Hinduism*, pp. 281–99. Delhi: Oxford University Press.
Bose, Sugata and Ayesha Jalal, eds. 1999. *Nationalism, Democracy & Development: State and Politics in India*. Delhi: Oxford University Press.
Bose, Sugata and Ayesha Jalal. 2003. *Modern South Asia: History, Culture, Political Economy*, 2nd edn. Delhi: Oxford University Press.
Bose, Sumantra. 1999.' "Hindu Nationalism" and the Crisis of the Indian State: A Theoretical Perspective'. In Sugata Bose and Ayesha Jalal, eds., *Nationalism, Democracy & Development*, pp. 104–64. Delhi: Oxford University Press.
Bougle, Celestin. [1908] 1991. 'The Essence and Reality of the Caste System.' In Dipankar Gupta, ed., *Social Stratification*, pp. 64–73. Delhi: Oxford University Press.
Brown, Donald E. 1988. *Hierarchy, History and Human Nature: The Social Origins of Historical Consciousness*. Tucson: University of Arizona Press.
Buddhist Scriptures. Selection and trans. Edward Conze. 1959. London: Penguin.
Caldwell, Robert. [1856] 1875. *A Comparative Grammar of the Dravidian or South-Indian Family of Languages*. London: Trubner.
Carpenter, Edward. [1889] 1921. *Civilisation: Its Causes and Cures*. New York: Charles Scribner's Sons.
Carrithers, Michael. 1992. *Why Humans Have Cultures*. Oxford: Oxford University Press.
Carus, Paul. 1997. *The Gospel of Buddha*, rpt. Chennai: Samata Books.
Casolari, Marzia. 2000. 'Hindutva's Foreign Tie-up in the 1930s: Archival Evidence', *Economic and Political Weekly*, 22 January.
Chakravarti, Uma. 1989. 'Whatever Happened to the Vedic Dasi?: Orientalism, Nationalism, and a Script for the Past.' In Kumkum Sangari and Sudesh Vaid, eds., *Recasting Women: Essays in Colonial History*, pp. 27–87. Delhi: Kali for Women.

———. 1993. 'Conceptualising Brahmanical Patriarchy in Early India: Gender, Caste, Class and the State', *Economic and Political Weekly*, pp. 579–85. 3 April, vol. 28, no. 14.

———. [1987] 1996. *The Social Dimensions of Early Buddhism*. Delhi: Munshiram Manoharlal.

———. 1998. *Rewriting History: The Life and Times of Pandita Ramabai*. Delhi: Kali for Women.

———. 2002. 'From Exclusion to Marginalisation? Hegemonic Agendas and Women's Writing.' In Sujata Patel et al., eds., *Thinking Social Science in India*, pp. 115–32. Delhi: Sage.

———. 2003. *Gendering Caste: Through a Feminist Lens*. Calcutta: Stree.

———. 2006. *Everyday Lives, Everyday Histories: Beyond the Kings and Brahmanas of Ancient India*. Delhi: Tulika.

Chalam, K.S. 2007. *Caste-based Reservations and Human Development of India*. Delhi: Sage.

Champakalakshmi, R. and S. Gopal, eds. 1996. *Tradition, Dissent and Ideology*. Delhi: Oxford University Press.

Chanana, Dev Raj. [1960] 1990. *Slavery in Ancient India*. Delhi: People's Publishing House.

Chandra, Sudhir. 1992. *The Oppressive Present*. Delhi: Oxford University Press.

Chatterjee, Debi. 2010. *Ideas and Movements Against Caste in India*. Delhi: Abhijeet Publications.

Chatterjee, Partha. 1986. *Nationalist Thought and the Colonial World: A Derivative Discourse?* London: Zed Press.

———. 1989. 'Caste and Subaltern Consciousness'. In Ranajit Guha, ed., *Subaltern Studies VI*, pp. 169–209. Delhi: Oxford University Press.

———. 1993. *The Nation and Its Fragments*. Princeton: Princeton University Press.

Chatterji, Angana. 2008. *Violent Gods: Hindu Nationalism in India's Present—Narratives from Orissa*. Gurgaon: Three Essays.

Chatterji, S.K. 1998. 'Some Emerging Issues in Independent India.' In Sebasti L. Raj, SJ, ed., *Fifty Years After Freedom*. Delhi: Indian Social Institute.

Chattopadhyaya, D.P. [1959] 1992. *Lokayata: A Study in Ancient Indian Materialism*. Delhi: People's Publishing House.

———. [1976] 2001. *What is Living and What is Dead in Indian Philosophy*. Delhi: People's Publishing House.

———. [1989] 2008. *In Defence of Materialsim in Ancient India*. Delhi: People's Publishing House.

Chaturvedi, Parashuram. [1950] 1964. *Uttar Bharat ki Sant Parampara*. Allahabad: Leader Press.
———. 1954. *Kabir Sahitya ki Parakh*. Allahabad: Leader Press.
Chaudhuri, Nirad C. 1974. *Scholar Extraordinary: The Life of Friedrich Max Müller*. Delhi: Orient Paperbacks.
———. [1951] 1987. *The Autobiography of an Unknown Indian*. London: The Hogarth Press.
———. 1999. *The Continent of Circe*, rpt. Bombay: Jaico.
Chomsky, Noam. 1996. *Powers and Prospects*. Delhi: Madhyam Books.
———. 1998. *On Language*. New York: The New Press.
Choudhary, Prasanna Kumar and Shrikant. 2001. *Bihar Mein Samajik Parivartan Ke Kuchh Ayam*. Delhi: Vani Prakashan.
Cox, O.C. 1970. *Caste, Class and Race: A Study in Social Dynamics*. New York: Monthly Review Press.
Crane, Ralph J. 1992. *Inventing India: A History of India in English-Language Fiction*. London: Macmillan.
Crook, Nigel, ed. 2001. *The Transmission of Knowledge in South Asia*. Delhi: Oxford University Press.
Dahiwale, S.M., ed. 2005. *Understanding Indian Society: The Non-Brahmanic Perspective*. Delhi: Rawat.
Dalmia, Vasudha. 2003. *Orienting India: European Knowledge Formation in the Eighteenth and Nineteenth Centuries*. Delhi: Three Essays.
Dalmia, Vasudha and Heinrich von Stietencron, eds. 2007. *The Oxford India Hinduism Redaer*, with Introduction by Dalmia, pp. 1–26. Delhi: Oxford University Press.
Dalton, Dennis. [1983] 2012. *Mahatma Gandhi: Nonviolent Power in Action*. New York: Columbia University Press.
Dangle, Arjun, ed. 1992. *Poisoned Bread: Modern Marathi Dalit Literature*. Bombay: Orient Longman.
Das, Arvind N. 1983. *Agrarian Unrest and Socio-Economic Change in Bihar 1900–1980*. Delhi: Manohar.
Datta, B.N. [1944] 1983. *Studies in Indian Social Polity*. Calcutta: Nababharat Publishers.
Dayananda Saraswati. [1875] 2002. *Light of Truth,* the English translation of *Satyarth Prakash*, rpt. Delhi: Sarvadeshik Arya Pratinidhi Sabha.
Delany, Sheila, ed. 1971. *Counter-Tradition: The Literature of Dissent and Alternatives*. New York: Basic Books.
Deleury, Guy. 2005. *India: The Rebel Continent*, tr. Florence D'Souza. Delhi: Macmillan.

Deoras, Balasaheb. 1984. *Sri Balasaheb Deoras Answers Questions*. Banglore: Sahitya Sindhu.
Desai, A.R. [1948] 1991. *Social Background of Indian Nationalism*, 5th edn. Bombay: Popular Prakashan.
Desai, Meghnad. 2009. *The Rediscovery of India*. Delhi: Penguin.
———. 2012. 'Hind, Hindi, Hindu, Hindutva', *The Sunday Express*, 1 July.
———. 2013. 'The Hindu Rate of Backwardness', *The Sunday Express*, 28 July.
Deshpande, Ashwini. 2011. *The Grammar of Caste: Economic Discrimination in Contemporary India*. Delhi: Oxford University Press.
Deshpande, G.P., ed. 2002. *Selected Writings of Jotirao Phule*, with Introduction, pp. 1–21. Delhi: LeftWord.
Deshpande, Satish. 2004. *Contemporary India: A Sociological View*. Delhi: Penguin.
Dhani, S.L. 1984. *Politics of God: Churning of the Ocean*. Panchakula: D D Books.
Dhammapada. Translations of Juan Mascaro (London: Penguin, 1973) and Eknath Easwaran (London: Routledge, 1986).
Dharmakirti. 2010. *Bhauddha Dharma Nahi Hai Hindu Dharma Ki Shakha*. Delhi: Samyaka Prakashan.
Dharma Theertha, Swami. [1941] 1992. *History of Hindu Imperialism*. Madras: Dalit Educational Literature Centre.
Dharmaveer. 1997. *Kabir ke Aalochak*. Delhi: Vani Prakashan.
Dharwadker, Vinay, tr. 2003. *Kabir: The Weaver's Songs*, with Introduction, pp. 1–96. Delhi: Penguin.
Dirks, Nicholas B. 2002. *Castes of Mind: Colonialism and the Making of Modern India*. Delhi: Permanent Black.
Doniger, Wendy and Brian Smith, eds. 1991. *The Laws of Manu*, with Introduction, pp. XV–LXXVIII. Delhi: Penguin.
Dreze, Jean and Amartya Sen. 1998. *India: Economic Development and Social Opportunity*. Delhi: Oxford University Press.
———. 2011. 'Putting Growth In Its Place,' *Outlook*, 14 November.
Dubey, A.K. 2001. 'Anatomy of a Dalit Power Player.' In Ghanshyam Shah, ed., *Dalit Identity and Politics*, pp. 288–310. Delhi: Sage.
Dumont, Louis. [1970] 1998. *Homo Hierarchicus: The Caste System and Its Implications*, revised English edn. Delhi: Oxford University Press.
Durkheim, Emile. [1912] 2001. *The Elementary Forms of Religious Life*, tr. Carol Cosman. Oxford: Oxford University Press.
Dutt, R.C. 1889–90. *A History of Civilisation in Ancient India*, based on Sanskrit Literature, 3 vols. Calcutta: Thacker, Spink & Co.

Dutt, R. Palme. [1940] 1989. *India Today*. Calcutta: Manisha.
Dwivedi, H.P. [1940] 1999. *Kabir*. Delhi: Rajkamal.
———. [1959] 1997. *Hindi Sahitya ki Bhoomika*. Delhi: Rajkamal.
Edwardes, Michael. 1986. *The Myth of the Mahatma: Gandhi, the British and the Raj*. London: Constable.
———. [1967] 1999. *British India 1772–1947*. Delhi: Rupa.
Edwards, David. 2001. *The Compassionate Revolution: Radical Politics and Buddhism*. Delhi: Viveka Foundation.
Embree, A.T. and Stephen Hay, eds. 1991. *Sources of Indian Tradition*, vols. I & II, 2nd edn. Delhi: Penguin.
Eppsteiner, Fred, ed. 1988. *The Path of Compassion*. Berkeley: Parallax Press.
Fanon, Frantz. 1963. *The Wretched of the Earth*, tr. Constance Farrington. New York: Grove.
Farquhar, J.N. 1999. *Modern Religious Movement in India*, rpt. Delhi: Low Price Publications.
Flood, Gavin, ed. 2003. *The Blackwell Companion to Hinduism*. Oxford: Blackwell.
Foucault, Michel. 1980. *Power/Knowledge: Selected Interviews and Other Writings 1972–77*, ed. Colin Gordon. New York: Vintage.
———. 1990. *The History of Sexuality*, vol. I. London: Penguin.
———. 1991. *The Foucault Reader*, ed. Paul Rabinow. London: Penguin.
Franco, F. and Sarvar V. Sherry Chand. [1989] 2009. *Varna: Ideology as Social Practice*. Delhi. Critical Quest.
Freire, Paulo. [1970] 1996. *Pedagogy of the Oppressed*, tr. Myra Bergman Ramos. London: Penguin.
French, Patrick. 1998. *Liberty Or Death: India's Journey to Independence and Division*. London: Flamingo.
Frykenberg, Robert Eric. [1989] 2001. 'The Emergence of Modern Hinduism.' In G.-D. Sontheimer and Hermann Kulke, eds., *Hinduism Reconsidered*, pp. 82–107. Delhi: Manohar.
Fuchs, Stephen. 1965. *Rebellious Prophets: A Study of Messianic Movements in Indian Religions*. Bombay: Asia Publishing House.
Fukuzawa, Hiroshi. 1998. *The Medieval Deccan: Peasants, Social System and Status 16th to 18th Centuries*. Delhi: Oxford University Press.
Galanter, Marc. 1984. *Competing Equalities: Law and the Backward Classes in India*. Delhi: Oxford University Press.
Gandhi, M.K. [1921] 1967. 'Speech at Suppressed Classes Conference, April 13, 1921.' In *The Complete Works of Mahatma Gandhi*, vol. 23. Delhi: Publications Division, Govt. of India.
———. 1970. *My Theory of Trusteeship*. Bombay: Bharatiya Vidya Bhavan.

———. 1979. *The Complete Works of Mahatma Gandhi,* vol. 1. Delhi: Publications Division, Govt. of India.

———. 1993. *The Penguin Gandhi Reader,* ed., Rudrangshu Mukherjee, with *Hind Swaraj* (1909) and *Varna Vyavastha* (1934). Delhi: Penguin.

———. 1994. *What is Hinduism?* Delhi: National Book Trust.

———. [1927] 1996. *The Story of My Experiments with Truth.* Ahmedabad: Navajivan Publishing House.

Gavaskar, Mahesh. 1999. 'Colonialism Within Colonialism: Phule's Critique of Brahmin Power.' In S.M. Michael, ed., *Dalits in Modern India.* Delhi:Vistaar Publications.

Geetha, V. and S.V. Rajadurai. 1998. *Towards a Non-Brahmin Millennium: From Iyothee Thass to Periyar.* Calcutta: Samya.

Geetha,V. 2002. *Gender.* Calcutta: Stree.

Gellner, Ernest. 1983. *Nations and Nationalism.* Oxford: Basil Blackwell.

George, K.M. 1991. *Kumaran Asan.* Delhi: Sahitya Akademi.

Ghose,Aurobindo. 1937. *Essays on the Gita,* 2 vols. Calcutta:Arya Publishing House.

———. 1948. *Speeches.* Calcutta:Arya Publishing House.

Ghurye, G.S. [1932] 2000. *Caste and Race in India,* 5th edn. Bombay: Popular Prakashan.

Gill, S.S. 2001. *Gandhi: A Sublime Failure.* Delhi: Rupa.

Gita. See under *Bhagavad Gita.*

Golwalkar, M.S. 1939. *We, or Our Nationhood Defined.* Nagpur: Bharat Prakashan.

Gooptu, Nandini. 1993. 'Caste, Deprivation and Politics:The Untouchables in U.P. Towns in the Early Twentieth Century.' In Peter Robb, ed., *Dalit Movements and the Meanings of Labour in India,* pp. 277–98. Delhi: Oxford University Press.

Gore, M.S. 1993. *The Social Context of an Ideology: Ambedkar's Political and Social Thought.* Delhi: Sage.

Govinda, Anagarika. 1961. *The Psychological Attitude of Early Budhhist Philosophy.* London: Rider & Company.

Goyal, D.R. [1979] 2000. *Rashtriya Swayamsewak Sangh,* 2nd revised edn. Delhi: Radhakrishna.

Goyal, Santosh. 1992a. 'Social Background of Officers of the Indian Administrative Service,' Appendix II. In Francine Frankel and M.S.A. Rao, eds., *Dominance and State Power in Modern India,* vol. 1. Delhi: Oxford University Press.

———. 1992b. 'Social Background of Top Corporate Officials in the Private and Public Sectors,' Appendix IV. In Francine Frankel and

M.S.A. Rao, eds., *Dominance and State Power in Modern India*, vol. 2. Delhi: Oxford University Press.

Gramsci, Antonio. [1971] 1996. *Selections from the Prison Notebooks*, tr. Quintin Hoare and Geoffrey N. Smith. Chennai: Orient Longman.

Grewal, J.S. 1999. 'Ideas Operative in Early Sikh History.' In J.S. Grewal et al., eds., *The Khalsa Over 300 Years*. Delhi: Tulika.

Guha, Ranajit. [1983] 1999. *Elementary Aspects of Peasant Insurgency in Colonial India*. Delhi: Oxford University Press.

———, ed. 1982–9. *Subaltern Studies: Writings on South Asian History and Society*, vols. 1–6. Delhi: Oxford University Press.

———. 1989. 'Dominance Without Hegemony and Its Historiography.' In idem, ed., *Subaltern Studies VI*, pp. 210–309. Delhi: Oxford University Press.

Guha, Ranajit and Gayatri Spivak, eds. 1988. *Selected Subaltern Studies*. Oxford: Oxford University Press.

Guichard, Sylvie. 2010. *The Construction of History and Nationalism in India: Textbooks, Controversies and Politics*. London and New York: Routledge.

Gupta, Dipankar, ed. 1991. *Social Stratification*. Delhi: Oxford University Press.

Gupta, S.K. 1985. *The Scheduled Castes in Modern Indian Politics: Their Emergence as a Political Power*. Delhi: Munshiram Manoharlal.

Guru, Gopal. 1995. 'Dalit Women Talk Differently', *Economic and Political Weekly*, 14 October, pp. 2548–50. Also in Anupama Rao, ed. (2003), *Gender and Caste*, Delhi: Kali for Women, pp. 80–5.

———. 1999. 'The Dalit Movement in Mainstream Sociology.' In S.M. Michael, ed., *Dalits in Modern India*. Delhi: Vistaar Publications.

———. 2001. 'The Language of Dalit-Bahujan Discourse.' In Ghanshyam Shah, ed., *Dalit Identity and Politics*. Delhi: Sage.

———. 2002. 'How Egalitarian Are the Social Sciences in India?' *Economic and Political Weekly*, 14 December. Also in A. Vanaik and R. Bhargava (2010), *Understanding Contemporary India: Critical Perspectives*, pp. 283–302. Delhi: Orient BlackSwan.

———, ed. 2009. *Humiliation: Claims and Context*. Delhi: Oxford University Press.

Hall, Stuart. 1996. *Stuart Hall: Critical Dialogues in Cultural Studies*, edited by David Morley and Kuan-Hsing Chen. London: Routledge.

Hamilton, Sue. 2001. *Indian Philosophy: A Very Short Introduction*. Oxford: Oxford University Press.

Hansen, Thomas Blom. 1999. *The Saffron Wave: Democracy and Hindu Nationalism in India*. Delhi: Oxford University Press.

Haq, Jalalul. 1997. *The Shudra: A Philosophical Narrative of Indian Superhumanism*. Delhi: Institute of Objective Studies.

Hardgrave, Robert. 1968. 'The Breast-cloth Controversy and Social Consciousness in Southern Travancore'. *Indian Economic and Social History Review* 5.2, pp. 171–87.

———. 1969. *The Nadars of Tamilnadu: The Political Culture of a Community in Change*. California: University of California Press.

Hardy, Friedhelm. 2007. 'A Radical Reassessment of the Vedic Heritage: The Ācāryahṛdayam and Its Wider Implications.' In V. Dalmia and H. Stietencron, eds., *The Oxford India Hinduism Reader*, pp. 29–49. Delhi: Oxford University Press.

Harriss-White, Barbara. 2004. *India Working: Essays on Society and Economy*. Delhi: Cambridge University Press.

Harriss, John. 2006. *Power Matters: Essays on Institutions, Politics and Society in India*. Delhi: Oxford University Press.

Harvey, Peter, ed. 2001. *Buddhism*. London and New York: Continuum.

Hawley, J.S. and Mark Juergensmeyer, eds. 1988. *Songs of the Saints of India*. New York: Oxford University Press.

Hay, Stephen, ed. 1988. *Sources of Indian Tradition*, vol. 2, 2nd edn. New York: Columbia University Press.

Hess, Linda and Sukhdev Singh. 1986. *The Bijak of Kabir*, with Introduction by Hess, pp. 3–37. Delhi: Motilal Banarsidass.

Hobsbawm, Eric. 1990. *Nations and Nationalism since 1780: Programme, Myth, Reality*. Cambridge: Cambridge University Press.

Hobsbawm, Eric and Terence Ranger, eds. 1983. *The Invention of Tradition*. Cambridge: Cambridge University Press.

Holder, John H., tr. 2006. *Early Buddhist Discourses*. Indianapolis: Hackett.

Ilaiah, Kancha. 1996. *Why I am Not a Hindu*. Calcutta: Samya.

———. 2000. *God as Political Philosopher: Buddha's Challenge to Brahminism*. Calcutta: Samya.

———. 2004. *Buffalo Nationalism: A Critique of Spiritual Fascism*. Calcutta: Samya.

———. 2009. *Post-Hindu India: A Discourse on Dalit-Bahujan Socio-Spiritual and Scientific Revolution*. Delhi: Sage.

Inden, Roland. [1990] 2000. *Imagining India*. London: Hurst.

Irschick, Eugene. 1969. *Politics and Social Conflict in South India*. Berkeley: University of California Press.

Ishwaran, K. 1983. *Religion and Society among the Lingayats of South India.* Delhi: Vikas.
Iyengar, K.R.S., ed. 1994. *Guru Nanak.* Delhi: Sahitya Akademi.
Jaffrelot, Christophe. 1997. 'The Ideas of the Hindu Race in the Writings of Hindu Nationalist Ideologues in the 1920s and 1930s: A Concept Between Two Cultures.' In Peter Robb, ed., *The Concept of Race in South Asia*, pp. 327–54. Delhi: Oxford University Press.
———. 1999. *The Hindu Nationalist Movement and Indian Politics.* Delhi: Penguin.
———. 2003. *India's Silent Revolution: The Rise of the Low Castes in North Indian Politics.* Delhi: Permanent Black.
———. 2004. *Dr Ambedkar and Untouchability: Analysing and Fighting Caste.* Delhi: Permanent Black.
Jaini, Padmanabh, ed. 2001. *Collected Papers on Buddhist Studies.* Delhi: Motilal Banarsidass.
Jaiswal, Suvira. 2000. *Caste: Origin, Function and Dimensions of Change.* Delhi: Manohar.
Jatava, D.R. 1997. *Social Philosophy of B.R. Ambedkar.* Jaipur: Rawat.
Jayaswal, K.P. 1930. *Manu and Yajanvalkya.* Calcutta: Butterworth.
Jenkins, Laura Dudley. 2003. *Identity and Identification in India: Defining the Disadvantaged.* London and New York: RoutledgeCurzon.
Jha, D.N. 2001. *Ancient India in Historical Outline.* Delhi: Manohar.
Jhabwala, S.H. [1960] 1991. *Gita and Its Commentators.* Bombay: Popular Prakashan.
Jodhka, Surinder S. 2012. *Caste.* Delhi: Oxford University Press.
John, Mary E., ed. 2008. *Women's Studies in India: A Reader.* Delhi: Penguin.
Jondhale, Surendra and Johannes Beltz, eds. 2004. *Reconstructing the World: B.R. Ambedkar and Buddhism in India.* Delhi: Oxford University Press.
Jordens, J.T.F. 1985. 'Medieval Hindu Devotionalism.' In A.L. Basham, ed., *A Cultural History of India*, pp. 266–80. Delhi: Oxford University Press.
Joshi, Barbara. 1986. *Untouchable! Voices of the Dalit Liberation Movement.* Delhi: Select Books Service Syndicate.
Joshi, Lal Mani. [1969] 2007. *Brahmanism, Buddhism, and Hinduism.* Delhi: Critical Quest.
———. [1973] 2012. *Aspects of Buddhism in Indian History.* Delhi: Critical Quest.
Joshi, Laxmanshastri. 1992. *Jotirao Phule.* Delhi: National Book Trust.
———. 1996. *Critique of Hinduism and Other Religions.* Bombay: Popular Prakashan.

Juergensmeyer, Mark. 1982. *Religion as Social Vision: The Movement Against Untouchability in 20th-Century Punjab*. Berkeley: University of California Press.

Kadam, K.N. 1993. *Dr B.R. Ambedkar: The Emancipator of the Oppressed*. Bombay: Popular Prakashan.

Kailasapathy, K. 1987. 'The Writings of the Tamil Siddhas.' In K. Schomer and W.H. McLeod, eds., *The Sants: Studies in a Devotional Tradition of India*, pp. 385–411. Delhi: Motilal Banarsidass.

Kakar, Sudhir and Katharina Kakar. 2007. *The Indians: Portrait of a People*. Delhi: Penguin.

Kalupahana, David J. 1976. *Buddhist Philosophy: A Historical Analysis*. Hawaii: University Press of Hawaii.

Kanungo, Pralay. 2002. *RSS's Tryst with Politics: From Hegdewar to Sudarshan*. Delhi: Manohar.

Kaufmann, Walter. 1974. *Nietzsche: Philosopher, Psychologist, Antichrist*, 4th edn. Princeton: Princeton University Press.

Kautilya. 1997. *The Arthashastra*, tr. R. P. Kangle. Delhi: Motilal Banarsidass.

Keer, Dhananjay. [1954] 1971. *Dr. Ambedkar: Life and Mission*. Bombay: Popular Prakashan.

———. [1964] 2000. *Mahatma Jotirao Phule: Father of Indian Social Revolution*. Bombay: Popular Prakashan.

Keith, A.B. 1948. *A History of Sanskrit Literature*. Oxford: Oxford University Press.

Kejariwal, O.P. 1988. *The Asiatic Society of Bengal and the Discovery of India's Past*. Delhi: Oxford University Press.

Ketkar, S.V. 1909. *History of Caste in India*, 2 vols. New York: Ithaca.

Khare, R.S. 1984. *The Untouchable as Himself: Ideology, Identity and Pragmatism among the Lucknow Chamars*. New York: Cambridge University Press.

Killingley, Dermot. 1993. *Rammohun Roy in Hindu and Christian Tradition: The Teape Lectures 1990*. Newcastle: Grevatt & Grevatt.

Klass, Morton. [1980] 2004. *Caste: The Emergence of the South Asian Social System*. Delhi: Manohar.

Kochhar, Rajesh. 2000. *The Vedic People: Their History and Geography*. Delhi: Orient Longman.

Kohn, Margaret and Keally Mcbride. 2011. *Political Theories of Decolonisation: Postcolonialism and the Problem of Foundations*. New York: Oxford University Press.

Kolenda, Pauline. 1978. *Caste in Contemporary India: Beyond Organic Solidarity*. Prospect Heights, IL: Waveland Press.

Kopf, David. 1969. *British Orientalism and the Bengal Renaissance: The Dynamics of Indian Modernisation 1793–1835*. Berkeley: University of California Press.

Kosambi, D.D. [1965] 1992. *The Culture and Civilisation of Ancient India in Historical Outline*. Delhi: Vikas.

———. [1956] 1999. *An Introduction to the Study of Indian History*. Bombay: Popular Prakashan.

———. [1962] 2000. *Myth and Reality*. Mumbai: Popular Prakashan.

Kosambi, Dharmanand. [1940] 2000. *Bhagwan Buddha: Jeevan aur Darshan*. Allahabad: Lokabharati Prakashan.

Kothari, Rajni. 1986. 'Flight Into The 21st Century', *The Times of India*, 27 April.

———. 1988. *The State Against Democracy: In Search of Humane Governance*. Delhi: Ajanta Publications.

———, ed. [1970] 1991. *Caste in Indian Politics*. Hyderabad: Orient Longman.

———, ed. [1970] 2003. *Politics in India*. Hyderabad: Orient Longman.

Kraft, Kenneth. 1999. *The Wheel of Engaged Buddhism: A New Map of the Path*. New York: Weatherhill.

Kriplani, Krishna. 1981. *Dwarkanath Tagore*. Delhi: National Book Trust.

Kulke, Hermann and Dietmar Rothermund. [1986] 2004. *A History of India*. 4th edn. London and New York: Routledge.

Kumar, Arun. 2001. *Rewriting the Language of Politics: Kisans in Colonial Bihar*. Delhi: Manohar.

Kumar, Raj. 2009. *Dalit Personal Narratives: Reading Caste, Nation and Identity*. Delhi: Orient BlackSwan.

Kumar, Ravinder. 1968. *Western India in the Nineteenth Century*. London: Routledge and Kegan Paul.

———. 1987. 'Gandhi, Ambedkar and the Poona Pact, 1932'. In Jim Masselos, ed., *Struggling and Ruling: The Indian National Congress 1885–1985*. Delhi: Sterling.

Kunhappa, Murkot. 1988. *Sree Narayana Guru*. Delhi: National Book Trust.

Lal, Shyam et al., eds. 1998. *Ambedkar and Nation-Building*. Jaipur: Rawat.

Lalitha Dhara, ed. 2011. *Phules and Women's Question*. Mumbai: Dr Ambedkar College of Commerce and Economics.

Lannoy, Richard. [1971] 1999. *The Speaking Tree: A Study of Indian Culture and Society*. Delhi: Oxford University Press.

Lee Tucker. 2006. *Child Slaves in Modern India*. Delhi: Critical Quest.

Lerner, Gerda. 1986. *The Creation of Patriarchy*. New York: Oxford University Press.

Ling, T.O., ed. 1981. *The Buddha's Philosophy of Man: Early Indian Buddhist Dialogues.* London: Dent.

Lingat, Robert. [1967] 1998. *The Classical Law of India*, tr. J.D.M. Derrett. Delhi: Oxford University Press.

Lobo, Lancy. 2004. *Globalisation, Hindu Nationalism and Christians in India.* Jaipur: Rawat.

Lorenzen, David. 1996. *Praises to a Formless God.* New York: State University of New York Press.

———. 2006. *Who Invented Hinduism? Essays on Religion in History.* Delhi: Yoda Press.

Louis, Prakash. 2000. *The Emerging Hindutva Force: The Ascent of Hindu Nationalism.* Delhi: Indian Social Institute.

———. 2003. *Political Sociology of Dalit Assertion.* Delhi: Gyan Publishing House.

Lucacs, Georg. [1923] 1993. *History and Class Consciousness: Studies in Marxist Dialectics*, tr. Rodney Livingstone. Delhi: Rupa.

Ludden, David, ed. 1996. *Making India Hindu: Religion, Community, and the Politics of Democracy in India.* Delhi: Oxford University Press.

MacGuire, Randall and Robert Paynter. 1991. *The Archaeology of Inequality.* Oxford: Blackwell.

Machiavelli, Niccolò. [1513] 2003. *The Prince.* London: Penguin.

MacMunn, George. 1984. *The Indian Social System*, rpt. Delhi: Discovery Publishing House.

MacPherson, Stewart. 1982. *Social Policy in the Third World.* Sussex: Wheatsheaf Books.

Madan, T.N.. 1987. 'Secularism in Its Place', *Journal of Asian Studies*, 46. 4, pp. 747–59.

———, ed. 1991. *Religion in India.* Delhi: Oxford University Press.

Mani, Braj Ranjan. 2007. *Resurgent Buddhism: Ambedkar's Predecessors in Modern India.* Delhi: Critical Quest.

———. 2014. *Knowledge and Power: A Discourse for Transformation.* Delhi: Manohar.

———. 2014. 'The Dark Side of Knowledge: Canon and Caste', the Mahatma Phule Memorial Lecture, 5 March, University of Pune.

Mani, Braj Ranjan and Pamela Sardar, eds. 2008. *A Forgotten Liberator: The Life and Struggle of Savitribai Phule.* Delhi: Mountain Peak.

Mani, Lata. 1989. 'Contentious Traditions: The Debate on Sati in Colonial India.' In K. Sangari and S. Vaid, eds., *Recasting Women: Essays in Colonial History*, pp. 88–126. Delhi: Kali for Women.

Manickam, S. 1993. *Slavery in the Tamil Country: A Historical Overview*. Madras: The Christian Literature Society.
Mann, Thomas. 1939. *Culture and Politics*. USA: Survey Graphic.
Manusmriti. See (translations of) Doniger and Smith (1991); and Olivelle (2005).
Marger, Martin N. 2005. *Social Inequality: Patterns and Processes*. New York: McGraw-Hill.
Mariategui, Jose. 1996. 'Gandhi' [1930]. In idem, *The Heroic and Creative Meaning of Socialism: Selected Essays of Jose Mariategui*. New York: Humanities Press.
Markovits, Claude, ed. 2002. *A History of Modern India 1480–1950*. London: Anthem Press.
Marshall, P.J., ed. 1970. *The British Discovery of Hinduism in the Eighteenth Century*. Cambridge: Cambridge University Press.
Marx, Karl. [1845] 1970. *The German Ideology*. New York: International Publishers.
———. [1859] 1971. *A Contribution to the Critique of Political Economy*. London: Lawrence & Wishart.
———. 1978. [Writings in] *The Marx–Engels Reader*, ed. Robert C. Tucker, 2nd edn. New York: Norton.
Masson, Jeffrey and Susan McCarthy. 1996. *When Elephants Weep: The Emotional Lives of Animals*. New York: Delta Book.
Meenakshi, K. 1996. 'The Siddhas of Tamil Nadu: A Voice of Dissent.' In R. Champakalakshmi and S. Gopal, eds., *Tradition, Dissent and Ideology*, pp. 111–34. Delhi: Oxford University Press.
Mehrotra, S.R. 1971. *The Emergence of Indian National Congress*. Delhi: Vikas.
Mehta, Pratap Bhanu. 2012. 'Breaking the Silence: Why We Don't Talk About Inequality', *The Caravan*, October issue.
Mehta, Ved. 1977. *Mahatma Gandhi and His Apostles*. London: Penguin.
Mencher, Joan. 1991. 'The Caste System Upside Down.' In Dipankar Gupta, ed., *Social Stratification*, pp. 93–109. Delhi: Oxford University Press.
Mendelsohn, O. and M. Vicziany. 2000. *The Untouchables: Subordination, Poverty and the State in Modern India*. Delhi: Cambridge University Press.
Menon, Dilip. 1994. *Caste, Nationalism and Communism in South India: Malabar 1900–1948*. Cambridge: Cambridge University Press.
———. 2006. *The Blindness of Insight: Essays on Caste in Modern India*. Delhi: Navayana.

Metcalf, Thomas. 1990. *Modern India: An Interpretive Anthology*. Delhi: Sterling Publishers.
———. 1998. *Ideologies of the Raj*. Delhi: Cambridge University Press.
Michael, S.M., ed. 1999. *Dalits in Modern India*. Delhi: Vistaar Publications.
Michelet, Jules. [1846] 1973. *The People* [*Le Peuple*], tr. John P. McKay. Urbana: University of Illinois Press.
Mishra, B.B. 1983. *The Indian Middle Classes: Their Growth in Modern Times*. Delhi: Oxford University Press.
Mitra, Ashok. 1995. *Caste and Class in Indian Society*. Calcutta: The Asiatic Society.
Mohanty, Manoranjan, ed. 2004. *Class, Caste, Gender*. Delhi: Sage.
Monier-Williams, Monier. 1887. *Brahmanism and Hinduism*. London.
———. 2003. *Hinduism and Its Sources*, rpt. Delhi: Munshiram Manoharlal.
Mookerjee, R.K. 1956. *Ancient India*. Allahabad: Indian Press.
Moya, Paula, et al. 2001. *Reclaiming Identity: Realist Theory and the Predicament of Postmodernism*. Hyderabad: Orient Longman.
Müller, F. Max. [1859] 1968. *A History of Ancient Indian Literature*. Delhi.
———, ed. 1982. *Vinaya Texts*, in *The Sacred Books of the East*, vol. XIII, rpt. Delhi: Motilal Banarsidass.
———, ed. 1998. *Dhammapada* and *Sutta Nipata*, in *The Sacred Books of the East,* vol. X, rpt. Delhi: Motilal Banarsidass.
———. [1883] 2000. *India: What Can It Teach Us?* With Introduction by Johannes H. Voigt. Delhi: Penguin.
Mukherjee, Hiren. 1991. *Gandhiji: A Study*. Delhi: People's Publishing House.
Mukherjee, Prabhati. 1988. *Beyond the Four Varnas: The Untouchables in India*. Delhi: Indian Institute of Advanced Study/Motilal Banarsidass.
Mukherjee, S.N. [1974] 1993. 'The Social Implications of the Political Thought of Raja Rammohun Roy.' In R.S. Sharma and Vivekanand Jha, eds., *Indian Society: Historical Probings,* pp. 356–89. Delhi: People's Publishing House.
Mukta, Parita. 1997. *Upholding the Common Life: The Community of Mirabai*. Delhi: Oxford University Press.
Munda, Karia, et al. 2000. *2nd Report of Parliamentary Committee on the Welfare of Scheduled Castes and Tribes*. Delhi: Govt. of India.
Nabha, Bhai Kahn Singh. 2006. *Sikhs: We are Not Hindus*. Amritsar: Singh Brothers.
Namboodiripad, E.M.S. [1958] 2010. *The Mahatma and the Ism*. Delhi: LeftWord.

Nanda, B.R., ed. 1980. *Essays in Modern Indian History*. Delhi: Oxford University Press.
Nanda, Meera. 2002. *Breaking the Spell of Dharma and Other Essays*. Delhi: Three Essays.
———. 2004. *Prophets Facing Backward: Postmodernism, Science, and Hindu Nationalism*. Delhi: Permanent Black.
Nandy, Ashis. 1980. *At the Edge of Psychology: Essays in Politics and Culture*. Delhi: Oxford University Press.
———. 1983. *The Intimate Enemy: Loss and Recovery of Self Under Colonialism*. Delhi: Oxford University Press.
Narasu, Lakshmi. 2002. *Religion of the Modern Buddhist*, ed. G. Aloysius. Delhi: Wordsmiths.
———. [1922] 2003. *A Study of Caste*. Delhi: Blumoon Books.
———. [1907] 2004. *The Essence of Buddhism*. Delhi: Winsome Books.
Narayanan, M.G.S. 1975. 'Historical Perspectives on Ancient India', *Social Scientist,* no. 39, October issue, pp. 3–11.
Narke, Hari, ed. 1993. *Mahatma Phule: Sahitya Aur Vichar*. Bombay: Govt. of Maharashtra.
Nath, Trilok. 1987. *Politics of the Depressed Classes*. Delhi: Deputy Publications.
Natarajan, S. 1959. *A Century of Social Reform*. Bombay: Asia Publishing House.
Natrajan, Balmurali and Paul Greenough, eds. 2009. *Against Stigma: Studies in Caste, Race and Justice since Durban*. Delhi: Orient BlackSwan.
Nehru, Jawaharlal. 1929. Presidential address at Lahore Congress Annual Session.
———. [1946] 1996. *The Discovery of India*. Delhi: Nehru Memorial Fund/Oxford University Press.
———. [1936] 1999. *An Autobiography*. Delhi: Nehru Memorial Fund/Oxford University Press.
Nemade, Bhalchandra. 1997. *Tukaram*. Delhi: Sahitya Akademi.
Nichols, Beverley. 1946. *Verdict on India*. Bombay: Thacker & Co.
Nietzsche, Friedrich. 1968a. *Twilight of the Idols* [1889] and *The Anti-Christ* [1895], tr. R.J. Hollingdale. Harmondsworth: Penguin.
———. [1880s] 1968b. *The Will to Power*. New York: Random House.
———. [1883-5] 1974. *Thus Spoke Zarathustra*, tr. R.J. Hollingdale. Harmondsworth: Penguin.
Noorani, A.G. 2000. *The RSS and the BJP: A Division of Labour*. Delhi: LeftWord.

Novetzke, Christian Lee. 2008. *Religion and Public Memory: A Cultural History of Saint Namdev in India*. New York: Columbia University Press.

Nurullah, Syed and J.P. Naik. 1951. *A History of Education in India*. Bombay: Macmillan.

O' Flaherty, Wendy Doniger. [1981] 2000. *The Rig Veda: An Anthology*. Delhi: Penguin.

O'Hanlon, Rosalind. 1985. *Caste, Conflict and Ideology: Mahatma Jotirao Phule and Low Caste Protest in Nineteenth-Century Western India*. Cambridge: Cambridge University Press.

———. 1994. *A Comparison between Women and Men: Tarabai Shinde and the Critique of Gender Relations in Colonial India*. Delhi: Oxford University Press.

Oldenberg, H. [1882] 1927. *Buddha: His Life, His Teachings, His Order*. Calcutta: The Book Company Ltd.

Olivelle, Patrick. 2005. *Manu's Code of Law*. Delhi: Oxford University Press.

Omvedt, Gail. 1976. *Cultural Revolt in a Colonial Society: The Non Brahman Movement in Western India 1873–1930*. Bombay: Scientific Socialist Education Trust.

———. 1994. *Dalits and the Democratic Revolution: Dr Ambedkar and the Dalit Movement in Colonial India*. Delhi: Sage.

———. 1995. *Dalit Visions*. Delhi: Orient Longman.

———. 2003. *Buddhism in India: Challenging Brahmanism and Caste*. Delhi: Sage.

———. 2008. *Seeking Begumpura: The Social Vision of Anti-caste Intellectuals*. Delhi: Navayana.

Oommen, T.K. 2013. 'Analyzing India's Social Transformation: The Missing Subaltern Perspective', the Ambedkar Memorial Lecture on 5 February at NISWASS, Bhubaneshwar.

Orsini, Francesca. 2002. *The Hindi Public Sphere 1920–1940*. Delhi: Oxford University Press.

Paine, Thomas. [1791] 1984. *Rights of Man*. New York: Penguin.

———. [1794] 2004. *The Age of Reason*. New York: Dover Publications.

Pande, G.C. 1974. *Studies in the Origins of Buddhism*. Delhi: Motilal Banarsidass.

———. 1978. *Shramana Tradition: Its History and Contribution to Indian Culture*. Ahmedabad: L.D. Institute of Indology.

Pandey, Gyanendra. 1990. *The Construction of Communalism in Colonial North India*. Delhi: Oxford University Press.

———. 1991. 'Hindus and Others: The Militant Hindu Construction', *Economic and Political Weekly,* 28 December.
Pandian, J. 1987. *Caste, Nationalism and Ethnicity.* Bombay: Popular Prakashan.
Pandian, M.S.S. 2007. *Brahmin & Non-Brahmin: Genealogies of the Tamil Political Present.* Delhi: Permanent Black.
———. 2010. 'Writing Ordinary Lives.' In G. Pandey, ed. *Subaltern Citizens and Their Histories,* pp. 96–108. New York: Routledge.
Panikkar, K.M. 1938. *Hinduism and the Modern World.* Allahabad: Kitabistan.
———. 1961. *The Foundation of New India.* London: Allen & Unwin.
Panikkar, K.N. 1998. *Culture, Ideology, Hegemony: Intellectuals and Social Consciousness in Colonial India.* Delhi: Tulika.
Panini, M.N. 1996. 'The Political Economy of Caste.' In M.N. Srinivas, ed., *Caste: Its Twentieth Century Avatar.* Delhi: Viking Penguin.
Pankratz, James N. 2001. 'Rammohun Roy.' In Robert D. Baird, ed., *Religion in Modern India,* 4th revised edn., pp. 373–87. Delhi: Manohar.
Parekh, Bhiku. 1989. *Colonialism, Tradition, and Reform: An Analysis of Gandhi's Political Discourse.* Thousand Oaks, CA: Sage.
Pargiter, F.E. 1922. *Ancient Indian Historical Tradition.* London: Oxford University Press.
Patil, Sharad. 1982. *Das-Shudra Slavery.* Delhi: Allied Publishers.
Payne, Robert. 1969 [1997]. *The Life and Death of Mahatma Gandhi.* Delhi: Rupa.
Periyar, E.V. Ramasamy. 2000. *Collected Works of Periyar E. V.R.,* compiled by K. Veeramani. Chennai: Periyar Self-Respect Institute.
———. 2009. *Women Enslaved,* tr. G. Aloysius. Delhi: Ctitical Quest.
Phule, Jotirao. 1991. *Collected Works of Mahatma Jotirao Phule,* 2 vols., tr. P.G. Patil. Bombay: Educational Department, Govt. of Maharashtra.
———. 1996. *Mahatma Jotiba Phule Rachanavali,* in Hindi, ed., L.G. Meshram Vimalkirti, with *Tritiya Ratna* (1855), *Sarvajanik Satya Dharrma Pustak* (1890). Delhi: Radhakrishna Prakashan.
———. 2002. *Selected Writings,* ed., G.P. Deshpande, with *Slavery (Gulamgiri* 1873), *Cultivator's Whipcord (Shetkaryacha Asud* 1883). Delhi: LeftWord.
Pimpley, P.N. and S.K. Sharma. 1985. '"De-Sanskritisation" of Untouchables: Arya Samaj Movement in Punjab.' In idem, eds., *Struggle for Status.* Delhi: B.R. Publishing.
Pollock, Sheldon. 1985. 'The Theory of Practice and the Practice of Theory in Indian Intellectual History', *Journal of the American Oriental Society,* No. 105: 3, pp. 499-519.

Prasad, R.C., tr. 1990. *Tulsidas' Shri Ramacharitamanasa.* Delhi: Motilal Banarsidass.
Prashad, Vijay. 2000. *Untouchable Freedom.* Delhi: Oxford University Press.
Procter, James. 2004. *Stuart Hall.* London and New York: Routledge.
Queen, Christopher S., and Sallie B. King, eds. 1996. *Engaged Buddhism: Buddhist Liberation Movements in Asia.* Albany: State University of New York Press.
Quigley, Declan. 1999. *The Interpretation of Caste.* Delhi: Oxford University Press.
Radhakrishnan, S. [1923] 1962. *Indian Philosophy,* vol. 1. London: George Allen and Unwin.
———, tr. 1992. *The Bhagavad Gita,* rpt. Delhi: Oxford University Press.
———. [1956] 1997. 'Foreword' to P.V. Bapat, ed., *2500 Years of Buddhism.* Delhi: Publications Division, Govt. of India.
Radice, William, ed. 1999. *Swami Vivekananda and the Modernisation of Hinduism.* Delhi: Oxford University Press.
Rai, Alok. 2001. *Hindi Nationalism.* Delhi: Orient Longman.
Rajashekhar, V.T. 1993. *Dialogue of the Bhoodevatas.* Bangalore: Dalit Sahitya Akademy.
Ranade, M.G. [1900] 1961. *Rise of the Maratha Power and Other Essays.* Bombay: University of Bombay.
Rangarajan, L.N., ed. 1992. *Kautilya: The Arthashastra.* Delhi: Penguin.
Rao, Anupama, ed. 2003. *Gender and Caste.* Delhi: Kali for Women.
———. 2010. *The Caste Question: Dalits and the Politics of Modern India.* Delhi: Permanent Black.
Rao, M.S.A. 1979. *Social Movements and Social Transformation.* Delhi: Manohar.
———. 2000. *Social Movements in India.* Delhi: Manohar.
Rao, Parimala V. 2010. *Foundations of Tilak's Nationalism: Discrimination, Education and Hindutva.* New Delhi: Orient BlackSwan.
Rao, V. Venkata. 1976. *A Century of Tribal Politics in North-East India 1874–1974.* Delhi: S. Chand & Co.
Ratner-Rosenhagen, Jennifer. 2012. *American Nietzsche: A History of an Icon and His Ideas.* Chicago: University of Chicago Press.
Ravikumar and R. Azhagarasan, eds. 2012. *The Oxford India Anthology of Tamil Dalit Writing.* Delhi: Oxford University Press.
Raychoudhuri, Tapan. 1988. *Europe Reconsidered: Perceptions of the West in Nineteenth Century Bengal.* Delhi: Oxford University Press.
Ray, Himanshu P. 1994. *The Winds of Change: Buddhism and the Maritime Links of Early South Asia.* Delhi: Oxford University Press.

Ray, Niharranjan et al., eds. 2000. *A Sourcebook of Indian Civilisation*. Calcutta: Orient Longman.

Rege, Sharmila. 2006. *Writing Caste, Writing Gender: Reading Dalit Women's Testimonios*. Delhi: Zubaan.

———, ed. 2013. *Against the Madness of Manu: B.R. Ambedkar's Writings on Brahmanical Patriarchy*. Delhi: Navayana.

Rhys Davids, C.A.F. [1909] 1980. *Psalms of the Early Buddhists* (I. Psalms of the Sisters; II. Psalms of the Brethren). London: The Pali Text Society.

Rhys Davids, T.W. [1902] 1981. *Buddhist India*. Delhi: Motilal Banarsidass.

———. [1899] 2000a. *Dialogues of the Buddha*, vol. 1. Delhi: Motilal Banarsidass.

Rhys Davids, T.W. and C.A.F. Rhys Davids. [1910 and 1921] 2000b. *Dialogues of the Buddha*, vols. 2 & 3. Delhi: Motilal Banarsidass.

Rig Veda. [1981] 2000. *The Rig Veda: An Anthology*, tr. Wendy Doniger O' Flaherty. Delhi: Penguin.

Robertson, B. C. 1999. *Raja Rammohun Roy*. Delhi: Oxford University Press.

Robinson, Rowena and Sathianathan Clarke. 2003. *Religious Conversion in India: Modes, Motivations, and Meanings*. Delhi: Oxford University Press.

Rodrigues, Valerian. 2008. *Dalit-Bahujan Discourse*. Delhi: Critical Quest.

Rolland, Romain. 1951. *Inde, Journal 1915–1943*. Lausane: Vineta.

Roy, Arundhati. 2003. 'Gujarat, Fascism and Democracy.' In Chaitnya Krishna, ed., *Fascism in India*. Delhi: Manak.

Roy, Kumkum. 1996. 'Vedic Cosmogonies: Conceiving/Controlling Creation.' In R. Champakalakshmi and S. Gopal, eds., *Tradition, Dissent and Ideology*, pp. 9–19. Delhi: Oxford University Press.

Roy, Kumkum, Kunal Chkrabarti and Tanika Sarkar. 2005. *The Vedas, Hinduism, Hindutva*. Kolkata: Ebong Alap.

Roy, Rammohun. 1945–8. *The English Works of Raja Rammohun Roy*, eds. K. Nag and D. Burman. Calcutta: Sadharan Brahmo Samaj.

Roy, M.N. 1937. *The Historical Role of Islam*. Bombay: Vora & Co.

———. 1940. *Gandhism; Nationalism; Socialism*. Calcutta: Bengal Radical Club.

———. 1950. *India's Message: Fragments of a Prisoner's Diary*, vol. II. Calcutta: Renaissance Publishers.

Rude, George. 1995. *Ideology and Popular Protest*. London: University of North Carolina Press.

Said, Edward. 1978. *Orientalism: Western Conceptions of the Orient.* London: Penguin.

Sainath, P. 1996. *Everybody Loves a Good Drought.* Delhi: Penguin.

———. 1998. 'Dregs of Destiny', *Outlook,* 19 October.

Sangharakshita. 1985. 'Buddhism.' In A.L. Basham, ed., *A Cultural History of India.* Delhi: Oxford University Press.

———. 1986. *Ambedkar and Buddhism.* Glasgow: Windhorse Publications.

Sankrityayan, Rahul et al. 1990. *Buddhism: The Marxist Approach.* Delhi: People's Publishing House.

Saradamoni, K. 1980. *Emergence of a Slave Caste: Pulayas of Kerala.* Delhi: People's Publishing House.

Sardar, G.B. 1978. 'Saint-Poets of Maharashtra: Their Role in Social Transformation.' In S.C. Malik, ed., *Indian Movements,* pp. 101–38. Shimla: Indian Institute of Advanced Study.

Sardesai, S.G. 1979. *Class Struggle and Caste Conflict in Rural Areas.* Delhi: People's Publishing House.

———. 1994. *Progress and Conservatism in Ancient India,* rpt. Delhi: People's Publishing House.

Sarkar, Jadunath. 1973. *Shivaji and His Times,* rpt. Delhi: Orient Longman.

Sarkar, N.K. 1978. *Social Structure and Development Strategy in Asia.* Delhi: People's Publishing House.

Sarkar, Sumit. 1983. *Modern India 1885–1947.* Delhi: Macmillan.

———. 1996. 'Indian Nationalism and the Politics of Hindutva.' In David Ludden, ed., *Making India Hindu,* pp. 270–93, Delhi: Oxford University Press.

———. 1997. *Writing Social History.* Delhi: Oxford University Press.

———. 2002. *Beyond Nationalist Frames: Relocating Postmodernism, Hindutva, History.* Delhi: Permanent Black.

Sarkar, S.C. 1928. *Some Aspects of the Earliest Social History of India.* London: Oxford University Press.

Sarkar, Tanika. 1996. 'Imagining Hindurashtra: The Hindu and the Muslim in Bankim Chandra's Writings.' In David Ludden, ed., *Making India Hindu,* pp. 162–84, Delhi: Oxford University Press.

Sastri, Nilkanta and Srinivasachari. 1980. *Advanced History of India.* Delhi: Allied Publishers.

Satish Chandra. 2001. *Historiography, Religion and State in Medieval India.* Delhi: Har-Anand.

Satyamurthy, T.V., ed. 1996. *Region, Religion, Caste, Gender and Culture in Contemporary India.* Delhi: Oxford University Press.

Satyanarayana, K. and Susie Tharu, eds. 2011. *No Alphabet in Sight: New Dalit Writing From South India*. Dossier 1: Tamil and Malayalam. Delhi: Penguin.
Savarkar, V.D. [1923] 1999. *Hindutva—Who is a Hindu?* Mumbai: Savarkar Rashtriya Smarak.
Savitri Chandra. 1978. 'Dissent and Protest in Hindi Bhakti Poetry.' In S.C. Malik, ed., *Indian Movements*, pp. 139–58. Shimla: Indian Institute of Advanced Study.
Schomer, Karine and W.H. McLeod, eds. 1987. *The Sants: Studies in a Devotional Tradition of India*. Delhi: Motilal Banarsidass.
Schouten, J.P. 1995. *Revolution of the Mystics: On the Social Aspects of Virashaivism*. Delhi: Motilal Banarsidass.
Schweitzer, Albert. 1936. *Indian Thought and Its Development*. New York: Henry Holt & Co.
Scott, James C. 1985. *Weapons of the Weak: Everyday Forms of Peasant Resistance*. Oxford: Oxford University Press.
———. 1990. *Domination and the Arts of Resistance: Hidden Transcripts*. New Haven and London: Yale University Press.
Seabrook, Jeremy. 2000. *No-Nonsense Guide to Class, Caste and Hierarchies*. Oxford: New Internationalist.
Seal, Anil. 1968. *The Emergence of Indian Nationalism: Competition and Collaboration in the Late Nineteenth Century*. Cambridge: Cambridge University Press.
Sen, Amartya. 1999. 'On Interpreting India's Past'. In Sugata Bose and Ayesha Jalal, eds., *Nationalism, Democracy & Development*, pp. 10–35, Delhi: Oxford University Press.
Sen, Amiya P. 1993. *Hindu Revivalism in Bengal 1872–1905*. Delhi: Oxford University Press.
———, ed. 2003. *Social and Religious Reform: The Hindus of British India*. Delhi: Oxford University Press.
Senapati, Nilamani. 1975. *Mahima Dharma*. Cuttak: Dharma Granth Store.
Shah, Ghanshyam. 1990. *Social Movements in India: A Review of the Literature*. Delhi: Sage.
———, ed. 2001. *Dalit Identity and Politics*. Delhi: Sage.
———, ed. 2002. *Caste and Democratic Politics in India*. Delhi: Permanent Black.
Sharma, Arvind. 2001. 'Swami Dayananda Saraswati.' In Robert D. Baird, ed., *Religion in Modern India*, pp. 388–409. Delhi: Manohar.
Sharma, Jyotirmaya. 2003. *Hindutva: Exploring the Idea of Hindu Nationalism*. Delhi: Penguin.

———. 2007. *Terrifying Vision: M.S. Golwalkar, the RSS and India.* Delhi: Penguin.

———. 2012. *Cosmic Love and Human Apathy: Swami Vivekananda's Restatement of Religion.* Delhi: HarperCollins.

Sharma, R.S. 1980. *Indian Feudalism,* 2nd edn. Delhi: Macmillan.

———. 1983. *Perspective in Social and Economic History of Early India.* Delhi: Munshiram Manoharlal.

———. [1958] 1990a. *Shudras in Ancient India,* 1958, 3rd revd. edn. Delhi: Motilal Banarsidass.

———. 1990b. *Ancient India.* Delhi: NCERT.

———. [1959] 1991. *Aspects of Political Ideas and Institutions in Ancient India,* revised edn. Delhi: Motilal Banarsidass.

———. [1983] 2001. *Material Culture and Social Formations in Ancient India.* Delhi: Macmillan.

Sharma, Ursula. 2002. *Caste.* Delhi: Viva Books.

Shirer, William. [1961] 1991. *The Rise and Fall of the Third Reich.* London: Mandrin.

Shrivastava, Aseem, and Ashish Kothari. 2012. *Churning the Earth: The Making of Global India.* Delhi: Penguin.

Shyam Chand. 2002. *Saffron Fascism.* Delhi: Hemkunt Publishers.

Sidhanta, N.K. 1929. *The Heroic Age of India.* London: Kegan Paul.

Simeon, Dilip. 1986. 'Communalism in Modern India', *Mainstream*, 13 December, pp. 7–17.

Singh, Darshan. 1996. *A Study of Bhakta Ravidasa.* Patiala: Punjab University publication.

Singh, Iqbal. 1987. *Rammohun Roy: A Biographical Inquiry into the Making of Modern India,* vols. II & III. Bombay: Asia Publishing House.

Singh, Kumar Suresh. 2002. *Birsa Munda and His Movement 1872–1901: A Study of a Millenarian Movement in Chotanagpur.* Kolkata: Seagull.

Singh, Yogendra. 1986. *Modernisation of Indian Tradition.* Jaipur: Rawat.

Sircar, D.C. [1957] 1998. *Inscriptions of Asoka.* Delhi: Publications Division, Govt. of India.

Smith, Brian K. 2012. *Veda and Varna.* Delhi: Critical Quest.

Smith, David. 2003a. 'Orientalism and Hinduism.' In Gavin Flood, ed., *The Blackwell Companion to Hinduism,* pp. 45–63. Oxford: Blackwell.

———. 2003b. *Hinduism and Modernity.* Oxford: Blackwell.

Solomon, J. and I. Back. 1994. 'Conceptualising Racisms: Social Theory, Politics and Research', *Sociology* 28, 1, pp. 143–61.

Srinivas, M.N. [1966] 1972. *Social Change in Modern India.* Delhi: Allied Publishers.

———. [1962] 1985. *Caste in Modern India*. Bombay: Media Promoters.
Sunil, K.P. 1991. 'And Justice for All . . . ', *The Illustrated Weekly of India*, 8–14 June, pp. 16–19.
Szasz, Thomas. 1974. *The Second Sin*. London: Routledge and Kegan Paul.
Tagore, Devendranath. 1909. *The Autobiography of Maharshi Debendranath Tagore*. Calcutta: S.K. Lahiri.
Tagore, Rabindranath. [1925] 1997. 'The Cult of the Charkha.' In S. Bhattacharya, ed., *The Mahatma and the Poet*, pp. 99–112. Delhi: National Book Trust.
———. 1927. 'The Shudra Habit', *Modern Review*, May issue.
Talwar, Vir Bharat. 2001. *Hindu Navjagaran ki Vichardhara: Satyarth Prakash: Samalochana Ka Ek Prayas*. Shimla: Indian Institute of Advanced Study.
Taylor, Charles. 1992. *Multiculturalism and 'The Politics of Recognition'*, ed. Amy Gutmann. Princeton: Princeton University Press.
Thapar, Romila. 1975. *The Past and Prejudice*. Delhi: National Book Trust.
———. [1966] 1984. *A History of India*, vol. I. Harmondsworth: Penguin.
———. [1961] 1999a. *Ashoka and the Decline of the Mauryas*. Delhi: Oxford University Press.
———. 1999b. 'The Tyranny of Labels'. In K.N. Panikkar, ed., *The Concerned Indian's Guide to Communalism*. Delhi: Viking.
———. 2001. 'Syndicated Hinduism.' In G.-D. Sontheimer and H. Kulke, eds., *Hinduism Reconsidered*. Delhi: Manohar.
———. 2008. *The Aryan: Recasting Constructs*. Gurgaon: Three Essays Collective.
Tharu, Susie and K. Lalita, eds. 1991 and 1993. *Women Writing in India*, vol. I: 600 BC to the Early Twentieth Century; vol. II: The Twentieth Century. Delhi: Oxford University Press.
Thorat, Sukhdeo and Katherine Newman, eds. 2010. *Blocked by Caste: Economic Discrimination in Modern India*. Delhi: Oxford University Press.
Tidrick, Kathryn. 2006. *Gandhi: A Political and Spiritual Life*. London: I.B. Tauris.
Tolstoy, Leo. 1987. 'On Patriotism' [1894]. In idem, *Writings on Civil Disobedience and Non-Violence*. Philadelphia: New Society Publishers.
Trautman, Thomas R., ed. 2005. *The Aryan Debate*. Delhi: Oxford University Press.
Turner, Bryan S. 1983. *Religion and Social Theory*. London: Heinemann.
Upadhyay, Prakash Chandra. [1992] 2007. *The Politics of Indian Secularism*. Delhi: Critical Quest.

Upadhyaya, B.S. 1989. *Feeders of Indian Culture.* Delhi: People's Publishing House.
Vanaik, Achin. 1990. *The Painful Transition—Bourgeois Democracy in India.* London: Verso
Van der Vir, Peter. 1996. 'Writing Violence.' In David Ludden, ed., *Making India Hindu,* pp. 250–69, Delhi: Oxford University Press.
Varma, Pawan. 1998. *The Great Indian Middle Class.* Delhi: Penguin.
Varma, V.P. [1954] 1974. *Studies in Hindu Political Thought and Its Metaphysical Foundations.* Delhi: Motilal Banarsidass.
———. 1956. 'The Origins of Buddhism', *The Journal of the Bihar Research Society,* Buddha Jayanti spl. issue, vol. 2.
Vaudeville, Charlotte. 1993. *A Weaver Named Kabir.* Delhi: Oxford University Press.
———. 1996. *Myths, Saints and Legends in Medieval India.* Delhi: Oxford University Press.
Verardi, Giovanni. 2011. *Hardships and Downfall of Buddhism in India.* Delhi: Manohar.
Vishwanathan, E.S. 1983. *The Political Career of E.V. Ramaswami Naicker.* Madras: Ravi and Vasanth Publishers.
Vishwanathan, Gauri. 2001. *Outside the Fold: Conversion, Modernity, and Belief.* Delhi: Oxford University Press.
Vivekananda, Swami. 1988. *Caste, Culture and Socialism.* Calcutta: Advaita Ashrama.
———. 1991. *Inspired Talks.* Madras: Ramkrishna Math.
———. 1998. *The Nationalistic and Religious Lectures,* ed. Swami Tapasyananda. Calcutta: Advaita Ashrama.
———. [1951] 1999. *The Complete Works of Swami Vivekananda,* 8 vols. Calcutta: Advaita Ashrama.
Voigt, Johannes H. 1967. *F.M. Max Müller: The Man and His Ideas.* Calcutta: Firma K.L. Mukhopadhyaya.
Walker, Benjamin. 1983a. *Hindu World,* vol. I. Delhi: Munshiram Manoharlal.
———. 1983b. *Hindu World,* vol. II. Delhi: Munshiram Manoharlal.
Webster, John C.B. 2000. *Religion and Dalit Liberation: An Examination of Perspectives.* Delhi: Manohar.
Weil, Simone. [1955] 2001. *Oppression and Liberty,* tr. Arthur Wills and John Petrie. London: Routledge.
Williams, Paul with Anthony Tribe. 2000. *Buddhist Thought.* London and New York: Routledge.
Woodward, F.L. and E.M. Hare. 1932–6. *Anguttara Nikaya,* translated as *The Book of Gradual Sayings,* 5 vols. London: Pali Text Society.

Zacharia, Benjamin. 2011. *Playing the Nation Game: The Ambiguities of Nationalism in India*. Delhi: Yoda Press.

Zavos, John. 2000. *The Emergence of Hindu Nationalism in India*. Delhi: Oxford University Press.

Zelliot, Eleanor. 1979. 'The Indian Rediscovery of Buddhism.' In A.K. Narain et al., eds., *Studies in Pali and Buddhism*, pp. 389–406. Delhi: B.R. Publishing.

———. 1996. *From Untouchable to Dalit: Essays on the Ambedkar Movement*. Delhi: Manohar.

Zelliot, Eleanor, and Rohini Mokashi-Punekar, eds. 2005. *Untouchable Saints: An Indian Phenomenon*. Delhi: Manohar.

Index

Aborigines/non-Aryans 60, 66, 68, 89, 93, 193, 196, 223, 228, 234, 269, 325, 328
Achhutanand, Swami 53, 222, 298, 327–30
Adi-Andhra 326
Adi-Dharma, in Punjab 293, 331–2
Adi-Dravida/Dravidians, *see* Dravidian movement
Adi-Hindu movement, in Uttar Pradesh 327–31
Adivasis/tribals (original inhabitants) 33, 196, 286, 394n; and egalitarian culture 99, 201; tribal revolts 297
Agganna Sutta 114 ff., 123
Agrahara 164
Ajivikas 84, 92
Ajit Keshkambal 99
Akhil Bharatiya Brahman Mahasabha 222
Alberuni 38
Alekha or Mahima Dharma 296–7
Allama 171
Alvars and Nayanars 164
Althusser, Louis, his thesis of Ideological State Apparatuses 22–3
Ambapali 117
Ambedkar, B.R. 21, 22, 24, 27, 28, 30, 33, 35, 36, 44, 45, 47, 52–6, 57n, 188n, 248–9, 252, 253, 289n, 292, 294, 298, 304, 310, 316, 318, 319, 326, 327, 332, 337, 339, 349 ff.; and Buddhism 120–2, 126, 131 ff., 156, 350, 394, 402; and Constitution 389 ff.; clash with Gandhi over caste and separate electorate 356 ff.; fight against caste 349 ff.; Mahad struggle 351–3; on base-superstructure dogma 21–2; on Gandhi and Gandhism 382–5; on nation and nationalism 385 ff.
anicca and *anatta(vada)* 106–7
Annie Besant 340
Annihilation of Caste 351
anuloma-pratiloma marriage 131, 169–70
anti-caste/anti-brahmanic ideology and movement(s) 23–4, 33–40, 52–6, 84 ff., 90, 98–100, 111–17, 140 ff., 253 ff., 292 ff; 349 ff.; as nationalism from below 295 ff., 332 ff.; education as a focal point of 56, 254–5, 271–4, 294, 296, 302–3, 350; *see also* Ambedkar, Buddha, Buddhism, Iyothee Thass, Mukti movements, Narayana Guru, Periyar and Phule
arajaka 86
Arjuana 74, 75, 79, 80
Arthashastra, see Kautilya
Aryan/Indo-Aryan/Vedic-Aryan 37, 42, 49, 59 ff., 89, 164, 191 ff., 227, 228, 234, 240, 244, 247, 248, 269, 270, 310, 316, 324, 326, 327, 328, 330, 331, 336n; Aryanisation 164, 165; battles with indigenous people 37; *see also* Colonialism, Orientalism and Dayananda
Aryan race theory 42, 43, 50, 51, 191 ff., 240, 244, 262
Arya Samaj 209, 214 ff., 222, 255, 284, 327–8, 331
Asan, Kumaran 298, 302–4
Ashoka the king 38, 51, 94, 104, 124, 125, 127–30, 135, 136; his edicts, inscriptions 128; his dhamma 128; his introduction of uniformity in law 129–30

Ashvaghosa 100, 127
Asiatic Society of Bengal 192
astika-nastika, the contexual meaning 92–3; *nastiko vedanindakah* 92
asura(s) 93; *asura-views* 93; *Asuropanishad* 99
atishudra/antyaja/panchama, the origin of 69
Attenborough, Richard 14, 47
Atthangika Magga 105
Aughars 88
Aurobindo Ghosh 50, 76, 77, 214, 219, 244
avarna–savarna, the meaning and making of 66–7
avatara, doctrine of 76, 201, 269
Ayyankali 298, 307–8
Ayyappan, K. 53, 298, 302, 305, 306, 307, 308, 333

Bahinabai 181
bahujan hitaya 101, 111
Bajaj, Jamnalal 377
Bali Raja 269, 270, 286, 289n; and Vaman 269
Banerjee, Surendranath 211, 285
Bankimchandra Chatterjee 50, 214, 224, 236, 244
Bansode, Kisan Faguji 327
Basava 142, 169–71
Bengal Brahman Sabha 224
Bentinck, William 208
Bhagavad Gita 30, 72, 73 ff., 102, 183, 192, 201, 233, 239n, 329; the myth and truth of 73–80
Bhagyareddy Varma 298, 326
bhakti (devotion) 40
Bhakti movement, *see* Mukti movement(s)
Bharati Dasan 322
Bharatendu Harishchandra 237
Bhattacharya, Jogendranath 224
Bhils 196, 235, 331
Bhima Bhoi 296–7
Bible 219, 241
Birla, Ghanshyam Das 377

Bodhisattva 105, 133
Brahmadeya 69, 134, 164
Brahmana (the Supreme Spirit) 70; Atman-Brahmana 102, 107, 109, 110
Brahmanas (texts dealing with rituals) 59, 66, 94, 108; *Shatapatha Brahmana* 63, 68, 108
Brahman(s) 24 ff.; etymology and meaning of 69–70; *see also* Caste, Brahmanical *and* Brahmanism
Brahmanical: cosmogony 78–9; knowledge-production, the classical basis of 24–5; patriarchy, *see* Women; polity and state 81–4; 'lawless laws' 354
Brahmanical social order, *see* Caste
Brahmanism, as ideology and politics of hierarchy 11 ff., 24 ff.; its backlash against Buddhism 130 ff.; its backlash against Mukti movements 183 ff.; its forgeries for brahmanisation of culture 134 ff.; its makeover as Hindusim 43–4, 199–201; its nexus with colonialism as well as Hindu nationalism 191 ff.
Brahmi script 127
Brahmo Samaj 209, 210, 211–12, 213, 255, 284
breast-cloth controversy 295
Brihadratha 130
Brihaspati 90
Buddha/Gautam Siddhartha 5, 38, 39, 51, 74, 90, 96–7n, 98 ff., 171, 232, 257, 289n, 297, 301, 304, 326, 349, 394; against caste and brahmanism 111–17; against Vedic-Upanishdic metaphysics 107–10; life and philosophy 100 ff.; political ideas 122 ff.; theory of dependent origin 106, 108, 109; *see also* Buddhism
Buddhism/Buddhist(s) 31, 32, 35, 38, 39, 40, 50, 51, 53, 74, 76, 78, 84, 87, 88, 90, 92, 93, 94, 96n, 97n; 98–139, 141, 142, 147, 150, 151, 163, 164, 171, 192, 200, 201, 219, 231, 232, 233, 249, 257, 304–5, 309–10, 311, 326,

339, 350, 371, 394, 396n; Buddhist Sangha 92, 123; contributions of 125 ff.; global spread of 125–6; role of brahman-Buddhists in the decline of 132 ff.; the myth of Upanishadic influence on 107–8; violence against 183 ff.; women in Sangha 116–17, 118–19; universities (at Taxila, Nalanda, Vikramshila) 127; *see also* Buddha

Carlyle, Thomas 383
Carpenter, Edward 396
caste/caste system/brahmanical social order 11 ff. (figures often throughout the text); and class 28; and patriarchy 28–9; as a system 24 ff.; brahman-kshatriya nexus 81, 148; caste indoctrination 65 ff.; mythical (Rigvedic) origin of 61, 66, 95n; nationalist glorification of 222 ff.; patronage by ruling groups 82; reproduction of 399–401; in judiciary 404–5; *see also* Ambedkar, Gandhi, Nehru, Periyar and Phule
Census(es) 12, 312, 337–9; the Gait circular 338–9, 394–5n
Chaitanya 184
Charvaka(s), *see* Lokayata
Chetty, Thyagaraj 312, 313
Chokhamela 142, 174, 177–9, 188n
Chola dynasty 164
Chomsky, Noam 23
Christ, Jesus 216, 231, 289n
Christianity 32, 33, 53, 144, 200, 204, 210, 216, 217, 219, 231, 233, 241, 243, 257, 265, 266, 277, 293, 305, 339; Protestant reformation 144
Christian(s)/missionaries 44, 209, 213, 226, 231, 248, 249, 250, 252, 265, 266, 273, 308, 319, 341, 367
Civil Rights League 308
Colebrooke, H.T. 192, 193, 198, 239n
colonialism/colonial: 12, 13, 40 ff., 189 ff., nexus with caste elites and brahmanism 12, 40–3, 190 ff.; knowledge/Orientalism 12–13, 191–201
communalism 24, 34; brahmanic roots of 31 ff.; and brahmanic Hindu nationalism 236–8, 244 ff.
Congress/Indian National Congress 44, 45, 223, 236, 237, 251, 255, 285, 286, 287, 288, 306, 307, 312, 316–18, 321, 324, 331, 332, 333, 334, 335n, 337 ff.
Contemporary India, discriminations in 397 ff.
counter-tradition, the meaning of 19
Crony capitalism 397
cultural nationalism 233 ff.
culture of silence 35

Dadu Dayal 140, 142, 146, 159, 184
dalit(s)/ati-shudras/scheduled castes, *see* caste *and* dalit-bahujans
dalit-bahujan(s)/lowered castes 11 ff., 33 ff., 52 ff., 226, 235, 248, 250; 253 ff., 291 ff., 337 ff; *see also* Phule, Ambedkar and Periyar
Dalit Panther's manifesto 333
danda 64, 82 ff.; *dandaniti* 26, 82–4
Darwin, Charles 218
Dasa/Dasyus 37, 42, 60, 93, 328
Dasan, Bharati 322
Dayananda Saraswati 44, 48, 50, 194, 214 ff., 220, 227, 244, 253, 346; castigation of Kabir 146, 216; Vedic fanaticism, *Satyartha Prakash*, and *shuddhi* 214–19
Delhi Sultanate 148, 150
Devanagari script 127
Dhamma 101, 102, 106, 109, 110, 122, 128, 394, and dharma 139n
Dhamma-cakka-ppavattana 106
Dhammaghosa 125
Dhamma-mahamartya 130
Dhammapada 104, 111, 139n
dharma 26, 30, 49, 71, 76, 81, 83, 92, 215, 231, 299; etymology of 70, 96n; *dharmadanda* 32; *Rajadharma* 83
Dharmakirti 108–9
Dharma Sabha 211–12

Index

Dharmashastra(s)/*smriti(s)* 11, 24, 29, 31, 35, 39, 55, 68, 70, 71, 72, 73, 83, 85, 93, 94, 134, 169, 206, 221, 262, 267, 274, 330, 386
Dharmasutras 39, 72
Disraeli, Benjamin 195
dominance and resistance, concomitance of 19 ff.
Dravidian people/culture/language/literature 66, 164, 193, 234, 308 ff., 328, 336n
Dravidian movement 308 ff., 336n; *also see* Iyothee Thass and Periyar
Dronacharya 15, 55, 79
Duncan, Jonathan 190
Dutt, R.C. 50, 223–4

East India Company 189 ff.
Ekalavya 15, 80, 405
Ekanath 173–4, 183

Fa Hsien 126
Fanon, Franz 22, 189
feudalism/feudal forces 76, 134–5, 142, 147, 154, 191, 298, 380; caste-feudal(ism) 81, 140, 183, 189, 201, 206, 297, 335
Foucault, Michel 253, 271
Freire, Paulo 21
French Revolution 260, 352

Gana (tribe) 92
Gandhi, Mohandas 11, 12, 14, 15, 44, 45, 46–8, 54, 58n, 76, 77, 78, 156, 193, 195, 197, 199, 227, 236, 239n, 251, 306–7, 317, 320–2, 328, 331, 332, 334, 335n, 337, 341 ff., 402, 403; castigation of modernity: *Hind Swaraj* 374–6; harijanisation of dalits 364 ff.; critiques and critics of 377–85; support of caste 368–72; support of varnashrama and brahmanic Hinduism 15, 46–7, 341, 371; his trusteeship 342, 343, 351, 370, 384
gender, *see* women
Ghosh, Jogendrachandra 224–5

Gita, see *Bhagavad Gita*
Godse, Nathuram 77, 251, 322
Gokhale, G.K. 376
Golwalkar, M.S. 194, 246–7, 249, 250
Gorakhnath 147, 151, 163; *Gorakh-Gita* 175
Gora Kumbhar 142, 177, 182
Gramsci, Antonio 22–3, 253; his concept of hegemony 22–3
Grihyasutras 221; *Gautamadharmasutra* 30
Gulamgiri 35, 256, 262–3, 269, 273, 288
Gupta period 135, 138
Guru Granth Sahib/Adi Granth 146, 161
Gyaneshwar 76, 77, 144, 145, 173–4, 183

Halhed, Nathaniel 192, 198
Hall, Stuart 23
Haralayya and Madhuvayya, their martyrdom 142, 169–70
Harappan culture, *see* Indus Valley civilisation
Harshavardhan 87, 88, 126, 127
Hastings, Warren 191, 192
Hedgewar, K.B. 45, 248, 250
Hegel, G.W.F. 54
Hindi movement 237; Hindi-Hindu-Hindustan 237, 324
Hindu Mahasabha 244, 245
Hinduism/Hindus (figures often throughout the text); folk Hinduism 201, 219; neo-Hinduism, construction of 190, 190 ff.; Hindu nationalism, its link with European fascism 244 ff.; Hindu majoritarianism, the bluff of 33; syndicated Hinduism 43–4, 200–1; *see also* Gandhi, Nationalism and RSS
Hindutva 14, 244 ff.
hiranya garbha 82
Hitler, Adolf 240, 243, 244, 245
Hsuan Tsang 38, 87, 126; attempt on his life by brahman fanatics 87–8
Hunter Commission on education 272–3

Indic religion 32

Index

Indus Valley (or Harrapan) civilisation 37, 60, 89, 129, 330; no connection with Rigvedic Aryans 60
Islam, *see* Muslim(s)
Itihasa-Purana 11, 184, 267
Iyothee Thass 35, 53, 56, 222, 226, 298, 304, 308, 309–12, 336n; and Buddhism 120, 309–10; on brahmanical culture and epistemology 311–12

Jabali 93
Jagjivan Ram 367
Jain(s)/Jainism 31, 38, 88, 92, 93, 96n, 97n, 99, 100, 147, 164, 192, 201, 216, 219, 311, 371, 396
Janabai 177
Jataka stories 127
jati, *see* caste
Jatibhed-Vivekasar 261
Jones, William 191, 192–3, 198
Justice Party 312–16, 320, 324

Kabir 51, 53 140, 142, 143, 145, 146, 148–57, 161, 162, 163, 166, 168, 184, 185, 186, 188n, 210, 257, 289n, 327, 328, 349; attempt of his brahmanisation 145, 149–50; life, struggle, creativity 148 ff; Kabirpanth(i) 156, 188n, 257, 329
Kalama Sutta 5, 103
Kali 73, 98
Kalidas 192
Kaliyuga 74, 79, 85, 154, 185, 187, 239n, 374
kallumalai 308
kamma 117, 133
Kanishka 126, 127
Kannada 324; *see also* Virshaivas
Kanshi Ram 362
Kapalikas 88
karma 65, 70, 71, 76, 107, 117, 201, 214, 231, 268, 269
karma-kanda 38, 92, 93, 144
Karna 79, 80, 362, 405
Katha-sarita-sagar 137, 202

Kautilya 15, 38, 83, 84, 129; his *Arthashastra* 64, 83, 84, 129
Kautsa 90
Kayastha Pathshala 222
Khilafat 347
Krishna 73, 74 ff., 79–80, 102, 174, 245, 258
Kshatriya(s), *see* caste; and Khattiya(s) 115
Kumarila Bhatta 147

Lajpat Rai 50, 235, 339
Lokahitavadi Gopal Hari Deshmukh 258, 259–60, 267
Lokayata, Lokayatika(s)/Charvaka(s) 35, 90–2, 93, 99; *Lokayatasutra* 99
Lokhande, N.M. 281–2
lowered castes, *see* caste *and* dalit-bahujans
Lucknow Pact 340

Macaulay, T.B. 202, 203
Machiavelli 243
Mahabharata 64, 68, 81, 83, 85, 93, 95, 134, 135, 136, 184, 221; *see also Bhagavad Gita*
Mahabodhi Society 126
Mahadevi, Akka 142, 172
Mahaparinibbana Sutta 102, 117
Mahaprajapati Gautami 117
Mahasammata, theory of 38, 123–4
Mahavir, Vardhamana 90, 99, 100
Mahayana 126, 133–4, 138n
Mahendra 125
Majjhima patipada 105
Makkali Gosala 99
Malaviya, M.M. 45
Malayalam 301, 305, 324, 335n; *see also* Narayana Guru
Mangoo Ram 222, 298, 331
Manu 29, 38, 67, 71, 96n, 186, 190, 192, 198, 208, 209, 217, 228, 229, 239n, 241, 242, 244, 249, 328, 340; his real identity (Sumati Bhargava) 131
Manusmriti 29, 30, 58n, 68, 69, 70, 71, 72, 81, 83, 96n, 131–2, 134, 190, 192, 207, 208, 241, 325; burning of 320,

351, 353; colonial resurrection of 190–1
Maomaris 297
Mariategui, Jose 383
Marx, Karl/Marxian 13, 20–3, 61, 253, 346; his key ideas 21–2
Marxist(s)/communists (of India), 22, 37, 92, 252, 323–4, 381, 382
Materialist philosophy in ancient India, *see* Lokayata
Matsyanyaya 26, 64
Maurya(s) 95, 129–30, 132, 134; *see also* Ashoka
Max Müller 14, 42, 50, 58n, 95, 194, 195–6, 198, 239n, 240, 284
McDoland, Ramsey 358
Megasthenes 38
Menander 125
Metta Sutta 103–4
Michelet, Jules 397
Mirabai 142, 162
mlechchha 31, 68
M.N. Roy 238n; on Gandhi and Gandhism 381–2
moksha 91, 92, 277
Monier-Williams, M. 193–4
Morley–Minto reforms 338
Moses 198
Muhammad the prophet 216, 231, 232, 289n
Muktabai 272
Mukti or Bhakti movement(s) 40, 140–88; against caste 140 ff.; brahmanic backlash 183 ff.; Buddhist-shramanic roots of 141–2, 146; *janbhasha(s)* preferred over Sanskrit 144, 182; sant-poets of the north 148–62; subaltern, decaste and women sant-poets 142; Tamil Siddha(s) 142, 163–8; Varakaris 173–83; Virashaivas 169–73
Muktayakka 172
Muslim(s)/Islamic religion, rule, or ideas 31, 32, 33, 41, 43, 44, 45, 49, 51, 53, 82, 132, 141, 142, 148, 149, 150, 151, 153, 155, 156, 160, 165, 187, 189, 190, 192, 194, 196, 198, 189, 200, 203, 205, 210, 213, 216, 217, 221, 224, 226, 231–2, 233, 234, 236, 238, 246, 248, 249, 250, 251, 252, 263, 264, 265, 266, 269, 283, 293, 304, 308, 319, 327, 331, 339, 340, 341, 342, 344, 345, 346, 347–9, 357, 359, 360, 398
Muslim League 339, 340, 349
Mussolini, Benito 243, 245

Naidu, Sarojini 377
Naidu, M.V. 313
Nair, T.M. 312, 313
Namashudras 296
Namdev 142, 146, 157, 174, 175–7, 188n
Nanak, Guru 51, 140, 142, 146, 159–61, 162, 184, 210
Nandnar 163
Naoroji, Dadabhai 285
Narasu, Laxmi 323
Narayana Guru 53, 56, 222, 226, 294, 298 ff., 333, 335n; his debate on caste with Gandhi 307; SNDP movement 302 ff.
Nathpanthi(s)/Nath-Siddhas/Nath-Yogis 40, 146–7, 148, 150, 151, 163, 175–6
nationalism 11, 44–54, 222 ff., 282 ff., 291 ff., 337 ff.; and caste 222 ff.; cultural nationalism 233 ff.; Hindu nationalism and Hindutva 244 ff.; *also see* Ambedkar, Congress, Gandhi, Nehru, Periyar and Phule
Nazism 240, 243, 244
Nehru, Jawaharlal 44, 45, 46, 48–51, 54, 58n, 133, 197, 199, 334, 348–9, 351–2, 355, 393; and caste 11, 351–2, 395n; his brahmanic *Discovery of India* 48–51; on Gandhi and Gandhism 378–81
nibbana (nirvana) 104, 133
Nietzsche, Friedrich 240 ff.; and Manu 241, 242; his vicious ideology 240–4
nirguna 143
nirguna and *saguna* 184; the conflict of 184–6

Non-Cooperation movement 347
Non-Brahman Manifesto 312
non-brahman movements, *see* anti-caste movements
Nyaya school 92

orientalism/orientalists 42, 50, 191 ff.; *also see* colonialism
Other Backward Classes (OBCs)/ shudras, *see* caste *and* dalit-bahujans

Pal, B.C. 50, 219, 235
Pala dynasty 88
Paine, Thomas 260
Pali language 35, 126, 133, 136; Buddhist-Jain texts in 38, 86, 93; Pali Buddhist canon 38, 39, 100, 116, 126, 138–9n
Pambattti Sittar 140, 142, 167–8
Parashara 208
Parashuram 269
paribbajaka (parivrajaka) 99
Parshva 100
Pashandas 84
Patanjali 93, 130; on shramanic-brahmanic antagonism 38, 93
Patel, Vallabhbhai 355, 359
paticca samuppada 106, 108, 109
Patil, Mukundrao 291
patriarchy, *see under* women
Periyar, E.V. Ramaswami 24, 33, 35, 36, 44, 45, 47, 52–6, 57n, 291, 292, 298, 304, 315, 316–24, 333, 335n, 382; and Ambedkar 316, 318, 324–5; and Gandhi 320–2; on nationalism 318; on non-brahmanism 319
Peshwa(s)/Peshwai 257–8, 260, 261, 270
Phule, Jotirao 24, 27, 33, 35, 36, 44, 45, 52–6, 57n, 156, 188n, 222, 223, 226, 248, 253–90, 292, 294, 298, 304, 316, 319, 326, 333, 402; a new religion, vision of 53, 55, 333, 337, 349; his bahujanvad: the community of the oppressed 253, 256, 264–5, 274, 289n; vision and campaign for education 254, 255, 263, 271–4; history from below, attempt at 255; on caste 253, 260, 261 ff.; on colonialism 288; on nation and nationalism 282–8; for women's liberation 274–9; for cultivators and workers 279–82
Phule, Savitribai 256, 275, 276, 294
Poona Pact 360–3
Poona Sarvajanik Sabha 284, 290n
Praja Mitra Mandali 325
Prakrit language(s) 35, 127, 136, 137, 138, 194
Prarthana Samaj 209, 255, 284
Prinsep, James 135, 192
Purana(s) 98, 134, 145, 149, 151, 155, 167, 185, 210, 248; *Bhagwat Purana* 192; *Shiva Purana* 192
Puran Kassapa 99
Pushyamitra Shunga 130–2; his persecution of Buddhists 130–1

Quran/Koran 153, 154, 191, 219, 232

race/racialism, 26, 66–7, 115; *also see* Aryan(s) *and* Aryan race theory
Radhakant Deb 207, 211, 212
Radhakrishnan, S. 48, 76, 77, 107, 351
Rai, Lajpat 50, 235, 339
Rajagopalachari, C. 76, 77, 80
Rajah, M.C. 326
rakshas(as) 31, 68; *rakshasisation* (demonisation) 31
Rama the god 73, 137, 153, 184, 186, 213, 309, 336n; reference as Shambuka-slayer 186, 309
Ramabai, Pandita 277–8, 290n
Ramakrishna Mission 229
Ramakrishna Paramhans 225, 229, 278
Ramananda, the myth of 145–6, 149–50, 188n
Ramayana 135, 136, 137, 184 ff., 221, 309, 329; Valmiki's *Ramayana* 93, 186; *Ramcharitamanasa* 184, 185–8
Ram Charan 327–8, 330
Ramdas 183
Rammohun Roy 43, 44, 50, 198, 199, 202, 203 ff., 220, 222, 253, 274

444   Index

Ranade, M.G. 50, 144–5, 173, 234, 236, 238, 266–7, 285, 286, 287, 288
Rashtriya Swayamsevak Sangh (RSS) 244 ff.
Ravana 31, 309, 336n
Republican Party 350
Ravidas/Raidas 53,140, 142, 143, 145, 146, 157–9, 161, 162, 184, 185, 187, 188n, 327, 328, 329; his utopia of a world without misery 157
reservation/affirmative action 313–14, 315, 317–19, 320
Rigveda, *see* Veda(s)
Risley, H.H. 337
Romain Roland 58n
Round Table Conference(s) 353, 356–8, 388, 390
Rousseau, J.J. 383
Ruskin, John 383, 396

Sabba Sutta 102–3
Sadhu Jana Paripalan Sangham 308
Sahajiya/Sahajyani Buddhism 146, 151, 176
Sahodara Sangham 306
Said, Edward 253; his *Orientalism* 196–7
Sakyas 84, 115, 116, 122, 124; *also see* Buddha *and* Buddhism
Samadharma, the Dravidian vision 323
Sanatana Dharma 43, 46, 203, 204, 214, 226
Sanjay Belathaputta 99
Sanghamitra 125
Sanskrit 14, 35, 42, 59 ff., 68, 72, 75, 87, 94, 126, 133,134, 135ff., 144, 146, 164, 181, 182, 191, 192, 193, 194, 195, 214, 215, 216, 221, 227–8, 232, 264, 301, 308, 336n, 371; and Hindi 237; forgeries/interpolations in 94–5
Sanskritisation/brahmanisation 134, 135, 164
Sanskritisation, thesis of 27, 57n.
sati 205, 206, 207, 274
Satnamis and Satnami Mahasabha 296

Satyashodhak Samaj 188n, 248, 256, 257, 263–4, 270, 277, 278, 281, 287, 289n, 316
Savarkar, V.D. 48, 50, 227, 244, 245, 246, 250
savarna, *see Avarna-savarna*
Savata Mali 142, 177, 182
Sayana 31, 196, 239n
Self-Respect movement 316 ff.
Sen, K. C. 50, 193
Separate electorate, *see* Poona Pact
Shahu Maharaj 298
Shaivism/Shaivite(s) 53, 164, 165, 175
Shambuka 15, 55, 309, 405; the story of 186
Shankara/Shankaracharya 30, 65, 76, 77, 78, 93–4, 108, 134, 147, 201, 232, 233, 262; his attack on Buddhism 134
Shashanka (of Gaud) 88
Shastra(s) 190, 191, 209, 218, 226, 262
Shetkaryacha Asud 257, 276, 280, 287
Shibnath Sastri 210
Shiva/Adinath 73, 175, 258, 300
Shivaji, Chhatrapati 257, 261, 269–70; brahmanic humiliation of 289–90n
Shoonyavada 133, 134
Shraddhanand 365
Shraman (saman)/shramanic tradition 35, 37 ff., 56, 88 ff., 140, 141, 146, 200, 201; its conflict with brahmanism 37–8, 88–90; its leaders in the sixth century BCE 99; the etymology and meaning of 96–7n.; *see also* Ambedkar, Buddha, Buddhism, Mukti movements, and Phule
Shruti-smriti 25, 59, 88; *see also* Vedas and Dharmashastras
shudra(s), *see* caste *and* dalit-bahujans; etymology of 31
Siddha(s) 88, 309; *see also* Nathpanthis
Sikhism/Sikhs 32, 33, 40, 51, 56, 159–61, 192, 201, 210, 216, 331, 357, 360
Singaravelu, M. 323–4
Sita 15, 55, 230, 405

Index

Sivavakkiyar 142, 165–6
Social Darwinism 83
Sree Narayana Dharma Paripalana Yogam (SNDP) 302 ff.
Stri-Purush Tulana 278
Subramania Bharathi 168
Sufi(ism) 40, 56, 88, 141, 148, 165
Surdas 184
Sutta Nipata 111, 112
Swatantra Samudayam 305

Tagore, Debendranath 213, 220
Tagore, Dwarkanath 210, 212–13
Tagore, Rabindranath 156, 168, 235, 238; his critique of Gandhi 377–8
Tamil/Tamilian 138, 163 ff., 308 ff., 336n, *also see* Dravidian, Iyothee Thass and Periyar
Tamil Buddhism/South Indian Buddhist Association, *see* Iyothee Thass
Tamil Siddhas' movement 163–8
Tantrism/Tantrik 133, 146, 147
Tarabai Shinde 277, 278–9
Taylor, Charles 54
Telugu 324, 325
Theendal 298, 307, 335–6n
Theragatha 116
Theravada 138n
Therigatha 116, 118–19
Thiruvalluvar 161
Tilak, B.G. 45, 48, 50, 54, 76, 77, 227, 233, 234, 235–6, 244, 245, 248, 270, 278, 285, 355; his perverse nationalism 340
Tipitak, the Pali canon 138–9n.
Tipu Sultan 189
Tirumular 163, 165, 168
Tolstoy, Leo 337, 383, 396n
Toynbee, Arnold 14
Trilochan 157
Tritiya Ratna 254, 264, 271
Triveni Sangh 297
Tuka the poet 142, 143, 179–82, 257
Tukaram Tatya Padwal 261
Tulsidas 40, 144, 184, 185–8

Tukaram Tatya Padwal 261

Upali 116
Upanishad(s)/Upanishadic/Advaita/ Vedanta/Vedantic 37, 39, 59, 65, 66, 70, 74, 90, 92, 100, 101, 102, 104, 107, 108, 110, 126, 134, 194, 195, 201, 203, 204, 210, 223, 225, 226, 230, 232, 239n, 268, 284, 301; *Allopanishad* 108; *Brihadranyaka Upanishad* 102, 108; *Chandyoga Upanishad* 93, 99, 239n

Vaikkon temple agitation 295, 307, 335n, 341
Vaishya(s)/bania(s) 29, 64, *see* Caste
Vaisheshika 92
Vallabhacharya 184
Varakaris' movement 173–83
Varna 24, 26, 131; *also see* Caste
Varnashrama Dharma/varna dharma 29, 43, 66, 81, 85, 90, 160, 171, 184, 204, 227, 246, 300, 307, 317, 321, 342, 343, 344, 345, 351, 372, 377, 390, 394, 403
Vasettha Sutta 111
Veda(s)/Vedic 24–25, 30, 31, 37, 39, 42, 49, 59–68, 71, 72, 73, 79, 89, 90, 92, 93, 94, 100, 101, 102, 104, 107, 110, 126, 130, 134, 135, 145, 146, 149, 151, 152, 153, 154, 155, 166, 167, 180, 194, 198, 201, 202, 203, 204, 207, 209, 210, 213, 226, 248, 304, 322, 325, 327, 330, 363; ideology of 61, 62–4; *Purush-sukta* 61, 66, 67, 95, 188n; *Rigveda* 31, 59 ff., 89, 95, 195, 223, 239; *see also* Dayananda Saraswati
Veda-Purana/Veda-Upanishad/Vedic-brahmanism, *see* Veda(s), Purana(s), *and* Upanishad(s)
Vedanta 14, *see* Upanishad(s)
Veda Samaj 209
Vidyasagar, Ishwarchandra 208, 211, 225–6, 339n
Vidyapati 184

Vipassana 105
Virashaiva Mahasabha 325
Virashaivas' movement 169–73
Vithoba/Vittal 174 ff.
Vivekananda, Swami 13–14, 44, 48, 50, 196, 199, 218, 219, 225, 226 ff., 239n, 244, 253, 278, 290n, 346; the myth of 226–33
Vokkaliga Association 325
Voltaire 144
Vratya(s) 68
Vrishalas(s) 84

Walangkar, Gopal Baba 339
Wilkins, Charles 192, 198
Wilson, H.H. 193, 198

Women/gender/patriarchy 12, 28, 29, 34, 41, 65, 71, 74, 85, 96n, 111, 116–19, 141, 147, 161–2, 172, 202, 242, 253, 254, 354, 355, 381; and the 19th reform movements 205 ff., 217–18, 220–1, 226, 230, 231, 320, 322; brahmanic patriarchy 28–9, 58n, 274–5; in Buddhist Sangh 116–19

Yajna 61, 68; *ashwamedha* 62, 91; *rajsuya* 62, 130
Yajnavalkya 29, 131, 229; and Gargi 102; *Yajnavalkya Smriti* 72
Yoga 74
Yuddhishthira 80